The Velvet Philosophers

Barbara Day

First published in Great Britain in 1999

by The Claridge Press
33 Canonbury Park South
London NI 2JW
Tel: 0171 226 7791
Fax: 0171 354 0383

CIP data for this title is available from the British Library

ISBN 1-870626-37-0 Hardback
ISBN 1-870626-42-7 Paperback

Cover and title page illustrations: Jessica Gwynne
Cover design and typesetting: Horsell's Farm Enterprises
e.mail: shf@easynet.co.uk
Printed and bound by Antony Rowe Ltd

The Velvet Philosophers is also published in Czech. For details contact: The Jan Hus Educational Foundation in Brno,
tel: (00 42 0) 5 42210269
e.mail: vnjh@janhus.anet.cz
www.vnjh.sk

CONTENTS

Acknowledgements

I would like to thank all those in the Jan Hus Educational Foundation, and those connected with it, who have taken the time and the trouble to talk to me about their experiences, who have searched their personal archives for relevant materials, who have corresponded with me, and who have read various sections to check their accuracy.

Much of what happens in this book I have had to reconstruct from memories of events now up to twenty years old. Many of these memories conflict with each other, but I have done my best to establish the accuracy of what I have written down. I apologise now for any mistakes I may have inadvertently made, and for the incompleteness of what I have written. One of the main handicaps I faced was the virtual non-existence of any research into the subject by Czech and Slovak specialists, and I would plead for it to be undertaken as a matter of urgency.

A list of those interviewed appears at the end of the book, but a special thank you goes to Kathy Wilkes, Roger Scruton, Jessica Douglas-Home, Catherine Audard, Alan Montefiore, Alena Hromádková, Jiří Müller and Miroslav Pospíšil, with whom I have had an ongoing dialogue. Those who have searched through their own or other archives to find relevant documents include Kathy Wilkes, Roger Scruton, Jessica Douglas-Home, Helen Ganly, Catherine Audard, Nathalie Roussarie, Christopher Kirwan, Ralph Walker, Sir Anthony Kenny, H. Gordon Skilling, Jessica Strauss, Theodore de Boer, Henri Veldhuis, Wolfgang Stock, Zdena Tominová, Jiří Fiala, Vilém Prečan, Jiří Gruntorad (*Libri Prohibiti*), Milan Jelínek and Jiří Müller.

References to the archives of the Jan Hus Educational Foundation (Great Britain), Association Jan Hus (France), Jan Hus Educational and Cultural Fund (USA), Jan Hus Fund/Fonds Jan Hus (Canada) and Academica Copernica (Germany) appear as JHEF, AJH, JHECF, JHF and AC respectively, preceded by the initials of the individual holding those specific papers. Professor Gordon Skilling's papers are held by the archives of the University of Toronto, to which we are also grateful for access and photocopying.

I would like to thank the Charles Douglas-Home Memorial Trust and the Research Support Scheme of the Open Society Fund for having provided the funding without which this work would not have been possible, and the Ford Foundation which provided institutional support through the Jan Hus Educational Foundation in Brno.

Barbara Day
May 1999

Introduction

This is the story of a group of men and women from both sides of the iron curtain for whom philosophy was a matter of life and death — the life or death of an independent culture and society (as described by Václav Havel in his letter to President Gustáv Husák in 1975). They worked together for more than ten years, until Czechoslovakia's 'velvet revolution' brought them out of the underground into the open. Over the ten years from 1979 to 1989 a few disappeared from sight and many more were added, but the core remained the same. The work was not fragmented by personal and political rifts, as often happens in underground movements; those involved subordinated differences of view to the tasks that had to be done. The range of the acceptable political spectrum was represented on both sides: in the West, from French ex-communists through British Labour to traditional conservatives; in Czechoslovakia, from those who later joined the Czech Social Democratic Party through to those who were to play a future role in right wing Czech and Slovak political movements. Some of the Czechs and Slovaks involved rose to high political office after 1989; others were to play leading roles in education and culture.

What they shared was a belief in education: in learning how to think independently and how to act as a free individual in accordance with one's conscience. In the West this belief (or at least the possibility of the belief) had been taken for granted; in Czechoslovakia, after forty years of totalitarianism (under the Nazis and the Communists) it was — for those who dared to be open about it — a burning issue. At one end of the age range were those who remembered the pre-war democracy of the First Republic; at the other, young people aware that they were growing up in a society of false answers and dissimulation. It was in this situation that teachers and students turned to the great thinkers of human civilisation, from ancient Greece to the 20th century, to read what they wrote and to discuss what they meant by what they wrote.

The western philosophers who visited these 'home seminars' during the years from 1979 to 1989 spoke on their return with awe of the courage of their Czech and Slovak colleagues and of their resilience in the face of exhausting and degrading employment, police interrogations and the continual risk of arrest and prison. Relatively few of these visiting lecturers had previous experience of travelling behind the Iron Curtain; what little information they had acquired from the western press was confused and contradictory, and most were unprepared for what they found. Educated in a democratic society, their inbred assumption was that bodies such as the police and customs authorities were the responsible servants of a responsible government. That this was not the case in a totalitarian state immediately set up tensions; there were those who were genuinely troubled by the clandestine nature of their visits. They also found it disturbing to visit a society where intellectuals of their own calibre were living an impoverished existence on the edge of society. Visitors' reports testify that the sighting of a uniformed figure or a stranger's attempt to draw them into conversation could bring dryness to the throat and a pumping of the heart. Reports frequently agonise over the writer's own response at moments of stress; had they said too much, or not enough, or to the wrong person? In deciding not to risk a second attempt to visit a known dissident, were they acting with due caution or contemptible cowardice? Was it a sensible precaution to be 'shuffled hurriedly down a series of back streets', or dramatic excess? How real were the dangers? As one lecturer reported (having been persuaded by the Czechoslovak police not to deliver his promised lecture to Ladislav Hejdánek's seminar): 'I left Prague later [the next] morning with a troubled conscience and a deep concern for the victims of thought-policing'.[1]

The western visitors included eminent academics and artists, political observers and theologians; but very few of them had experienced anything other than an open society and a rule of law. Perhaps the most difficult thing for them to come to terms with was the knowledge that there were no certain guidelines. Nothing evokes greater fear than the unknown, and it was this fear that governed the life of most Czechs and Slovaks from 1948 to 1989, with a brief respite during the 'Prague Spring' of 1968. After the war, the decline in living standards and the failure of the Communist Party's post-war promises had led to a search for scapegoats — a witch hunt. Amongst those who died were eleven leading Communist politicians, prosecuted in what were known as the Slánský trials.[2] But thousands more disappeared in the 1950s — lawyers, priests, shopkeepers, small businessmen. Without warning, someone could be intercepted on the way home or taken from his bed in the small hours of the morning. It was enough for a witness to say 'I don't like those people there, they're behaving in an anti-régime manner'; or 'That man over there is sitting in an anti-socialist way.' In the 1950s someone could be sentenced to years of imprisonment for lending someone the wrong kind of book — a book from abroad, or from the First Republic. Denunication was common, from motives of revenge, envy, or self-preservation. After years of imprisonment men returned to their families bearing horrific scars of torture, unable to speak of what they had experienced.

Czechoslovakia was itself a prison; for nearly two decades after 1948 only the privileged were allowed to travel. Information about conditions in western society was entirely negative. Many people then imagined the opposite, that westerners lived a life of luxury in which benefits were provided by a state apparatus as totalitarian as Communism but more successful. (This image of the West has persisted well into the 1990s.) Travel to the West, whether on holiday, business, or academic exchanges, was confined to Party members whose behaviour was monitored by special agents (even travel within the eastern bloc was not easy). Many young people considered the possibility of leaving the country 'illegally'. To prevent this, the borders with Germany and Austria were fortified with high fences, stretches of ploughed ground and watch towers. Nevertheless, some people tried. More than three hundred died, blown up by mines (which were in use until the end of 1965), electrocuted or shot by border guards. Their bodies were photographed sprawled on the bare ground or hanging on the barbed wire. The records are incomplete, and it is still difficult to bring those responsible to justice.[3]

The relaxation of the mid-1960s can be seen now as an illusion, but the perception among many people at the time was that 'there would be no more fear'.[4] The post-invasion 'normalisation' process of the 1970s reversed that expectation, and the memories and fears of the 1950s returned. Although the process of repression was more subtle and the show trials and executions were not repeated, the governing principle was still that of fear. Since the worst crime was to hold an independent opinion, virtually every member of the population was a potential criminal. The majority endeavoured to lead a life style in which no one, or only their closest family and friends, heard their real views. Nevertheless, in the 1970s the proportion of the population which suffered for their opinions was much larger than in the 1950s, even though the punishments were the relatively 'minor' ones of being banned from following their profession or seeing their children excluded from education. This method of control could only be achieved by an information structure which reached into every part of the nation's life.

Although the Communist Party was returned to power at every 'election' and filled every position of influence from the President downwards with its 'nomenklatura', there was one body with greater power, and that was the secret police. In a country where information was a rare commodity, the secret police held enormous reserves. One of its main roles was the collection of information; the secret police not only monitored what was going on inside and outside the country, they had the power to interrogate anyone, especially dissidents with contacts abroad. No other office had this access and this power. In accordance with the structure of the Communist hierarchy, the information was transferred to the General Secretary of the Party, thus enabling him to remain in his position of power. The secret police, however, had prior access to the information, and if they chose they could withold it.

The second main role of the secret police was repressive. It was they who watched for any manifestation of independence, regardless of content. Any initiator of an independent activity was considered potentially 'hostile'. It was difficult for western philosophers to understand why a discussion about Plato between half a dozen people in a private flat should be a crime.

The threat to the authorities was that this was an 'organised activity' outside the control of the Communist Party. The police term for these private discussions (known by their participants as *bytové semináři*, or home seminars) was 'anti-university', and the Jan Hus Educational Foundation set up by British philosophers in 1980 was (when the police found out about it in 1986) designated a 'Centre of Ideological Subversion'.[5] The visiting lecturers, by supporting the actions of the 'internal enemy' were considered to be interfering in the affairs of a foreign country.

Various measures were taken by the secret police against the home seminars even before the time of the western visitors. By the late 1970s it seemed as though they would tolerate those which did not advertise themselves, but were prepared to use brutal tactics against what were known as the 'open' seminars. One reason for this was laziness: if they knew where the seminars were operating, they were in a position to intervene when the order came; whereas if they tried to close down all the seminars they knew they would start somewhere else and be more difficult to trace. Later, the police took a more devious course: to infiltrate, acquire information and make life difficult for those involved by minor, untraceable irritations; this way they hoped the activities would in time self-destruct. Apart from the notorious case of Jacques Derrida's imprisonment, the police attitude towards the westerners was one of persuasion, in an attempt to convince them that their contacts consisted of Trotskyites and criminal elements. After the early 1980s the secret police avoided direct contact with the visiting philosophers, although some were placed on the Index of Undesirable Persons.[6]

The ten years of the western philosophers' work with the underground university in Czechoslovakia did not pass without difficulties, loss and tragedy. Some of those involved died before or soon after the Velvet Revolution, in some cases violently. Others suffered exile, prison, legalised brutality, broken marriages, alchoholism, illness, and other disappointments and betrayals. Nor did the longed-for arrival of democratic government ensure personal happiness; many looked back with nostalgia on the close-knit dissident community which supported its members in times of persecution, and whose values were uncompromised by the requirements of public responsibility. Most of them however recognised that what they had learned in the seminars of the underground university had to be put to use in the creation of a new society. In their new roles in political life, the civil service, the educational system and the non-governmental sector, they worked to apply the principles and standards learnt from a patchy but intense study of philosophy, political and social science, psychology and history. They were working against immense odds — the active opposition of the 'old guard', the indifference of those who had spent their whole life in a dependency culture, the opportunism of post-Communist society. They were among the first to recognise that the transition of the Czech and Slovak Republics to fully-fledged open societies would not be a matter of a few years, but of at least two generations. The endowment they had received in the underground seminars they held in trust, an inheritance to be passed on to their children and grandchildren.

'Bolted Down under Hoods of Steel'

To use the name 'underground university' for the independent
and unofficial education system which existed in Czechoslovakia under the Communist regime is romantic and inaccur-
ate, but difficult to avoid. Many of those working within it
avoided the title both because of its lack of accuracy and because there was a danger that it undermined the legal basis of
their activities. In the second half of the 1970s the Czechoslovak
Socialist Republic subscribed to international agreements
guaranteeing its citizens the right to free speech and free
assembly; groups of people meeting to discuss a theme from
philosophy, art or literature could not be (but were) described as
'anti-state activities'. However, the term 'underground university' implies an organisation, something along the lines of the
'flying university' in Poland, and the activities in
Czechoslovakia never achieved this degree of sophistication.
This was largely due to the much harsher policies taken by the
Czechoslovak authorities; in Poland the demarcation between
what was allowed and what was not, was not so sharp, and much
of the 'unofficial' teaching took place on 'official' premises. In
Czechoslovakia, seminars were held in people's homes because
there was nowhere else to hold them, and in secret because of
the constant fear of police intervention. Another term which it is
almost impossible to avoid using is that of 'dissident', in
refering to those who organised and attended these seminars.
The philologist Karel Palek[1] objects to the use of the word when
describing those such as himself involved in unofficial cultural
work. Translation and writing was not 'dissidence'. For him the
term (scarcely used in the 1970s) implies an oppositional political stance, a field in which he was never involved. Many of

those who taught in the so-called 'underground university' would take the same attitude, since their activities needed no justification. Nevertheless, in a totalitarian society, any activity which does not conform to established rules is regarded by that society as oppositional, and it becomes difficult to avoid the use of the word 'dissident'.

The first 'home seminars' under the Communist regime in Czechoslovakia were held in the 1950s by teachers expelled from the universities because of their 'bourgeois background' and belief in academic freedom. Amongst them was the philosopher Jan Patočka. Patočka's name is inseparable from Czech philosophy and from Charter 77. He was born in 1907, when the Czech lands of Bohemia and Moravia were still part of the Austro-Hungarian Empire. After 1918, under the First Republic, Czechoslovakia was very much an integral part of Europe, an advanced industrial nation with high educational standards and a flourishing cultural life. During this period Patočka studied philosophy at the Charles University in Prague, spending the year 1928-1929 at the Sorbonne in Paris. The two living philosophers who were to have the greatest influence on his thinking were Edmund Husserl, born in Moravia of a German-speaking Jewish family, whom Patočka met in Paris;[2] and Husserl's pupil Martin Heidegger, whom Patočka met in Freiburg in 1933.[3] Another important influence was the philosopher Tomáš Masaryk, President of Czechoslovakia from 1918 to 1936. Masaryk's death in 1937 was for Patočka and for many Czechs the end of an era.

In the 1930s the combination of the Depression and the influx of academics leaving Hitler's Germany created a critical situation in Prague, and although Patočka started teaching at the Charles University in 1934 and was habilitated as an associate professor in 1936, he did not obtain a permanent position. Nevertheless, he was secretary of the Prague Philosophy Circle, shared in the organisation of the World Philosophy Congress in Prague in 1934, and invited Husserl to Prague in 1935. The publication in 1936 of *The Natural World as a Philosophical Problem* created considerable interest and established him as a philosopher of European status. In this, his first book, Patočka argued that philosophy can be used by man as a tool for diagnosis, thus enabling him to recover his instinctive sense of the reality of the natural world in the face of scientific concepts which alienate him from his actual environment.

On 17th November 1939 the Nazis closed the Czech universities, and Patočka spent the wartime years as a manual labourer. In spite of having no hope or expectation of publication it was during this period that he worked on his theory of pre-Socratic philosophy which, when eventually published — not until the 1990s — filled four volumes. After the end of the war Patočka returned to the university. It was an extraordinary time to be teaching; the lecture halls were crowded with a five-year back-log of students, recent witnesses to the breakdown of society and its values in the countries of Central Europe. Patočka's intention was to deliver the essentials of philosophy as a basis for rebuilding an authentic way of life, concentrating on ancient Greek philosophy as a route to the rediscovery of the sources of European civilisation.

When the Communists seized power in 1948 Patočka escaped arrest but after a year of uncertainty was, with many other teachers, expelled from the university. The ideologists of Marxism-Leninism tried to ensure his teaching was not allowed to reach disciples either by word of mouth or the written word. Over the next few years only two of his studies were published (1949 and 1952) in the Protestant monthly *Křeśťanské noviny* (Christian News). For a short time he worked in the Masaryk Library and then in the Comenius Archive of the Institute of Education; the study of Comenius's work became a contributing element to the development of his own philosophy, and after 1958, when he began to work in the Institute of Philosophy as a librarian, he was able to write studies on the philosophy of science. At the same time he held seminars in his villa apartment not far from the Břevnov monastery in western Prague for a group of his former students (many of them now engaged in manual work). Other teachers, for the same reason, were also teaching from home, and these occasional seminars continued until, in the early 1960s, it gradually became possible to work openly. By 1965 the Communist Party was at war with itself, and although official philosophy still followed the Marxist-Leninist line, reform was in the air.

In the liberated atmosphere of 1968 Patočka was finally made professor and returned to the Charles University. One of his colleagues, a Party member with political influence, was Professor Milan Machovec, whose specialisms were Virgil, Ancient Philosophy and Scholasticism. It was even possible to hold philosophy seminars for a wider public, and for a few years these took place at the revived Philosophical Society; at the ecumenical seminary in Jircháře Street; in some departments of the Socialist Academy; and with Machovec himself at the Arts Faculty of the Charles University. (The ecumenical seminars known as the Jircháře Colloquia began in the early 1960s in the apartment of the protestant theologian J.C. Hromádka. Up to two hundred people gathered in the seminary refectory on Thursday evenings, including non-church members and even Marxists. After the invasion by Soviet troops in August 1968 and the 'normalisation' of public life, a new Dean was appointed to the Faculty and the seminars were closed in 1970.)

In 1972 Jan Patočka was forced into retirement. One of his post-graduate students, Ivan Chvatík, chose to continue to study with him, and gathered together others to form a discussion group which would meet weekly at Patočka's home from early evening to midnight. The group included students like Chvatík, others who were forbidden to study, and some who held teaching positions in the Charles University. At the same time Patočka continued to give lectures on an occasional basis, as the guest of institutes whose heads were not too frightened to invite him. These were attended by no more than around 20 to 30 people, and after a few years such 'semi-official' events gradually came to an end.

It is the year 1970 rather than 1968 which marks the break in academic, intellectual and cultural continuity in Czechoslovakia. Journals were closed down, the teaching of certain subjects was curtailed, and expulsions of teachers from universities and secondary schools began. It was a time of deep depression in the country, when many people saw no future ahead and decided to find ways to emigrate. The home seminars of this period were not a gesture of defiance, but an attempt to maintain a space for normality under imposed 'normalisation'; teachers and students were simply trying to continue their interrupted studies. The expelled professors worked at home instead of in their university departments, and their students were those who had previously attended the university seminars — in some cases, students still registered at university continued with both their official courses and their unofficial discussions. One exceptional case was that of Professor Miroslav Katětov, a mathematician so renowned (especially in the Soviet Union) that the Charles University did not dare to expel him. Katětov's Wednesday seminar ran uninterruptedly from 1970 to the present day, and he used the opportunity to invite lecturers expelled from teaching.[4] Another 'semi-official' venue was a psychiatric clinic, where Dr. Nesnídalová organised monthly lectures by Patočka, Petr Rezek, Jiří Němec and others. No one knows how many such seminars (in different subjects) operated at this time; the sociologist Jiřína Šiklová believes there were around forty. Her own group, which gathered Catholic and Protestant Christians together with reform Communists was based mainly on historical themes. It lasted from 1971-1973, when it dispersed because of police intervention. In 1974 the philosopher Jiří Němec began a seminar mainly for young people which covered literature, music, philosophy and theology — 'not religious instruction, just the regular Bible knowledge everyone should have that they weren't getting in school'.[5] Jan Patočka taught not only at his own home, but at seminars arranged by others: in 1973-74 Ivan Chvatík arranged for him to give a series of eleven lectures on Plato and Europe, each at a different venue; and in 1974 he gave a series of eight lectures in the picturesque surroundings of the photographer Jaroslav Krejčí's studio on Kampa Island in the Malá Strana (Small Quarter) of Prague. Petr Pithart remembers that these were in the nature of university seminars, when Patočka would simply talk and explore ideas with them. However, there was little unity between the different groups; the exclusivity was often caused not by reasons of security, but out of old divisions and rivalries carried over from the old days — the disciples of Patočka remained separate from those of Machovec, and they from those of the philosopher and former reform Communist Karel Kosík. In the autumn of 1975 Machovec tried to remedy this by setting up a larger seminar in the Pařížská Street apartment of one of his former students, Dana Horáková. This met once a fortnight and covered a variety of themes, on the principle that if anyone was prepared to take the risk of leading such a seminar, their subject must be worth attention. Julius Tomin, who was later to initiate the participation of western lecturers, was a co-organiser, and a regular speaker. About 30 to 40 people attended, including Jiřína Šiklová, Ivan Chvatík, Martin Palouš and both the Havel brothers. But this seminar was more of a gathering of experienced minds than a teaching ground for young students.

From this point of view, 1977 does mark a new development in the underground university, directly attributable to the appearance of the petition of Charter 77. It is appropriate that Jan Patočka's philosophy helped to inspire the Charter, and that he was one of the first three spokesmen. The creation of Charter 77 was given a direct impetus by the United Nations' International Covenants on Civil and Political Rights and on Economic, Social and Cultural Rights, and by the Final Act in the Helsinki conference of 1975. The Czechoslovak Republic, with other states, had been a signatory to the Covenants and the texts were published in Czechoslovakia in October 1976. The Charter systematically details all the points at which current practice in Czechoslovakia departed from the articles of the Covenants, including the right to freedom of expression; the right to education; the right to 'seek, receive and impart information and ideas';[6] and the right to freedom of religious confession. It points out that decisions affecting the lives of citizens are often made unconstitutionally and illegally by unauthorised persons, without recourse to any authority outside the Communist Party — thus creating a violation of the right to freedom of association.

Other violations of human rights included interference with privacy and with correspondence; interference with the process of justice; and denial of freedom of movement and freedom in choice of employment. The Charter, however, was not simply a criticism of the authorities; it also drew attention to the responsibility of every citizen for ensuring that the agreements should be observed. This, from the Communist Party's point of view, was the most dangerous part of the Charter: the establishment of a moral authority and the revival of a civil society which was not under its control. The authors were aware of this, and explicitly stated that Charter 77 was not an 'organisation': it had no membership and was not the basis for oppositional political activitity. '(It) is a loose, informal and open association of people of various shades of opinions, faiths and professions united by the will to strive individually and collectively for the respecting of civil and human rights in our own country and throughout the world...'[7] Charter 77 was, as a petition, presented entirely legally under Czechoslovak law. Nevertheless, it came as an unpleasant shock for the Czechoslovak authorities. It had seemed as though during the 1970s the process of normalisation had been successful in subduing the population, without recourse to show trials. International attention, lulled by the apparent lack of reprisals in the year following the August invasion, had moved on. The tightening of controls had taken place at an administrative level; every member of the Communist Party and every non-Party member in a position of responsibility had been required to sign a statement saying that they agreed with the 'intervention by fraternal armies'. For an outsider, it seems strange that the nation which had acted so positively in 1968 should become so submissive, but it is necessary to take into consideration the twenty years from 1948; memories of executions, prison sentences and uranium mines[8] were still fresh. No one wanted to see a return of that horror, least of all to their family and children.

Those who refused to sign were dealt with by removing them from positions of influence. Teachers would be downgraded, often by moving them to a different school (chosen to cause the maximum inconvenience in travel). University teachers were — if they were lucky — moved to research institutes where they had no contact with students. Many of them were not allowed that opportunity, and they embarked on a descending spiral which led to a job as a window cleaner or night watchman. Others did not even try to make a career. Pavel Barša from Brno worked in the Academy of Sciences for a year after graduating in 1978, then left from choice to work as a cleaner, night watchman and stoker, whilst performing as a musician in the 'unofficial culture'. Karel Palek, who graduated from the Charles University as a philologist in 1972, realised that there was no future for him in academic life, and refused to follow a substitute career in translation. After trying out the boiler rooms in the Tyrš House in the Malá Strana and the Alcron Hotel near Wenceslas Square, he came to the Stomatological Clinic in Charles Square. Conditions were good; it was a gas-fired boiler which needed little attention, and with a small desk and a large ash tray (for cigars) he settled down for thirteen years work as a samizdat critic and editor. In 1983 Roger Scruton[9] visited the boiler room: '...lit from above by little windows at ground level through which an oily light filtered downwards over a collection of kitsch.... Fidelius is a student of kitsch, which he sees as a precursor of the imagery of Communism.' 'Communist culture,' he argues, 'is really kitsch with teeth.'[10] Other stokers were not so fortunate; the work could involve 24-hour shifts of heavy labour. Daniel Kroupa and Martin Palouš started work at four in the morning, shovelling piles of coke to heat the Tyrš House. They would discuss philosophy leaning on their shovels, and read volumes of Marx whilst sitting on heaps of coke; probably the last workers of the Communist age to do so. The fumes damaged Kroupa's health, and he moved to the Michle water-works. Even in such lowly jobs as these they would often be monitored by the secret police.

It was not a way of life which appealed to the average member of the population. Most people preferred to conform to what was required of them in exchange for some private space of their own. This was the period of the '*chata culture*', when families turned to their own resources to create a private world: in some cases an island of moral values treasured in defiance of the outer, political world; in others, a stronghold of consumerism and material acquirement. The *chata* or country cottage could represent either of these extremes. At one level the country cottage represented traditional, 'Czech' values. The Czechs, even at the end of the 20th century, are not at heart a city society. Many of them have parents or grandparents still living in one of the villages which thickly strew the map of Bohemia and Moravia. Towns and cities are deserted at weekends, whilst in summer whole families move to the country and working members commute to the town. Sometimes the destination is the parents' home or a cottage inherited from a family member (such a place is properly a *chalupa* rather than the modern '*chata*'). Those without property in the family search for something to buy (in this way, many old German houses in the Sudetenland have been rescued and restored as holiday homes, whilst other homes were bought from agricultural workers moving into modern accommodation). Those without the inclination to care for an older property build from scratch, creating the down-market colonies of *chata*s. The cottage represented, however fictionally, a return to an older way of life where one was not troubled with moral questions such as whether or not to fulfil one's 'socialist obligations'. There were many positive results. Children were out of the pollution of the towns, whilst their parents exercised themselves with the practical tasks of a simpler way of life. Country lore and country customs could be passed on and fostered. On the other hand, the *chata* became a dreamworld into which to retreat, and in many cases was turned into the materialisation of dreams. Wages in Czechoslovakia were not high, but there was not much to spend them on, and after 1970 it was extremely difficult to travel abroad. It was possible, through inventive use of what materials were available, to furnish a cottage in some luxury. Families who had to squeeze into small flats in high-rise blocks in town realised their fantasies of gracious living in the countryside. Others rejected this approach, preferring an authentic and primitive life style.

The idealised values of this way of life were illuminated in a whole genre of 'village' films, above all those directed by Jiří Menzel (whose 1971 *Skřivánci na niti* [Skylarks on a String] based on Bohumil Hrabal's comedy about political undesirables in the 1950s labour camps could not be released until after 1989). The village films include *Na samotě u lesa* (An Idyllic Site by the Forest, 1976) about a starry-eyed city family trying to buy a cottage from a hard-of-hearing villager, and *Vesničko má středisková* (My Sweet Little Village, 1985) in which a village cooperative thwarts the plans of Party functionaries to send the village simpleton to Prague and convert his inherited cottage to their own use. Menzel's films featured the wisdom of homely values, the preservation of traditional customs, the pretensions of naive newcomers, the impersonality of city life and the cameraderie of the country pub. For obvious reasons, they barely touched on the harsher realities of living under a totalitarian regime, and then only on superficial details (queuing in the local hardware store for unavailable items).

In retrospect, Menzel's films can be seen as a clear attempt to steer the nation's retreat into an inner, family life towards a reflective, evaluative philosophy (a recurring character in his films is the pragmatic doctor, young or old). However, many

Czechs were at the same time abandoning any concept of civic responsibility or interest in a wider society. It is this torpid, sleep-walking world which Václav Havel describes in his writings of the 1970s. Ernest Gellner, the British social scientist of Czech-Jewish origins who became a patron of the Jan Hus Foundation, wrote: 'Consumerism, government by perpetual bribery, is not a viable permanent option for mankind — for ecological reasons, because of the diminishing marginal effectiveness of bribes, because of the self-defeating nature of nominally material, but in fact symbolic bribes, which neutralize each other when everyone has access to them.'[11] However, there were three (three in particular) sections of society which resisted the spell. It is to Havel's credit — although he was strongly criticised for it during the 1980s — that he united these three streams in Charter 77. In January 1977 they were represented by himself and his fellow spokesmen, Professor Patočka and Jiří Hájek, Czechoslovak Foreign Minister in Dubček's government in 1968.[12]

Jiří Hájek is representative of the 'sixty-eighters': Communists who grew up in the Party and who, from the late 1950s, allied themselves with the reform movement. After the invasion they were the ones blamed for having tried to lead Czechoslovakia out of the socialist camp, and there was no way back to the fold even for those who who were willing to try. In the aftermath of 1968 it was the reform Communists who were punished first and most acutely. It was clear that those who had earlier been active politically were in the wilderness for as long as Moscow held control over the satellite countries. Since most of them were, as they had already shown, ambitious and energetic men and women who had grown up believing in themselves as an elite, they did not find it easy to accept their new status. Some of them emigrated. Among those who were still in Czechoslovakia at this time were Pavel Kohout, Petr Pithart, Zdeněk Mlynář,[13] Rita Klímová, Miroslav Kusý and Milan Šimečka.

The second group, represented by Jan Patočka, had nothing in common with the first group except a rejection of the present state of affairs. Those who could loosely be said to be in this grouping had never believed in Communism, and had either opposed it in 1948 or grown up with a gradual realisation of the evil of any totalitarianism, whether of the right or of the left. Many of those involved in the seminar movement tended to belong to this loose grouping: Daniel Kroupa, Jakub Trojan, Milan Balabán, Alena Hromádková. This second strand of the Charter is sometimes called the 'religious' strand, and included both catholics and protestants. Although Patočka himself was never a 'believer' in the sense of accepting the creed of one or other of the churches (his father had been a strong atheist), he had a natural sympathy with those individual Christians (including a number of underground priests) who had refused to compromise themselves in State-led movements. Their natural allies were those who had left Czechoslovakia in 1948, and their descendants. However, these exiles were strongly suspicious of the ex-Communist signatories of the Charter, and of their natural allies, the emigrés of 1968.[14] These relationships made the Charter a much more ambiguous document in the western world than it was in Czechoslovakia itself; although Havel himself has said (in a television programme made for the 20th anniversary of Charter 77) that when the lists of signatories were being collated, he was surprised by many of the names — those of ex-Communists — on the lists brought in by Zdeněk Mlynář (who in 1977 became an exile in Vienna).

Václav Havel represented, politically speaking, the liberal wing. After his success as a playwright in the mid-1960s Havel had openly opposed the 'normalisation' process and consequently his work could not be published or produced in his home country. Living on his royalties from abroad, he was deeply involved in the 'unofficial culture' — the theatrical avant-garde, poets, artists, rock musicians, amateur film makers — which formed a bohemia within Bohemia. All artistic activity in socialist Czechoslovakia was supposed to be directely or indirectly financed and controlled by the state apparatus. An artist had to be licensed before he could exhibit or sell his work; in the 1970s even an amateur theatre group was not allowed to exist unless it came under the patronage of a factory, Culture Centre, or similar. Therefore most of this group survived in poorly paid, often irregular jobs, practising their 'real' activities on a risky and — in the eyes of the authorities — illicit basis. No one knows how many unrecorded cases there were in the 1970s of harassment of groups or individuals; nor how many isolated young people decided to suppress their desires and hopes of expressing themselves in their own way, and conform with the future that Communism had marked out for them.

Such people as these were won over to the Charter as a result of the show trial of the rock group the Plastic People of the Universe earlier in 1976. Jan Bednář, who later became a student in the 'underground university' remembers how the corridors of the court house became a meeting place for those who realised that the State was presenting a show trial; disparate individuals drawn together by their indignation began to form alliances. Strenuous efforts by Havel and other dissidents publicised the trials in the foreign press, and won for the defendants a reduced sentence. After 1977 the Charter became a patron of such groups and individuals, and of new aspirants. The suppression of activities upheld by international agreements — such as the holding of unofficial concerts, theatre performances and art exhibitions — could from then on be referred through Charter 77 to the authorities. Naturally, it did not mean that such activities would not continue to be harrassed; but it meant the end of individual isolation and the beginning of solidarity. The reaction of the Czechoslovak authorities was to try to prevent those who stepped within this community from mixing with people from other walks of life.

Shortly after the publication of the Charter,[15] all the first wave of signatories were harassed and interrogated, none more so than the three spokesmen. Václav Havel was arrested on the 14th January 1977. Patočka, collapsing after police interrogation, was still being questioned when he died from a brain haemorrhage on 13th March. For several months Jiří Hájek remained the only spokesman for the Charter, a fact which reinforced the feeling of some people that it was a grouping of former reform Communists. Milan Machovec's seminar continued to meet until the police arrived at the end of January. When told that they had been ordered to close down the seminar, Julius Tomin reacted belligerently: 'If they come, they come,' he responded.

When Julius Tomin signed the Charter at the end of 1976 he was in his late thirties. Growing up in the 1940s and 1950s, he studied English and Russian, and subscribed to Tolstoy's and Gandhi's views on non-violence. (Later, during raids on the philosophy seminars, his passive resistance often resulted in injury as he was dragged through doors and down stairs, and flung into police cars and vans.) After serving a prison sentence for his refusal to do military service he tried to leave Czechoslovakia for Sweden, but was picked up in Poland and sentenced to another year. Whilst in prison he studied Marxism (since any other serious literature was unavailable) and resolved that instead of opposing the regime he would work to try and make it more humane. After serving his sentence, and whilst employed as a forester in Slovakia, he wrote to Professor Machovec about his desire to study philosophy. Machovec called Tomin for interview and was impressed by his ability and enthusiasm. It was the mid-1960s, a comparatively relaxed period, and Machovec arranged for Tomin to return to university under his supervision to write his doctorate in classical philosophy (Tomin now learnt ancient Greek to read the texts in the original). In the atmosphere of the 1960s, Tomin associated himself with the reform Communists, participating in a Marxist-Christian dialogue which led to a two month lecture tour of North America followed by a year (1968-69) at the University of Hawaii. On his return he was refused an academic post and worked for five years as a turbine operator, to be sacked when his employers discovered him teaching philosophy to his colleagues. He became nightwatchman in the zoological gardens near the chateau of Troja; a post which allowed time for study and writing; one of his papers, 'An Evaluation of an Experiment after five Years' — the experiment being the Communists' redeployment of dissident intellectuals in manual jobs — was published in a West German anthology. Tomin married his wife Zdena in the early 1960s, at a time when he was working as a ward assistant in a psychiatric hospital and she was a therapist.

Julius and Zdena were the parents of two sons, the eldest of whom, Lukáš, reached his 14th birthday in 1977 (the second son, Marek, was six years younger). Fourteen was at that time the age when children in Czechoslovakia applied to move on from 9 year school to the final three years of their secondary education, either at a gymnasium or at a specialist school in economics, the arts, languages or a practical subject. Lukáš, intelligent and questioning, should have been a clear candidate for a gymnasium education followed by university. However, Lukáš's parents were not only 'intellectuals' but also 'enemies of the state'. Zdena Tomin remembers seeing an order in the police records: 'Lukáš Tomin not to be admitted to higher education under any circumstances.'[16] They knew that Lukáš had no chance of a gymnasium education — the most he could hope for was an apprenticeship. With his own sons and the children of other Charter signatories in mind — Ludvík Vaculík's two sons and those of Otka Bednářová; Ivan Klíma's son and daughter; Jiří Ruml's son Jan; the daughters of Jiří Gruša and of Rudolf Battěk; the seven Němec children — Tomin started his own seminar in ancient philosophy. During the week he would study a passage of Plato in the original Greek, and then, once a week, expound it to the group of students.

Some of the Charter signatories, re-forming themselves after the shock of Patočka's death, felt that the home seminars, like the 'unofficial' activity of artists, could refer to the Charter as their patron. Since the Czechoslovak authorities had signed an international Covenant guaranteeing the right to 'seek, receive and impart information and ideas of all kinds, regardless of frontiers', there was no reason why a seminar should not be held openly in a private flat (nor why specialists from abroad should not be allowed to speak at such a seminar). Many of them were facing the same problems as the Tomins, with children who would not even be allowed to sit for the school leaving certificate. At the age of 15 the only jobs open to them would be manual jobs — labouring, gardening, hospital care. (This awareness of having been denied the opportunity to study affected many of them deeply, even in the successful careers they followed after 1989.) It is said that, about this time, the term 'Patočka University' began to be used, and a complete timetable drawn up, including courses in sociology, psychology, history, history of art and literature. I have been unable to find anyone who participated in this kind of planning, nor anyone who can name someone who did. Most people involved in the Prague seminars insist that at this time they would not have dreamt of creating any such 'Patočka University' since the term implied an organised structure which, unlike the sessions held by individuals in their own specialism, was not clearly and demonstrably legal within the existing framework of the law.[17]

There is at the same time a vagueness in people's recollections about what happened when during these years; Daniel Kummerman[18] remembers them as 'a period without shape', when events happened which are still fresh in his memory, but which he cannot place in any time frame.

The term 'Patočka University' certainly did exist as early as 1980, since in her duplicated brochure 'Unofficial Philosophy Courses in Prague' Dr. Kathy Wilkes[19] wrote: 'Some people have christened the unofficial seminars in Czechoslovakia the "Patočka University"'... However, this title is substantially misleading. It suggests a parallel with the System of Academic Courses (otherwise known as the "Flying University") of Poland which does not exist.... Furthermore, to call this assortment of courses the "Patočka University" is potentially dangerous.... One of the reasons for harassing Tomin is that he purports to be running an alternative university...'.

Some of the seminars which took place in the late 1970s and 1980s will be described in later chapters dealing with the visits of the Western academics: the theology seminars, including those of Jakub Trojan and Milan Balabán; Ladislav Hejdánek's open seminar; the Kampakademie at the home of the Palouš family; seminars run by Rudolf Kučera and Petr Rezek; the Brno and Bratislava seminars; and the Cambridge Diploma course and Miroslav Červenka's 'Evening University', both of which began in 1987. Of these, the most elegant tone was set by the Kampakademie in the home of the Palouš family on Kampa, the picturesque 'island' which forms part of the west bank of the Vltava. Kampakademie was set up in the early 1970s by Martin Palouš and Daniel Kroupa, but western visitors often assumed it was the creation of Martin's father Radim Palouš,[21] who had been a student of Jan Patočka in the 1940s and 1950s. In the early 1970s Radim Palouš was teaching at the university and was not expelled until he signed the Charter in 1977; Martin, expelled as a teacher the same year, managed to graduate in time. The original intention of the 'Academy' was for the study of Plato, but subsequently the group translated Heidegger with Ladislav Hejdánek and Aristotle with Zdeněk Neubauer. In time the Kampakademie became a gathering of like minds such as the Havel brothers and Pavel Bratinka, and eventually 30 or 40 people might gather on an evening when a western lecturer was anticipated. Once a year in the 1980s the nucleus of the group would gather at Václav Havel's cottage at Hrádeček.

Another prestigious seminar was that of the logician Ivan Havel, which began in November 1977 as a re-assembly of the group which had formerly met in Pařížská Street. Unusually, a complete list of these meetings, held on alternate Mondays, has been reconstructed, with subjects ranging from geometry through history to theatre.[22] Havel's purpose was to mix dissidents with friends from the universities and the Academy of Sciences, and for the first two years, until the police began to monitor attendance, this succeeded. Even after police intervention some people in official positions continued to attend, because they did not want to miss the expertise of the lecturers. Petr Pithart also aimed to break down barriers at the 'Five o'clock teas' organised by his wife from approximately 1980-1986. Invitees were carefully chosen, and one of the dissidents would give a non-controversial talk: Ivan Klíma on Kafka, Jiří Stráský[23] on mountain climbing as a life philosophy, or Jan Sokol[24] on the medieval philosophy of hours. Pithart also ran short courses for groups of around fifteen young people at a time. The participants were all known to his children or friends, and were selected from around 100 families in Prague who, although not dissidents, were 'in the know'. Some home semin-ars had a cultural or artistic focus; the most famous of these was that held by Václav Ševčík in the villa area of Baba in western Prague, which included film shows and exhibitions and attracted people from all over the country. One of the most consistent and systematic seminars in philosophy was taught from the early 1970s to the late 1980s by Zdeněk Pinc, who used it as a model for the Institute for Basic Education he founded at the Charles University in the 1990s. Another long-term seminar was taught by Daniel Kroupa, also the co-founder of the Kampakademie. From 1978 to 1983 he worked with a group from which a number of the later professional philosophers (Filip Karfík, Lenka Karfíková, Josef Moural) emerged; in the later 1980s he ran a number of broader-based courses. Philosophy was also taught by Ivan Dubský, Emanuel Mandler, Egon Bondy (in conjunction with Milan Balabán's seminars on Judaism) and Zdeněk Neubauer, who would appear at different venues. Over several years from 1977 Neubauer gave a series of lectures on 'The Philosophical Problems of Cybernetics', initially held at the Faculty of Mathematics and Physics, and from 1980 to 1984 at the Střední dům armády (Central Army House) and advertised as 'schooling for non-Party members'; Jiří Fiala remembers that it was eventually betrayed by the fact that none of the participants appeared to be asleep. From there the seminar moved to 'Lávka' on the Smetana Quay, and in 1988 (by now with alternating lecturers) to the Lekářský dům (House of Medicine).[25] From 1983 onwards a seminar on the philosophy of geometry was led by Petr Vopěnka[26] and other philosophers (including Radim Palouš) at the Faculty of Mathematics and Physics.[27] (Ivan Dejmal remembers that every year the police put a stop to the seminars, but that they would start up again the next year under another title.) Such 'semi-official' seminars were very exceptional; most groups met in small numbers in each others' homes, and were careful about monitoring who was invited to join the seminar. In most cases the idea of foreign participation would have been unwelcome, since the police attention it would attract might prove an obstacle and discouragement.

The phenomenon of samizdat, or 'home publishing', although often treated independently, is indivisible from the home seminars. In the first place it could never have been manufactured without the participation of the band of people for whom intellectual freedom was more important than police intervention. The demands it made on their resourcefulness are unimaginable in the West: the need to find competent typists who would risk a prison sentence for what they were undertaking, and bookbinders who would bind the works produced, as well as the editing of texts and the collection, collation, correction and distribution of large quantities of typescript whilst evading detection. The publishers also saw it as a challenge that the volumes should be as elegantly produced as possible.

The content of samizdat was related to the seminars in two ways. One kind of samizdat emerged originally from those groups which met to read and discuss each others' works and whose members, to facilitate the discussion, prepared their own writings in sufficient copies to share around the group. In course of time, as the production of samizdat became more organised and professional, such writings found their way into the hands of people who would never have had the courage to attend a seminar, but gained a sense of freedom from reading in the safety of their homes. The other kind of samizdat[28] was intended for the teaching seminars, and arose out of the desperate need for materials and textbooks. Publications in English which deal with Czech and Slovak samizdat tend to concentrate on the first kind of samizdat, on original writing. Paul Wilson has noted how small and circumscribed was the Czechoslovak operation compared with Poland, with its thousands of readers and large press runs;[29] the Poles were publishing not only their own writing, but translations of the most up-to-date text books on, for example, ecology and information technology.[30] Czech samizdat was in many ways a much more personal enterprise. Zdena Tominová wrote of the danger that 'the emotional value attached to [the writings]... may sometimes be greater than the actual literary value of the writing itself'.[31] In Brno in the second half of the 1980s the Jan Hus Foundation saw it as a priority to contribute towards the translation and samizdat publication of texts which were standard in the West but which were completely unavailable in Czech or Slovak.

In spite of the problems caused by the police action against the Charter, in the autumn of 1977 Milan Machovec started to lead a basic course on the history of philosophy, the essential problems to be found in philosophy, and the representatives of the main movements. It was attended by the university age children of dissident parents and other young people unable to study, and initially had a large attendance. However, in the course of the year the authorities became aware of the seminar and a police guard was set on the flat, taking names of those entering and leaving. What happened next is not entirely clear; according to some reports the seminar moved first to the home of Ivan Hoffman in Havelská Street in the centre of Prague, and only later to the flat of Julius Tomin in Keramická Street. Tomin remembers that he had for a time given up his Plato group in favour of Machovec's seminar, but now renewed it. Jan Vaculík believes that it was around this time that Machovec divided the young people into two groups: those who seriously wished to study, whom he taught in secret, and those who were prepared to risk the raids. Nevertheless, those still attending Tomin's seminar included Jan Ruml (son of the dissident Jiří), Jan Bednář (younger son of Otka Bednářová) and Markéta Němcová, the eldest of Jiři and Dana Němcová's family. Without the (often controversial) activities of Julius Tomin, the home seminars in Czechoslovakia would probably have remained as closed groups. It was Tomin who, from early 1978 to mid-1980, insisted that the principles of the Charter be adhered to, even in impossible conditions. Husband and wife had both been among the earliest Charter signatories, and Zdena was even more deeply involved in Charter 77 politics than Julius; she became Charter spokesperson in January 1979, and remained so for a difficult thirteen months, during which three of her fellow spokesmen were imprisoned.

Not long after the Plato seminar had opened at the Tomins' home, Tomin became involved in a different kind of seminar with a new audience. In the days of normalisation, the prestigious faculties of the Charles University — the Faculties of Law and Arts — were virtually closed to all but the 'nomenklatura', the children of parents with an impeccable class and political background, destined for key positions in the Communist Party. Independently minded young people did not even apply to the Charles University, preferring to study at the ČVUT, the Technical University, where it was still possible to get a sound education without an excessive emphasis on political indoctrination, and where there was more hope of finding good teachers than in the heavily purged Charles University. In the late 1970s such young people, living as much of a bohemian student life as was possible under a totalitarian regime, could not help observing the kind of society they were living in, and were more critical of the 'chata culture' than their parents. Loose groups began to form, initially indistinguishable from normal student groupings. One such group centred around a small attic studio in Krakovská Street, just off Wenceslas Square, rented by a student of architecture, Vladimír Prajzler. (Accommodation, especially student accommodation, has always been scarce in Prague and most students either live at home or are crowded into hostels. Controlled rent flats such as this one are still passed down through family members.) Many of Prajzler's friends came from outside Prague, towns such as Šumperk and Ústí nad Labem, so the flat became something of a commune, with students dossing down overnight and turning it into an outpost of the underground. Much of their time would be spent at unofficial rock concerts or making their own films; other evenings they would sit in debate over numerous bottles of Moravian wine — an atmosphere, as Prajzler describes it, of 'nihilism with a human face'.

Eager for new opinions, the group decided to invite a member of the older generation to talk to them. (One of the Šumperk students, Luděk Bednář, attributes the initiative for expanding the Krakovská seminar to his fellow-Šumperkian, Pavel Lašák, who subsequently gave up university and was on military service before the more dramatic events took place.) The students' first choice was Karel Kosík, then working at the National Museum, who courteously refused, but proposed Julius Tomin. Tomin agreed, but with some apprehension. There was the constant danger of police provocation, and the promised assembly might turn out to be leather jacketed thugs with truncheons. To reassure him, two students collected him from his flat and accompanied him to Krakovská. He found waiting for him twenty to thirty Technical University students, deeply attentive and eager to follow his exposition of Ancient Greek philosophy. Originally intended as a single event, it led to a course of ten seminars in Greek philosophy, held on a mid-week evening in the flat in Krakovská. The eagerness of the young people was to find out what philosophy had to say to them about 'how to live in this world of Communism and lies'. After Tomin, other visitors were to speak to the group at Krakovská: the charismatic priest Svatopluk Karásek, who had played with the Plastic People, lectured several times, as well as Jan Kratochvíl, musician and philosopher, and Professor Drozd, a specialist in Russian literature. Krakovská was eventually to become one of the venues for the Oxford philosophers. Aware of the dangers of a police raid, the students repainted the walls of the communal flat and restored it to a semblance of respectability.

As well as lecturing to Prajzler's group, Tomin invited them to join his Plato seminar at Keramická Street — a handful did so, including Prajzler himself; Lenka Dvořáková, a student at the Faculty of Engineering (who came to describe herself as a student of 'land surveying', in a Kafkaesque attempt to make sense out of a course in which she found no sense); Aleš Havlíček, who studied nuclear physics; and Luděk Bednář (unrelated to Otka Bednářová and her sons), who had found nuclear physics dangerously political and switched to electrotechnics. In Prajzler's recollection, the dissidents' children were a little taken aback by the ideas and attitudes of these educationally privileged newcomers; Jan Bednář does not think that this was true, but Prajzler's memory is corroborated by Zdena Tominová, who remembers that there was always a certain edge between them, and that sometimes the Technical University students were suspected of being informers. Ludvík Vaculík's son Jan — who against all the odds had been successful in obtaining a college place and who no longer attended the home seminars — remembers that the irony of the situation was that whereas the dissidents' children saw the seminars as a fragile route to a 'normal' life, there were those amongst the newcomers eager for excitement outside the narrow routine of their own lives.

Tomin's decision to start an open seminar was not originally a way of testing the authorities, but a genuine desire to introduce young people to the Ancient Greeks and especially Plato, who was as close to him as Machovec or any contemporary pedagogue. He loved argument, debate, the crossed swords of protagonist and antagonist; which was also new and exciting for Czech students of the 1970s, accustomed in their university lectures to sit and take notes of authorised opinions. Kathy Wilkes was later amused to find that the teaching of Plato was anathema to the authorities: she agreed that Plato certainly offered a political theory, but one which was generally thought to support rather than subvert totalitarianism.[32] Socrates, she suggested, might have been a different matter, especially after he became a symbol to many Czechs through the songs of the exiled singer Jaroslav Hutka. But Tomin's teaching, she noted, undermined the standard view of Socrates as a free spirit, and followed Nietzsche in portraying him as the *eminence grise* behind Plato's totalitarianism.

In the period between 1977 and 1980, Tomin ran courses on Presocratic Philosophy, Plato, Aristotle, Aristophanes, Hume, William James, Wittgenstein and Berkeley, based on the gift from Germany of eight copies of Berkeley's *Principles of*

Human Knowledge, a work of epistemology and metaphysics which, Kathy Wilkes later observed, must have baffled the listening cops.[33] It also baffled some of the students, who felt it was not what they had expected; however, it was good for their English, and at least they had books, so most of them continued. The complete lack of books for their studies and the need to rely on their own notes and memories was a motivation for many of the students to become involved in samizdat distribution in the 1980s.

In May 1978, when the course was gradually winding down for its second summer break, Tomin presented his students with a new idea. He was doing his best for them, he said, but they needed something more. With their permission he would write to some western universities and suggest that their professors became involved in the teaching. With the help of those present on that occasion — the Vaculík brothers, Jan Bednář, Jan Ruml, Vladimír Prajzler and Ivan Dejmal — Tomin drafted a letter in both English and German to be sent to two English-speaking universities (Oxford and Harvard) and two German universities (Heidelberg and the Free University in Berlin).

In the letter, which neatly fills one side of A4 paper, Tomin describes how he came to set up the seminar, and the attention it has received from the Ministry of the Interior — 'to (their) credit let it be said that they have hitherto not put any further obstacles in our way, at least not directly; they are content to carry out persecution of individuals by sacking them from their jobs, preventing young people from studying at secondary schools, and so on. At times, though, they still threaten us: "We'll destroy you — you and your Plato!"'[34] Julius describes his frustration at having foreign mail confiscated and being unable to buy English or German newspapers and journals. But, he points out, there is still one possibility — foreign visitors can come to Czechoslovakia.

He is broad in his description of what subjects they would welcome — 'We wish to understand the world we live in... We shall welcome natural scientists who will try to bring closer to us the world of the natural sciences... We wish to understand the society we live in — we shall welcome economists and sociologists... We wish to understand Man — we shall welcome psychologists, philosophers, theologians... We wish to understand the development of mankind — we shall welcome anthropologists, historians, futurologists, ecologists... There is only one condition — you need to have the desire to come and see us, to share with us the fruits of your own study and research.'[35] And to close, he arrives at the practical point of when they should come: 'we meet to study philosophy in my flat every Wednesday at 6 p.m., from September to June... Ideally, we should like to set aside an agreed day for your lectures, for instance the first Wednesday in the month between October and June.'[36]

In line with his beliefs, Tomin posted these letters in the normal way, but at the same time gave copies to trusted visitors for posting outside Czechoslovakia. One of these visitors was the General Secretary of Amnesty International, Paul Oestreicher, with whom the Tomins had stayed in London in 1968, and who had remained a good friend. Oestreicher made copies for distribution to such people as George Theiner, editor of the London-based journal *Index on Censorship*. George (Jiří) Theiner had been educated in Britain during the war; in Stalinist Czechoslovakia he spent the years from 1950-53 in labour camps attached to the Silesian coal mines. He worked as an editor and translator in the Prague of the 1960s, and then, in exile for the second time after the Soviet invasion, became editor of *Index on Censorship* where he worked for the rights of all those living in oppressed countries, not only Czechoslovakia. Bill Newton-Smith, secretary to the Sub-Faculty of Philosophy in Oxford, remembers receiving one copy of Tomin's letter from Theiner and another from an All Souls don who had been visiting Prague.

There are conflicting opinions as to whether copies travelled through the secret courier service set up by the Czech emigré Jan Kavan: Tomin believes absolutely not, whereas Kavan is sure that he did handle the letter. It is possible that a copy was given to one of Kavan's couriers, since at least one of them (Heather Allen) was visiting the Tomins. Jan Kavan and Julius Tomin represented two completely different approaches to the issue of how to behave within a totalitarian regime: on the one hand, an emphasis on secrecy and disguise; on the other, a determination to carry on 'as normal', to hold on to one's rights even to the point of sacrificing what little space for freedom the

régime might grant.[37] In the early days of the Oxford philosophers' visits the contrasting personalities of Kavan and Tomin
had a complex influence on the development of the British
response to the situation in Czechoslovakia.

In the 1970s and 1980s Jan Kavan was a key figure in
relationships between the West — especially the British — and
the Czechoslovak dissidents. His father Pavel had been an active
Communist in the post war period, and became a member of the
post-1948 government. When the regime found itself unable to
fulfil its grandiose promises and in a series of show trials sentenced its own members to death and imprisonment, Pavel
Kavan was one of those jailed. Shortly after his release in 1960
he died from a heart attack. His wife Rosemary, an
Englishwoman, remained committed to Communist ideals. Jan
Kavan was active in the student movement in 1968, and
immediately after the invasion fled to Britain, where — in common with other Czechoslovak students at that time — he was
given an opportunity to study at university, in his case the
London School of Economics.[39] He thus belongs to the generation of 'reform Communists' and was regarded with distrust by
many of those emigrés who had fled from Communism in 1948.
Unlike other student exiles, who either integrated into British
life after completing their courses or used Britain as first base on
a longer odyssey, Kavan clung to a shoestring life in bohemian
London, determined to stay in contact with the opposition
movement in Czechoslovakia — at that time fragmented and in
disarray. In 1969 he founded the Solidarity Fund 'in response to
the needs of Czechoslovak citizens who were suffering from the
effects of imprisonment, job discrimination, unemployment and
civil disabilities imposed on them for their political and social
beliefs'.[40] Most of Kavan's circle in Britain were idealistic
young intellectuals, left-wing revolutionaries involved in human
rights movements. In February 1976 he established the Palach
Press Ltd., an agency 'with the aim of providing accurate information about Czechoslovakia and placing literary samizdat with
Western publishers.'[41] The Palach Press was to be the public face
of the secret and confidential Solidarity Fund. Kavan's timing
was opportune, in that the Palach Press was established shortly
before the drama of Charter 77 opened. In 1977 Petr Uhl[43] set up
the publication of *Informace o Chartě* (Information about the

Charter; commonly known as *Infoch*) which published or summarised documents issued by the Charter spokesmen and other
letters and communications. Uhl later described *Infoch* as 'that
proverbial tree which every man has to plant at some
point in his lifetime'.[44] In the VONS[45] trials of 1979 Uhl was
sentenced to five years imprisonment; his wife Anna Šabatová[46]
continued publication in his absence. As part of the Palach
Press's information service Kavan translated and summarised
the contents of *Infoch* for the western media and other
subscribers.

During the early years of his operations Kavan relied on
underground couriers to communicate with his sources. These
were mainly young Britons with no apparent connection with
Czechoslovakia. An individual would travel as a tourist no more
than twice a year, carrying easily concealed letters; typed single-
spaced on one sheet of thin A4 paper, these were wrapped in
another sheet of thin paper to avoid the bulk of envelopes.[47]
Visits were agreed with the previous traveller, or by coded postcards. Meetings between the couriers and Kavan's contacts in
Prague were arranged with complicated precautions to ensure
secrecy. In other cases the courier's role was not to carry letters,
but to hold discussions with Kavan's contacts and bring information about particular projects. In 1977 Kavan asked the
young teacher Heather Allen to visit Julius Tomin; Tomin,
sitting at the kitchen table bottling mushrooms, described to
Allen his seminars on classical Greek philosophy and his students' ability to relate the issues and principles to their own
everyday life. Allen returned overflowing with enthusiasm. For
her, the rewards of the work as a courier for Kavan were to
'bring voices back and send them out to the world'.

Belonging to the same circle of left-wing intellectuals was
the sociologist Steven Lukes, who from the late 1960s to early
1980s was based in Oxford. Lukes was one of those members of
the British left who had been emotionally moved by the events
of the late 1960s, and had been eager to establish contacts not
only in Czechoslovakia but in the rest of eastern Europe. In 1969
he had met two Czechs on study visits to Oxford: the young
lawyer Petr Pithart and the student Jana Fraňková (at that time
still Vaňatová), completing her degree at St Hilda's College as
part of the British support for Czechoslovak students stranded

after the Soviet invasion. Pithart, as a young and talented 'reform Communist' was destined for a golden career; the last thing he anticipated was to return to an occupied Prague to spend two decades in poverty as a samizdat historian. Vaňatová-Fraňková, whose mother had been a strong Communist, graduated in English Literature in 1971 and returned to Prague to live a precarious existence on the edge of the dissident ghetto. Lukes also met the sociologist Alena Hromádková who, during the dying days of freedom in 1969, was passing through Oxford on what was to be her last visit abroad for twenty years. A strong Catholic, daughter of parents who had remained loyal to the ideals of the First Republic, she had had no experience of the world of Communist 'nomenklatura'. Lukes visited them in Prague during the 1970s and all three — Pithart, Fraňková and Hromádková — were to be important contacts for the Jan Hus Foundation over the coming years.

There are several conflicting stories of how Julius Tomin's letter, posted in May 1978, reached the Oxford philosophers the following December. What is important is that it did reach them, and that it was read out to the Sub-Faculty of Philosophy by the Canadian philosopher of logic Bill Newton-Smith at its meeting on Monday 29th January 1979.

Oxford comes to Prague

The Oxford academic community was not at this time known for its interest and participation in international affairs — Ernest Gellner on one occasion referred in frustration to the 'North Oxford narodniks [narrow-minded nationalists]'.[1] Bill Newton-Smith did not expect the Oxford dons to show a great deal of interest in the letter from a dissident Czech philosopher. Charter 77 was already two years old in January 1979, and there had been no recent newsworthy events to stir the British conscience. 'Letter from Czechoslovakian philosophers' appeared as the final item on the Sub-Faculty's agenda which included, *inter alia*, the timetabling of philosophy examinations and the rate of payment per lecture for visitors from abroad.

Newton-Smith was surprised when the Sub-Faculty voted not only to send philosophers to Tomin's seminar, but even recommended financial support. Kathy Wilkes's recollection is that the matter was settled in barely two minutes: 'Of course we were going to send lecturers to the Prague seminars; it was normal practice to respond to invitations from academic colleagues.' Others who were present at the meeting think there may have been resistance from philosophers who had already established contact with Czech and Slovak universities, resistance which was to surface a few months later. Nevertheless, the minute for January reads: 'It was agreed that the Chairman [J.L. Mackie] should send a letter of support to the Czechoslovakian philosophers. It was agreed to ask the Lit. Hum. [Literae Humaniores] Board to make a grant to cover the cost of sending two members of the Philosophy Sub-Faculty to meet with the Czechoslovakian philosophers.'[2] (The letter was not written; in March it was agreed to wait until more information had been received.[3]) Bill Newton-Smith was to play an important role in the future of the Jan Hus Foundation; so was Alan Montefiore, at that time Herbert Samuel Fellow in Philosophy at Balliol College, who remembers that he was one of those at the meeting who volunteered to visit Tomin's seminar. Nevertheless, his visit was not to take place until the end of the year. As it turned out, the first visitor was to be crucial to the whole development of the relationship between Oxford and Prague.

Kathy Wilkes was (and is) a woman who welcomes challenges — intellectual, moral and physical.[4] Her interest in philosophy began at the age of thirteen, and was encouraged by her brothers and father, headmaster of Radley College. In the 1960s women were not admitted to the historic Oxford colleges, and after having been the only girl to study at Radley College, Wilkes found herself in the all-female atmosphere of St. Hugh's. Nevertheless, she graduated in Classics and went on to read for her doctorate at King's College Cambridge as their first woman student. Wilkes was proposed as the first visitor to Tomin's seminar because, she claims, she was on sabbatical and had more time than the other philosophers. Newton-Smith, who remembers making the proposal over lunch at Balliol, objects that this was not the only reason: 'I knew that she was the right person to begin with; she was energetic and outward-looking and would get the project off to a good start.'

For more information about the situation in Czechoslovakia they turned to Steven Lukes who, a member of the Sub-Faculty of Social Sciences and a Fellow at Balliol with Alan Montefiore and Bill Newton-Smith, was in touch with what was happening in the Sub-Faculty of Philosophy. His friendship with many of the philosophers and his intimate involvement with the beginnings of the Jan Hus Foundation subsequently led many Czechs to think he must have been a leading member of the Foundation; yet he avoided any formal connection, and his name rarely appears in the records. Lukes, alarmed by what he considered to be the philosophers' ignorance about conditions behind the Iron Curtain, introduced them to Jan Kavan. Their first encounter must have taken place in February or March 1979; Kavan remembers that all his early meetings took place with Kathy Wilkes, with whom he had many detailed conversations, and that he did not meet Newton-Smith or Montefiore until much later.

Wilkes had therefore been well briefed when she went to London on Friday 23rd March 1979[5] to ask the Czechoslovak Embassy for an eleven day tourist visa. Nevertheless, Lukes was still doubtful about the philosophers' competence, and travelled ahead to Prague to enlist the assistance of Alena Hromádková and Jana Fraňková. Tomin himself ignored Lukes's message asking for a 'secret' meeting at Gottwaldova metro station, and was not happy when Lukes visited his flat by torchlight; nor, it turned out, did he approve of the security briefing his first Oxford philosopher had received from Kavan and Lukes. Tomin's guiding principle was that if one's actions are not illegal or dishonourable, then they should be carried out in the open. To this end he always made public the dates and times of his seminars. When the Oxford visitors started arriving regularly, Tomin would take them to lunch talking openly in fluent English — at a time when many Czechs, if they even dared to have English-speaking friends, would ask them to speak in low tones or not at all in public. For Tomin, this was a sign of their subjugation.

When, however, on 9th April — the Monday of Holy Week — Wilkes arrived in Prague, Tomin was delighted by his visitor and prepared to put the issue behind him (later it was to emerge in a more serious form). After nearly a year, the message he had cast into the waters had brought results; and only now did Kathy Wilkes discover that her visit was the only response to Tomin's appeal to the four universities: '...since he had by then virtually given up hope of any response, my visit held greater significance than I had ever imagined.'[6] That day and the following were divided between discussion with the Tomins and sightseeing with Hromádková, who became Wilkes's guide to Prague for the rest of her stay, and Fraňková. Wilkes's first seminar, on Aristotle, took place on the Wednesday evening at the flat in Keramická Street; starting at the usual time of 6.00 p.m.,it lasted until midnight.[7] Wilkes subsequently observed that: '...the discussions were the most stimulating that I have experienced. It was imposible to receive a "standard's counter" to a familiar argument, because they have had no chance to learn of the "standard" arguments; all comments were first-hand; absolute concentration was sustained throughout the sessions — not surprisingly, given that they were willing to take risks to attend.'[8]

On Maundy Thursday Wilkes met the students in the Old Town Square; two days later she rose at five in the morning to stay in Hromádková's primitive country cottage in the Orlické Mountains near the Polish border in the north of Bohemia.[9]

Returning to Prague on Easter Tuesday, Wilkes was taken by Julius to the Krakovská seminar, where she lectured on commissurotomy[10] from 6.00 p.m. until 11.30 p.m. On Wednesday the students waited for her under the statue of St Wenceslas and she returned to Krakovská for another seven-hour discussion. Thursday was Wilkes's final night in Prague, but she gave what was perhaps the most demanding seminar of her ten day visit. Tomin had publicised the news of his first visiting western academic, and on that evening Kathy Wilkes was more nervous of the distinguished gathering (of around 25 people) than of any possible intervention by the police. Amongst those present were the philosophers Radim Palouš and Petr Rezek, and the writer Ludvík Vaculík, who wrote an account of the seminar in his diary, later published as *Český snář* (The Czech Dreambook). Vaculík had nearly failed to arrive for the lecture; that morning he had been called in by his police interrogator, a certain Major Fišer. He was questioned about his feuilleton 'Attempt at - another genre' — about the source of his idea, how the feuilleton came to be published in *Listy*[11] and what fee he had received. The rest of the three hour interrogation was filled first with a standard exchange of views about the constitution, the law, free speech and Charter 77 and then — exceptionally (and probably as a result of the proximity of Easter) — with Vaculík's exposition of the symbolic meaning of Christ crucified between the two thieves. Fišer sat listlessly, whilst a new, more active colleague listened with greater interest, eventually saying 'I don't go along with you. But then, we're not Christians'. Which Vaculík took to be self-evident.

Exhausted, Vaculík went home and fell asleep over a book. By the evening he was reluctant to make the trip across Prague, but felt bound to respond to Tomin's excitement over the visitor. On arrival, 'my first surprise was that an Oxford professor could be so young and feminine and at the same time so confident and wise...'.[12] He was impressed by her choice of dress, which reminded him of academic robes: black trousers of a shiny material, smartly creased, and a matt grey blouse, its fullness

gathered above the bust and at the waist. His second surprise
was that he was actually able to follow the arguments of Kathy
Wilkes's lecture (which Tomin translated block by block). What
thrilled Vaculík and the rest of the students was the freedom of
Wilkes's expression, the relaxed way in which she felt able to
expound her own views without regard to doctrine or reliance on
established opinion. She took her examples from literature,
philosophy and psychology, and, with their help, thought
through her own ideas.

The subject of the lecture was the 'Identity of Human
Personality' and Wilkes's first point of reference was John
Locke: if a prince and a cobbler exchanged brains, who would
then be the prince and who the cobbler? And — since identity is
social as well as subjective — which would each wife recognise
as her husband? For whereas the cells of the body are renewed
throughout life, memory endures and accumulates. Human
personality is like a rope made up of fibres of experience —
principles, desires and hopes. The longer the fibres, the stronger
the personality. Is the adult the same person as the child? The
individual can deliberately cultivate certain elements whilst
resisting other influences. 'Personality' is not something which
is permanent and limited: it is the expression of its own
development.

Vaculík recorded that Wilkes ended with an open-ended
example from literature, of the young son of a Russian land-
owner who vows that when he inherits he will divide the
property between his muzhiks, only to regret the decision thirty-
five years later. The reference formed the basis of a discussion
which lasted nearly as long as the lecture. At first the group was
engaged mainly by the effect of experiments showing the relative independence of the brain from the body. Tomin himself
was actively engaged in the discussion — 'I have an unforgettable picture', Wilkes wrote later, 'of Dr. Tomin using every
resource of intonation, gesture and posture to convey impartially
the views he was reporting, opposing, or propounding, often
carried away by the argument to such an extent that he had to be
stopped to wait for translation.' It was at his prompting that the
group moved to the more abstract issues involved, and Vaculík
was interested to discover that the young people returned mainly
to the question of personality being governed by moral

principles. Ivan Dejmal recalls that it was an enormous theme which presented many questions. Vaculík described in *The Czech Dreambook* how he decided to provoke the group by offering the specific example, known to everyone there, of the writer Pavel Kohout.[13] Kohout had been consistent in his attempts to live his life according to specific principles, to such an extent that in his youth his efforts had outpaced his understanding. When his understanding matured, he had replaced his previous misguided attempts by a still greater striving to renew and strengthen his personality. To accuse Kohout of having made an about-face was a misunderstanding. A life based on moral principles cannot be achieved all at once; it is a process of trial and error. Kohout had been consistent and steadfast in his search for truth. Vaculík's choice of example threw the rest of the group into silence, a silence broken only by Tomin's translation into English. According to Vaculík, Kathy Wilkes praised him for his contribution, but it seems, at 10.30 p.m., to have brought the seminar to an end.

Wilkes left the country the next day. As well as the seminars and contact with students there had been time for much talk and discussion with the Tomins. It was an inspiring and stimulating time for all three of them. Much of the discussion was about philosophy; at that time, Kathy Wilkes' main interest was in philosophy of mind and analytical philosophy. The chief focus of Tomin's work was Plato; Wilkes subsequently observed that 'Tomin's views, formed in unavoidable isolation from secondary literature, were based on in-side-out familiarity with the entire Greek corpus. Persecuted though they are, he and his colleagues are free to ignore as faintly comic the intellectual demarcation lines of the West...'.[14] Very often Tomin and Wilkes held opposing opinions, but part of the joy of this visit was the discovery that differences helped to deepen the relationship. Tomin explained that he exploited the fact that, legally, the authorities could not make his own position any worse than it was already. They also discussed Tominová's work as Charter spokesperson, and the moral problems — such as the loss of the children's education — caused by living under totalitarianism.

Like many visitors to the Czechoslovak capital on many different occasions, Kathy Wilkes returned overwhelmed and elated, her head full of plans and possibilities. On 7th May 1979 she reported to the Sub-Faculty of Philosophy. She recommended that it apply to the Lit. Hum. Board for funds not only for travel, but also for books — 'I took with me books to the approximate value of £50, and these were eagerly seized upon — to illustrate, one reprint given to one of the students had apparently been read by 40 people a week later.'[15] She also urged '...individual members of the Sub-Faculty to go in any case, suggesting only that their names were known officially to the chairman and the secretary of the Sub-Faculty so that, if there were to be trouble with the police, such people could declare themselves to be there qua Oxford philosopher rather than qua individual; moreover, by far the easiest way to arrange such visits is for each one to be discussed by the preceding visitor with Tomin, which would presuppose some organization here.'[16] As a result of the meeting, it was agreed that the secretary Bill Newton-Smith would co-ordinate the visits, working closely with Wilkes. Uppermost in Wilkes's mind was the need to publicise the plight of the Prague philosophers, as they struggled to uphold civilised values and academic standards in a society where the slightest displeasure on the part of the authorities could result in a ruined life. The first reference to Tomin's seminars appeared in an article in the *New Statesman* in May,[17] which referred to the collapse of professional ethics and moral standards in the Communist countries. A few days later Kathy Wilkes published her own article in *The Guardian*[18] and at the end of the month an article specifically about the Tomin seminars appeared in the Oxford magazine *Isis*.[19] The Sub-Faculty of philosophy had agreed, with money from the Literae Humaniores Board, to send as the next visitor the Canadian philosopher Charles Taylor, Chichele Professor of Social and Political Thought at All Souls College. On Tuesday 5th June Wilkes came (with books for the Prague students purchased with a grant from the Lit. Hum. Board) to Lukes's rooms in Balliol College to brief Taylor.[20]

Whilst the Oxford philosophers were pressing a normally indifferent British press and public to take notice of the Czech philosophers, a situation was unfolding in Prague which was to influence both the development of the seminars and the future of the Tomin family. It began with one of those incidents which in a police state can either be attributed to malicious brutality or interpreted as a step in a more complex plan. On the same June evening as Wilkes, Lukes and Taylor were sitting in Balliol discussing the Prague seminar, Zdena Tominová was on her way home from a visit to Jiří Gruša and his family.[21] Entering the main door of no. 4 Keramická Street, she was attacked by a masked man. Passers-by rescued her, but not before she had been severely beaten. An ambulance was called and she was hospitalised with concussion. The news reached Tomin, on night duty at the zoo, who visited her at the Na Františku hospital. Returning to work in an emotional state, he neglected his rounds to write a letter to President Husák; he was convinced there had been an attempt to murder Zdena and that he was to have been accused of the murder. The following day Zdena issued a statement connecting the attack with her constant surveillance by the secret police.[22]

It was usual and more convenient for the secret police to attack women than men; Julius, although not heavily built, was formidably strong and if he had fought back it would have taken several policemen to overcome him. The attack on Zdena was probably unconnected with the philosophy seminars; she had built up important contacts in the western peace movement, and had been chosen as one of the three Charter spokespersons for 1979. A week earlier, on 29th May, her fellow spokesmen (Václav Benda and Jiří Dienstbier) had been detained by police. Zdena had immediately issued a Charter statement, pointing out that the timing of the arrests had been chosen to coincide with Pope John Paul II's visit to Poland, on which western interest was focused.[23] Earlier on the day of her attack, replacement spokesmen (Jiří Hájek and Ladislav Hejdánek) had been chosen. Nevertheless, once the attack on her had been 'investigated' and a police guard put on the Tomins' flat 'for their own safety' there were threatening implications for the philosophy seminars. On Wednesday June 6th the regular seminar took place; on Thursday, Julius gave a talk on Charter 77 to a visiting group of West German 'tourists' at a rendez-vous in the Vikarka restaurant in the Castle, under the nose of President Gustáv Husák. The next day, Friday 8th June 1979, the second Oxford visitor, Charles Taylor, arrived at the Tomins' flat at the time agreed with Kathy Wilkes. Zdena had just returned from hospital, her face still badly bruised. Julius was exhausted through lack of sleep and emotional strain. The Tomins' telephone line had been cut, which was usual at times of crisis. With scarcely an hour or two before the seminar, Taylor ran through his repertoire of themes and Julius chose Marxism: 'Because I can translate that in my sleep.' The students listened dutifully, but, it emerged later, were deeply disappointed by the subject of the lecture.[24]

The weekend had arrived; Taylor was looking forward to seeing the Bohemian countryside described by Kathy Wilkes, so it was arranged that the second seminar would take place in a quarry near the castle of Karlštejn not far from Prague. The June weather was fine and warm, and photographs taken by Zdena Tominová show the students stretched out in the long grass, carefree and relaxed.[25] Sitting by a campfire in the June evening Taylor spoke for four hours on Romanticism. Many of those present remember this as the most successful seminar they attended. The following evening Taylor made his way to the student flat in Krakovská Street, where the subject of his third lecture was 'Quine[26] and the Foundations of Language'. After the seminar and a few half-litres of Czech beer, Taylor and the students sat through the warm summer night on the banks of the Vltava. 'It was for me an unforgettable experience,' he wrote later, 'I've rarely encountered such eagerness to discuss philosophy.'[27] Several of the students remember that of all the visitors, Taylor was most on their wavelength. A fourth lecture, on recent developments in philosophy in the West, was given at the Paloušes' home, for the Kampakademie.

Charles Taylor arrived back in Britain on Monday 11th June;[28] the same evening the Sub-Faculty in Oxford listened to his report on the Czech seminars and agreed that the Chairman should write to the Czechoslovak Embassy in London expressing the philosophers' concern over the recent treatment of their colleagues in Czechoslovakia, and should release the letter to the press.[29] Wilkes, Taylor and Newton-Smith were to help with drafting the letter. There was still one more visitor due: Richard Hare, White's Professor of Moral Philosophy at Oxford University, travelling to Prague on Monday 2nd July 1979.

In Central Europe the summer begins precisely on 30th June; the Technical University students had already held their last gathering in the flat in Krakovská Street before they dispersed for the summer. They had invited Zdena Tominová; not to lecture, but to discuss the purpose and future of Charter 77. Spring 1979 had been a difficult time for the Chartists; the arrests and police brutality had led many signatories to question its significance. By now, a 24-hour police guard had been established on the Tomins' home and Richard Hare's lecture was held at a different address, in Ivan Dejmal's flat in nearby Kamenická Street. Hare, described by the Master of Balliol Anthony Kenny as 'the most influential moral philosopher in Britain' had made it clear that in view of the increasingly controversial nature of the project, he would go to Prague only to teach philosophy — no political subtext was to be read into his visit. There was no Krakovská seminar, and he gave only the one lecture in Prague. Dejmal remembers that Hare engaged the Czech listeners with his life story, and how it had formulated his ideas on philosophy. Vladimír Prajzler attended the lecture, and remembers Hare (an extremely tall man) as being 'dignified but interesting'.

As the respite of the long vacation of 1979 drew to an end, Ludvík Vaculík's son suggested to Tomin that, as part of the recently initiated and promising programme of foreign visitors, they should invite to the seminar Thorolf Rafto, Professor of Economic History from the University of Bergen in Norway. The elderly and distinguished 'highly individual humanist', famous for his work in human rights, was visiting Prague. It was agreed that Rafto should lecture on 'The Meaning of History' on 5th September 1979, the first seminar of the autumn. It was to be held in the Dejmals' flat (the police guard on the Tomins' flat had been lifted during the summer but re-imposed when Tomin received a letter with news of an award from the Friedrich Eberhard Stiftung in West Germany). However, Tomin and Rafto arrived to find a police guard had been posted also on the Dejmals' flat. Retiring to the first-floor café of the Hotel Belvedere, they saw from its windows a police car draw up outside; shortly afterwards its occupants, according to Tomin's description, literally tore Rafto from his hands. At the same time the police raiding Dejmal's flat drove off with the two daughters of Ladislav Hejdánek. For the next twenty-four hours, in spite of a complaint by the Norwegian Ambassador to the Czechoslovak Ministry of Foreign Affairs, Rafto disappeared. The police, who had put him on the train to Berlin, denied all knowledge of his existence; eventually Rafto reappeared in Berlin with the East

German dissident Robert Havemann. Back home, he told Wilkes in a telephone conversation that he was convinced that the police were after him personally, and that nothing must stop the philosophers' visits; it was quite impossible to exaggerate their importance.

At the time of Rafto's abduction the Technical University students Vladimír Prajzler, Luděk Bednář and Lenka Dvořáková were still on holiday in Bulgaria. Returning to his flat in Krakovská Street a few days later, Prajzler began to prepare for his final year at university. Early in the morning of Monday 10th September the doorbell rang. Two plain clothes policemen (without a search warrant) confiscated letters and documents, and took Prajzler to the police station in Bartolomějská Street where he was interrogated for 17 hours before being locked in a cell. The Tomins had briefed the students to remain silent in such an eventuality; thinking of the detention of the activists from the Committee for the Defence of the Unjustly Prosecuted (already held without charge for four months), Prajzler could not help wondering whether he had been locked up for a few hours or several years. On Wednesday he was released; twenty metres down the street he was arrested again, and held till the Friday. Early on the same day (Wednesday) Bednář and Dvořáková, not knowing of Prajzler's detention, had returned to the Krakovská flat and been picked up by the police; Dvořáková was interrogated for several hours, and Bednář held for the full two-day period. (Over the next few months the students became familiar with the 48-hour detention system, and learned never to go anywhere without a toothbrush and a supply of cigarettes.) The three of them, together with more of the students who had been rounded up, were held individually in adjoining rooms. The aim of the police was to obtain information on the philosophy and literature seminars, not only those they were attending, but any others of which they might have heard. More than ten years later, Prajzler discovered that one of the Krakovská students had been secretly recording the June discussion with Tominová in the attic flat, and had passed the recording to the police. As it turned out, that was the last student seminar to have been held in Krakovská Street.

Prajzler and Bednář were not surprised to receive letters from the Dean of their Faculty soon after their release, announcing their expulsion from university on the grounds that they were 'active member(s) of an organised group which influenced university students against the socialist position'. Prajzler's letter later disappeared, probably in a police search.[30] During that summer vacation, Aleš Havlíček had been travelling with friends to Poland for the Pope's visit and been injured in a road accident. The Technical University authorities expelled him later, ostensibly on the grounds that he had not fulfilled examination requirements. Twenty-year-old Lenka Dvořáková from the industrial town of Ostrava, about to enter the third year of a course at the Faculty of Civil Engineering, also received a letter from the university, differently worded, but telling her not to return to her studies. One of the charges made against her was that she had organised a group in her room to read and discuss Dostoyevsky. A similar letter of expulsion was received by Tomáš Liška, studying at the Film Academy. Along with their university places, the expelled students lost their grants and hostel beds, and had to earn a living and find accommodation as best they could: Havlíček as a boilerman at the Hotel Jalta, Dvořáková as a model at art school. Luděk Bednář remembers that the Tomins were like parents to them, and that he lived for a while in their Keramická flat .

Far from dissuading western academics from visiting Prague, the situation stimulated greater interest. But the financial resources of the Sub-Faculty of Philosophy were limited. It would only be possible to send a small handful of philosophers a year, and Kathy Wilkes foresaw the time when the Literae Humaniores Board would say 'enough'. It was necessary to inspire philosophers from other universities who would raise their own funding, or even travel at their own expense. Over the next few years she sent out more than a hundred letters; it is impossible to know how many philosophers were approached in this way, how many agreed, and how many refused.

One philosopher who initially refused to go was Roger Scruton, at that time lecturer at Birkbeck College, London University. In mid-May 1979, during a philosophy conference held at Cumberland Lodge in Windsor Great Park, Wilkes tried to convince Scruton of the importance of visiting Tomin's seminars.[31] Scruton was reluctant. He had too many things he wanted to do; a visit to Czechoslovakia was not part of his programme and would take up too much time. But in September he was to attend a conference on aesthetics in Cracow in southern Poland. Eventually he was persuaded that it would be an effective use of time for him to take the train from Cracow to Prague. Also persuaded was Anthony Savile of King's College London, who on his way from London to Cracow lectured to Tomin's students on 'Beauty', with Zdena Tominová translating.

Scruton arrived on Monday 24th September for a three-day visit. For his lecture to Tomin's seminar, he spoke on Wittgenstein's private language argument. He remembers that there were about 25 people present, including the 'dapper figure' of Radim Palouš. Among the young people were Markéta Němcová, Tomáš Liška and Lenka Dvořáková. After the seminar, from 6.00 till 9.00 p.m., Scruton and the Tomins went to a restaurant; the next day he met Tomáš and Lenka on the quiet, wooded Shooters' Island in the Vltava. As he talked to them he realised how hungry they were for the outside world, for access to a wider culture and literature. He heard about their expulsion from university, and realised that Tomin's seminars, important as they were, provided only a small part of the education they should be getting. He also wondered how much opportunity they had to express their own ideas; the seminars were dominated by Tomin, and the young students were overshadowed by his powerful personality. In conversation with the students, Scruton began to realise what a vital role the seminars played in passing on to the new generation traditions of independent enquiry; he also thought how much more effective they could be if the teaching were freed from the influence of personality. He began to wonder about the number of young people in Czechoslovakia like Tomáš and Lenka, enquiring minds who did not know about Tomin's lectures and who had no guide or tutor at all. Scruton resolved that he would try to open up the traffic between Prague and the outside world, search for other connections, for manifestations of free speech and ideas which did not expose themselves so publicly as did Tomin. And for the first time the possibility arose that ways might be found for the caged students to visit the West.

By this time, Tomin himself had received an invitation to go to Oxford, to give the Vaughan Memorial Lectures at Balliol College; invitations were shortly to follow from the Cambridge

Classics Faculty; from University College and Bedford College, London; and from the British Aristotelian Society. He had written in a letter to Wilkes: 'At first [the Cambridge invitation] turned my head. I wanted to go right now. I lived several weeks (perhaps only a week, it just looked ages) in a happy dream of living as a visiting scholar in Cambridge. My wife was very much for it — she wanted to send me here alone, she cannot leave now. Well, I brought it so far that I went to the passport office to take the application forms. And then I realised that I cannot go.'[32] His reason was that in Prague he was as free as it was possible for anyone to be, whereas if he went to England he would have to act in such a way as to be allowed to return: 'I would have to pervert myself for the time being... when I come to England I want to get more freedom and not to be less free.'[33] The Cambridge invitation had been sent through official channels, and Tomin had received it via the Ministry of the Interior. The same day the police called in Ladislav Hejdánek and told him: 'Now Tomin is leaving.' They made no secret of the fact that he should accept these invitations, and preferably take his family and belongings with him — for good.

They had ways of making their point clear. On a Friday early in October 1979 (shortly after Roger Scruton's first visit) Tomin travelled to northern Bohemia to give a seminar in the village of Řepčice. On his arrival he found the village surrounded by police with dogs. Refusing to get into a police car, he was picked up and put inside, and taken first to a police station and then the psychiatric hospital at Dolní Beřkovice. Over the next days he insisted on the illegality of his detention, refusing even to take the opportunity of an offer to send a message home. Zdena, at home in their third-floor flat behind the 24-hour police guard ('for your own safety') heard the students singing in the street and knew they had something to tell her; slipping past the guards with a rubbish bag, she exchanged it for Julius's rucksack and told the students to run. It took her three days, trying one office after another, before a policeman softened and told her where to find Julius. At noon on the Tuesday morning she persuaded the doctors at Dolní Beřkovice to sign him into her care. A month later Tomin was summoned to a Prague psychiatric hospital, where he went accompanied by Eva Kantůrková[34] and the visiting antipodean philosopher Thomas Mautner. The bizarre and threatening nature of these encounters burned deeply into Tomin's memory, and the conviction that there was a conspiracy was to certify him as 'psychopathic paranoia querulans' (as he remembers being described in a newspaper report of the time) and commit him to a psychiatric institution for life remained with him even after he left Czechoslovakia.

Soon after Tomin's detention, on 22nd October 1979, what were known as the 'VONS trials', the most serious show trials since the 1950s, opened in the smallest room of the court in Spálená Street in Prague. VONS had been founded in 1978, to follow cases in the civil and criminal law in which ordinary citizens had been illegally accused of offences against the state. In the dock, accused of criminal subversion of the republic in collusion with foreign agents, were Otka Bednářová (mother of Jiří and Jan Bednář), Václav Benda, Jiří Dienstbier, Václav Havel, Dana Němcová (wife of Jiří Němec and mother of seven children) and Petr Uhl. Sentences given on the third day of the trial ranged from five years for Uhl to three for Bednářová and Benda; Němcová was allowed a suspended sentence on health grounds. Inevitably, the trial had a serious effect on the morale of the students.

By now, pressure was also being put on Ivan Dejmal, in whose flat the seminars were being hosted. Dejmal was an environmentalist who had been in his last year at university in 1970 when he was charged with 'anti-state activities' as a member of the Revolutionary Socialist Party and subsequently with 'undermining the morale of the army' into which he had been forcibly drafted; he was not released from prison until 1976. On the 2nd November 1979 Dejmal was one of twelve people detained 'on suspicion of preparing a criminal act of terror'[35] — specifically, of plotting to assassinate President Gustáv Husák. For Dejmal there was a real possibility that he might be put on trial alongside the VONS committee. He and the other participants in the philosophy course were asked 'whether the course discusses theoretically the problem of terrorism', and eventually he was told that the course would be stopped 'with maximum publicity — so that everybody in the flats would know what kind of charlatan philosopher they have there'.[36] After forty-eight hours the group had their hair cropped and were released.[37] It is not likely that the authorities, certainly not the senior officers, seriously thought that the group was plotting to assassinate Husák. The purpose was intimidation, particularly in cases where the police thought someone might weaken under the humiliation of exposure.

Alan Montefiore of Balliol College recalls the feeling of tension amongst the students during his visit in the Christmas vacation of 1979; the normally courteous Jan Bednář asked aggressively: 'Why are you here? Are we some sort of zoo, that you come to stare at us?' Montefiore was travelling with his partner, the French philosopher Catherine Audard, and with Steven Lukes and his second wife Nina, a lawyer who was following for Amnesty International the appeal against the sentences imposed in the VONS trial. The tension at the seminar, which took place in Ivan Dejmal's flat, was aggravated by the presence of a Swedish news photographer. Initially all the westerners refused to be photographed, but after a harangue from Tomin, Montefiore and Audard agreed to be included. Tomin's attitude towards the visitors so upset Alena Hromádková that she refused to attend any more of his seminars. In his lecture, Montefiore continued the theme of Richard Hare's philosophy, following from Hare's visit in July. Possibly because of the Christmas season, there was no police raid; the visitors were struck more by the hostility of the Hotel Flora waiters than that of the police. Montefiore's seminar started at 10.00 p.m.[38] and ended at 3.00 a.m., allowing an hour or so sleep for those like Markéta Němcová who had to get up at 5.30 a.m. for work the next day.

Following Scruton's September visit, the philosophers had been thinking of ways to arrange for some of the students to study at Oxford; not to make emigrés of them, but to enable them to return to Czechoslovakia with a qualification which the Communist authorities could not ignore. The day after the seminar Montefiore and Audard met Lenka Dvořáková, Jan Bednář and Tomáš Liška in the café Slavia. (Earlier in December, Dvořáková had surprised the British philosophers by finding her way to England for a short visit, where she had met Kathy Wilkes and Roger Scruton.) Each of the students had to weigh up the opportunity for him- or herself. The temptation was to be very great for Markéta Němcová, who longed all her life to follow courses as a normal student.[39] In 1979 she recognised that if she did leave Czechoslovakia, the Communists would never allow her to return. Her mother, after several months detention, was now on a suspended sentence. Markéta was the eldest of the seven children and she believed it her duty to stay. Luděk Bednář, a conscientious objector, was shortly to start living in semi-hiding to avoid military service (in Czechoslovakia under the Communists there was no alternative to service in the army). He did not immediately refuse the offer from the Oxford philosophers, but neither did he take it up, knowing the risks involved.

The three students who did meet the Montefiores were those who were seriously considering the offer. Jan Bednář, whose doubts were similar to Markéta's, eventually left in 1982, one of the darkest years for the dissident community. He completed an Oxford degree and embarked on a career with the BBC. Years later, asked why he had decided to return to Prague in the 1990s, he replied: 'Because I always felt I had not left of my own free will.' Twenty-one-year-old Tomáš Liška, on the other hand, desperately wanted to leave. Like Tomin and Luděk Bednář, he was a conscientious objector and had already spent a period in prison. He was involved in the underground world of pop and rock music, and in August he had been picked up by the police in Poland (in company with Markéta's brother David) and transferred against his will to a Prague psychiatric hospital. He was already under-nourished and emaciated — visitors remember sunken eyes burning in a pale face — and his greatest fear was of being sent back to prison, where he was afraid he might die. Liška also commenced a degree course at Oxford, but fled from there to Paris and on to Berlin. After ten unhappy years he too returned to Prague in 1990. Lenka Dvořáková had a different motivation for leaving. Her close collaboration with Roger Scruton became a closeness of another kind, and for a while they discussed the possibility of marriage. Obstacles, hesitations and emergencies hampered this plan as they hampered so many others. When eventually Dvořáková got married, it was to Jan Payne, a doctor and fellow student at Hejdánek's seminar, whose family had for many years hosted the seminars given by Jakub Trojan, a protestant clergyman who had lost his licence.

On New Year's Eve 1979 Montefiore and Audard had supper with Wilkes. Three days later Wilkes lunched with Lukes and Scruton before setting out the next day for Prague. Over the next twelve days she had a packed programme, meeting not only the students and other old friends but also leading members of the intellectual community: Jiří Gruša, Eva Kantůrková, František Pavlíček,[40] Jan Sokol and the wife of Josef Daniš, the lawyer who had dared to defend accused Charter signatories. On the 12th January she attended a performance of the banned actress Vlasta Chramostová's Living Room Theatre. There were several seminars in the programme, including one on the 14th January for the Kampakademie.

The discussions which Wilkes had in the course of her visit convinced her even more of the importance of publicising the conditions in which her colleagues in Prague were living (this had also been emphasised by Thorolf Rafto). As in the past, it was difficult to interest the western press in 'a faraway country of which we know little'. Wilkes wrote to the Master of Balliol, Anthony Kenny: 'Scruton is going to see if he can interest any paper in a package-deal: his rough handling at Julius's apartment plus the two arrests [of Vladimír Prajzler and Luděk Bednář].'[41] Opportunities for publicity improved with the return to work in January 1980 of the employees of *The Times* newspapers, after a lockout of nearly a year. The newspaper group included *The Times Literary Supplement*, *The Times Educational Supplement* and *The Times Higher Educational Supplement*. The first edition of the *THES* to appear published Julius Tomin's letter of May 1978 on the front page, accompanied by an article by John O'Leary. In February 1980 the *THES* published a full page article by Paul Flather,[42] written in cooperation with Alan Montefiore.[43] Steven Lukes also made use of the re-emergence of *The Times* and published his description of Tomin's seminars: 'The lectures take place in a crowded apartment, with Dr. Tomin translating, at times explosively interjecting his own comments, but patiently and carefully pursuing the argument wherever it leads. Abstraction is no barrier to rapt attention. One lecture on Kant, dealing with the most difficult and intricate points, lasted five hours and the audience never faltered. There is a constant sense of drama. Questions are insistent and probing, and the answers matter. The lecturer is treated with respect but not deference. Any retreat from the argument into "professional" expertise is noticed and deplored.'[44] He also wrote about a session 'in a beautiful apartment in north Prague' on Marxism and Morality: 'The discussion was alive and exciting, but the topic was a disaster, and the problem, of course, was Marxism, not morality. In Czechoslovakia today Marxism is intellectually dead. The humanist Marx of the 1960s is long past.'[45]

During the same days Bill Newton-Smith, Fairfax Fellow in Philosophy at Balliol College and secretary of the Oxford Sub-Faculty of Philosophy, on sabbatical leave at Nijmegen University in Holland, was preparing to leave for Prague. His visit had been brought forward at short notice and arranged by telephone.[46] It was the 7th March, and just before boarding the plane to Prague at Amsterdam airport he bought the latest issue of the *New Statesman*. It proclaimed in red on the front cover: 'Inside Prague: Philosophy and the police state'; inside was a four page article by Julius Tomin. Tomin was described in the introduction to the article as the 'intellectual prime mover behind the 'Patočka University' or 'parallel university' in Prague' and Tominová as 'an important member of the Charter 77 movement, and associated with the Committee to Defend the Unjustly Prosecuted.'[47] Mention was made of the visits to Tomin's seminars by western academics. Newton-Smith read the article with some misgivings.

Tomin began his article with a description of the charges awaiting the Dejmal and the other seminar members who had been arrested the previous November. This led him to 'another aspect of the whole affair, namely the arbitrary handling of concepts. Here, the arbitrary treatment of concepts goes hand in hand with the arbitrary treatment of reality; above all, the people.'[48] Tomin gave examples of the authorities' 'arbitrary use of concepts' such as 'terror and 'fascism'. The article juxtaposed the analysis of politics by the Greek philosophers against the pseudopolitical thought of Marxism in contemporary Czechoslovakia. He identified 1977 as the year when the state, unable to handle the problem of Charter 77, handed over authority to the security services. Most of the population remained happy to function within the system of security. But the identifiable individuals who made up Charter 77 had put themselves outside the security net. 'One finds oneself in the realm of inner freedom and then one faces the question of how to live so that the free life would be worth the sacrifice. That is where philosophy can help.'[49]

Newton-Smith, for whom the preparations had so far been very relaxed, began to anticipate trouble. He was due to give two seminars on successive evenings and was also carrying messages for Jan Kavan, who had given him instructions that, in order to shake off the secret police, he should pick up taxis at random in the street to take him to the addresses he had been given. After checking into the Albatross Hotel on the Vltava, Newton-Smith set out to visit the Tomins. A few minutes before he arrived Julius, Zdena and Lukáš had been served with a summons to appear at the central police station. Tomin believed the summons was connected with the *New Statesman* article. However, the present business was philosophy. Newton-Smith was not disappointed: 'I have never encountered someone with so much dedication to philosophy that actual and impending problems of the magnitude facing him were set aside. For the next five hours we had an intense, non-stop discussion of the problems of perception and the nature of truth.'[50] The next day they continued the discussion. Tomin explained to Newton-Smith the difference between Oxford students and those in Prague, who needed to know why they were risking prison for the study of such a thing as philosophy. Lunching in the Expo 57 restaurant[51] with its magnificent views over Prague Newton-Smith found this hard to believe.

The lecture (on 'The Rationality of Science)' took place in Ivan Dejmal's flat, and started at 7.30 that evening: 'The eager, concentrated attention of the dozen students created an intellectually exciting atmosphere. Their excitement was infectious and I was looking forward to their reactions.'[52] Fifteen minutes into the session the door bell rang. Dejmal, who normally monitored the arrivals, was engaged in transcribing the lecture; another student ran to open the door to what he assumed to be a late arrival, and rushed back in order not to miss a word of the lecture. Seven policemen, some in uniform and some in plain clothes, burst in behind him. The uniformed police took the names and details of the students, whilst the secret police demanded that Newton-Smith accompany them. Tomin was ordered to translate their orders to Newton-Smith, which he refused to do. As Newton-Smith was dragged from the flat his last sight was of Tomin, hands bleeding from struggles with the police, taking up his lecture and reading from the point where they had been inter-rupted.

Newton-Smith was interrogated by three policemen in the police complex in Bartolomějská Street, where he was warned that the seminar was associated in some way with the Charter 77 movement. The police, who had endeavoured to keep agents on his tail from the moment of his arrival, asked whom he had been to see that afternoon; 'No one,' answered Newton-Smith truth-fully, since his attempt to visit one of Kavan's contacts by taxi had ended in linguistic miscomprehension. Warned that if he ever tried to return to Czechoslovakia he would be under close surveillance, he was told that Tomin was an 'enemy of the state' and any attempt to revisit him would result in major trouble. If he was interested in lecturing, it was suggested, he could contact the Academy of Sciences. His notebook and lecture were con-fiscated, and as he was escorted from the room two and a half hours later he had the satisfaction of hearing the interpreter embark on an explanation of the rationality of science.

Bohemia was under blizzard conditions, and flights from Prague airport were grounded. Newton-Smith's hopes that he might be driven to Vienna were dashed: 'And a line to Reuters as well,' retorted the policeman. After collecting Newton-Smith's belongings from the hotel the party set out for the nearest western frontier. Newton-Smith commiserated with the interpreter on the lateness of the hour. 'That's all right,' she replied, 'I was warned yesterday I would be needed this evening for the interrogation of a Canadian academic.' Lost in the forests of western Bohemia, the Soviet-made car broke down. Newton-Smith produced a pen-knife with which the driver set to work on a fault in the ignition, and distracted his guard with the whisky intended for the second seminar whilst he wrapped incrimi-nating addresses in snowballs and hurled them into the forest. At the border his passport and luggage were returned, and he was dropped from the car to walk into Germany. It was 3.30 in the morning.

Newton-Smith's experience, which was unpleasant rather than dangerous (the dons were more concerned about what further harassment might be facing Tomin and his students), gave the Oxford philosophers an opportunity to confront the Czechoslovak authorities with evidence of the illegal behaviour of the police. Newton-Smith and Montefiore were dons at Balliol, one of the oldest Oxford colleges. On Monday 10th March 1980 (whilst Tomin was waiting to be interrogated at his local police station) the Master of Balliol, Anthony Kenny, wrote a formal letter of protest to Dr. Zdeněk Černík, the Czechoslovak Ambassador, asking what had been 'improper' about Newton-Smith's behaviour. 'I cannot conceive how there can have been anything illegal in reading a philosophical paper on the role of reason in scientific thinking to a private group of students.'[53] He requested a meeting. During the week Kathy Wilkes publicised the scandal on Radio Oxford, the BBC (*Newsnight*) and Radio Free Europe.

In Prague, on the Tuesday of that week, the three Charter spokesmen (Rudolf Battěk, Marie Hromádková and Miloš Rejchrt) addressed a letter to the Ministry of the Interior, the Federal Assembly, the Ministry of Foreign Affairs, the Ministry of Education and the Arts Faculty of the Charles University, protesting against the violation of a private home, of the right to education and free speech. The next day, the 12th March, Radim Palouš was lecturing on 'Konkrétní fenomenologie smyslu' (The concrete phenomenology of meaning), again in Ivan Dejmal's flat. The seminar was raided by the police and an Eton school-leaver, Angus Cargill, was deported, accused of 'interfering in Czechoslovak internal affairs'.[54] Two days later Dejmal was called for interrogation and told that the philosophy course would not be allowed to continue, regardless of what the law might say, because they (the police) did not wish it. The international situation, they said, was not developing in a peaceful direction and 'as far as we are concerned, relationships with Great Britain are not a priority'. Dejmal was warned that if the philosophy seminars did not stop he would be put under close supervision, his telephone would be cut, and he would eventually be imprisoned.

Precisely a week later (19th March) Professor Kenny was received at the Czechoslovak Embassy in London, not by the Ambassador as he had requested, but by his second-in-command, Minister-Counsellor Dr. František Telička. Professor Kenny subsequently recapitulated the content of the conversation in a letter to Dr. Telička.[56] They mutually deplored the fact that the incident 'could be seen as an impediment to normal cutural relations on academic matters', and Telička reluctantly allowed that maybe the police had been 'over-zealous'. Whilst admitting that there could be no objection to a visitor discussing philosophy with a group of Czechs, Telička claimed that Newton-Smith's lecture to the students had differed from the text handed in to the police; even if that had been true (in the brief 15 minutes of the lecture) Kenny wondered how the police could possibly have known before making their illegal entry. Telička invoked the cultural agreement between the two countries; as far as Kenny was aware, this did not ban any other cultural activities. When Telička claimed that Tomin's activities were illegal, Kenny replied that 'it would be important for Oxford philosophers intending to visit Prague to know under what law and in what respect Dr. Tomin and his associates were regarded as forming an illegal society', and demanded a copy of the relevant law. Dr. Kenny pointed out no one had been involved in any deception: 'There was no attempt to conceal the interest of Balliol College in the philosophy of Dr. Tomin. I had myself sent to the Ambassador a copy of my letter inviting Tomin to lecture in the College.'[57] The conversation concluded by Kenny telling Telička that the philosophers would be delighted to accept invitations to lecture at the Charles University, provided that the lecture was open to the general public. Telička replied that this went without saying, because of the open nature of Czech society.

The following day (20th March) Kenny found it necessary to add a postscript to his letter. On the day of his meeting with Dr. Telička fourteen more over-zealous policemen had raided Dejmal's flat, during the continuation of Radim Palouš's lecture. This time they entered by breaking down the door. Eight of the 27 participants were detained for 48 hours: Palouš and Dejmal, together with Miloš Rejchrt (protestant minister and Charter spokesman); Tereza Kohoutová (daughter of the writer Pavel Kohout); Karel Šling (son of Otto Šling, executed in the 1950s show trials); Jiří Středa (an industrial worker) and Tomin himself who, practising passive resistance, was dragged down two flights of stairs to the police car.

Part of the purpose of Anthony Kenny's visit to the Czechoslovak Embassy on 19th March had been to ask for clear guidelines as to what was and was not permitted to academic

visitors to Czechoslovakia. This was part of the policy of openness pursued by Tomin on the basis of Charter 77's insistence on
the right to assembly. Dr. Kenny also needed to know on his
own behalf, as he and his wife were due to leave for Prague in
the second week of April. On April 2nd, when Tomin was
preparing to work with his students on Aristotle's *Metaphysics*,
police blockaded the house in Keramická Street. He came out to
talk to the students waiting on the pavement, but refused to obey
a command to accompany a policemen. Dragged to a car and
taken to Bartolomějská police station, interrogated for three
hours, thrown on a pile of coal in neighbouring Konviktská
Street, he then returned home to continue his lecture. On 7th
April Tomin wrote to President Gustáv Husák: 'Maybe you
remember, Mr. President, that at the beginning of the 1970s I
sent you my studies on Aristotle. At that time I was working as
a mechanic in a condenser on a low-pressure turbine at the
Holešovice electricity station. As the central Marxist idea I discussed the thesis of how to overcome the division between
physical and intellectual work. In my view this was not an issue
concerning an idea whose realisation would be possible in some
distant future once our police force had prepared the proper conditions... I wanted to bring Marx's idea right into daily life, or at
least into my life... May I invite you to the lecture to be held next
Wednesday 9th April at seven in the evening? There is the
possibility that your presence would persuade the Ministry of
the Interior to instruct their forces to abandon the intervention
they have assured me will take place.'[58]

On the evening of April 9th the police took Tomin from
home before the start of the seminar, barefoot and without his
spectacles. Lukáš, accompanied by seven or eight of the students, went to Bartolomějská with Julius's shoes and spectacles
and other items. Whilst the students were waiting outside the
police came to collect their identity cards; shortly afterwards
some were called into the police station and put in cells. Jiří
Středa's hair was forcibly shorn; Tomáš Liška and Luděk
Bednář were warned that if they continued to take part in 'illegal
gatherings' they would be charged with article 98 — subversion
of the Republic. Pavel Šmída subsequently addressed a complaint about his treatment to the Ministry of the Interior and the
General Procurator.[59]

That was Friday; the next day, Saturday 12th April, the Master of Balliol and his wife sat in the Tomins' flat in Keramická Street surrounded by Julius, Zdena and Lukáš, a French visitor (Jacques Laskar) and seventeen attentive students (Šmida, after his beating the day before, was absent). They were looking forward to Anthony Kenny's seminar, a contrast between the ideals of Aristotle's *Nicomachean* and the *Eudemian Ethics*. As was always the case with the home seminars, they had assembled quietly, arriving in twos and threes in order not to disturb the neighbours. As was also the rule, no alcohol was being drunk, nor was anyone smoking. Kenny remembered that 'Radim Palouš objected to Aristotle's identification of philosophy with the good life. His argument was succinct: "If the good life was the same thing as philosophy, then a better philosopher would be a better man. But Plato was a better philosopher than Socrates, but he was not a good man."'[60] And then: 'We had more than an hour reading Aristotle together and we had the impression that the police were going to leave us alone. We were discussing the passage where Aristotle says that philosophy is the most noble of all pursuits when the police came in.'[61] Sweeping up in several cars, they had announced their arrival by sirens, loud ringing of the doorbell, and banging on the door. Zdena, trying to check whether they had a search warrant (they had not), was pushed aside by the force of at least fourteen policemen. Everyone except Radim Palouš was taken in relays to Bartolomějská; waiting for the cars to return, the police amused themselves by herding the students into one room, pulling the girls' hair, and forcibly searching Lukáš. Books, letters and other items lying around the flat were examined and the materials they intended to take with them piled in the hall. Zdena went from room to room, trying to limit the damage: 'Eventually I was alone in the flat with my elder son and two of the policemen. To my angry and insistent question as to whether they had had enough, the darkhaired policeman in the short leather jacket thrust his face into mine and demanded: "Do you want a slap across the face?" Perhaps he was really going to give me one, it would have been in accord with everything that had gone before... (if it hadn't been for the uniforms, the whole thing would have been like a raid by gangsters). But the other young man led him out, the door banged, and that was the end, except for the unlawful detention for the last fifty hours of my husband and friends.'[62]

Anthony Kenny, his American-born wife and Jacques Laskar, who had been the first to be driven off to Bartolomějska, were held until three in the morning and interrogated in separate rooms. 'The most difficult thing was to convince the police that the meeting at the flat was entirely philosophical.... (they) would not believe this. The chief interrogator said to me: "If you wish to fight Communism, you must do it in your own country." I said: "You are quite mistaken if you think that the reason I came to Prague is to fight Communism. It was to pursue philosophy with philosophers."'[63] Kenny later wrote to *The Times*: 'Over the last 10 years I have hardly ever taken a holiday which did not involved giving or listening to philosophy lectures and seminars. Philosophers commonly do not regard philosophy as a chore to be pursued only during official working hours.'[64] The Kennys were delivered to the same border-crossing with West Germany as Newton-Smith, and, carrying their luggage, walked through the woods of Rozvadov in the frosty dawn of an April morning. Tomin and his students remained locked up for something over the statutory 48 hours.

By now the diplomatic issues were becoming serious. The Foreign Office was unable to ignore the treatment of a Fellow of the British Academy and asked for an explanation as to why normal consular access had not been granted and the British Ambassador not informed. The British Ambassador, Peter Male, twice spoke to the Deputy Minister of Foreign Affairs, who maintained that tourists had no right to give lectures, and that these could only take place in accordance with the Anglo-Czechoslovak Cultural Agreement.[65] The Czechoslovak authorities were uncomfortable but intransigent. Ambassador Černík had received a more detailed briefing than before his earlier meeting with Kenny, and when summoned to the Foreign Office told them that he had been 'instructed to inform Mr. Blaker[66] that Dr. Kenny's activities had not conformed with Czechoslovak laws'; specifically that he had violated sections 8 and 13 of the agreements between the UK and Czechoslovakia on academic visits.[67] This made nonsense of the Czechoslovak government's agreement at Helsinki to abide by international law, nor was the British Foreign Office able to find any Czechoslovak law or regulation of relevance;[68] but in the two years since the publication of Charter 77 the authorities felt they had successfully implemented the policy of isolating Charter activists. The flow of Oxford philosophers was unforeseen and inconvenient, but they believed time was on their side; by making it impossible for Tomin's seminars to operate, they felt his declared aim — the teaching of philosophy — would sound futile and quixotic even to his supporters. The Tomin family had already been offered permanent emigration, which they had refused, but the authorities were expecting them to leave eventually. Meanwhile the seminars remained one of the causes backed by the Charter; on 23rd April the Charter spokesmen addressed a letter to the Rector of the Charles University, Dr. Zdeněk Češka, concerning the violations of the law which had occurred during and after the philosophy seminars: 'We turn to you, so that you, with the weight of authority which comes with the office of the Rector of the time-honoured Charles University, can get these scandalous events put right.'[69]

In Oxford, the item that had tailed at the end of an agenda just over a year before had now become a major issue, and Kenny's complaint to the Czechoslovak Ambassador had been followed by one from the Sub-Faculty of Philosophy (Kathy Wilkes was now the secretary). However, there was some unease about the turn of events. The Vice-Chancellor had not been pleased about the publicity surrounding Dr. Kenny's visit to Prague, and, unlike the Foreign Office, refused to protest on behalf of the University to the Czechoslovak authorities.[70] The acting chairman of the Sub-Faculty, Ian Crombie, suggested that the visits to Prague might have to come to an end; pressure was being put on the Lit.Hum. Board to discontinue funding. Some members — in particular Jonathan (L.J.) Cohen, a philosopher of science — had established official relationships with Czech universities, and feared that these would be endangered by their colleagues' romantic ventures. They would probably have endorsed Dr. Černík's advice to Her Majesty's government, that it request Balliol College to desist from future activities of the same kind and rather to establish an exchange with the Czechoslovak Academy of Science. Nevertheless, at the meeting on 5th May 1980 the following statement was agreed: 'Item 9a: the Sub-Faculty of Philosophy at Oxford University intends to continue to give support to the philosophy discussion groups in Czechoslovakia conducted by Dr. Julius Tomin and his colleagues. The Sub-Faculty, in response to Dr. Tomin's request, will continue to arrange for visits to Czechoslovakia by philosophers from other universities as well as by those from Oxford. It will, in consultation with Dr. Tomin, continue to seek for ways in which philosophers from outside Czechoslovakia can meet to discuss philosophy with their colleagues inside the country in conformity with Czechoslovak law and without police intervention.'[71] Mr. L. J. Cohen asked for his abstention to be recorded.

Under Item 9b, the Sub-Faculty agreed that a five-member committee should be set up to arrange the programme of visits, and under 9c that the Literae Humaniores Board be asked for a grant to cover their expenses. The 5th May 1980 marks the first occasion on which a formal organisation came into being whose task was exclusively to liaise between western philosophers and their Czech and Slovak colleagues. The statement in item 9a contained three basic principles which became fundamental to the Jan Hus Educational Foundation's operations over the next ten years: that the purpose of its activity was the discussion of philosophy; that this was in conformity with current Czechoslovak law; and that activities would be based on requests from the Czechoslovak side. The committee included four of the founding members of the Jan Hus Foundation: Kathy Wilkes, Charles Taylor, Alan Montefiore and Bill Newton-Smith. The fifth member was the philosopher Michael Dummett, whose place in the Foundation would be taken by Roger Scruton — already extremely active, but a member of London University rather than Oxford.

The number of visiting philosophers was expanding (the opposite reaction to that anticipated by the Czechoslovak authorities), and there were beginning to be risks of misunderstandings and inappropriate behaviour which could put Tomin and his students at risk. One of the first actions taken by the Oxford committee was the production of an eighteen page brochure, written mainly by Kathy Wilkes in consultation with Tomin, with, as appendices, the English text of Charter 77 and a copy of Tomin's 1978 letter.[72] Wilkes opened the main text with an outline of Tomin's career, including his long involvement in home seminars. This was followed by a description of his seminars, his students, the harassment of his seminars from 1978-1980 and, in greater detail, the more serious events from March 1980. Wilkes described the origin of the Oxford connection, and in particular the non-political content of the seminars. This was of particular importance because of the Czechoslovak authorities' attempts to link the lectures with the activities rather than the principles of the Charter, and their suggestions that Tomin's students were engaged in subversive activity rather than studying pure philosophy. The brochure served as a briefing for future lecturers and can be counted as the first of the Jan Hus Foundation's documents.

In the meantime the Tomin family had been considering the events of the past year, and what the future might hold. At the end of February 1980 Tominová had come to the end of a tempestuous year and one month as Charter spokesperson, but police harassment had grown worse rather than eased. It had been Tomin's decision to invite the Oxford lecturers, and no one regretted it, but the police had made it impossible to hold the lectures in the way Tomin had originally intended. Some of the young people had decided for themselves that they were no longer interested; others had been withdrawn by their parents. The police action was illegal under Czechoslovak law, but it was difficult to reiterate this point when the consequences were threatening the physical and mental health of the young people. Tomin decided to change his teaching methods. Seminars would be held once a month, visiting lecturers would still be welcomed, but for the rest of the time they would study from notes and translations; students could visit Julius at his flat for individual discussions (the 'Socratic method'). Another idea was to hold seminars in the Šárka valley, a wild, rugged park in the west of Prague. If matters improved, they would return to the normal pattern. Following Dr. Kenny's expulsion, the next seminar was scheduled for a month later, on 7th May — two days after the meeting in Oxford of the Sub-Faculty of Philosophy. At 3.00 p.m. Tomin was summoned to his local police station; three and a half hours later he was transferred to Bartolmějská. Two policemen bantered over his head: 'So this is a philosopher?' 'Some philosopher, a child could see through his philosophy.' 'What an idiot, he needs to be in the

psychiatrists' hands.' 'It seems he's got a doctorate. I'd like to know what for.' 'He does everything for money. He bought that as well.' Then one turned on Julius: 'We've already told you, enough of these lectures, and you're going to listen to us! And stand up when we're talking to you!'[73]
When Julius had not returned by 9.00 p.m. his students prepared a statement affirming their right to attend lectures on Aristotle and declaring that they would join him in the hunger strike he had announced from the 7th to the 18th May. Half an hour later the flat was raided and eleven students detained for 48 hours — including Lenka Dvořáková, Ludék Bednář, Jan Bednář and Markéta Němcová with her sister Pavla and brother David. They were warned that the next time they attended a philosophy seminar they would be arrested and charged, probably under Article 202 — criminal hooliganism.

Alarmed by the worsening situation, the philosophers resolved to give the students their moral support; Scruton made a flying visit to Prague (10th-12th May), followed by Wilkes (who had just returned from a meeting with philosophers at the Sorbonne in Paris) on the 16th May. Unable to find a hotel room, she stayed with the Tomin family and, in line with the principle of openness, fulfilled the legal obligation of registering her address with the police. On Sunday the students took her to the Karlštejn quarry, where she gave an impromptu 'underground' seminar whilst they sheltered from the rain in a cave. On the morning of Monday 19th, during a leisurely farewell breakfast, three plain-clothes policemen and an interpreter arrived at the flat and took Wilkes into custody. In the course of the interrogation she was asked why she lectured to criminals and not to the Academy. 'If they are criminals,' she asked, 'why aren't they in prison?' Once the question had been re-phrased, she replied: 'Because they invited me and the Academy didn't.' She was accused of abusing her tourist visa, and Oxford University of financing subversive activities. Sandwiched between two stout policemen she was driven to the airport where Liška, Šmida and Dvořáková waited for her with red roses. In spite of her female guard's attempts to stop her (the male guards did their best to distance themselves from this embarrassing foreigner), Wilkes continued to communicate with them through the glass screen which separated the duty-free shop from the public area. On her return, she wrote how, in a week of contrasts, 'the refusal of the police to let thought contaminate action contrasted with the insistence of the students upon their inseparability'.[74] Another contrast she noted was the policemen's embarrassment in front of the tourists compared with the students' disregard of the risk of being picked up by the police after Wilkes' departure.

On her return, Wilkes discussed with Scruton the consequences of emigration of a number of Czechs; possibly the Tomins and their two sons with Dvořáková, Liška and Bednář. They weighed up the practicality of such plans — emigration, immigration, finance, education, occupation and, especially, psychological shock. Nevertheless, they did not at that time doubt the desirability of the plans: 'Have you a list of colleges which can offer suitable scholarships?' Scruton wrote to Wilkes in June. 'Can you find out when and to where Lenka [Dvořáková] should apply, and what are the chances of success. It would be good for her to settle down in the knowledge that there was something waiting for her at the end of all this, and I think it is best if it were arranged as soon as possible, so that she can then put her mind to obtaining a visa. Obviously she has got to get out anyway, as have the others... I do think that what she said is true, that this possible exodus of "anti-socialist-minded" elements to Oxford will provide the motive that will make everything at last intelligible to the Secret Police, and hence lead to preventative measures.'[75] Wilkes's plans had been made in consultation with Tomin and with VONS, one of whose members subsequently wrote to Jan Kavan: '...some of Tomin's students wish to take advantage of the fund and use it for their study course in England. We furthermore agreed in principle that the Fund should be used to purchase and to facilitate transport of text books and literature and other necessary things connected with it. Obviously the Fund should also be used to cover the expenses connected with arranging the safe transport of the parcels over here. We can see other possibilities and opportunities but it makes sense to think about them seriously only when we get more details about the foundation of the Fund and the amount of money at its disposal.'[76] The reference to 'the expenses connected with arranging the safe transport of the parcels over here' refers to Kavan's messenger service, which at this point was regularly carrying letters between Wilkes and the Tomins. The wording of the letter raises a question as to whether the Chartists initially assumed that they were to play a decision-making role in the spending of funds raised by the Oxford philosophers; at this time many western agencies were channelling donations (usually for humanitarian purposes) through the Charter leadership. It would not, however, have been in accord with the philosophers' programme, which focused on the exchange and development of ideas rather than financial aid. In the event it did not become a major issue, largely because the Jan Hus Foundation expanded its own network and worked with seminar leaders rather than the Charter spokesmen.

The possibility of arranging for Tomin's students to study in Britain, combined with a continued programme of work in Czechoslovakia, was going to cost money on a scale never imagined a year earlier. The Sub-Faculty of Philosophy had already set up two bank accounts for the receipt of donations: the Prague Book Fund, which was set up in November 1979 with an unsolicited grant from the Australasian Philosophical Association, and the Patočka University Fund, set up in March 1980. In June 1980 the Lit. Hum. Board refused to make a grant for the expenses of the five-member committee on the grounds that philosophers from other universities were also making visits to the Prague seminars. Roger Scruton, trained in law, recognised that it was time for the work of the committee to be superseded by an organisation that could be registered under the Charities Law of Great Britain. The Jan Hus Educational Foundation held its first meeting at 12.00 noon on Tuesday 8th July 1980.[77] But as far as finding wealthy contributors, he foresaw the problem that was to haunt the Jan Hus Foundation for the next ten years: '...if you are thinking of composing a suitable circular letter, which does not have the faintest shadow of political meaning, and which lays emphasis on the harmlessness, worthiness, etc. of Julius's cause, its bold, patriotic inspiration, and the fact that neither you nor anyone involved either wants to overthrow or cast discredit on the Czech regime, or reprove it for revealing the unacceptable face of communism (a doctrine likely to be unacceptable to anyone in a position to contribute)... it will need tenacity of purpose and ruthlessness of approach.'[79]

After Tomin had refused permanent emigration, the police

offered a 5-year visa, which, after some delay, he accepted. The visa was valid for the UK and Australia; he attributed the latter to the recent visit of David Armstrong, a philosopher from Australia, who had visited Prague in July (ostensibly on trade union business) and talked to the Tomins on several occasions. His approaching departure was kept secret, so that even Christopher Kirwan,[80] who arrived on 28th July, did not know of it. Kirwan was disappointed to find no students, since the British philosophers had overlooked the inviolability of the summer holiday. In one thing he was able to be useful, more than he realised at the time. Marek Tomin had broken his leg at summer camp, and the Tomins were asked to collect him by car. For Kirwan, as a western tourist, it was relatively easy to hire a car and collect the boy.

On 1st August, less than three months after her expulsion, Kathy Wilkes arrived back in Prague, having confused the Czechoslovak authorities by obtaining a new passport in her full name of Vaughan-Wilkes. She found the Tomins ready to leave. Their documents were prepared, and the authorities were happy to say good-bye, though not without making life difficult for as long as possible. She agreed without hesitation to the adventure of leaving by hired car, obtained in the same way as Christopher Kirwan had obtained his. The car, a Soviet-made Zhiguli, was loaded under the eyes of the police outside the flat in Keramická Street. With five people to carry (and Marek's leg in plaster) there was little room for personal luggage; it was agreed that each member of the family could take one treasured possession. For Julius, it was his Greek philosophers; for Zdena, the 40-year-old typewriter which she had once physically defended from a raiding policeman.[81] Lukáš took his guitar, and Marek his collection of geological specimens.

Heavily overloaded, Wilkes drove the Zhiguli precariously towards West Germany, knowing that the slightest infringement of traffic rules in a country where she had never driven before would bring the weight of the 'law' down upon them. On the border, the police had last-minute instructions to confiscate Julius's doctoral certificate. (The intention was to damage his reputation abroad by denying the Charles University had ever awarded him a doctorate.) Julius refused. Several times they were waved forward to the crossing point and forced to reverse as the red and white pole came down. After five hours, whilst the five of them remained locked inside in the car, they were allowed to cross.

Over the border (and with a change of car) they crossed Europe, stopping briefly in Switzerland and Paris. For British-born Wilkes, it was a shock to see how western consulates treated this bunch of East bloc refugees. In Britain, after a week in the country, Wilkes introduced the Tomins to the academic community. Tomin was excited and enthusiasic: interviewed by the BBC for *The World this Weekend*, he declared: 'I must say that I had a quite critical attitude towards philosophy in the West. I just thought that it is where you do philosophy because you have a good living standard, good salary, and these kind of things. And I thought that, when this person from Oxford comes and lectures to my students, my students need more, because philosophy for them cannot mean a way of nice living at the university and then having a nice job. They need a philosophy which somehow has the strength to give strength to their lives. And I wouldn't imagine that the academics from Oxford would come and contribute anything to this. But then came Kathy Wilkes, and her subject was Socrates and then, in another lecture, philosophy of mind. These two subjects were, just by chance, the subject to which I devoted most of my attention for the last 15 years. And we had, by chance, the most opposite views on these two subjects. So this was a real find and Kathy Wilkes was able to sustain it and I was able to sustain it; and the students saw for the first time in their lives, that there can be a strong intellectual fight which brings people not apart, doesn't make enemies, but makes them close to each other. And for me, this was a fascinating revelation — that people from Oxford may come and may just heighten the level of all our discussions, even my own work. So I have, I think, on the background of this experience, some ground for hope that I'll find here a strong intellectual life, which will challenge me to living my life in philosophy as strongly as I lived in Czechoslovakia.'[82]

This brings to an end the story of Julius Tomin's seminars in Prague. It should bring to an end Tomin's role in this book. But although the Jan Hus Foundation — to be constituted in a few months time — would be solely committed to supporting Czechs and Slovaks working in their own country, it was impossible for individuals who had attended Tomin's seminars in Prague to ignore him now he was in Oxford. At first it seemed as though all that was needed was a period of re-adjustment. Kathy Wilkes rented a house in Oxford for the family. Julius had a year's lecturing ahead of him, first at Balliol College and then in Cambridge. Funds were raised to ensure the boys' education.

Within the year the problems foreseen by the more sceptical philosophers began to make themselves felt. (One of them was Ralph Walker, a philosopher from Magdalen College who became a trustee of the Jan Hus Foundation in 1983. He was to play an important role in preparing structured courses for the Czech students; but in the Sub-Faculty of Philosophy he had voted against the invitation to Tomin, on the grounds that someone with his background would be ill-equipped to deal with the competitive academic world of the West.) At the end of the first year, Julius, surprised and hurt that a tenured position had not been found for him at Oxford, accused the philosophers of bad faith. A fund set up by the philosopher and Vice-Provost of Worcester College, David Mitchell (under the patronage of the Northern Dairies Educational Trust) yielded enough to keep the family for another two years, but it had become apparent that Julius would not find a job answering his ambitions within that time, or ever. The problem was not to do with his intelligence or ability, but with the lifetime spent under totalitarianism. During that time he had learnt how to be courageous, steadfast and inspiring, but these were not qualities listed in job descriptions for British academic posts, which required people who could work as part of a team, carry out set tasks, and act as a consistent mediator and guide for students. The fact that some of his theories on Plato were dismissed by other academics was less important than the narrowness of his specialisation; his knowledge of certain parts of Plato's work was more thorough than that of any philosopher in Oxford, but his limited acquaintance with the breadth of western philosophy would have been unacceptable in any of the posts for which he diligently applied. For Julius, the rejection letters confirmed a suspicion that the world was in the grip of a conspiracy; that he was being silenced by a similar 'nomenklatura' as had kept him out of the academic world in Prague. His reactions were the same as those in his previous life: he fired off bitter letters of accusation and

denunciation in multiple copies to universities, individual philosophers and newspapers, and held hunger strikes to publicise his
grievances. One of his main targets was Kathy Wilkes, who
retreated from her high-profile role, but tried to find ways of
supporting the family.

Tominová, in time, left Oxford. After some difficult years she
made a name for herself with the novels *Stalin's Shoe* (1986)
and *The Coast of Bohemia* (1987), portraying dissident life in
Prague (including the seminars). Eventually she became a reporter for the Czechoslovak service of the BBC. Marek settled
quietly and successfully into the routine of an English public
school, adopted English as his second native tongue and after
1989 established himself as an interpreter. Lukáš, the brilliant,
passionate teenager who, first for the sins of his family and then
for his own beliefs, had been thrown out both from secondary
school and from a manual apprenticeship, found it difficult to
come to terms with the English educational system. After a year
at London University he escaped to Paris and then, after 1989,
back to Prague where, like his mother, he wrote and published
in English. In 1995, at the age of 32, he was found dead in the
Šárka valley, where the philosophers and their students had
taken their Socratic walks.[83]

Principles and Policies

It was late summer, 1980. Much of Europe's attention was focused on Poland, where, following Pope John Paul's visit in the summer of 1979, there was a growing sense of spiritual and cultural identity. August saw the strikes in the Gdansk shipyard, the rise of Lech Wałęsa, the historic agreement between the strike committee and the government and the growth of the Solidarity movement. Czechoslovakia, on the other hand, appeared to be even more in the grip of the post-1968 'normalisation' process; Charter 77 seemed more like a last cry for help than the start of something new. The early 1980s were to be an especially grim period for Czechoslovak dissidents and their children. Several leading members of the dissident community were in prison, at the start of long sentences; they included Václav Havel and Otka Bednářová. The Charter was not showing any signs of becoming a popular human rights movement and for many potential signatories was too closely associated with the reform Communists. This had come about because of the death of Patočka and imprisonment of Havel early in 1977, which left JiříHájek as the only spokesman for most of that year. To add to the Charter's problems, Havel had, during his first prison term in 1977, signed a statement which was distorted by the authorities to imply that he had renounced the Charter; the consequences, which he describes in *Letters to Olga*, had caused some people discouragement during the early months of the Charter. Early in 1980 the Chartists had tried to broaden their base by naming a total of seventeen spokesmen, of whom Rudolf Battěk, Miloš Rejchrt and Zdena Tominová were responsible for authorising documents. (The seventeen included Jiří Bednář, brother of the seminar student Jan Bednář.) It was nevertheless difficult for these documents and other information to be circulated, and the movement was better known abroad than at home, a situation which made it easy for the state-controlled media to accuse Chartists of 'blackening the name of Czechoslovakia abroad'. Attacks in the press, which began immediately in the first days of January 1977, were only the beginning of a tide against the Charter. On 28th January a meeting was held in the National Theatre urging artists and cultural workers to sign an endorsement of governmental policy; the document was later infamously known as the 'Anti-Charter'. In the name of 'life, joy and beauty', the Anti-Charter condemned the unpatriotic sentiments of 'a tiny group of renegades and traitors (who) have cut themselves off from their own people and isolated themselves from their real life and real interests'.[1] This denunciation subsequently made the rounds; those required to sign were members of the Communist Party and the handful of non-Party members holding responsible positions. Very few of them had the opportunity to read the Charter, but they were threatened with dismissal should they refuse to sign the Anti-Charter. The Communist authorities succeeded in establishing a psychological distance between Charter signatories — including their families — and the rest of the population which, at the beginning of the 1980s, was particularly critical for young people of university age.

The first eighteen months of the British philosophers' co-operation with the home seminars in Prague had come to an end. They had been months full of enthusiasm, excitement and incident, friendships and misunderstandings, and — most importantly — genuine study and debate. Luděk Bednář remembers that he found the British visits amazing, a new world; until then they had belonged to a closed society, but now they caught a glimpse of what they had always longed for. The British were convinced they must continue. When Kathy Wilkes asked one of the students why she came in spite of the risks, her answer was: 'I must; for me it is life.'[2] Many years later, Markéta Němcová remembered that the visits of western philosophers were the one thing they had to look forward to in a grey and dismal life.

The Charter signatories and their children had every reason to feel excluded from 'life, joy and beauty'. Very often, the only work they could get was physically hard, often dirty and uncomfortable, and involved long and unsociable hours. (British visitors remember the times when Markéta Němcová fell asleep during seminars; since she rose at five, spent the day moving heavy patients and then delivered messages around Prague for the Chartists and seminar leaders, it was not surprising she was tired.) Many employers deducted the hours and days spent in detention and interrogation by the police from their employees' holiday entitlement; Němcová was once left with five days holiday for the whole year.[4] Not only was the work dull and demanding, but there was no prospect of anything better. The police would make it as difficult as possible for members of dissident families to get any kind of job by threatening potential employers. (When Julius Tomin was first on hunger strike in June 1977, a police order went out that Zdena was to lose her job as interpreter 'because she is the only bread-winner in the family'.) The laborious monotony of their work was depressing especially for the young people, but even worse was the loss of friends and the impossibility of a normal social life. Colleagues at work, with no experience of political discrimination, assumed that they were some sort of lawbreakers. (Jan Bednář remembers that once the police came to arrest him while he was at work as nightwatchman. On his return he found that the colleague on duty with him had spread the word that he had been arrested for a criminal offence.)

Police action against Charter signatories was also the cause of broken marriages. It was difficult for a wife to tolerate a situation where police could break in at night and take her husband from their bed. There were situations where she offered her husband a straight choice between emigration and divorce. Unlike the rest of the population, the Chartists did have the opportunity to emigrate; the authorities were glad to see the back of troublesome elements. However, many of those who had signed the Charter for reasons of conscience felt that this would be a betrayal of their intention. In the case of families, the issue was often the children; when father was taken away by police in the middle of the night, some kind of explanation had to be found before the children left for school in the morning. Most people were living in communities where they were well known (moving house is far less common in central Europe than in the West, and many rented flats are 'inherited' through generations).

Zdena Tominová has described the shame of walking to the shops with head down and eyes lowered for fear of meeting an acquaintance, since if they greeted her they would certainly be called for interrogation by the secret police following close behind.

The children of the dissidents at least grew up with an awareness of moral values. The situation was more problematic with young people who had entered the Charter movement and were attending seminars of their own accord. Many of them were as stable and well-balanced as their dissident contemporaries, but others, who came because of the attraction of what was forbidden, were also liable to take risks with sex, drugs and alchohol. The Charter was blamed for the death of a gymnasium student who had attended Tomin's seminar, where she had met Jaroslav Hutka of the Plastic People of the Universe. With great daring, she organised a concert for him at her school. The rejection she faced by schoolfriends, teachers and family subsequently led her to suicide. Very often the older Chartists found themselves acting *in loco parentis*, guiding and advising young people who had become alienated from their parents. The repeated press attacks, usually against named individuals, were a further source of humiliation. Gradually the circle began to diminish. Some emigrated, others took refuge in alcoholism. Amongst those who emigrated was Markéta's father, Jiří Němec, who in 1981 left Prague for Vienna, where the Institut für die Wissenschaften vom Menschen found funds for him to work as an editor and researcher. Like other exiles coming from isolated Czechoslovakia, he was mortified to discover that the plight of the dissident intellectuals was far from being a priority in the rest of Europe.

In these circumstances, the appearances of the western philosophers, who came expressly to meet and talk to the young people, who listened as well as lectured, were like beacons in an unending waste of lost time. Every visit was in its own way stimulating — even the less successful lectures, where the visitors had made assumptions about the background level of knowledge of their audience and expected the students to be conversant with the latest western theories. Confronted with actual and concrete questions, most of the lecturers realised it was more useful to give a straight exposition of a text or to open up a problem for discussion than to continue with an abstract argument in a field where the students had no landmarks. The best of them — the students still give Charles Taylor as an example — adapted quickly to the situation and were able to be both scholarly and relevant. Friendships were established which have now lasted almost twenty years. The students appreciated the irony of the situation. Absolute beginners in philosophy, some of them with barely a secondary education, they found themselves working in tutorial groups (the Oxbridge system, but scarcely known in Central Europe) with some of the leading scholars of the time.

The British understood that whilst the visiting philosophers must be prepared to risk grotesque encounters with the secret police, long and boring hours in police stations and eventual deportation, these harassments did not count in comparison with the long-term mental and physical suffering which the Communist authorities were capable of inflicting on their own citizens. If the visits were to continue, it was necessary to be attentive to the needs and wishes of the Czechs, and to establish an efficient organisational team in Britain which would ensure that the right people visited the seminars, and that they were fully briefed about the situation they would find.

In Prague, plans had already been made for the continuation of Tomin's seminar in the academic year 1980-1981. Many of the Czech dissidents had previously had no time for Tomin's 'crazy ideas'. Academics such as Milan Machovec, Jiří Němec and Jakub Trojan who had been quietly tutoring small groups of students feared that the open seminars were provocative and risked attracting the wrong kind of person; not only the young tear-away eager for sensation, but also police informers. They felt that whilst the police must know about their tutor groups, as long as they did not attract attention to them they would be allowed to work undisturbed. The publicity that Tomin had attracted had been destructive and had culminated in the break-up of his seminar; however, as Hejdánek later noted, the end result had been positive. The Tomin experience established a landmark from which all future activities could be measured, and gave the tutors the possibility of saying to the police: 'Then what is allowed?'.

Following the expulsion of Bill Newton-Smith in March 1980, Tomin had visited Ladislav Hejdánek in Vinohrady, a district into which the prosperous Prague bourgeoisie had expanded at the end of the nineteenth century, close-packing it with streets of tall and decorative apartment houses. It was in one of these, Slovenská Street, that Hejdánek lived with his family. Hejdánek had begun to study mathematics and philosophy at the Charles University before the Communist takeover, one of his teachers being Jan Patočka. Another had been the evangelical theologian J.L. Hromádka, founder and first chairman of the World Council of Churches. Hromádka had argued that it was morally feasible to support Communism without betraying one's loyalty to Christianity, a belief to which Hejdánek did not subscribe. After his graduation in 1952 he had worked as a labourer, before finding a low-paid post in the Institute of Epidemiology and Microbiology; by getting up at three in the morning he continued to study, write and publish articles on philosophy (in *Vesmír*, *Plamen*, *Tvář* and the *Křesťanská Revue*). In 1968 he was invited to join the Institute of Philosophy at the Faculty of Sciences; in 1971 he was expelled from the Institute and charged with 'attempted instigation'. He spent the next eighteen years as a night watchman, coal stoker and stockroom clerk. A spinal disorder which caused constant pain, headaches and giddiness led to periods in hospital and a small sickness benefit. In September 1977 Hejdánek, at the age of 50, was appointed Charter spokesman in place of the imprisoned Havel; he remained so through 1978, and then stepped in again when Jiří Dienstbier was imprisoned in June 1979. One of the first Charter documents was a letter to President Husák with nineteen signatories (including Tomin) protesting against the brutality used against Hejdánek when he had been detained by the police.

When Tomin came to see Hejdánek in March 1980 he proposed that they should prepare a protest over the police harassment of philosophy and have it signed by every philosopher in Czechoslovakia. Hejdánek explained that in his view no one would sign except those already outside the system and that neither the authorities nor anyone else would take any notice. Angry and upset, Tomin left the flat. This incident and the knowledge that Tomin was planning to emigrate weighed on Hejdánek's mind. At this time there were three seminars meeting in his flat. One had been set up for students at the School of

Evangelical Theology, which until 1948 had been a faculty of the Charles University (and became so again after 1989). Teachers at the school were aware of the inadequacy of the courses taught there, and used Hejdánek's seminar to maintain contacts with phenomenological theology. Another seminar was for former members of the Jircháře Colloquia and a third was for younger students.

Apart from the trials of 1972 (when Hejdánek had almost been imprisoned) the seminars had continued without interruption, in spite of the 24-hour police surveillance imposed after he had become Charter spokesman. Over the next few months, however, Hejdánek came to the decision that he would combine the three groups into one open seminar. Mindful of what had happened to Tomin's Technical University students, he warned that anyone who had anything to lose should stay away. The new seminar convened in the academic year 1980-1981 consisted of elements of all three seminars, together with some of Tomin's old group (including Dvořáková and Liška) and a handful of new students who had heard about the seminar, possibly from Radio Free Europe. Hejdánek became convinced in time that at least two of the new students were police informers, but decided to disregard the risk. He reasoned that it was all to the good if secret policemen reflected on the content of the philosophy lectures. (John Procopé, a Cambridge philosopher whom Scruton was at this time considering as a potential visitor and donor, later came to the same conclusion. Interrogated by the Czech police in February 1981, he noted that the interpreter appeared to know something about the subject. 'The more we talked, the more he reminded me of the intellectuals with whom I had been consorting. He had the same eagerness for uncommon knowledge, the same air of a soul in love with ideas. Perhaps he was himself a student, called in to help with translation. Perhaps he had attended these seminars in disguise. Perhaps he had heard recordings of them at the police department. The seminars were said to be bugged. "If they really do listen in to these seminars," I reflected, "there must be some highly cultivated policemen in Prague by now."')[5] Hejdánek's seminar was to run for over nine years, from autumn 1980 to autumn 1989, meeting almost without fail every Monday night between the 1st October and the 30th June. It was to this seminar that the Oxford philosophers intended to continue to send visitors. It also became the venue for the visiting Dutch and French philosophers. For eighteen months, until the turn of 1981-1982, Hejdánek's seminar was more or less tolerated by the authorities. The theme of his seminar for 1980-1981 was the philosophy of science, and for 1981-1982 the philosophy of history. His aim was to counteract the political bias of the Czechoslovak educational system (he was quoted as saying: 'You can't even find a good Marxist philosopher in Czech universities'[6]) by offering his students a variety of viewpoints, a choice of theories. This was why the visiting lecturers were so important, offering a range of ideas current in the West. His requests were similar to those of Tomin: visitors should come at regular intervals; the subject of their talk should be sent in advance; if possible, materials and books relevant to the next speaker should be brought by the preceding visitor. In practice over the years, it sometimes happened that visitors arrived at short notice, or did not arrive when expected. For this reason, Hejdánek always had a theme prepared, to be laid aside in the eventuality of a foreign lecturer arriving. With visitors arriving from different countries, clashes sometimes occurred. Hejdánek would have been justified in feeling that the organisers in the free West should be capable of sorting this out between themselves. However, philosophers were often disappointed when, although their dates had been given well in advance, they arrived to find another speaker holding the floor. To accommodate sore feelings which occasionally arose when distinguished western academics jostled each other in his crowded flat, Hejdánek would often convene several seminars in the course of one week.

The Oxford connection with Hejdánek had been set up before Tomin's departure; among those who visited both philosophers in August 1980 had been Alan Montefiore and Catherine Audard. The first British visitor of the new year 1981 was Christopher Kirwan, who had been disappointed not to meet any students the previous summer. In the course of three days in January he gave his lecture 'St Augustine on the beginning of time' to three groups: a gathering of theologians in Zdeněk Neubauer's flat, a group of four historians at the home of Stanislav Sousedík, and Hejdánek's seminar. Sousedík gave Kirwan a typescript prepared by Ivan Mueller, a Czech living in

Freiburg, of his edited version of John Wyclif's *De Universalibus*. Kirwan took on the task of finding a publisher, and in 1984 it was published as an *editio princeps* by the Clarendon Press in Oxford.[7] Later in January Roger Scruton was back in Prague, lecturing on 'Fantasy and Imagination' for Jiří Němec's seminar (with translation by Tomáš Liška and Martin Palouš) and Aristotle's Theory of Virtue for Hejdánek (translation by Lenka Dvořáková). The Czechoslovak authorities were still refusing exit visas to both Liška and Dvořáková; however, when Scruton returned at the beginning of April it seemed that by autumn 1981 both of them would be undergraduates at Oxford University.

During the whole of this time, Hejdánek's flat remained under the surveillance of uniformed police and four or five raids by the secret police took place; but instead of raiding the seminar within the first twenty minutes, as they had done with Tomin, the police usually waited until the lecture had lasted for an hour or so. Nor were the students detained and beaten, as they had been in the spring of 1980. The only western visitor to be detained during this time was John Procopé, in early February 1981. Entering the dark hallway of Hejdánek's block of flats, he was confronted by two uniformed and one plain-clothes policemen who informed him that 'dnes večer Dr. Hejdánek nebude mít čas' ('Dr. Hejdánek will not have time this evening'). Interrogated in the station in Bartolomějská Street, Procopé delivered an abbreviated version of his paper 'On God's wrath and Christian Meekness in the thinking of some Church Fathers' which, although of interest to the young interpreter, failed to impress his interrogator — 'a dark-haired man in a green suit, somewhat like the young George C. Scott in appearance,' whose manner was 'relaxed and not unfriendly'. He told Procopé that the people he had been consorting with were Trotskyites: 'Such people,' he continued, 'cannot be allowed to disrupt the country. We, the responsible of East and West, must see to stability... Above all, we must not go the way of Poland.' It was a new perception for Procopé, whose audience the previous evening had listened quietly to his paper on 'Boethius and the Consolation of Philosophy'. Delivered to the airport, Procopé — grateful that unlike Newton-Smith and Dr. and Mrs. Kenny he had not been pushed out of a car to cross the border on foot — reflected that:

'There is nothing so charming... as a Czech policeman when he puts on the charm. There had been no conflict of wills. Suppose there had. What would I have done then? And what had happened to the people whom I had met?'[8]

As a result of Procopé's experience, the next visiting lecturer changed his mind about travelling behind the Iron Curtain and was replaced by John Lucas of Merton College in Oxford (who, in the space for 'occupation' on the visa application form, had entered the one word 'don'). Lucas remembers being taken around Prague's back streets, nightwatchmen's lodges and hospital boiler rooms by Tomáš Liška, spreading the message that on the Monday night there would be a seminar on 'Foreknowledge and Free Will'. Elaborate arrangements were made for messages to reach England should he be arrested. In March, Hejdánek's seminar was visited by Jack Skorupski, professor of Moral Philosophy at Glasgow University and Daniel Dennett of Tufts University in the United States. Scruton had delivered their papers during his January visit; however, Dennett later reported: '... my paper had arrived safely, but not been viewed as a version of the talk I would give. No translation of any of it had been prepared, so Tomáš [Liška] — with help from Martin Palouš — managed a near-simultaneous translation, sentence by sentence, of my remarks, which were of course a much truncated and simplified version of the paper ("True Believers")....'[9] Scruton returned in April, intending to lecture on Kant's ethics to Hejdánek's seminar. That evening, however, he found Hejdánek waiting in the street for him; after a weekend of difficult bargaining with the police, Hejdánek had reached an agreement with them that if Scruton did not lecture, they would allow the seminar to continue and Scruton to leave the country without deportation.[10]

The 1981 visits to Hejdánek and the other seminars in Prague had taken place under the auspices of the as-yet unregistered Jan Hus Educational Fund (*sic*). The founders had met in July 1980; the first official meeting was held on Monday 10th November. At the second, the same month, Charles Taylor was appointed the first Chairman of the future Foundation. At the back of their minds, they were aware of the enormousness of the task they had taken on and of the nature of the enterprise; it could have been described as quixotic, except that the windmills they were confronting really did house the dark powers of a totalitarian state. Behind the 'young George C. Scott in a green suit', the listless Major Fišer and the podgy young men in leather jackets was an apparatus with its roots in the Soviet Union. The British Foreign Office, although it had protested against Anthony Kenny's detention, was not going to welcome romantic adventures. It was essential to get the Trust's plans in order, to identify their immediate and concrete aims, and to allocate the accumulating tasks. The matters discussed reflect the programme of the next nine years. One of the important issues at the first meeting was the need to obtain charitable status, for without charitable status there could be no serious fund-raising. However, the founders were optimistic and in November 1980 set themselves a target of £75,000 to be raised and invested (the whole issue of raising funds for investment was to recur over the next ten years, and was never resolved). Newton-Smith wrote to Jessica Strauss Pittman, who was in the process of founding a sister-trust in America: 'The appeal is to cover all intellectual and cultural activities and we will be focusing exclusively on Europe so we won't get wires crossed with you.'[11] The appeal was eventually launched in June 1981, after registration in April. Another proposal — which also became a recurring issue — concerned an approach to Robert Maxwell for funding.[12] The publishing tycoon at that time had his headquarters at Headington in Oxford and both Newton-Smith and Montefiore had dined with him there. Newton-Smith wrote to Jessica Strauss Pittman: 'We saw Maxwell (who is a Czech) who will give some money and advice. He stressed that our line should be that we want to keep C. in the European cultural and intellectual tradition and this seems to go down well.'[13] In fact, Maxwell never showed much sentiment towards the pre-war democracy into which he had been born, and never made even a token donation to the Oxford philosophers' fund.

The committee was more successful with appeals to the Oxford and Cambridge colleges and to individual philosophers in Britain; hundreds of letters were written, most of them by Kathy Wilkes and Roger Scruton. But the case for the Jan Hus Foundation had not been helped by the launch of the appeal for Julius Tomin earlier in the year; a number of colleges and individuals indicated that, having made a substantial contribution towards the support of the Tomin family, they felt that for the time being they had done their duty by Czechoslovakia. In spite of the fact that the sums collected were modest, a legend grew up both in the West and Czechoslovakia that the Jan Hus Foundation was in possession of a lavish endowment. The impressive list of patrons may have given rise to the legend; in fact, only a small number of the patrons made any substantial contribution (at Christmas 1981 the Duke of Norfolk, mildly distressed at a suggestion that he might make a covenant in the Foundation's favour, sent £5 as a good-will gift).

The first set of accounts for the Jan Hus Foundation run from 13th November 1979 to 31st July 1982 (once the Foundation was formerly registered, the Trustees chose August to July as their financial year, as roughly corresponding to the academic year). In this period of twenty and a half months a total of £7,523.57 was raised from approximately 130 donors (the number cannot be exact, because in the early days some receipts are marked with a name and question mark, or 'not known'). The average donation works out at something under £60 each, but in fact most individuals donated £10 or £20; there were eighteen three-figure donations, and one of £1,000. Amongst donating colleges were Christchurch, Keble and Emmanuel in Oxford and Kings in Cambridge. There were a few well-known names: Sir Adrian Cadbury, Harold Pinter, Karel Reisz and Lord Weinstock, all of whom continued to support the Foundation in later years. An early donor was Diana Phipps, a member of the Czech Šternberk family, who, after 1989, was to recover the family castles in Bohemia.[14] Most of the donors were academics, some of whom had already, or would in the future, visit the underground seminars (usually paying their own costs).

During this period the Patočka University and Prague Book Fund accounts were still in existence, and transactions took place between the three accounts before they were incorporated into one. Out-going grants and donations from the three accounts amounted to £6,780.89 between November 1979 and July 1982; these included payments to Hejdánek, purchase of books, and some refunds of visiting lecturers' expenses. Over the twenty and a half months, the sum of £375 was spent on secretarial expenses, £163.05 on printing and postage (which did not reflect the real cost, borne by individual trustees) and

£618.63 on legal fees in connection with the registration of the Foundation as a charity.

Another important issue for the committee was the policy and programme for the coming year. If funds could be raised, it would enable them to go ahead with a new part of the philosophy programme — the awarding of research stipends for the Czech philosophers. At the first meeting a six-month stipend of £100 a month (provided by John Procopé) was agreed for Hejdánek. £100, even at the exchange rate fixed by the Czechoslovak authorities, was still an adequate monthly income in Prague (the standard stipend was later fixed at £60 per month). It had been ascertained that it was only when money was officially transmitted through a bank that a Czechoslovak citizen could claim exemption from the charge of 'parasitism', or living off the state. Hejdánek was willing to be used as a test case; his December stipend was despatched through the bank and reached him six weeks later, the authorities accepting that the sum was sufficient, for legal purposes, to count as an adequate income. The question of how best to pay stipends continued to be an issue: in September 1981 Montefiore reported: 'On the one hand, currency is more profitable and, *en principe*, anonymous. On the other, it carries a clear legal risk; and some people are against the principle. As against this, there is now more worry about the long term risks of receiving stipends.'[15] The method of paying stipends in cash was usually preferred by recipients working in low-paid but undemanding jobs, as they were able to remain part of the officially-employed labour force whilst still continuing with their academic work. The main problem for the Foundation was the risk of confusion and misunderstandings. Up to ten or twelve stipends were sometimes running simultaneously, of different amounts and over different time schedules. Visiting lecturers had to memorise their instructions and work from a list of names which they were allowed to write down only in code. A typical early briefing for one visitor (who was given £983 to distribute in five parts) ran to one and a half single-spaced typed pages, ending with the words: 'Do not utter names indoors, and enter quietly everywhere.'[16]

Decisions about stipends were made by the Trustees on the basis of applications and requests which fitted the criteria of the Foundation — criteria which were in the making, and which were constantly reassessed. Essentially, the purpose of a stipend was to support academic work which would promote the development of independent learning. The work could take the form of organising and preparing seminars;[17] of translating into Czech or Slovak a key text in the humanities or social sciences; or of researching a subject not on the ideologically-biased syllabus of the Czechoslovak universities, and presenting it in a form which made it available to students on the underground courses. Stipends were also provided for those involved in the practical work of producing samizdat. The stipends offered were not intended for research work which was not oriented towards the seminars, and were not 'welfare' payments (although a candidate's circumstances were often taken into consideration). Results were expected, and the quality of work debated. A reporting schedule was attached to all the stipends. This sometimes caused difficulties, as recipients were understandably reluctant to make a report in writing which would subsequently be carried through airport checks, and so their reports would be oral, sometimes passed along a chain before reaching the Trustees in Britain. In other cases the reporting schedule was taken very seriously; the Luther scholar Jan Litomiský from Pelhřimov in southern Bohemia[18] sent regular reports by normal postal service to London during the period of his stipend from 1987 to 1989. The standard stipend of £60 a month, when converted at the official rate of around 9 or 10 crowns to the pound, just about covered living expenses. A number of recipients did not use the stipend for personal expenses, but put it towards samizdat production and other 'professional' expenses. In a 'Note on validation' written in the early 1980s, Roger Scruton suggested: 'In my own opinion, the only indisputably publishable work that has come to us recently from our contacts in Prague has come from Pithart and Fidelius; but their stuff is of a truly high standard. All the rest falls just below the mark. Nevertheless, by the standards of a second-rate English university, the research, teaching and publication undertaken by those whom we support is, on the whole, extremely successful, and we should, I believe, try to see it as a whole, with the less good stuff "carried" by the excellent stuff. If we compare what our people achieve on a budget of 15,000 a year or less, with what the University of Bradford (say) achieves with a budget of millions, we should be proud, not of ourselves, but of them.'

Another important issue for the meetings held in late 1980 was the choice of appropriate visiting lecturers. The Foundation was no longer urging all philosophers to visit Prague. Although the long term aim was to set up regular teaching courses, there were still arrangements to be made for the second half of the academic year. Alan Montefiore's next visit was already planned; other visitors suggested at the Foundation's first meeting included Sir Karl Popper, born in Vienna but resident in Britain. Newton-Smith, who knew him professionally, thought that the possibility would interest him, but Popper was now 78, and although in the late 1980s he was actively interested in the publication of his work in samizdat (in Brno), he never did go to Czechoslovakia.[20] As well as Hejdánek's seminar, contact had already been made with the seminars led by Palouš, Trojan, Sousedík and Neubauer. During his visit in January 1981, Scruton had learnt that Alena Hromádková, who was becoming an essential guide and adviser for the British visitors, belonged to a small group studying political science; whilst another of the students, Daniel Kummerman, ran a group for which he would appreciate a speaker on the philosophy of Hannah Arendt.[21] There was also Petr Rezek, one of Patočka's original seminar and now a passionate and lively member of Hejdánek's seminar. Rezek was to become a vital colleague for the Foundation in years to come. The Foundation was also eager to support seminars operating outside Prague; early in 1981 Scruton heard about a seminar in Brno led by Zdeněk Vašíček, and Dvořáková promised to go down and collect information; and about another in Bratislava led by Miroslav Kusý. (In fact, it was to be three years before the Foundation worked regularly in Brno, and five years before it made contact with Bratislava. The delay may partly have been due to the fact that members of the Foundation had been warned in Prague about the violently repressive action taken by police against Zdeněk Vašíček's seminar in Brno.)

The Jan Hus trustees met monthly between January and July 1981. During this time the registration as a charity was completed, and news came that steps to register the French Association Jan Hus were going well; in a few months time Jessica Strauss Pittman would have put together 'a small working group' of directors for the American fund. Initial contact was made with Charter 77 Foundation in Sweden, led by the emigré Czech physicist František Janouch, which raised funds for humanitarian support for those who suffered as a result of upholding the principles of the Charter. (It was hoped initially that Charter 77 Foundation might make a donation to the work of the Jan Hus; in fact, Janouch was interested in the reverse possibility, that the JHEF might make a donation to Charter 77 Foundation.) It was agreed that a policy document should be drawn up for distribution to contacts inside Czechoslovakia. It was also established as a key principle that every visiting lecturer should provide a written report on his or her return from Czechoslavakia.

The possibilities — if money and time could be found — seemed to be unlimited. Visiting lecturers were being sought in the fields of philosophy, sociology, theology, music and art. Books had to be provided for the courses, but there were already rumours that some of the books taken to Prague had found their way onto personal bookshelves, and were no longer in circulation. The possibility of founding a library was discussed, and where this could be housed. Meanwhile, to refute charges of exclusiveness, an offer of a book exchange was made to the English Library of the State Library in the Klementinum. (In 1948 the British Council had been forced to close its library, but an English-language library was later established within the State Library — which was also the university library — to which the British Council supplied new books. It was exceptional in having an open shelf policy, and survived until 1997 when it was incorporated into the main library.) The head of the English Library responded promptly and positively to the letter from the Jan Hus Foundation,[22] and the exchange lasted up to and beyond 1989. As well as being of practical value, the book exchange established an important principle of JHEF policy; that it was not 'a tool of the opposition', but was, on the contrary, an independent body willing and able to cooperate with receptive and open-minded official institutions.

The issue of books and their transportation was an important and difficult one. Books were to become a major expense for the Foundation in the future, especially academic texts which could often only be obtained from specialist sources; although publishers were often generous in supplying free copies, it took time and diligence to find the right person to approach. An important contact was the publisher Norman Franklin, who became a patron and used his influence with other publishing houses. As many donations as possible were obtained, either from authors or from publishers. Every new potential avenue was sought (although a visit by Newton-Smith to the book display at the Hegel Congress in Germany in the summer of 1981 proved disappointing). The specific problems involved in purchasing books for Prague were summarised in a four-page report prepared by Kathy Wilkes in April 1984, which opens with six reasons as to why 'the present state of affairs is wholly unsatisfactory'. Book lists were being sent to her without any explanation as to why those specific books were important, and no indication of priorities. In future, she proposed, applicants should be asked to provide more details, and more information as to who would be using the books. She suggested that the 'new secretary' (yet to be appointed) should be asked to keep records of what books had been sent and to whom, and should obtain catalogues from British publishers to be distributed in Prague. Above all, she asked that Trustees should visit Prague as frequently as they possibly could: 'Non-Trustees, as we have learned from dozens of reports, usually cannot provide the JHEF with the details needed — they often do not know what to ask of whom — nor can they communicate so directly and helpfully with our contacts. This suggestion has independent merits, but for the book problem it would help with the important task of keeping people in Czechoslovakia informed about what we are doing, and why. I do not think that such a policy would lead to more Trustees being refused a visa. Those of us who do not get visas are refused for reasons unconnected with the JHEF.'[23] Every visitor packed one bag with books, prepared to explain to border guards that they were preparing a paper for a forthcoming conference. Seminar leaders warned that books should not be sent through the ordinary post for fear of theft (although books for the Klementinum library could safely be sent by this method).

The remaining possibility was to smuggle in the books. One channel through which this could be done was the Volkswagen van into which Jan Kavan had in 1971, with the help of the English activist Michael Randle, fitted concealed compartments. The van had been successfully smuggling books and materials into Czechoslovakia for ten years, but the operation was always short of money. Kavan believed he could convey all the Foundation's books — at a price. Early in 1981 he made an offer to transport a minumum of 700, possibly up to 1,500 books (depending on their size) for a payment of £3,000. The trustees agreed to the offer in principle, but, with limited funds available, proposed an initial payment of £500 for the transport of 100-150 books. Kavan's reply shows a scarcely suppressed irritation at what he felt to be the parsimonious attitude of the British. After years of operating on a shoe-string, he betrayed some resentment of this new, high-profile, and, to the outsider's eye, well-supported organisation. Without financial support from the Jan Hus Foundation, he implied, the van service might not be able to continue: 'Last but not least we would like to mention the fact that we are expected by people in Czechoslovakia to continue to transport also other books, mainly in Czech and that this service is regarded by all the different groups in Czechoslovakia as vital and that was one of the reasons why they asked you to consider helping the [Solidarity] Fund as one of your projects which should receive a priority.'[24]

When writing this, Kavan did not yet know about the dramatic events of the previous day (27th April 1981); events whose consequences have still not been resolved at the end of the 1990s. As a result of what is believed (but not by everyone) to have been a tip-off from an informer in Prague, the Volkswagen van (driven by Giles Thonon, a French lawyer, and Françoise Anis, law student and President of a Paris section of the League of Human Rights) was stopped on the border by Czechoslovak customs officers. In the secret compartments were discovered not only Kavan's materials from Britain but also materials from the emigré publishers Pavel Tigrid in Paris and Jiří Pelikán in Rome, and the publishing house Index in Munich. On 6th May, the Czechoslovak Press Agency announced that Thonon and Anis had been carrying not only 'anti-state printed matter and records aimed against the socialist social system' but also 'instructions for the conduct of criminal activity in Czechoslovakia' and that there was proof that Czechs and Slovaks had 'participated in this criminal activity'. Most compromising of all for Kavan was the rumour that a list of names and addresses had been discovered in the van. In the

Thames TV feature *The Last Round-Up?* made in May 1981 the reporter Julian Manyon claimed that these were the names of Kavan's dissident contacts. Kavan immediately complained to the Broadcasting Complaints Commission, and in 1985 his complaint was upheld. However, in 1992 Pavel Tigrid's list of Prague contacts[26] was discovered in the files of the secret police, and was proved to have been carried in the van; the B.C.C. consequently anulled its ruling. Amongst other papers found in the StB files were allegations by an agent in the London Embassy that Kavan — by 1992 a leading member of the Czech Social Democrat Party — had from 1969 been giving information about his emigré compatriots. In 1996 he was cleared of the allegations and in 1998 he became Foreign Minister of the Czech Republic.

However, whilst still appreciating Kavan's efforts on their behalf, many of the dissidents decided not to use his channels in future; in September 1981 Alan Montefiore reported: 'We heard some criticism in Prague of the "irresponsibility" of sending in two messengers carrying material belonging to three or four organisations at once.'[27] The Jan Hus Foundation was not directly involved in the crisis, although it had its effect on their work in Prague and, in the long term, also in Brno. Of a large number of dissidents detained, seventeen were charged with 'subversion of the Republic on a large scale in co-operation with a foreign power';[28] seven of them (including the seminar student Jan Ruml[29]) remained in prison without trial for a year.

The French Philosophers

It is quite surprising that the first support for the underground philosophers in Czechoslovakia should have come from the British philosophers and not from the French who traditionally were more involved in politics. The French had reasons to be specially affected by what was happening in Czechoslovakia. There had been a tradition of friendships and cultural links since long before the Second World War. During the first part of this century, significant cultural and educational links had been established with France, a country which represented the wider world beyond the boundaries of the Austro-Hungarian Empire. Czech artists and writers such as Alfons Mucha, Franz Kupka and the Čapek brothers were amongst those who had lived and worked in Paris. The Czech surrealists were well known in France, and after the war Toyen settled in Paris. During the First Republic a substantial Czech community established itself in France. Jan Patočka had studied at the Sorbonne; his work was translated into French and known to French philosophers, whereas few British and Americans had heard his name.

The Soviet invasion of Czechoslovakia in August 1968, and, to a lesser extent, Charter 77 and the trial of Václav Havel and the other VONS leaders in October 1979[1] had made a deep impression on the French left, both Communist and non-Communist; there were also memories of the Munich agreement of 1938, which many French viewed as a betrayal. There had been closer links between French intellectuals and the Czech academic establishment and more regular visits and exchanges than was the case with the British. However, despite the fact that support had been organised in France for Czech political dissidents[2], nothing had been done in the field of academic philosophy. This began with the visit of the French philosopher Catherine Audard with Alan Montefiore and Steven Lukes to Julius Tomin's seminar in December 1979. On their return, whilst Montefiore worked with Wilkes, Scruton, Taylor and Newton-Smith on the setting up of the Jan Hus Educational Foundation in Oxford, Audard decided to initiate a structured support for Czechoslovak philosophers in France. She approached a number of friends and colleagues as well as human rights activitists such as Michel Broué and Jean-Jacques Marie, asking for their help and advice on the creation of an 'Association Jan Hus' modelled on the British trust. Among those who immediately responded to her appeal were Jacques Derrida, Jean-Pierre Vernant and Maurice de Gandillac. Another philosopher who would have seemed to be a natural leader of the AJH was Paul Ricoeur, who had been close to Jan Patočka during Patočka's stay in Paris between the wars, and had a long personal involvement with Czech philosophers and theologians. Ricoeur was approached by Audard, but, in view of the political situation, feared for the safety of his friends in Prague and thought that a movement with too much public exposure and involving possibly inexperienced and irresponsible 'intellectuals' was not such a good idea. Nevertheless, he became extremely supportive as soon as he saw that the AJH was acting cautiously and responsibly in its endeavours.

In March of that year (1980) Audard worked on the organisation of a protest against the Prague arrests, signed by 65 French philosophers, 39 from Great Britain, ten from Germany and seven from North America. In May she arranged a meeting in the Sorbonne, at which Kathy Wilkes and Alan Montefiore spoke to fifty French philosophers. The activities of the Oxford philosophers initially met with some surprise from their colleagues, who were amused to discover that British academics existed who could even find Prague on the map. The French took a different view of their involvement from the British, and saw no reason why they should not openly visit both the Charles University and the dissident seminars. Whereas the British had from the start insisted that the only issue with which they were concerned was philosophy, the French took a much more political attitude. The single-minded approach of the Oxford philosophers came in for strong criticism: 'The English are apathetic

about politics. You go to Prague and you end up talking about
Aristotle and about Berkeley. There is something absurd about
that to me. I am Marxist and I argue from that position. You
must go and you must talk about Marx, Engels and Trotsky, and
about changing the structure of the bureaucratic state in Eastern
Europe. That is what matters.'[3] Wilkes and Montefiore tried to
imagine the reactions of Tomin's students if they were to follow
Pierre Foujeyrollas' advice and lecture them on Marx, Engels
and Trotsky. However, their sincerity won over the French; who
nevertheless decided that if they were going to support the venture it would be in their own way. The movement involved the
most famous of French philosophers, Jacques Derrida, whose
wife's mother was Czech, and who had visited the country several times in the 1960s. He summed up the feelings of the meeting: 'This case is important because it is an international case. It
is symbolic and will arouse deep solidarity across all borders in
philosophical thinking. We have to let Tomin begin again as an
academic. We have to let him think, speak, exercise himself in
what he is qualified and trained — being a philosopher... Most
of the Oxford philosophers have come to the campaign from a
liberal position, which is legitimate, of course. But probably that
is not enough. I think we cannot avoid making it more political.
The case has proved that the Czechoslovaks have signed but not
applied the Helsinki Agreement on human rights — they have a
very different ideology in mind, very different information, and
very different rules of argument. The lesson of Dr. Tomin's case
is that the practical side of philosophy is very important for us
all. We have learnt that we must have very definite political priorities. I am very glad that it is Oxford philosophers who came
to visit us today. It makes the point very much clearer.'[4]

Ladislav Hejdánek's memory is that Paul Ricoeur was the
first of his visitors from the AJH, in the summer of 1980. In fact,
Ricoeur travelled independently, visiting several Prague seminars (including that of Zdeněk Neubauer), but he did bring with
him news of the launching of a new initiative. Whilst in Prague
Ricoeur was followed by police but the seminars were not interrupted (although several participants were later interrogated).
Some of the Czechs had the feeling that the authorities were rather impressed by the visit of the internationally renowned professor. For Hejdánek it was a good augury; not only was Ricoeur

the most distinguished visitor he had received, but more than thirty years before Hejdánek had attended one of his lectures. It had been at a conference of the World Student Christian Fellowship in Brussels in 1947, not long before the Communist putsch in Czechoslovakia. A firm friendship developed. Ricoeur continued to visit Prague, but did not formally join the AJH for several years, being concerned that the presence of too many foreign visitors was going to cause problems for the Czechs.

In Paris, Catherine Audard took on the responsibility of setting up an organisation in parallel with the British Foundation; it was decided that a 'Comité de soutien aux représentants de la culture vivante en Tchéchoslovaquie et aux étudiants victimes d'interdits professionnels' should be created.[5] A meeting was arranged, to include the participation of Julius Tomin and Paul Ricoeur, for 21st December 1980. Under French law, the organisation had to take a different form from the British; it was created as an 'association', with members who paid an annual subscription and attended an annual Assemblée générale. The French organisation was thus both more structured and more public than that in Britain, which, beyond the central core of active Trustees, maintained only a loose and unofficial network of donors, visiting lecturers and well-wishers.[6] Twenty-six philosophers attended the first official meeting, held at the École Normale supérieure on 1st February 1981; they included Jacques Derrida, Maurice de Gandillac, Jean-François Lyotard and Jean-Pierre Vernant. Officers were appointed (Vernant as President, Derrida as Vice-President, Audard as Secretary and her father Jean Audard as Treasurer) and recent reports read from Christopher Hill and Roger Scruton. By 15th May, more than 50 members had signed up, and a réunion was called for 31st May. Audard wrote: 'Malgré les événements récents[7] le nombre des visites de professeurs ou d'étudiants français continue á se développer et elles sont tres attendues par les groupes à Prague. Tous les témoignages concorde pour souligner à quel point notre appui est vital pour eux. Il faut donc continuer et amplifier ce mouvement, mais, étant donné la situation actuelle, il est nécessaire de bien préparer ces visites et que ceux qui ont l'intention de partir cette année ou l'an prochain disposent de toutes les informations que possède notre Association. Il suffit pour cela qu'ils m'écrivent dès que possible pour prendre contact.'[8] On 4th August 1981 the statutes of the Association Jan Hus were registered with the *Journal officiel des déclarations d'associations* (three months after the British Jan Hus Foundation's registration with the Charity Commission).

For a long time the subscriptions (100 francs for active members, 500 francs for benefactor members, 30 francs for students) remained the only funding for the Association Jan Hus. With a budget of 9,000 francs in its first year, the Association was able to provide 50 or so books and one three-month stipend of 2,000 francs a month, and organise four visits. Only the most basic expenses of administration could be covered, and most philosophers paid their own travel costs to Prague; for this reason, a reconstruction of the list of early French visitors is even more difficult than that of the British. In 1982 the first application for funding was made to the French Ministère des Relations Extérieurs, but it was several years before funds were forthcoming from the French government.[9] Meanwhile, it was necessary to attract as many new members as possible, and an appeal went round all the universities in France: 'La nécessité de créer un vaste mouvement de solidarité autour de ces étudiants et de ces enseignants, ensuite, une telle Association est devenue évidente pour tous ceux, venus de Paris, d'Oxford ou d'ailleurs, qui ont pu les rencontrer et prendre conscience de leur situation. Beaucoup ont été exclus de l'Université et sont dans l'impossibilité de poursuivre leurs études et leurs travaux dans le cadre des institutions. Pour vivre, ils font des métiers manuels et sont le plus souvent exclus de la vie intellectuelle officielle. Ils ont beaucoup de difficultés à rester en contact avec leurs collègues d'autres pays et sont très privées de ce manque d'échanges. Voyager est presque impossible. Les livres les plus classiques sont très difficiles á trouver.'[10]

One of the first French philosophers to visit Ladislav Hejdánek's seminar was Jacques Derrida, who arrived in Prague on Saturday 26th December 1981. Even before his departure from Paris airport Derrida felt he was under observation. On Sunday 27th two secret police followed him wherever he went; eventually, hoping to have shaken them off, he called at Hejdánek's apartment to hand over money and materials entrusted to him by Audard. Later that evening, a group of around ten people gathered there for the seminar. Derrida arrived in the darkness of a December night; Hejdánek and the students remember that he was uneasy and nervous, telling them how he was being followed. They warned him about possible hidden microphones; he was struck how freely they spoke about the police. As for the group, it was enough that the celebrated philosopher was actually there among them. Derrida delivered a lecture based on what he was at that time teaching about Descartes in Paris. Miloš Rejchrt interpreted, and remembers the difficulty he had with the extreme language of deconstruction. Initially the students were silent. The abstract subject matter differed from the theology of the Dutch or the pragmatism of the British. Amongst those present was Tomáš Vlasák, a priest in the underground church who later joined the Cambridge Diploma course run by the British JHEF. With careful thought he asked the question: 'K čemu je ta filosofie?' What use is that philosophy? What does such an intellectual, formal way of thinking have to offer to those who are living on the edge of existence, who are seeking a meaning to life in a totalitarian society? A few minutes later, as Derrida left Hejdánek's apartment, uniformed police asked to see his passport. In the street, Derrida's wife's relations were waiting to collect him by car. Thoroughly disturbed, Derrida told them what had been happening to him. They found it hard to believe, but agreed that he should collect only his most essential belongings from the hotel and stay with them. Nevertheless, the following day the secret police followed him by car and on foot as though (Derrida's own description) he were electronically tagged.

On Tuesday 29th December Derrida collected his cases from the hotel and said goodbye to his relations at the airport. Passing through customs he was called into a private room where police with dogs searched his cases, eventually — at the third attempt, after a telephone call evidently asking for help — finding four packets of a brown powder concealed in the lining. Over the next few hours a protocol was written and photographs taken of him and his suitcases. Then he was taken to a police station where from 4.00 p.m. to 12 midnight he was interrogated about his life, his relationship with Czechoslovakia and Kafka (whose grave he had visited). 'Is Ladislav Hejdánek then a Kafkalogist?' they asked. At midnight he was charged with 'the production and traffic of drugs', and the team of lawyer, commissioner, interpreter and prosecution departed, leaving him in the guard of one policeman. 'Do you believe this charge?' Derrida asked the policeman. 'Of course,' replied the policeman, 'that's just how western intellectuals behave — look at the Beatles.'

The planting of the drugs was not a sudden whim of the police, but part of a larger strategy, known as Operation Isolation, devised to discredit Charter 77. This had first been thought of in December 1977, but the final strategy had been drawn up by Major (at that time) Karel Vykypěl[11] in March 1981. The aim of the action was to drive a wedge (to use the name of another StB operation) between Charter signatories, and discredit them in the eyes of the public. In phase 2 the police were, among other actions, 'to prepare, in cooperation with the 4th section of the 10th directorate SNB, compromising situations for Anna Šabatová-Uhlová, Ladislav Hejdánek and Jaroslav Bašta in connection with their links with emigrant and ideologically subversive centres... to arrange, as a means of preventing the participation of foreign emissaries and lecturers in the so-called anti-universities, situations which will lead to their being compromised (for example, trafficking in drugs) and consequently to the participants in the lectures being compromised.'[12] Jacques Derrida was to be the first victim, but the intended target was Ladislav Hejdánek.

Derrida was driven through the cold December night to Ruzyně jail, where a hostile prison officer locked him into a small and dirty cell furnished with one bunk. Here he meditated on the value of deconstructionist philosophy for those deprived of freedom: 'K čemu je ta filosofie? What use is that philosophy?'. At 5.00 a.m. the door was unlocked to admit a Magyar gypsy who, moved by the plight of this poor western bourgeois (Derrida's words), did his best to help by cleaning the cell. The two men had no language in common, but in exchange Derrida taught the other a game drawn on a piece of paper tissue. As the dull winter light began to dawn, Derrida was taken to be shaved, registered with the prison authorities, and put into prison pyjamas. Told to choose a pair of shoes 'from a pile like in concentration camps', he accidentally chose two left shoes. More photographs were taken; it was around midday on the 30th December. Derrida was led to another cell, occupied by four or five young Czechs who reminded him of the students he had met at the seminar: energetic, articulate and angry. They told him their stories — one had been imprisoned for trying to join his brother in the USA. Like the students, they were not afraid to say what they liked about the system and the police. The young men listened to Derrida with sympathy, and warned him that he faced a two-year sentence. As the lights in the cell went out that night, Derrida could only hope that the defence lawyer present at his interrogation had kept his promise to phone his Prague relations.

Meanwhile, Hejdánek and his students had been expecting Derrida to return to continue the seminar, as was the custom with the French visitors. When Derrida had not arrived on the evening of Monday 28th December, Hejdánek, with a French student who had joined the seminar, went to look for him at his hotel. Only his cases were there. Derrida, they were told, had not slept at the hotel. The student went to the French Embassy, Hejdánek to Agence France Presse. Both telegraphed to Paris. Early the following morning (Tuesday 29th December) the French Ambassador sent for the Czechoslovak Minister of Foreign Affairs, who said that he had no report of a Frenchman being detained. At this point, this was true; whilst the French Ambassador was talking to the Czechoslovak Foreign Minister, Derrida was collecting his cases from the hotel and being driven to the airport. For the rest of that day the Ministry continued — in good faith — to deny that Derrida had been detained. It was not until shortly before his transfer to Ruzyně that night that a statement was issued saying that Jacques Derrida had been arrested for 'the production and traffic of drugs'.

The defence lawyer kept faith with Derrida, and telephoned his wife's relations in Prague. They rang Derrida's wife in Paris during the night of 29th/30th December. Shocked and helpless, Mme. Derrida rang Catherine Audard and Alan Montefiore, who by chance were visiting Paris. Audard rang Roger Errera, a Conseiller d'État with personal experience of Czechoslovakia.[13] Errera gave her the home telephone number of the responsible official at the Quai d'Orsay, already warned by the French Embassy in Prague that Hejdánek was worried about Derrida's whereabouts. The French government did not hesitate to use the hot line to President Gustáv Husák. Early on the morning of

Wednesday 30th December the secret police realised they had made a catastrophic misjudgement; in their attempt to implement phase 2 of 'Operation Isolation' and discredit the visiting philosophers, they had provoked an international incident. They were also horrified by the speed with which retribution had arrived; they were not to know that Hejdánek had informed the French Ambassador of Derrida's arrest a full 16 hours before it had actually happened.

Between 10.00 and 11.00 p.m. on Wednesday 30th December, Derrida, exhausted from the previous sleepless night, was woken in his cell and returned to the police station. In front of the same group he had met the night before he was told that, whilst still considered to be guilty of the 'production and traffic of drugs', he was being expelled. He spent the rest of that night at the French Embassy before being put on the morning train to Paris. On the western side of the frontier he was met by a crowd of admiring French journalists. It was New Year's Eve 1981-82.

The 'Derrida case', far from discrediting the underground university and dissuading western professors from travelling, created greater solidarity between the Czechs and their foreign lecturers and, especially in France, stimulated academics to travel behind the Iron Curtain. From that time on Ladislav Hejdánek's seminar welcomed an unfailing stream of French philosophers, most of whom travelled at their own expense but within the context of the Association Jan Hus programme. Welcome as this was, it increased the workload for Catherine Audard, who by 1983 knew also that she would be moving permanently to London. The administration of the growing organisation was a cause of concern. In May, Audard persuaded a reluctant colleague, the librarian Nathalie Roussarie with whom she had been involved in human rights programmes, to accompany the philosophers Jacques and Hélène Brunschwicg on their July visit to Ladislav Hejdánek's seminar. Roussarie remembers that she met Radim Palouš and Petr Rezek on the same visit, and the impact that these meetings made on her. Shocked by the conditions in which the Czech teachers and students were working, she took on the post of Honorary Secretary to the AJH in September 1983 and, prepared by Audard, from then on became the organising strength of the association. Another factor in the success of the French operation was the presence in Prague of the French student Valérie Lowit. Lowit, the daughter of the Czech sociologist Tomáš Lowit, living in exile in Paris, was at that time living in Prague and able to make practical arrangements and memorise messages far more easily than the slightly dazed travellers.

At this time, the normal pattern for French visitors was for them to travel to Prague on Friday evening and settle in their hotel. On Saturday morning they would visit the contact named for them by Audard or Roussarie to exchange messages and materials. Other visits would be made on the advice of the first contact. During the day they were expected to phone the French Conseiller culturel to make an appointment for the Monday (during this period the British preferred to avoid official contacts, fearing they would draw the attention of the Czechoslovak authorities). There might be further visits on the Sunday, but the main business was on Monday night, the seminar with Hejdánek, 'qui peut durer assez tard'.[14] Visitors were recommended to stay until Wednesday, so that the seminar could be continued on the Tuesday evening. A report was expected as soon as possible after their return. One of the seminars occasionally visited was that of the Němec family in Ječná Street. David Němec remembers that during one of Jean Pierre Vernant's lectures on classical tragedy there was a loud banging on the door of the apartment. Outside stood the artist Magor (Ivan Jirous),[15] who removed one of David's paintings from the wall and demanded of Vernant that he should buy it from him, since he needed money for beer. Vernant offered him fifty crowns, accepted the picture, and solemnly continued with his lecture.

One of the most frequent visitors, Jean-Claude Eslin (co-editor with Olivier Mongin of the journal *Esprit*) remembers that there were two traditions of French philosophy involved in the Association Jan Hus, that of the former communists represented by Vernant and Etienne Balibar, and the tradition of the non-Communist Left represented by his own journal, with its strongly anti-totalitarian stance.[16] In France the two traditions normally kept their distance from each other, but in their work in Prague and in the AJH they were exceptionally united. Both Eslin and Mongin had studied the work of Jan Patočka, and came to the seminars with an understanding of Czech work in philosophy. Eslin felt that through the discussions in Prague, the French and the Czechs were beginning to restore the close relationship which had existed between them in pre-war Europe. (One of the most important subjects on which he lectured was the writings of Hannah Arendt, which Martin Palouš was at that time translating into Czech.) He found that the seminars worked on many levels — philosophical, cultural, political, historical and religious — and that they combined both tradition and innovation. Like many other visitors, he was impressed with the way in which men such as Rudolf Kučera, Karel Palek and Václav Malý could combine menial labour with demanding intellectual work. For Eslin, the visits to Czechoslovakia were an opportunity to get a wider view of Europe which he could pass on to his students at the Ecole Européenne des Affaires in Paris, Oxford, Berlin and Madrid.

The French interpreter at Rudolf Kučera's seminar was usually Karel Palek; at Ladislav Hejdánek and Jakub Trojan's seminars, Miloš Rejchrt.[17] Rejchrt was a priest in the protestant church who had lost his licence in 1972 and been forced to work as a stoker, at first in Česká Lípa and after 1976 in Prague, where he found the 48 hour detentions in Bartolomějská police station companionable and even stimulating. Of the French philosophers he valued most Jean Pierre Vernant and Paul Ricoeur, for their clarity of thought and expression (Ricoeur, he remembers, always avoided technical terms and, if it was necessary to use one, took care to explain it). One of his memories is a visit by André Glucksmann, who gave a fine lecture on the theme 'Truth and Error'. After the lecture, the group (which included Václav Havel) had supper in the National House in Vinohrady; the waiter, seeing they were having a good time, let them stay beyond closing hours, and Rejchrt remembers the sense of liberation, of living a normal life outside the fence of oppression and persecution which was the daily reality.

The Association Jan Hus played an important role in samizdat production, not only in raising funds for stipends and publication, but also in providing books and materials (the elegant appearance of *Střední Evropa* in later years owed much to French taste in Lettraset and similar aids). In 1986 the Association was also responsible for publishing Karel Palek's samizdat work *Jazyk a moc* (Language and Power) in France under the title *L'Esprit post-totalitaire*, in a translation by Erika Abrams and with a foreword by André Glucksmann. Further samizdat production was connected with the Association's work in Brno.

The work of the French Association Jan Hus ran from beginning to end in parallel with the work of the British Jan Hus Educational Foundation. The main co-ordinators were initially Catherine Audard and Alan Montefiore, shortly joined by Nathalie Roussarie and Roger Scruton, and eventually Barbara Day. Sometimes the two organisations, made up of powerful personalities, seemed to be in rivalry; sometimes there were disagreements about policy, and occasionally communication failed, leading to clashes in dates or duplication of materials. These failings however were trivial in comparison with the ten years of co-operation between two independent organisations, neither of which either claimed or yielded leadership. The focus of the work was in Czechoslovakia, on the colleagues for whom philosophy was not an academic pursuit but a day by day application. It was an approach which led to humility in their western colleagues. In the words of Jean Claude Eslin: 'What was new for us was not purely intellectual; it was always a mix of courage, new ideas, it was a mix of politics, religion, philosophy — a way of life. And so, for example, after that I think I never forgot to speak with my students, I never forgot Central Europe, the Prague traditions. It helped me to put away the conformist view of Europe for my students: the purely occidental, the purely 'European Union' view. I said always to my students, the European Union is just a part of Europe.'[18]

Seminars and Samizdat

It had been agreed amongst the Trustees of the Jan Hus Foundation that the coordination of visits should be the joint responsibility of Kathy Wilkes and Roger Scruton. Of all the Trustees, they were the two who had spent the most time visiting Czechoslovakia, giving seminars, talking to seminar leaders and students, meeting other members of the 'unofficial' community; they were also the two who had spent the most time looking for suitable visiting lecturers. Even after her expulsion in May 1980, Wilkes contrived opportunities to return to Prague, applying for visas at Czechoslovak Embassies as far flung as Rome, Washington and Beijing.[1] She believes that one invitation was arranged by the secret police themselves, as a reaction to her response — on the day she was expelled — to the question why she did not lecture at the Academy or the Charles University: 'Because they haven't asked me!' An invitation arrived from the Academy of Sciences to the Eirene Conference in Prague in September 1982; her paper on Stoicism was later published as part of the proceedings of the conference.[2] However, by 1983 the doors had closed, and the main burden of the work fell on Roger Scruton. Decision-making remained the responsibility of the board of trustees, and one of the major themes was how best to service the development of independent academic study in Czechoslovakia. Ladislav Hejdánek was an important figure, but there was increasing concern that the composition of his seminar was too *ad hoc* for a regular teaching programme, and that various factors — including the multiplicity of foreign visitors — made systematic study impossible. It was also a priority to set up regular teaching seminars at venues unknown to the police, and to create an environment for people which would not be disturbed by the threat of raids. Kathy Wilkes remembers that even before Tomin had left she had been discussing with Ralph Walker the possibility of structured courses on classical philosophy on the model of the Oxford syllabus. There was also Roger Scruton's awareness, felt on his first visit, that there was a far deeper pool of potential students to be sounded.

Up to the academic year 1981-1982 the main focus remained on Hejdánek's seminar, and in spite of the police surveillance, it was intended that lecturers should still go there. In July the American philosopher Richard Rorty travelled from Heidelberg to give a 'double' seminar, the first part on analytical philosophy and the second, to satisfy another group of students, on the philosophy of Charles Hartshorne. Rorty found his contact with Hejdánek and the students (which still included Liška and Dvořáková) unexpectedly stimulating; and Hejdánek's observation that the government wanted there to be no non-scientific intelligentsia in Czechoslovakia in the next generation remained in his mind. Rorty was followed in September by Alan Montefiore and Catherine Audard, who discussed with Hejdánek the possibility of extending the range of visits — 'loosely connected networks, with the contacts being between, say... historians and historians, mathematicians and mathematicians... lawyers, both academic and working; literary critics.... Those who would most appreciate such visits would be writers. Tom Stoppard's visit had provided inspiration that lasted for two years.'[3] On the basis of this, in November 1981 Stoppard (who, since his protest against Václav Havel's imprisonment in 1977, had been *persona non grata* with the Czechoslovak authorities) arranged a meeting at which Wilkes and Scruton talked to James Saunders, Piers Paul Read, Snoo Wilson, John Bowen and Melvyn Bragg about the seminars. It was however minuted at a meeting of Trustees in June 1982 that nothing had come of this; of this group of writers only Piers Paul Read (several years later) visited Czechoslovakia on behalf of the Foundation.

The 'Derrida affair' of December 1981 — never forgotten in Prague — had a number of consequences. The image of France as a whole, both its intellectuals and its government, was greatly enhanced in the eyes of many Czech dissidents.[4] They were rewarded in that, from then on, there was no shortage of French philosophers willing and eager to give seminars at their own expense in the programme of the Association Jan Hus. However, the international attention provoked by Jacques Derrida's arrest alarmed the British Foreign Office, which warned the Jan Hus Trustees that it would be advisable to suspend visits for the time being.[5] The German government took the same line as the British; when the philosophers Jürgen Habermas and Ernst Tugendhat visited Hejdánek's seminar in March 1982, they were told by the German Cultural Attaché in Prague that the German government would take no responsibility for them should they be arrested. Fortunately, the Czechoslovak authorities did not seem to know of these directives, and, it seemed, had been shocked and embarrassed by their *faux pas*. From the time of Derrida's imprisonment there were no serious incidents directly connected with lectures by foreigners at the underground seminars. Scruffy men in leather jackets continued to trail the visiting lecturers, they were often searched on arrival or departure, and on rare occasions deported; but, as a rule, the seminars were not raided whilst a foreigner was present. It appeared to have registered with the authorities that a case such as Derrida's was not a deterrent to the philosophers, but rather the reverse. Hejdánek became so accustomed to the pattern of raids that he made sure his announcements about dates of forthcoming visits were loud and clear enough to be picked up by a potential microphone or an informer in the group (he is convinced that when the Dutch professor Theo de Boer was deported in 1983 it was the result of a misunderstanding over his announcement). However, amongst the British there was a growing feeling that the uncertainty and insecurity caused by the threat of police action often made the teaching process more symbolic than useful. Kathy Wilkes confirmed the Trustees' anxieties in a report to a meeting held in Oxford in October 1982: '[Hejdánek's seminar] has been all summer under incessant police surveillance; the police occasionally disrupted meetings, but more typically checked the identities of participants and interrogated them subsequently. Several visitors over the summer had visited unchecked, possibly because they had entered the building before the police arrived. Hejdánek remains optimistic, but is almost alone in this; it seems improbable that the students will continue to attend if the autumn session repeats the pattern of the summer. Visitors to this seminar were encouraged to go to Rezek's apartment first.'[6] There was increasing concern that Hejdánek's mixture of attendees — which included philosophers and theologians, university professors and young people up from the provinces hoping for adventure — was not conducive to serious study. Reports were filtering back to Britain that students were dissatisfied, that there was little continuity in the contributions of the different visitors — British, French and Dutch — and that some of the lectures given by the foreigners were unintelligible to those attending. In October 1983 Scruton reported that Hejdánek was 'rather hurt and disturbed that no Englishmen had been to his seminar for so long',[7] and would welcome proper teaching seminars spread over two days, which would include instruction on essay-writing (which the group had tried, but found difficult). The next visitors on behalf of the JHEF were Lars Bergström of Uppsala University (Undetermination and Realism) in January 1984 and Christopher Kirwan (Augustine on evil) in April, when Hejdánek again asked for 'a fresh infusion of English people';[8] a request he repeated in December, on the occasion of David Papineau's visit ('on the mind-body problem, John Searle's Reith lectures, computer-influenced cognitive science, Chinese room arguments, etc.'[9]). However, by the time Donald Davidson (described by Ralph Walker as 'the most distinguished visitor ever sent by the Jan Hus Foundation" arrived in June 1985 to give an introduction to 'The Theory of Meaning', it would appear from Davidson's report that Hejdánek had almost given up hope of seeing any more Anglo-American visitors.

The sparsity of British visitors to Hejdánek's seminar between 1981 and 1985 does not seem to have been due to a deliberate policy on the part of the Jan Hus Foundation; nothing relevant appears in the minutes of the meetings, and Hejdánek himself still feels that it was never explained. Catherine Audard's view is that Hejdánek's students were not interested in analytical philosophy, in contrast with the group later organised by Petr Rezek. Some of the reasons for the Trustees' hesitation about sending lecturers have been mentioned — the police surveillance, the heterogeneous nature of the group, the large number of French and Dutch visitors. Ralph Walker also notes that

British visitors found the timing of the seminar — Monday evening — difficult, and that there had been constant problems in setting up a line of communication to Hejdánek. It is also noticeable that in the reports of this time there are constant references to misunderstandings about what has been agreed; visitors arrive on dates, times, and at addresses other than those when and where they are expected. Very often these misunderstandings occurred when messages from an unidentified source contradicted those left by an earlier visitor. It is not impossible that, in addition to their more overt activities, the secret police were carrying out a programme of disinformation through persons unknown. This can only be conjecture.[10] The number of these misunderstandings did, however, incline the Foundation to support seminars not yet known to the secret police.

An increasing number of seminars had been taking place at the home of Petr Rezek, one of Patočka's former pupils. Rezek had graduated from the Charles University in psychology, philosophy and aesthetics at the beginning of the 1970s. His original employment had been as a psychologist, but in the later 1970s, although not a Charter signatory, he preferred to work as a caretaker or boilerman and enjoy the opportunities for free speech and study. He had already shown himself active in setting up a seminar for practising architects on architectural theory, to which Roger Scruton had spoken in April 1981 (on the relative consequences of horizontal and vertical emphasis), another on modern aesthetics and art criticism, and a third on the aesthetics of opera. (A discussion between Scruton and Rezek about Wagner had lasted into the early hours of the morning.) He maintained a correspondence with, amongst others, Charles Taylor in Canada, and had brought together a study group of his own generation which included some ex-university teachers (mainly phenomenologists) and some still in official institutions. The group considered itself to be a continuation of Patočka's seminar, and called itself the 'Prague Philosophical Circle'. It was for this group that the British were first able to hold a regularly taught, sustainable course.

The first course for Petr Rezek's group, on 'Analytical Philosophy', was discussed in January 1981 with Christopher Kirwan (who became a Trustee of the Foundation that year) and agreed with Roger Scruton during his June visit. 'I think this might be one of our most worthy ventures,' Scruton wrote in his report to the British Trustees. Analytical philosophy, the field of the English-speaking world, was virtually unknown in the studies of philosophers brought up in the Central European tradition and now living in the closed world of Marxist-Leninist philosophy; this made it all the more attractive to enquiring minds who felt cut off from what was going on in the wider world. Scruton's programme consisted of 20 topics, later narrowed to 16, ranging from 'definite descriptions' through Russell, Wittgenstein, Grice, Davidson and Ryle through to 'reasons and causes'. (In the event, two of the original topics had to be omitted, but additional talks were given on consciousness, analytical ethics and 'reference and substance'.) The syllabus was accompanied by a reading list of 60 books, all of which the Foundation had to obtain by donation or purchase and send in with its lecturers. The plan was that, at approximately monthly intervals, a lecturer should fly to Prague on a three-day tourist visa, giving seminars on two of the topics to the same group at two different venues (for reasons of security).

The first visiting lecturer on the Analytical Philosophy course, at the end of September 1981, was Ralph Walker from Magdalen College, who had not yet been directly involved in the Foundation's work. (Walker later took the main responsibility for planning and organising the courses for Rezek's students, and for liaison with Rezek, who could at times be a demanding colleague.) Although Walker's talks went ahead as planned, the visit did not go as smoothly as had been hoped. His visit coincided with that of another visitor, the banker Jonathan Ruffer (a Foundation Trustee from 1981). Ruffer's task was to build up contacts in Christian organisations; on this occasion he met Hejdánek and Markéta Němcová, but there had been confusion over the timing of his visit, and a planned meeting with Jakub Trojan did not take place. Possibly because of the confusion, his meeting with Walker was observed by the secret police and Walker was followed to a meeting with Rezek. In consequence the police apprehended and interrogated Rezek, who persuaded them that Walker was an opera-loving friend whom he had met in 1968. Walker and Ruffer, returning on the same flight to London, were searched at the airport. Walker's notes on 'definite descriptions' and 'proper names' were photocopied by the airport police, whilst Ruffer, in spite of a body search, sucessfully managed to conceal in a trouser pocket a VONS report of a recent trial. Trustees waited in anxiety for a post card or message to warn them not to continue, but the police appeared to overlook the matter. In mid-November, as previously arranged with Rezek, Dorothy Edgington of Birkbeck College in London arrived in Prague to speak on Russell's Logical Atomism and Wittgenstein's *Tractatus*. She reported that: 'Clearly, [the students] had done the required reading, and I was impressed by the standard of the discussions. Petr Rezek's enthusiasm and organizational ability, in running this and other groups, is quite remarkable. He was exceptionally kind to me throughout my stay.... It is hardly necessary to add that I came away feeling great admiration for those I had met — for their courage and persistence, and for the sheer hard work which they put into these activities; and with a more vivid awareness of the values for which they fight.'[11] Edgington's visit was followed by one from Scruton in December, but in January 1982 the disruption caused by Jacques Derrida's imprisonment and the subsequent advice from the Foreign Office led the Trustees to decide that they would temporarily suspend the course, along with others planned on History of Art, Political Thought, and Literary Criticism. Visits by the philosophers Christopher Taylor and Anthony O'Hear, planned for January and February, were postponed. Rezek, who knew about the Derrida crisis but not about the advice given by the Foreign Office, was frustrated and disappointed by the interruption in communication. The silence was broken at the beginning of March with a visit from Jon Elster of All Souls, Oxford. After discussion with Elster and consultation with his students, Rezek decided to resume the Analytical Philosopy lectures with Elster speaking on 'reasons and causes'. In spite of a failure of communication in April (the philosopher Anthony O'Hear, expecting to lecture for Rezek and Hejdánek, arrived a few days later than expected, and missed them both) the lectures continued at intervals of six to eight weeks. Numbers attending ranged from ten to as few as three, when the seminar had to be held at short notice. In summer 1982 Rezek wrote to 'Lulu' (one of Roger Scruton's pseudonyms): 'many thanks for all I have got this time. I am glad that we shall continue the anal[ytic] c[ourse]. I suggest to finish it till

December — from the second half are numbers 11 and 12 the most interesting [Ryle's concept of mind and Wittgenstein's private language argument], and you can add what is important or not too difficult to arrange. I think we could get on with other themes later, perhaps irregularly. Some people are studying very hard, others would to like acquire only basic information, therefore I suggest this compromise. For the persons serious interested would a rapid sequence dangerous, because they could lose continuity, the other the interest if the c. would be too long.'[12] Rezek was considering the two kinds of students, those who worked hard and had been disappointed by the interruptions, and those who did not do any personal study, but attributed a symbolic significance to the events and were grateful for the information provided. The course was successfully completed and a final report made in 1983.[13] One of the most talented of the circle, Karel Hubka (who died in London in 1986), wrote in November 1984: '...the contact with the visiting lecturers from this country [Britain] was of immense importance, since often the manifestation alone of the existence of societies cherishing values different from those of the country the members of the Circle have to live in has a healing effect upon the rifts in the collapsing self-confidence of such a group... Broadening of the primarily existential horizon of PPC's philosophical community by means of lectures and discussions of various other mainstreams of contemporary philosophy came just in time to fuel new interests and instigate new questions.'[14] Another of the students, Pavel Kouba, has explained that for a group which had for years been specialising in Patočka's phenomenology, the introduction of a completely new tradition came like air through an open window.

The success of the Analytical Philosophy course — at least as a pilot venture — and the willingness of the philosophers to lecture at the underground seminars is the more impressive when compared with problems which arose over the course in History of Art, originally one of Rezek's priorities. The pattern was to have been the same as that for the course in Analytical Philosophy — twenty topics ranging from the Renaissance to modernism, two to be covered by each of ten visitors. Rezek emphasised 'the need for continuity and predictability, and the danger that the participants might be dismayed when promised visits fail to materialize'.[15] But of a number of art historians approached by Roger Scruton, the only one to travel to Prague was Michael Baxandall from the Warburg Institute, who gave a seminar for Rezek's group in January 1983. Most of the remainder wrote with polite explanations as to why it was impossible for them to undertake such a journey, and suggesting alternative lecturers. Not so Anita Brookner, who in October 1981 wrote scathingly that she had yet to hear from any of her friends behind the Iron Curtain that lectures on Delacroix would solve any of their problems, adding that she thought the plan was quixotic and extremely ill-conceived.[16] Brookner's letter is remarkable in that it is the only reaction of this kind to be found in the Foundation's archive.

Rezek could at times be an emotional and impatient colleague, but for the Foundation his co-operation meant a vital expansion of their programme. His passionate devotion both to the text — he was regularly supplied with the latest publications, especially the Loeb editions in the original Greek — and to the students (some of the later recruits were students from the Charles University) whose interests and security he was careful to protect. When it was clear to him that the students were beginning to get tired of the long-drawn-out course in analytical philosophy, Rezek began to think about a course on Aristotle, originally planned to start in April 1982. In April he asked (through Michael Flynn, a linguist from the Rijks Universitet Groningen) for 'all the books for the course, and a plan, as soon as convenient, together with six copies of Aristotle's *Metaphysics* in Greek... also... the Clarendon Plato Series, mentioning specifically the Gallop *Phaedo*, the McDowell *Theaetetus*, and the Gosling *Philebus*.'[17] During Kathy Wilkes' April visit he asked for 'any books, anthologies, commentaries etc. which we regard as particularly good (e.g., the Barnes/Schofield/Sorabji collections, Nussbaum's edition of the *De Motu*, Kirwan's and Annas' Metaphysics commentaries; also, if we can afford it, Bonitz.'[18] Some of these were taken in June by Christopher Taylor of Corpus Christi, Oxford who brought back a new request for cassettes for recording seminars. About the same time, Rezek wrote to Scruton: 'The second compromise I suggest [see above] is to start the Arist[otle] c[ourse] in September as arranged with K[athy]. We have no experience (or little) with A.'s Greek, we need time to obtain the necessary training. But because of motivation it is clever to open the c. with first two classes, and then go on after an intermission of 8-10 weeks; this means to arrange two other classes (= 1 visitor) before Christmas. In the meantime we shall study as usually. From January to June could come four visitors in this c.'[19]

The Aristotle course opened in September 1982, with three talks (at different venues) from Kathy Wilkes. This was the occasion when the secret police had obtained an official invitation for Wilkes to attend the Eirene Conference, and she used the opportunity to explore the 'grey zone' of scholars, with one foot in the 'official world' and another in that of the underground seminars. These were people who were thought to be too politically unreliable to be entrusted with a teaching post, but who were allowed to undertake research within a limited field, and who gave papers at the conference. They included the German-speaking scholar Stanislav Sousedík, one of the most highly-regarded members of the Analytical Philosophy course; Karel Hubka, a close friend of Rezek's who worked in the Pedagogical Institute of the Academy of Sciences on an edition of Comenius; and Hubka's wife Eva Stehlíková who, like Sousedík, worked in the Cabinet for Greek, Roman and Latin Studies.

As planned, the Aristotle course continued with a visit from Richard Sorabji in December (Sorabji was one of the most popular and successful visitors to Rezek's seminar), followed by Christopher Taylor (Corpus Christi, Oxford) and Jacques Brunschvicg (of the French Association Jan Hus) in the first half of 1983. The course was followed in April 1984 by one on Kant, organised and inaugurated by Ralph Walker. Walker planned altogether 17 topics, which began with sessions on Descartes, Leibniz and Hume, continued with 'Kant's Problem', and passed through 'Geometry, Spacial Order', 'Causality' and other topics to conclude in June 1986 (11 visitors later) with 'The First Antimony' and 'The Ontological Argument'. By then a Plato course was being planned; however, Rezek wrote (in German) to Ralph Walker about that and other matters:

'(2) I have already mentioned that the Plato translation is running a few months late and we can't begin without a text. I guess that it will be ready in Spring 87. But why have virtually no materials arrived so far? We could at least have read them! (I have already twice asked for the texts under the first headings. No result.) (3) I am a bit fed up with the groups, and disappointed too, and have become very doubtful about them. Should I perhaps once again try something else? Also the police are now more interested in what I am doing. So I should like to put off the 'two Critiques'.... (5) I have now ordered R. Sorabji's book three times... Last time I wrote to R. about the book. No reply. As I have now been trying to get it for two years, it is finally going to be sold out, isn't it?... (6) It seems that the Foundation prefers to send visitors rather than to carry on with routine work. It would e.g. be better to have the texts for Plato than a speaker who brings no written papers with him and who does not even send any afterwards. The money could be better used for other purposes (though perhaps with more effort). (5 [*sic*]) The money is not what matters. But I myself should like to know more about how it is to go with me in future. This time no word about that. I told you that I assume there must be other speakers in the series. But could I be informed, so that I can plan my work?.... (7 [*sic*]) I have set out one or two reproaches, because the conditions under which I work are very tense — I ask: What's it all for? Of course I know that without you and other friends we here should perhaps have already put an end to it earlier.

So don't be cross with me for having my doubts.'[20]

The Plato course went ahead in January 1988, organised by Christopher Kirwan. In the practical notes prepared for visiting lecturers he gave an outline of the way the group operated at that time: 'If possible write out your lectures in full and present a copy to Petr on your arrival. He will con them overnight... preparing himself to interpret. Eventually copies will be duplicated for use by the students; if you can take more than two copies yourself, some of the students will be able to follow your text as you read. Read, and Petr will translate... The audience, mostly young will have spent preliminary sessions under Petr's direc-

tion studying the relevant text of Plato and the secondary literature on my sheet... I think some of them know no Greek; they
rely mainly on an out-of-date Czech version and a better Slovak
one... Questions will be mixed, some foolish, some very acute.'[21]
Kirwan observed at the inaugurating seminar that: 'There was
evidence that Rezek had prepared the audience by serious study
of the text and secondary literature. So, a good start.'[22] The Plato
seminars lasted for a year, with visits from Lesley Brown
(Somerville, Oxford), Lindsay Judson (Christ Church, Oxford),
Christopher Taylor (Corpus Christi, Oxford), J.E. Tiles (Reading
University) and Ralph Walker. (Tiles arrived during the demonstrations of 28th October 1988, when, on the occasion of the
revival of their national day, Czechs came out on the streets in
anticipation of the 1989 demonstrations. He observed that 'it
appears not to have been the wrong weekend in Prague to try to
read Plato's epistemology and metaphysics as motivated by his
political concerns'.[23]) From start to finish, this Plato course ran
as had been envisaged from the first years of the Foundation.
There were no interruptions, and no major misunderstandings
Each speaker gave two seminars, the time of day varying, since
this was the weekend and the students had made a commitment
to the seminars — by this time, some of those attending were
also regular students at the Charles University. As had been the
case with the Kant course, all of the lecturers reported that they
were satisfied with (and in some cases highly impressed by) the
quality of the students, several of whom became teachers of
philosophy at the Charles University in the 1990s.[24]

Walker, during his visit in January 1989, discussed future
plans with Rezek. He reported that: '(Rezek) has been giving
public lectures on music and art, and they have been quite successful... His hope and plan is that he should run a series of public lectures on Aristotle's *Ethics,* in the small hall he has been
able to get for the lectures he has already been giving. He thinks
it would be best to start these in October, and has asked me to
compile a suitable bibliography and list of topics, much as
Christopher did for Plato. The public will not be able to do much
reading, of course — for them a short hand-out of translated
Aristotelian text might be prepared for each lecture (and I have
promised to give thought to choosing suitable extracts) — but he
hopes that a small group will be able to do more reading and

have a further discussion session after each meeting. If possible he would like two of us (or perhaps three) to go out to give lectures in the series, but for the most part he intends to give the talks himself.'[25]

The philosopher Jiří Fiala remembers that later in the year Rezek's lectures were banned for 'a stupid reason' (a false alarm over the mistaken identity of another lecturer had drawn the authorities' attention to Rezek's unwelcome presence). In June or July Rezek wrote to Walker: '...a problem has arisen because the hall (where I am lecturing on Husserl at present — I even have to give the lectures twice in succession; programme enclosed) does not want to put on any lectures in the autumn, for reasons which are not relevant. Either I shall talk them into allowing it, before the vacation comes, or else I shall try to find another institution.'[26]   In October 1989, however, a courier brought the message: '(Rezek's) Aristotle Course is not running as it was not possible to arrange it officially. He will try again possibly for the spring but more probably for next autumn and will write at least two months in advance.'[27]

Another important figure in Prague for the Jan Hus Foundation, from the early days of Tomin's and Palouš's seminars, was Pavel Bratinka (known under his code-name of 'Virgil').[28] In 1983 Scruton described Bratinka as: 'An energetic man, a Catholic, and an anti-communist, who has an enormous store of rage. He is also undeniably interesting, and with a sincere conception of what he has to do.'[29] Although a graduate in solid state physics, Bratinka's chief interest was political science and economics; from the mid-1960s he had been a regular visitor to the library at the American Embassy ('the only real library in Prague'[30]) and by 1979 was already finishing his translation of Friedrich von Hayek's *Road to Serfdom*. He was involved in many of the activities of the 'unofficial culture' (samizdat, and the treasury of Charter 77), and attached enormous importance to the underground seminars. 'They created a network of people of similar outlooks... a welcome respite from the ubiquitous presence of lies and nonsense elsewhere.'[31] He believed that, important as they were for intellectual development, the main significance of the seminars was in enabling people to come together and to create a political society. The help from outside played a major role in this; not only the constant inflow of teachers and literature, but also the encouragement and protection. The first time he attended a lecture by a foreigner was in June 1979, when E.P. Thompson lectured at the Paloušes' seminar. Later he met many of the Foundation's visitors, who were fascinated by their conversations with him during long walks through Prague. Robert Grant remembers that, crossing the Charles Bridge in 1986, Bratinka told him: 'The thing [Communism] can't last another ten years'. Grant found this difficult to believe. In January 1989 Ralph Walker reported that: '[Bratinka] has a bet with the First Secretary of the British Embassy that by the end of 1989 the government in Czechoslovakia will not be Communist. He accepts that this may be a bit optimistic.'[32]

Although Bratinka attended a number of seminars (including, as a strong Catholic, 'bible hours') he had never organised a seminar of his own. However, in conversation with Roger Scruton in January 1983, he showed interest in a course introducing the principal concepts of Western conservative thought, starting with Eric Voegelin.[33] The first visitor on this course was the sociologist from Middlesex Polytechnic, David Levy, who had previously visited Hejdánek's seminar (on a date not recorded, probably January 1982). (He remembers on that occasion being 'shuffled through back streets' to shake off the secret police, and memorising a complicated list of messages and deliveries.) In March 1983 Levy gave two lectures in Bratinka's flat to a group of five or six people, on Voegelin and on the relationship between politics and philosophical anthropology: 'It is close to their own tradition of thought but, in its particular, little known to them.'[34] However, after this good start the second lecturer, Sally Shreir, although meeting many of the Prague community, found that there had again been miscommunication about the seminar. On arriving at Alena Hromádková's flat she found that most of the evening was devoted to guitar-playing and singing: 'Pithart did not arrive until about 8.30 and Bratinka not until after 9.00.... Bratinka was evidently annoyed when he arrived, saying "I see there has been no philosophy tonight, only drinking and singing."... In the couple of minutes that I had to speak to him, [he] asked for volumes 1, 4 and 5 of Voegelin's *Order and History.*'[35]

The problem appears to have been resolved in time for the

visit by Ronald Beiner of the University of Southampton, who gave three working sessions, the second in Bratinka's flat (attended by eleven, including Ivan Havel) and the first and third at the home of Rudolf Kučera. These were devoted to the work of Hannah Arendt — the *Theory of Political Judgment* and the *Concept of Freedom*: 'The discussions were all extremely lively, and I was very impressed by how knowledgeable they were about the work of Hannah Arendt. The questions they raised were both intellectually very serious and deeply informed by their day-to-day political experience. They seemed to get much out of the exchange, and I know that I profited a great deal from it.'[36]

After the intensity of three visits in two months, the minutes of the Foundation noted that there was 'now a lull in the Conservative Political Thought course, and that it was unclear whether, and when, future visitors were needed.'[37] The identity of this group seems to shift (both Bratinka and Hromádková deny ever having been responsible for a seminar group) and it appears to have been incorporated into — or overlapped with — what Scruton described as 'Urbinus's group of neo-conservatives'.[38] 'Urbinus' was one of the code-names for Rudolf Kučera, who also wrote under the pseudonym 'Vrána' (Crow). Kučera was (and is) a political scientist[39] who was at that time engaged in back-breaking work as a labourer on a building site. This seminar, like many others, had come into existence as a gathering of teachers who had been thrown out of the universities in the 1970s, together with a few who were still able to teach. Unlike the orientation towards pure philosophy of Hejdánek's seminar, they concentrated on history and political science. Their first foreign visitor had been Steven Lukes, who continued to visit the seminar; after Lukes there came both the English and the French. Kučera remembers the greatest practical help — especially with the samizdat journal *Střední Evropa* — came from the circle around Olivier Mongin and the journal *Esprit*; as well as literature and expert opinion, they used to bring pens, knives, Lettraset, and gadgets for binding. However, the closest in political thinking was Roger Scruton. At this time the 'right/left' dichotomy meant little to them; the more important distinction was totalitarianism/democracy. According to Karel Palek, they were interested in 'conservatism' as a theme, as something with a concrete meaning, not as a right-wing political movement. Palek, who had joined Kučera's seminar in 1974, was one of the most important members of the group. Scruton remembers that in 1983 he was taken by Kučera to meet Palek — 'flamboyantly dressed in silk neckerchief and high-buttoned waistcoat, speaking impeccable French and supporting a Habsburg beard'[40] — under his code name 'Fidelius' (he was also known as 'Pius') and was greeted with the question: 'Are you Elizabeth?'. ('Elizabeth' was one of Scruton's code names.) Scruton subsequently published work by both Kučera and Palek in *The Salisbury Review*.[41]

According to the JHEF archive, Timothy Garton Ash spoke to the group in January 1984, although his subject has not been recorded; in February 1984 Robert Grant of Glasgow University made his first visit to Prague. The day after Grant's arrival Kučera was hospitalised, and Grant's only lecture was given to a small group in Bratinka's home. He spoke, without a text, on 'the relations between state and civil society, and what were the conditions of legitimacy'. 'My audience were sharp and critical. One of them, Václav Benda, had come out at considerable risk, since he is under constant surveillance....[42] I came in for a lot of flak. Clearly my audience were in fundamental sympathy with ideas that I was floating off almost for fun, or to see where they would lead. But they wanted a lot greater theoretical coherence than I had provided. Benda (or Mr. Benda, as they all called him) went straight to the main weakness. Take the Russians, he said; suppose the Soviet state actually is fully existentially representative. Suppose the Russian people are moral degenerates, and the Soviet state reflects them as they are, and rules over them with the nearest thing to full consent that can be imagined. Then the Soviet state must be legitimate in my terms. Have we any independent criterion by which to judge them?'[43]

In April 1984 Scruton met several members of the group, including (for the first time) Václav Benda, but does not seem to have given a seminar for them (although he gave two for Petr Rezek's Kant course). In July Professor Frank Bealey[44] gave a talk on the British Labour Party, after which there appears to have been a long interval until the seminar programmed to coincide with the samizdat publication of the Czech translation Scruton's *Meaning of Conservatism* in June 1985.[45] Although this was planned with immense care,[46] the Communist authorities were so concerned to prevent the seminar taking place that Scruton was detained whilst still in Brno and expelled from Czechoslovakia.

Of the seminars with which the Jan Hus Foundation was involved, this was the one in which the publication of samizdat was most closely integrated with the running of the seminar; so much so that by the end of the 1980s it was known to visitors as the 'Central Europe' seminar, after Rudolf Kučera's samizdat journal *Střední Evropa*. Kučera first had the idea for the journal in 1983, and discussed it with Roger Scruton: 'In brief, the idea is this: to gather together materials on the history and cultural-political identity of Central Europe, to found a journal that will publish samizdat contributions on this theme, and to initiate discussions and regular seminars among themselves.'[47] The first issue of the journal (at this stage known just as *Evropa*) was shown to Jessica Douglas-Home on her first solo visit to Prague in October 1984. At the end of the year a copy reached the Foundation through the underground channels and Scruton reported to Trustees: 'An excellent production, more scholarly than I thought it would be, with a decided tone of voice, and clearly attempting to say something different from the run of opposition literature.'[48] After summarising the contents he concluded: 'All the above seem to hang very well together, and show the fruits of the work on the history project, which has clearly set off a chain-reaction on the theme of recuperating history, and seeking in history for the true basis of self-understanding.'[49]

In September 1983 the Foundation had suggested a starting-grant of £50 for the journal, conditional on Scruton's discussion with Kučera: 'RVS should make it clear that the JHEF could not give long-term support to journals.'[50] This policy of not providing on-going financial support for journals was maintained by the Foundation throughout the 1980s. *Střední Evropa*, however, was supported by means of one-off grants for book purchases, translations, materials and equipment, and by a stipend for Kučera — with a view to all his work, including the seminars — which lasted from 1983 to 1989. The Foundation also provided contacts and advice: 'High level contributions from Western Europe to their journal would be very welcome;

but what would be most welcome of all would be consultation on the spot in Prague with an expert with special interest in the subject and prepared for an on-going collaboration with them. They would also like to find, if possible, an Austrian historian interested in the possibility of a similar collaboration — ideally someone with a special interest in the Jewish communities of their part of the world. They asked us to consult Ernest Gellner about this, and also to stress how much they would like to see him again... We were able to discuss all this with E.G. in Vienna immediately after our visit to Prague, and he has promised to do everything he can.'[51] From 1985 to 1989 foreign visitors to the journal and the seminar included Robert Grant (for a second time), John Rose, Steven Lukes, David Selbourne, Norman Podhoretz, Nora Beloff, Stephen Beller, David Levy and Mark Almond. In the course of the 1980s the *Střední Evropa* publishing project expanded from publication of the journal to the publication of translations and original work. By 1989 seven works had been published in samizdat, including one by Czeslaw Miłosz and two by Isaac Bashevis Singer, and another six were in preparation.[52] Another project, submitted by Vilém Prečan and supported by the Canadian Jan Hus Fund, was a history of samizdat by Petruška Šustrová.

Šustrová was one of Kučera's editorial board, which also included one of the former Technical University students, Luděk Bednář. Kučera's first colleague in launching the journal was his fellow-labourer from the building site, Jan Vít; a grant was provided by the Jan Hus Trustee, Tom Stoppard, for Vít to work on his first novel (in 1993 Vít became programme director for the private television station Nova). Translations from English were made by Bratinka and Bednář and from French by Karel Palek, who was as important to the samizdat as he was to the seminar. Palek was attracted by the 'working nature' of the seminar, and he felt the translations of the lectures to be more satisfying and concrete tasks than the abstract discussion of other seminars. The production of samizdat involved not only editorial but also organisational work. Palek remembers that he originally became involved in this through the VONS case studies, which he collected from Václav Benda and had re-typed and bound. He recalls that everyone working in samizdat had their own secret circle of typists, usually women with a typewriter at home who were otherwise unconnected with the 'unofficial culture'. After the typists had delivered the piles of papers, carried across Prague in shopping bags, there came the collation, done behind locked doors; some editors preferred a 'hierarchical' set of samizdat, one volume composed only of top copies, down to the last, composed of the tenth, twelfth or even fifteenth carbon copy. Palek preferred a more 'democratic' system, sharing the good and bad pages out equally between the volumes.

Scruton learnt of the full extent of Palek's samizdat operation in June 1983; amongst other works, it included 'a new autonomous press called Anamnesis dedicated, as its title suggests, to fighting against the loss of historical memory. For the coming year he plans, first, a series of Czech political thought, 1890-1978... Secondly, collections of documents concerning Czech political and cultural history during the first part of the century... Thirdly a series of political memoires...'.[53] He noted that 'The approximate price for each book must be (if it is to cover the cost of production): 60 crowns per hundred pages, plus 20 for binding.'[54] In October he reported: 'In brief: he has initiated the series 'Anamnesis', has continued to publish other books in samizdat, and is co-editor, and effective publisher, of *Kritický sborník*.[55] I saw copies of his samizdat publications, which are beautifully produced, and clearly very carefully selected and edited. I also saw pages, as yet unbound, of the first two Anamnesis volumes, and was able to verify that the translation of Hayek's *Road to Serfdom* is nearing completion. *KS* I saw in its entirety, and apparently copies have been sent out to Vašíček[56] in Bochum, whom I expect to see soon. So far two and three quarter years of quarterly publication, regular, well produced, about 100 pages each time, and of high intellectual quality. A very impressive production, which contains articles on all aspects of Czech culture, together with history, memoirs, bibliographies raisonnées of unobtainable authors, and so on. Also contains a review of everything published in samizdat. Highly sensitive, and no information about this to be transmitted outside the circle of our trust.... More tippex fluid required.'[57] By 1983, however Trustees were beginning to feel that the anticipated productivity was not being achieved; in 1984 Pius (Palek) replied with an account of his editorial activities, concluding:

'As for my own writings, the balance, up to (to)day, is quite deplorable... The principal reason of that 'creative' deficiency is a serious restriction of my global work capacity owing to some practical commitments I must assume in order to find a solution of certain private /familial/ problems /whose nature I have repeatedly explained in some occasions/... my immediate aim is producing a series of esays in language critique, oscillating more or less round the themes of nationhood, politics and experience.'[58] Palek's work in samizdat continued to be supported by the British to the end of 1985, when, after a visit to Prague by Alan Montefiore and Catherine Audard, it was agreed that 'Pius might be someone whom the [French] AJH would find it natural to take under their financial wing'.[59] In 1986 the Association Jan Hus arranged for the translation of Palek's *Jazyk a moc* and its publication by Grasset as *L'Esprit post-totalitaire*.

Support for samizdat featured consistently in the programme of the Foundation, which recognised the close link between samizdat and the seminars. The first grant specifically for samizdat was agreed in May 1982, for Petr Pithart and a team of historians to work on a Czech history. In July 1984 Paul Flather reported that this, 'the longest continuous project in Prague dating back to 1977, [was] progressing well. He says many new facts will be revealed, and new interpretations. It has reached the first Republic...'[60] In the first half of the 1980s grants or stipends were awarded to Eva Kantůrková; to Jana Fraňková for a translation of Hannah Arendt; to an 'anonymous Nietzsche scholar', who in spring 1988 was identified as Pavel Kouba, one of the students in Petr Rezek's seminar; to two 'anonymous critics' later identified as Stanislav Sousedík and Jan Lopatka; and to a number of smaller projects. A stipend was also paid, from early 1985 to the end of 1989, to František Šamalík, whom Petr Pithart described as 'a politico-legal historian of 18th-century Czechoslovakia, Marxist but not orthodox.'[61] Pithart continued: 'What he is doing is particularly worthwhile, because it represents something new in Czech historiography: he seeks not only to record and assess past events, but also to provide an account of all the ways in which a given event has been viewed from the time of its occurrence to the present.'[62]

In January 1983 Scruton returned from Prague with 'an embarassing request, but [Pithart] insisted that I put it forward and say that it comes from their most sincere and autonomous choice: that they be given a stipend to enable them to translate and publish in samizdat *The Meaning of Conservatism*, with a preface by me, and a postscript appending various key terms, defined according to my dictionary.[63] He insists that this is for them a most important project, and that the idea of an anti-liberal conservatism which explores the foundations of law and the rule of law is... etc.'[64] The following month the Trustees agreed an initial £250 towards the project. In March David Levy reported that: 'Cassandra's [Pithart's] translation of R.S. is going ahead. It will take two or two and a half years. Money for it is urgent since not only has C. given up other work to devote himself to it but he is having to consult legal experts etc. regarding particular terms.'[65] (Just over two years later it was the samizdat publication of *Smysl konservatismu* which led to Scruton's expulsion from Czechoslovakia.) After completing this project, Pithart turned his attention to the publication of Scruton's *Dictionary of Political Thought*. Funding for the project was initially refused by both the British and Canadian Trusts (Gordon Skilling believed that it would be adequate and cost-effective to send in more copies of the English text.) In April 1986, in the peaceful and police-free surroundings of the St. Agnes Convent, Pithart expressed his frustration to Barbara Day: '...he accepts that JHEF feel they cannot fund the translation, but points out that regardless who wrote it, it seems to be the only thing of its kind. None of the visitors he has asked have been able to suggest an alternative. He is grateful for private gifts, and for efforts to raise the money. This is his estimate of costs... over 2 years... £1,500-1,700, to include translation, consultation, revision and editing... In fact, it is a major undertaking, comparable to work done during the 19th-century National Revival; in that for many of the concepts expressed there is no vocabulary in Czech.'[66] The funding was raised, and in February 1987 Jessica Douglas-Home reported that the work was half-finished: 'At the moment it is being read by five specialists, i.e. psychologists, theologians, political scientists, economic scientists, who sometimes have to write more to explain certain terms where there is no Czech equivalent.'[67]

One of the Foundation's important colleagues in the field of samizdat was the historian Vilém Prečan, living in exile in West

Germany.[68] In 1986 a grant from the National Endowment for Democracy enabled him to establish the Czechoslovak Documentation Centre for the Promotion of Independent Literature, which from 1986 was housed in a castle in Scheinfeld belonging to Karel Schwarzenberg. In 1985 Roger Scruton visited Prečan to discuss questions of security and publicity, as well as the transmission of books, videos, equipment and messages to Czechoslovakia. The following spring Prečan returned the visit, with two particular issues on his mind: the Masaryk Conference to be held by the University of London that autumn, and the publication of an anniversary volume to mark ten years of Charter 77.

By early 1985 the Foundation had provided its first large piece of equipment for the samizdat press in Prague, a memory typewriter, in the safe-keeping of Pavel Bratinka. In May 1985 Ralph Walker reported that this would be used for the Kampakademie's new project, PARAF ('Parallel Philosophy'), and that it would be possible to produce 50 samizdat copies instead of the usual twelve.[69] Another major project, pursued in cooperation with the Kampakademie group, was the publication in Britain of originally samizdat works and their re-import in large(ish) quantities to Czechoslovakia. The first of these, Martin Heidegger's *End of Philosophy and the Task of Thinking* (translated into Czech as *Konec filosofie a úkol myšlení*) was printed in Britain in 1985. There was, however, a problem with transport as most British visitors travelled by air and had to be prepared for a search of their luggage at the airport; this was eventually solved with the help of two of the Foundation's important international contacts, Wolfgang Stock in Germany and Henri Veldhuis in the Netherlands. The second publication, *Voegelin & Patočka*, was a transcript of discussions held at the Kampakademie and edited by Radim Palouš under the pseudonym 'T.R. Korder' (a whimsical reference to the tape recorder on which they had recorded the seminars).

Both these editions came out under the joint imprint of Rozmluvy (Alexander Tomsky's emigré publishing house) and the Athenaeum Press, a publishing house established by the Foundation for this purpose and named after Roger Scruton's London club. Tomsky, however, as a good Catholic refused to be associated with the third publication, which was the translation by Pavel Kouba of Friedrich Nietzsche's *Untimely Reflections* (Nečasové úvahy). Once the practical problems of transport had been overcome, this project promised to be one of the Foundation's most valuable activities. It was proposed that the fourth volume in the Athenaeum series should be Pavel Bratinka's translation of Friedrich von Hayek's *Law, Legislation and Liberty*.

The Foundation's work with the underground seminars was inextricably enmeshed with its granting of stipends and its support of samizdat. As well as the major projects there were numerous associated projects radiating from the centre. Some of these concerned the Christian network, as for example the Foundation's association with the Harvest Trust, run by Matthew Hutton, who was in contact with Jakub Trojan, Miloš Rejchrt and the priest Pavel Smetana. Independently of the Harvest Trust, the Foundation co-funded (with the Scottish sisters Margaret Conway and Mary Clark) stipends for the priests Václav Malý and Radomír Malý. Under the fictional names of The Gower History Society and The Luther Trust (Barclays Bank was happy to cooperate) the Foundation provided official stipends for (respectively) the artist Ivan Jirous (known as Magor) and the translator of Martin Luther, Jan Litomiský, to enable them to continue with their work without facing charges of parasitism. In January 1989 the Foundation approved a grant for a project on human rights in Czechoslovakia submitted by Petr Uhl. In July 1989 an application was submitted by Jan Urban and Jiří Dienstbier for stipends for Rudolf Zeman and Alexandr Vondra;[70] this was agreed in October 1989, at the time that both of them were held in prison on charges relating to their publication of the samizdat jounal *Lidové noviny*. In another few weeks *Lidové noviny* was to be launched as one of the leading newspapers of democratic Czechoslovakia.

The North Americans

The Oxford philosophers knew that the potential for fund-raising in Britain was limited, and their thoughts soon turned to America. They were aware that American tax law made it difficult for donations to be made to charities outside the United States, and had been advised that the solution would be to register a sister-organisation in the States. They began to investigate this possibility at the same time as plans were being made to register the Jan Hus Educational Foundation under Charity Law in Great Britain.

An opportunity was provided by the presence in Oxford of Jessica Strauss Pittman, a graduate student from Baltimore, Maryland. Strauss Pittman, a political scientist with ambitions to become a senator, was related by marriage to a Czech family living in the 'grey area' of the 'unofficial culture'. It was through visiting a cousin married to a Baptist minister in Prague that Strauss Pittman and her husband had learned the 'rules' of how to survive life under totalitarianism. In the spring of 1979 she heard about the Oxford philosophers' contacts with Prague from her tutor Charles Taylor, and was amused and alarmed by what she felt to be their ignorance of conditions in Czechoslovakia. Very soon she was invited to join meetings with Kathy Wilkes and Bill Newton-Smith and began to advise on how to deal with the suspicions of police and immigration officials. Her practical suggestions later became standard practice for the Foundation — for example, she drew their attention to the fact that no tourist could explain away the presence in his luggage of ten identical copies of a work by Aristotle. It was safer for each traveller to take one copy each of a number of desired titles. In this way, multiple copies for the seminars could be accumulated gradually. Through the Oxford philosophers, Strauss Pittman made contact with Jan Kavan; she was quickly incorporated into his plans and network of contacts, and in summer 1980 visited Czechoslovakia as his courier.

Whilst on vacation in the States over New Year 1980, Strauss Pittman made the first steps towards gaining support for the new Jan Hus organisation. Through Jan Kavan she made contact with the translator and musician Paul Wilson. Wilson holds a unique position amongst English-speaking translators of Czech. He arrived in Czechoslovakia in the mid-1960s, in time to experience the euphoria of the Prague Spring and the despair of August 1968. Marrying a Czech wife, he assimilated into the local culture and even became a performer with the Plastic People of the Universe. After their trial in 1976 he was deported, and settled in Toronto, becoming the leading translator of work by Václav Havel, Bohumil Hrabal and Josef Škvorecký.[1] Wilson was also spending New Year 1980 in New York, and accompanied Strauss Pittman on a fund-raising visit to Jane Fonda's representatives. He remembers that he and Strauss Pittman were questioned about whether the money raised was to be used for 'right-wing purposes'. (In a letter written the following month Wilson described one of their interrogators as the 'Stalinist lady'.[2]) Nothing was raised from that source, but on the same visit Wilson 'got a line on some charitable foundations that might be eventually approached for help as soon as the Jan Huss Educational Trust or whatever it's to be called is "incorporated"'.[3]

In autumn 1980 Strauss Pittman returned to Baltimore with the mission to start what was eventually to be named the Jan Hus Educational and Cultural Fund. By late 1981 a 'small working group' of Directors had been put together.[4] It included Paul Wilson and fellow Canadians Charles Taylor and H. Gordon Skilling. (Skilling, a professor at Toronto University, is the leading western scholar on Czechoslovakia under totalitarianism. He lived in Prague as a student before the war and married his wife Sally in the Old Town Hall in 1937.[5] In the 1970s Skilling's historical research had drawn him close to the Chartists, about whom he wrote in Charter 77 and the Human Rights Movement in Czechoslovakia; in 1978 he had been required to leave the country, but returned in 1984.) On the American side were the sociologists David Stark[6] and Peter Steinfels[7] and the businessman Jack Moskowitz, whose primary interest was Poland. Strauss Pittman, on whom fell the burden of the work, was successful in obtaining pro bono legal assistance in incorporating the Fund under State of Maryland law. Her concern for the safety of her relations in Czechoslovakia led her to use the pseudonym Debra Black in all official communications: 'It sounds like extreme paranoia, but we have all experienced enough of the unpleasant effects of "connections" to understand my relatives' feelings on the subject.'[8]

The first meeting took place in a Park Avenue apartment in New York, lasting from 11.00 a.m. to 4.30 p.m. on 11th December 1981. (In Czechoslovakia at this time, regular visits were being made by the British, French and Dutch to Hejdánek's seminars; some of the dissidents imprisoned after the Kavan van incident in April had just been released; contact had been made with Jiří Müller in Brno; and in less than three weeks Jacques Derrida would be arrested at Prague airport.) As in the case of meetings of the British Foundation, a large part of the discussion was devoted to methods of fund raising. The Americans were optimistic, but it was recorded (by Strauss Pittman) that: 'No specific decisions were made concerning who would do which of these and when.'[9] Although the general aims and principles of the British and American foundations were similar, there was a major difference in that the 'underground university' was not the main focus of the Americans' attention. The addition of 'Cultural' to the title 'Jan Hus Educational Foundation' represented a more general interest in the activities of the 'unofficial culture'. Their brief was from the start much broader: Paul Wilson remembers that he saw their role as that of an 'Arts Council'; whilst Jessica Strauss Pittman was interested in focusing on small, targeted donations in the cultural sphere (from equipment for the Plastic People of the Universe to oil paints for a struggling artist). In a draft document prepared around this date, the Americans' 'Statement of Purpose' covered financial support for: 'Any individual or group who requires funds in order to pursue cultural and/or educational activities on a not-for-profit basis...'[10] A partial listing under *Eligibility for Receipt of Funds* included:

- professors/teachers in all fields

- students in all fields
- theologians/clergy of all religious denominations
- artists
- musicians
- writers
- uncertified actors, directors, performers of other sorts
- worker groups pursuing cultural/educational activities.[11]

Although under 'Distribution [of resources]' the Americans included 'the costs of visits by academics/artists invited by the Czechoslovak participants for specified purposes and occasions'[12], the expenses involved in travelling to Europe were too great for them to be involved in any regular seminar programme. Visits were arranged ad hoc, and usually incorporated into the British programme. American support focused on grants, usually one-off donations to a member of the dissident community for a specific project or urgent need. It was not to be expected that those inside Czechoslovakia who knew about the 'Hus Foundation' would always be able to distinguish between the different policies of the independent British and American organisations, and confusion sometimes arose, as in the case of a grant to the Plastic People described below. But in their broad principles the two organisations were in agreement; above all, in that both they and their Czech and Slovak colleagues were acting legally in the context of Czechoslovak law, and that, in suppressing independent intellectual and cultural activities, it was the Czechoslovak state itself which was in breach of the International Covenants it had signed in Helsinki in 1975.

Nevertheless, it was evident that the American Fund did not intend simply to be a fund raising body for the British. In September 1981 Kathy Wilkes wrote to Charles Taylor to suggest that since the British were likely to receive many more requests than the Americans, some of these could be passed on: 'This would obviate the necessity for people [in Czechoslovakia] to commit to paper and the post facts about themselves they'd rather the STB didn't know.'[13] She added: 'I can only say that in Prague the people I met weren't seeming to know quite how best to apply to you, much as they would have liked to.'[14]

Over the following months Debra Black (Jessica Strauss Pittman) worked to satisfy Inland Revenue Service requirements to qualify as a public charity, and to establish a network of patrons and friends of the Fund. Responsibilities were allocated to individual directors ('Mail campaign to human rights groups — Peter Steinfels... Overseeing the events [talks, benefits] held in various cities to raise funds — Jack Moskowitz',[15] etc.). Charles Taylor agreed to act as President and Treasurer and David Stark as Secretary. $10,000 was raised in the course of the year, $1,000 of which was sent to Prague via the British Foundation for the support of Petr Pithart's team working on a three-volume Czech history.[16] The rest remained to be distributed at the meeting held in Peter Steinfels' West End Avenue apartment on 3rd December 1982.

Amongst those present at this meeting was the Czech lawyer Vratislav Pechota, who had left Czechoslovakia after acting as adviser to the Charter 77 signatories, and was now lecturing at the Law School of Columbia University. Pechota, who was planning to establish an American branch of František Janouch's Charter 77 Foundation, had been working with Black on a proposal to merge it with the American Jan Hus Educational and Cultural Fund. Bill Newton-Smith, nominated by the British as their liaison with the North Americans, thought such a plan to be 'highly undesirable'.[17] Although he was unable to be present at the meeting, his discussions with Taylor, Skilling and Wilson led to the rejection of the proposal. Their chief reservation was that whereas the support given by Charter 77 Foundation was directly co-ordinated with the activities of the Charter activists, the American Jan Hus Fund, like the British, was committed to seeking out unaffiliated groups and individuals whose work the Fund considered, independently, to be worthy of support. The directors agreed instead that Charter 77 Foundation should be registered in its own name; Dr. Pechota and Jeri Laber of Helsinki Watch would represent the Foundation on the JHF board, whilst Debra Black and David Stark would represent the Jan Hus Fund on the Charter board. (Gordon Skilling was to sit on both boards independently.) 'The Hus Fund would continue to be the organization which raises funds for the purpose of supporting scholarly, literary, artistic and scientific work of individuals who have been prohibited from doing so freely in Czechoslovakia... The Charter 77 Fund will raise funds and adminster stipends to support the signators of Charter 77 as such. Each organization is pledged to cooperate with the other; and each recognizes the distinct mission of the other both in the nature of support activities and in the area of fundraising.'[18]

In making awards, the directors were more specific in defining their criteria. One important criterion was 'variety' in the fields of academic and cultural activity. They also hoped to spread the grants geographically, to find a balance between team and individual projects, and to encourage applications from young people. Fourteen applications were considered at the December 1982 meeting; most of which had been forwarded from the British foundation, although in the course of time the North American funds considered applications submitted by Jan Kavan, Vilém Prečan, Jaroslav Kořán (who later played an important role in the JHEF's literature programme, and at that time was travelling in the USA), the independently minded American diplomat Alice Le Maistre and contacts of Paul Wilson and Gordon Skilling. The award for Pithart's history project had already been dealt with; eight more applicants received $1,000 (one of them contingent on the British not having already made an award). The Plastic People were granted $300 for a new amplifier, and a young novelist $100 to produce the first chapter of a new novel. Three applications were deferred.

Strauss Pittman was determined to keep the American Fund as far as possible independent of the British, but there were practical problems connected with both the obtaining of information and the transmission of grants. Newton-Smith, returning from America, reported to the British trust: 'It is clear that Jessica would prefer to make grants directly to people in Czechoslovakia rather than via our organisation. However I am not convinced that they have either the sources in Czechoslovakia to obtain the requisite information, or the means to get the money to people in Czechoslovakia. The best prospects of influencing the Trustees in the right direction is to keep Wilson and Skilling fully in the picture. I am sure that they are impressed by the intensity of our operation and our degree of contact and I am sure they will do their best to steer the American Trust in the right direction.'[19] Some weeks after the meeting Strauss Pittman wrote to Kathy Wilkes with cheques to cover the grants to the young novelist and the 'Brno project' —

Jiří Müller's Brno samizdat publishing house.[20] Other grants were forwarded through Prečan and Kavan.

In the course of 1983 Strauss Pittman and the Directors ran the most ambitious fund raising campaign organised by the JHECF. A Board of Patrons included the poet Allen Ginsburg, the philosophers Donald Davidson and W.V. Quine, literary critic Northrop Frye and the writers of Czech origin, Josef Škvorecký and René Wellek. A brochure was published, using photographs supplied by the emigré photographer Ivan Kyncl,[21] at that time working with Jan Kavan in London. On January 14th 1984, the directors of the fund met at the home of Jack Moskowitz in Washington to decide on the disbursement of the funds raised through this campaign.[22] Wilson was unable to be present, but he wrote with a strong plea for a grant to be made to complete work on a 'Dictionary of Unconventional Czech' in the process of compilation by a team led by Jaroslav Kořán; the dictionary would 'include argot, slang, urban dialects, special slang pertaining to trades and professions, and vulgar and erotic expressions, from the early 19th century to the present time'.[23] (It does not appear that the grant was awarded.)

Although Charles Taylor reported to Roger Scruton after the January 1984 meeting that 'the outlook seems good', this was the last meeting of the American Jan Hus Educational and Cultural Fund. According to Taylor's letter, nine grants were made, most of them for academic or samizdat projects, but there is no evidence that any minutes of the meeting appeared, and in July 1984 Gordon Skilling wrote to complain that he had never received a list of grants awarded. The crisis seems to have been caused by the workload which had fallen on Strauss Pittman's shoulders; after working intensively on publicity and fund raising campaigns for Jan Kavan's Palach Press as well as for the Jan Hus Fund, she was disappointed at how little she had to show for hours of telephoning, letter writing and networking. Involved in post-graduate studies and recently having given birth to her first child, she felt that the other board directors had not taken up the responsibilities assigned to them. The British Trustees began to be concerned about the Americans' activities — they had heard worrying reports about visits to Prague by David Stark and Jack Moskowitz, who according to Alena Hromádková had breached the rules on security.[24]

(Nevertheless, it would appear that Stark had some valuable conversations with Hejdánek, Hromádková and Kořán.[25]) Gordon Skilling, after visiting Prague in June 1984, wrote to Strauss Pittman to complain about 'the confusion, if not chaos of our Hus Fund grants'.[26] Some money had arrived 'but with no clear indication as to how much each was to receive'; others, apparently promised a grant, had received neither money nor message. In January 1985 Skilling wrote to David Stark (who had replaced Taylor as President of the American fund) suggesting 'It is high time we had a meeting... Have we raised any money? if so how much?... I think we should continue sending funds, but on a smaller scale (I mean amount) and with stricter procedures of transmitting and accounting.'[27] In February 1987 he sent a final letter to Stark: 'Since I have not received any responses to my three letters back in 1985, nor any from Jessica Pittman, to whom I also wrote several times, I presume that the Hus Fund is moribund or dead.' He suggested that the balance in the acount 'be transferred to the Canadian fund as we have much we could do with it and it is a pity to see it lying wasted.[28] Some of it is due to the countless letters sent to the USA by myself and Charles Taylor, so that it would not be out of place to turn it over to us.'[29]

The Canadian fund had been set up originally as an adjunct to the American fund, to receive donations from Canadian donors. Strauss Pittman had originally hoped that this could be done through 68 Publishers, the Toronto publishing house run by Josef and Zdena Škvorecký. However, the Škvoreckýs were reluctant to be the receiving body for fund raising activities; they had learnt from experience that the emigré community might construe the arrangement as being of financial benefit to themselves.[30] Consequently, the three Canadians — Skilling, Taylor and Wilson — decided to set up an independent organisation (in spite of reservations on the part of the Americans who feared — correctly — that the new fund would absorb the energies of some of their most active members). A plan and timetable was drawn up at a meeting on 7th February 1983. Among the subjects discussed were honorary patrons (to include Margaret Atwood and Northrop Frye), advisers, incorporation and an appeal (targets included Czech hockey stars and Czechs in Australia). Close co-operation was to be maintained with the

Hus Funds in Great Britain and the USA.

At the next meeting on 15th March the three founders were joined by Josef Škvorecký, his wife Zdena Salivarová, John Reeves[31] and Gleb Žekulín[32]; Skilling was voted President, and a statement was drawn up: 'Grants will be made to individuals who are in difficult financial circumstances and who are trying to continue their creative activity in their spare time. The awards will be made on the basis of applications, stating the nature of the proposed work and the amount requested. Some funds will also be used for the purchase of books and periodicals and other materials needed for the pursuit of scholarly and artistic activities. Funds will also be used from time to time to assist in the translation and publication abroad of works produced by authors in Czechoslovakia or to give other forms of aid to independent cultural work.'[33] The fund was incorporated in Ontario under the title 'Jan Hus Fund — Le Fond Jan Hus'. In April 1984 the Directors met again, without the Škvoreckýs but with Žekulín's wife Lilit; as with the British and American organisations, efforts were being made to write to everyone who might make a donation or lead them to one. In June 1984 Skilling, during a visit to Czechoslovakia, obtained Václav Havel's recommendation[34] of the Jan Hus Fund, intended mainly for circulation in the theatre world. In July, however, Havel wrote (via Vilém Prečan's underground channels) to express his disappointment that a grant believed to have been made by the American fund to the rock group the Plastic People had never materialised.[35] In August Skilling replied by the same route that this appeared to have been a misunderstanding; the grant made by the Americans had been for equipment, not financial support.[36] ('Could it be the English Hus Fund?' he wondered.) 'I shall do my best,' Skilling promised, 'to get some money of this kind assigned to the PPU, and, of course, to Ivan Jirous [Magor], too, whenever we have more money to send. At the moment I do not think we have any in the USA, and the Canadian Fund has just started its appeal and has almost no money so far.'[37]

By spring 1985 the situation had improved, thanks in large part to a matching grant made by George Soros's Open Society Fund. Over $4,000 (Canadian) was available for distribution.[38] A grant was made to Jirous, but not to the Plastic People, who were referred to the British foundation (although during this period the European organisations kept strictly to academic projects and never considered the Plastic People for a grant). Other grants were made to projects recommended by Jiří Müller and Vilém Prečan, and to the actress Vlasta Chramostová, founder of the 'living room theatre', who was writing her memoirs. In June 1985 Havel wrote again to Skilling, thanking the Jan Hus Fund for the support for Ivan Jirous, and gently reminding him about the needs of the Plastic People. 'I know the Hus Foundation does not have a great deal of money at its disposal,' he added, 'which is why I am not making any other proposals, only to recommend an increase for those I have suggested already (Jirous and the PP). There are countless other ideas, but I will take these rather to the Charter 77 Foundation (Janouch), which has greater means. I have recommended Jirous and the PP to the Hus Fund mainly because Vráťa[39] and Paul are very close to them and at the same time close to the Hus Foundation.'[40]

Havel's letter was among the matters discussed at the JHF's meeting in January 1986 (held at the Skillings' home in Toronto), when, again, a grant for equipment, but not financial support, was made for the Plastic People; Paul Wilson was detailed to explain to Havel the reasons for this decision.[41] The Canadians had raised a substantial sum of money in the course of 1985, including a grant from the Ford Foundation.[42] Nearly $10,000 (Canadian) was disbursed in the form of 16 grants, amongst them such new categories as the Jazz Section and information technology. Some of the larger grants were for projects proposed by Vilém Prečan — for example, Petruška Šustrová's account of independent samizdat writing 1968 to 1985, and the publication of Ladislav Hejdánek's samizdat journal *Reflexe*. One of the issues debated was the question of making grants towards translation and publication in samizdat; this related in particular to an application from Jiří Müller in Brno for the Prameny series: 'Grant approved, subject to explanation as to why the books, which seem highly specialist in nature, should not simply be purchased in quantity and sent in. Some directors felt that the titles chosen might be read, by those interested, in original. Others, however, stressed the principles that the directors should not interfere in applicants' choice.'[43] This issue had already arisen at the previous meeting, when Wilson had been certain that a grant had been made towards the translation of Roger Scruton's *Dictionary of Political Thought* (one of Petr Pithart's most urgent projects) whereas Skilling was equally convinced that they had only agreed to send in copies of the English edition.

However, in spite of their success during this period, by February the Canadians had again run into problems of fundraising and administration. On 7th March 1987 Skilling, Wilson, the Škvoreckýs and the Žegulíns met and decided that although they would not terminate the Fund, it would remain at a low level of activity.[44] In March 1988 they forwarded the latest of the applications they had received to the Jan Hus Foundation in Britain. It was from a window cleaner asking for a stipend which would enable him to write a thesis with the title 'The International Standing of Czechoslovakia 1945-85.'[45] The stipend was approved. In 1997 the applicant, Jaroslav Šedivý, became Minister of Foreign Affairs for the Czech Republic.

Philosophy from the Netherlands

The story of Dutch involvement with the underground university in Czechoslovakia began with Hebe Kohlbrugge of Utrecht, who worked for many years with the Dutch Reformed Church. During the German occupation of Holland she was held in a concentration camp with women from Eastern Europe; after the war she travelled behind the Iron Curtain, where she established unofficial contacts with churches and Christians working in the oppressive conditions of Communism. She used these contacts to arrange for Dutch students to study at theological faculties in Romania, Hungary and Poland, where they learnt the language and came to know the system from within. Over the years she built a network of people she could trust and help across the whole region.

In 1978 an earthquake devastated many areas in Romania. One of Kohlbrugge's students studying in Cluj came back to Amsterdam and approached two other students, Jan Kraaijeveld and Henri Veldhuis, for help in driving to Romania with aid. Kohlbrugge gave them a list of people to visit not only in Romania but also on the journey through Hungary and Czechoslovakia. It was, Veldhuis remembers, the most dangerous journey of his life. On the return journey, they stopped in the Moravian village of Miroslav, to visit Jana and Vladimír Kalus, priests in the protestant church; Vladimír had lost his licence, but Jana was still allowed to practise. The family became a centre for a smuggling operation from Holland of works of theology and philosophy and the writings of Czechs and Slovaks published by the emigré presses. Through them, Veldhuis was introduced to the Prague dissidents Ladislav Hejdánek, Jakub Trojan and Miloš Rejchrt and, in 1979, learnt of the visits by British philosophers to Julius Tomin's seminars. Encouraged by the Czechs, Veldhuis began to make contact with Dutch philosophers who would be willing to visit the Prague seminars. The first to respond to Veldhuis's request was Professor Theo de Boer, one of the Netherlands' leading philosophers, with a reputation as a progressive thinker. Veldhuis is convinced that by showing his solidarity with the Czech dissidents de Boer had a decisive influence on the rest of the academic community. It was now December 1979, and Veldhuis had just received a copy of Kathy Wilkes' recently-issued 'Appeal for Assistance to Czechoslovakian Philosophers',[1] in which she asked for donations of books and money, and for philosophy lecturers willing to visit Prague. De Boer, who had written a book on Husserl, was willing to give courses not only on phenomenology but also on the philosophy of the social sciences. Although Veldhuis had his own connections, he suggested that de Boer should write to Wilkes and ask to be incorporated into the Oxford programme. In Wilkes's reply she explained that she was carrying out the role of co-ordinator at Tomin's request — 'he told me clearly that it would be impossible for him unless there was a single central organisation; that unless, to quote him, "Oxford arranges" things would get out of control. He made it clear that he could not guarantee that anyone who came without being sponsored by Oxford could expect to lecture to his groups.'[2] Tomin did not want more than one visitor a month: 'The reason... is that he is running two systematic courses for his students, and if there were two or three lectures on quite unrelated topics in one month, the development of his own seminars would get seriously disrupted.'[3] The months up to June were booked up, she told de Boer, but she would put him in her diary for October 1980; she would not yet tell Tomin, who 'simply doesn't want to have long-term arrangements in written form in his apartment, where a police raid might discover it.'[4]

By October the whole situation had changed with the emigration of the Tomin family. Wilkes, preoccupied with the situation in Oxford, failed to renew contact with the Dutch philosophers. In October de Boer went to Prague as he had planned, and in Hejdánek's apartment gave the first of a series of philosophy seminars which continued at the rate of four or five a year (in the course of nine years 18 Dutch philosophers made a total of 39 visits to Prague).[5] The British, under the impression that the Dutch were keeping their visits secret for security reasons, did not reestablish direct contact until 1987.

In 1981, a year after de Boer's first visit, Veldhuis began to organise a parallel series of visits by Dutch theologians[6] to Jakub Trojan's seminar. Trojan's circle was closely linked with those of Hejdánek, Milan Balabán and Alfred Kocáb. When, in 1974, Trojan lost his licence as a priest, he made use of his second degree to take a post as financial manager in a firm where the director refused to give him notice in spite of police threats (asking of Trojan only that he 'didn't make any trouble'). His theology seminar, which started in 1977 in direct response to the Charter, met alternate weeks during the academic year. His students — sometimes as many as twenty, sometimes as few as seven — formed an ecumenical group, including both catholics and protestants. In the early 1980s Trojan began to welcome visitors from Germany from the circle of Eberhard Bethge, biographer of Dietrich Bonhoeffer, and from Holland.

The organisation of the Dutch venture differed from that of the British and French in that it was not the work of a group of people who registered themselves as a charity or association, but of one man, Henri Veldhuis (now minister in a town near Utrecht).[7] Veldhuis kept the underground university operation entirely separate from that of his book-smuggling and other activities (he was a member of the Dutch foundation which supported Charter 77). His advantage in being able to do this was that he had the strong support of Hebe Kohlbrugge and, through her, of the Dutch churches, which gave generously and trustingly to causes supported by Kohlbrugge. Veldhuis, who himself made many visits to Czechoslovakia, was solely responsible for briefing the philosophers and theologians. He found that their understanding of Eastern Europe, gained very often from left-wing books and journals, was polarised and theoretical. 'It was an adventure to go to these socialist countries and to experience working there and to experience normal families,' remembers Veldhuis, 'the normal daily life of dissidents, what it means to be a dissident, to live in Prague, to do your work in that society, censoring what you think — some of the [visiting lecturers] were shocked. I am certain that for some of them it was a very important experience.'

As with the British and French operations, the Dutch placed great importance on the provision of literature for the seminars. Veldhuis and Kraaijeveld were also involved in a book smuggling operation, in which hundreds of books at a time — philosophy, theology, and books from the emigré press — were driven to Prague in the concealed compartments of a van. In 1984 a vigilant border guard picked up one of these consignments, and the drivers were imprisoned from September to November. Unlike the case of Jan Kavan's van in 1981, however, nothing was found which would compromise anyone in Czechoslovakia, and the affair ended without a scandal. (Veldhuis remembers: 'It was a wonderful lot of books, and we were proud of it, we collected only small ones, there were about 600.... [The guard] made a big study of the cab. He was very, very nervous. And in the end he decided to break open by force. And he took a risk because he knew by destroying it, then — and then he was as glad as a child when he found the books.') The philosophy lecturers, however, knew nothing of this operation. They took only such books as they could reasonably account for, together with an ingenious invention of Veldhuis's;a volume containing multiple copies of the text on which the visitor planned to speak, professionally bound in such a way that a customs officer's cursory glance would not notice anything strange. On arrival at the seminar the book would be broken up and the copies distributed.

Theo de Boer's first visit in 1980 set the pattern for all the Dutch visits to the underground university; he arrived on a Thursday and lectured at different venues on the next three nights (in the first years, they lectured for Petr Rezek's seminar; from 1984 to 1989 they visited Ivan Chvatík's group). The last seminar would be that of Hejdánek's on Monday, since it was the most open and therefore the most dangerous of the seminars. De Boer lectured both in German and English, but noted that his lectures had to be translated; he warned the Czechs that mastery of a world language should be a priority if they were eventually to take their place in Europe. On his first visit he spoke to Hejdánek's group on 'The Concept of Ideology'. On subsequent visits in 1981, 1982 and 1983 (always in March) he focused on the Jewish French philosopher, Emmanuel Levinas, who, himself imprisoned by the Nazis, had written on totalitarian systems of the 20th century. The impression made by Levinas' texts on the audience inspired Miloš Rejchrt to translate some of them from French; between two and three hundred copies of his translation were printed in Holland and smuggled back to Czechoslovakia.[8] Equally impressed was Ivan Havel, brother of Václav, who in 1982 was still in prison following the trials of 1979. Ivan transcribed de Boer's lecture notes, including entire articles by Levinas, and forwarded them to Václav. The notes and articles made a profound impression on Havel: 'The essay is magnificent, almost like a revelation, and it is compelling me to rethink many things more carefully'.[9] In Levinas, he reflected in his letter to Olga of 8th May 1982, 'I sense a storehouse not only of the spiritual traditions and millennial experiences of the Jewish people, but also the experience of a man who has been in prison. It's there in every line...'.[10] In subsequent letters he returned to Levinas' train of thought, on the 12th June writing: 'Levinas... stirred up the thoughts of a prisoner who then had to rethink many of the things he'd always thought about, and who thus became — perhaps — slightly better than he was.'[11]

On the occasion of his visit in March 1983 de Boer and his son were detained during a police raid on Hejdánek's seminar;[12] de Boer had again been talking about totalitarian systems of the 20th century, and this, the students noted, was a practical demonstration. Interrogated by police, de Boer asked his own question: why was it forbidden to come privately, in his own time, to foster the international communication of philosophy? The police, whose main aim was to discover whether there was any organisation behind his visit, retorted that he should have obtained permission from the Ministry of Education. In spite of the deportation, de Boer was able to return in March 1985. In 1986, on the occasion of the Erasmus Prize being awarded to Václav Havel, de Boer was asked to make the award to Havel in Prague (since Havel was not allowed to travel to Amsterdam). A television crew and a number of guests assembled in the Havels' apartment on the Vltava quayside. On arrival at Prague airport, de Boer was deported without explanation; back in the Netherlands he watched the ceremony on television, with his own speech (which he had sent in advance) read by Martin Palouš. The following year, 1987, the Free University of

Amsterdam paid tribute to Ladislav Hejdánek with an honorary doctorate. Hejdánek's speech was published with a Laudatio from Theo de Boer; in Hejdánek's enforced absence Jiří Němec[13] came from Vienna to accept the award. Nearly all the lecturers participating in Veldhuis's operation were Dutch; a few were from Belgium and Germany. It was one of the Belgians who was instrumental in putting the British and the Dutch back into contact. In November 1985 Professor Herman Parret of the Belgian National Science Foundation of the Universities of Louvain and Antwerp wrote to Bill Newton-Smith proposing cooperation with the Jan Hus Foundation. Parret did not yet know about Veldhuis's operation, but had travelled frequently to Czechoslovakia and had met Jan Patočka both in Prague and in Brussels.

Hermann Parret travelled to Prague on the third weekend in June 1986; the Jan Hus Foundation sent word ahead of his visit and it was arranged for him to lecture to Hejdánek's seminar on Sunday 22nd June. This would appear to have been a low point of the British trust's relations with Hejdánek; trustees were unaware that Hejdánek had changed apartments a few weeks previously, and had Parret not made contact with the Belgian members of Veldhuis's group shortly before leaving he would have gone to the wrong address. Parret returned from Prague distressed and indignant. His seminar had gone well and he had talked half the night with Hejdánek, but in verbal reports made to the JHEF he reproached them for their treatment of Hejdánek who, he said, 'was depressed and felt neglected by the British group'.[14] Parret's shock came partly from his discovery of the conditions in which Hejdánek and his students were living. Parret's perception was one of extreme poverty, both material and intellectual. 'He had the impression that most of the [the group] were in badly-paid jobs and studied in their spare time... H.P. was quite horrified by their lack of contemporary knowledge, although he felt they had a good classical grounding. He reported that they desperately needed books.'[15]

Parret compared British activities unfavourably with those of the group led by Veldhuis, whom he visited a few days later.[16] The Executive Committee of the JHEF discussed the issue at their meeting on 3rd July, and wrote to Parret that they were 'extremely... concerned by your experiences... The reason for our apparent 'neglect' has been our understanding that [Hejdánek's] seminars have been well supported by other outside organisations. However, we have agreed that one of our trustees should visit him in the autumn to discuss these matters, and that further visits should be arranged for speakers from this country.'[17] It was also agreed to make contact with Henri Veldhuis; however, it appears that this took another six months.[18] The first letter initiated a correspondence (somewhat cool at the outset) which continued through the remainder of the Foundation's work with the Prague seminars.

The Brno Operation

Prague was not the only city where underground seminars were held. Small groups could be found in nearly every town and city. Some of these made informal contact with groups in other centres, or with larger groups in Prague or Brno. Students used to come from different parts of the country to attend the Prague seminars, and they told about various efforts to set up seminars in their home towns. The largest number was in Brno, the second city in the Czech lands and the capital of Moravia. Brno had always had a rich and varied cultural background. As in Prague, there were before the last war both Czech- and German-speaking communities, and a rich dimension of Jewish life. Before the Iron Curtain came down, Brno, a short ride from Vienna, was abreast of everything new in culture, music and the theatre. The latest operas could sometimes be seen by Brno audiences before being staged in Prague or London, whilst at the beginning of this century Leoš Janáček was at the centre of its musical life — conducting concerts, holding music classes, founding an organ school and a permanent orchestra, editing a music journal. His tradition remained strong, providing a completely different musical focus from that in Prague. The Masaryk University (renamed the Purkyně University under the Communists) had a traditionally high standard of teaching, especially in linguistics. The review *Host do domu*, one of the best literary journals of the 1960s, was edited and published in Brno. Many of Czechoslovakia's best-known writers came from Brno, including Milan Kundera (who in 1974 accepted a teaching post in France and was consequently stripped of his citizenship by the Communists). Anther exile was Ivan Blatný, who died in a psychiatric hospital in Britain. But many others stayed, and contributed to the specific Brno culture; amongst them were Ludvík Kundera, philosopher, poet and cousin of the novelist; the philosopher Josef Šafařík, whose work influenced Václav Havel; and the poets Oldřich Mikulášek and Jan Skácel, who died days before the velvet revolution. Brno was also known for its theatres: in the mid-1960s the small satirical stage Večerní Brno (Evening Brno) held its own with the avant-garde Prague theatres, especially with work by the Brno playwright Milan Uhde.[1] An amateur theatre movement which began in the mid-1950s was important in engaging creative Moravian talent: Divadlo X (or Xka), a poetry theatre which flourished from 1957-1966 and again in the 1970s and 1980s; Quidam, which travelled to many international theatre festivals; and in the 1980s the group simply known as the Amateur Circle, to which the young philosopher Petr Osolsobě belonged. Petr Oslzlý[2] of Quidam was, in the late 1960s, one of the founders of the professional Divadlo Husa na provázku (Theatre Goose on a String).[3] The theatre became one of the driving forces in the unofficial culture and was the initiator of many country-wide theatre projects; the network thus formed provided a structural framework for the events of November 1989. In the mid-1980s the Theatre on a String was joined by HaDivadlo (HaTheatre, originally Theatre of the Haná region). Around these two theatres circled a constellation of artists, sculptors, ecologists, musicians and writers. It was largely due to the theatres' energetic efforts, led by Petr Oslzlý with the HaDivadlo dramaturge Josef Kovalčuk[4] and writer Arnošt Goldflam, that the atmosphere in Brno seemed less oppressive than that in Prague; although Czechs have noted that there were periods when the Prague authorities were notoriously more rigorous than those in Brno, and vice versa. But whereas in Prague the dissidents could expect to be physically barred from regular social events, in Brno it was easier for people to mix in the general crush at exhibitions, performances and festivals. As in Prague, an important role was played by the 'clubs' run by the Socialist Youth Union and the trades unions, where the club managers were allowed a certain measure of freedom.

Brno was almost as well supplied with seminars as Prague. Here too there were groups led by former university professors; for example, those of the psychologist Hugo Široký and of the structuralist Oleg Sus who, when he was demoted from university professor to library assistant, carried on teaching his students in the library in the late evenings. There was the M-klub[5], set up by the Moravian Chartists to study political science, and which revolved around several homes; this had between 30 and 40 members. The Klímas[6] and the Kantůreks[7] came from Prague to discuss political science with the Zlatuškas[8]. In the early 1980s a seminar attracting around 60 people, was held at Václav Čermák's; it was a history series which also covered Slovak history, and was visited by leading Slovak dissidents, travelling the short distance from Bratislava. Brno dissidents for their part would travel not only to Prague and Bratislava, but also to the historic university town of Olomouc, seat of the Archbishop, to take part in Vladimír Jochmann's seminar. There were catholic and protestant seminars, some of them run by secret members of the Dominican order. Around 30 people met at the home of the protestant priest Jan Šimsa. There was a group around the catholic poet Iva Kotrlá and her husband Zdeněk. Poetry was also discussed at the seminar of the actor and Charter signatory František Derfler, whilst the structuralists[9] held their meetings in the homes of Jiří Trávníček and Sylva Bartůšková. Psychologists gathered to discuss the forbidden topic of Jung, whilst the ecologists met at the Observatory. An important series of seminars (five in all) was held from February to June 1978. These were led by the philosopher Božena Komárková and were based on her unpublished writings from 1949 to 1965.[10] They were attended by a group which included Milan Uhde, Jiří Müller and Jaroslav Šabata.[11]

In 1977, in the aftermath of the Charter, plans were made for a comprehensive underground university for young people. It was from this date that Milan Uhde began to teach seminars in Czech literature (one of the earliest tasks of the JHEF in Brno was to give financial support for the lectures to be recorded on audio-cassette and circulated to other seminars). Another of those involved in the planning was the Brno archaeologist Zdeněk Vašíček (a Charter signatory), who had started to teach philosophy to the dissidents' children and other young people in Brno who had been unable to enter higher education. However, the reaction of the Brno police was more immediate and brutal than, at that stage (autumn 1977), that of the Prague police.

Uhde and Vašíček were warned that if they continued action would be taken, not against them, but against the young people attending the seminars.

In 1980 Zdeněk Vašíček found himself being persuaded to organise the first seminar to be given in Brno by a western lecturer. Alena Hromádková, stimulated by the ideas and new pathways being opened up by British lecturers in Prague, gave him no rest until he agreed to arrange the gathering. Roger Scruton, at that time the most frequent and adventurous of the visitors, heard about their plans during his visit to Prague in January 1981, and Lenka Dvořáková offered to go down to Brno to assess the situation. Vašíček was concerned that Brno should provide the best possible audience for such a seminar. Through various forms of persuasion he assembled the most distinguished of Brno's dissidents. Most of them belonged to the 1968 generation of dissent; some of them were former reform Communists, and the general political tendency was left-wing (after 1989 all of the group eventually became associated with the Social Democrat Party). They included reform Communists such as Jaroslav Šabata as well as some protestant Christians, including Jan Šimsa.

It was now the first weekend in April 1981. Scruton was driven by Lenka Dvořáková to visit her home in Ostrava, and from there to Brno. It was dark when they arrived, and it took them some time to find Vašíček's flat in a large house in the leafy suburb of Černá Pole. With the utmost caution they were ushered into the respectful silence of the room where the seminar was to take place.[12] Scruton, interpreted by Dvořáková, spoke on 'the absurdity of socialist views of legitimacy and the error of looking for an alternative in the doctrine of human rights' ('nervously at first,' he reported to the trustees in Oxford, 'but with increasing enthusiasm'[13]).

It seems that the long-awaited occasion may have been something of an anti-climax. The Brno dissidents had not known what to expect, but were taken aback by the expression of views deeply held but outside their experience. Out of confusion and respect for their guest they remained silent. Scruton, accustomed to the adventurous minds and penetrating questions of the young Prague students, found that the lack of response made it difficult for him to define and explain the provocative views he had just expressed. The evening seminar ended on a subdued note.

Nevertheless, the visit marked the start of the Foundation's work in Brno. The following day Vašíček introduced Scruton to Jiří Müller. In the late 1960s Müller had been a student specialising in the finance and management of the engineering industry at the Technical University in Prague and one of the main leaders of the student movement; from 1968 he was one of the chief organisers of resistance against the Soviet occupation and in 1969 the initiator of the student/worker political agreements. In March 1970 Müller presented himself for the defence of his diploma work, to be told that he was banned for 'repeated infringements of the principles of proper behaviour and civic duties'. In 1971 he was arrested for distributing leaflets advising citizens of their right not to vote in the elections, and in 1972 sentenced to five and a half years imprisonment for subversion of the Republic. On his release in 1976 he married Broňa, the daughter of patriots who had also spent years in prison. Müller's present objective was to find ways of breaking down the walls of the dissident ghetto. From the late 1970s to the present time he and Broňa had been working to build up a samizdat publishing operation, the largest in Moravia. Originally they had reproduced works being published under the Petlice imprint in Prague, but more recently they had started to issue their own publications of recent and contemporary Czech writers.

Scruton remembers their first meeting: '...[Müller] was crouching by a table, in a sparsely furnished flat in Brno, and his eyes looked out at me from under his fringe of hair like the eyes of a fox. What were my credentials? Was I reliable? Suddenly he smiled — a serene radiant acceptance, cancelling the severity of his Slavic face.'[14] Müller remembers that he had no initial expectations of anything from his meeting with Scruton, but when he heard him say that the British were willing to offer help in any possible and appropriate way, he invited him for a walk out of earshot of microphones and possible informers. He had not anticipated this opportunity, but used it to ask for support for the samizdat publishing house. At the time he was working ten hours a day in backbreaking physical labour in a fire extinguisher factory; Scruton proposed a six-month stipend to give him an opportunity to concentrate on the publishing work.

Money was also needed to buy paper and pay typists; Müller asked for 5000 crowns (at that time £100).

Three weeks later, at a meeting of Jan Hus Trustees held in Scruton's flat in Notting Hill Gate, the stipend for Müller was agreed; at the next meeting in May the grant of £100 was also approved. Within a few more weeks the stipend had been set up through the bank, and the £100 conveyed in cash via Prague to Brno. In the meanwhile, Müller had been arrested in connection with the seizure of Jan Kavan's van of smuggled literature and materials. Amongst the charges against him was one dating back to 1978, when a stock of samizdat published by Müller and bearing his name had been confiscated by the police at the home of the former actor Albert Černý. Nevertheless Müller, to his surprise, was released after two weeks, at the same time as the French smugglers and the Slovak Charter 77 signatory Miroslav Kusý.

In October 1981 Scruton returned to Brno. By now Zdeněk Vašíček had decided to emigrate and was making his final preparations. He was anxious about his future, and hoped that the Jan Hus Foundation might be able to help him find academic work. On this occasion Scruton visited the Müller family in their terrace house near the railway line. Evidence of the Foundation's efficiency in providing the stipend and grant had brought Müller great satisfaction; not only because of the usefulness of the money itself, but because he realised he had found someone who was both practical and trustworthy, and that there was sense in continuing the relationship. As a result of the seizure of his stock of samizdat, Müller was, for the time being, concentrating on other areas of work. The main subject of discussion was his commitment to the breaking down of barriers between the 'ghetto' and the 'grey zone'. At the turn of the 1970s and 1980s most Czechs were isolated from any sort of contact with the West. Any kind of travel abroad was strictly limited, and contacts with westerners on whatever basis were strictly monitored by Party officials. Even for those working officially in, for example, environmental organisations, it was difficult to obtain independent information, books, and other materials. It was chiefly in the field of the 'grey zone' that Müller wanted to recruit the support of the Jan Hus Foundation. Practical suggestions he made included the commissioning of articles which could be paid for officially through the bank. At the meeting of JHEF trustees in November 1981 it was agreed to put aside £500 for the needs in Brno.

Scruton had by now a good command of the Czech language, and spent the October evening discussing the translation of Czech poetry with the Müllers. The conversation lasted late into the night; too late for Scruton to return to his hotel. Over breakfast the next morning he raised again the question of philosophy seminars, outlining the sort of lectures and courses the Jan Hus Foundation could offer. Müller had been interested in finding new projects which would replace the samizdat which, after his imprisonment and the police impoundment of Černý's stock, he had had to put to one side. He felt that seminars made up of middle-aged dissidents missed the point; internal discussion within such a closed world was not going to make any impact on the future intellectual development of the country. At the same time, he was also against the principle of the open seminar as held by Tomin and even Hejdánek. It seemed to him to be immensely wasteful for valuable western scholars to be thrown out of the country, and for young people to exhaust their energy by spending two days of the week under police interrogation.

Müller believed that it was possible to work out another system which would be free of police intervention and which would have the maximum long-term effect on the development of the younger generation. He was interested in new projects, since the police were now aware of his samizdat operation. For the time being he shared his thoughts only with Broňa, who was now looking after their first child. For there to be any point to all the effort of travel and preparation, he decided, the seminars would have to be worked out as a long-term programme for a consistent group of people who would be able to implement what they were learning. This meant that the students would have to be people who lived in the outer world, beyond the dissident ghetto; and that to pass on what they were learning it would be necessary for them to stay in that society. The seminars would therefore have to be run by people who were still able to operate 'overground', and the Müllers themselves must not be seen to be associated with any of the foreign visitors. It was therefore essential to find the right people for this task, which Jiří Müller anticipated would last for many years, maybe a decade or more.

Müller's choice fell on Petr Oslzlý of the Theatre on a String. Oslzlý had originally been banned from higher education and put to work in a factory; he entered the Arts Faculty of the Purkyně University in 1968 (in the 1990s, after leaving the President's office and returning to Brno as head of the Theatre on a String, he was to become senior lecturer in the Masaryk University and Vice-Dean of the Theatre Faculty of the Janáček Academy). Theatre on a String disregarded the repertoire of the established theatres — still based on principles of socialist realism — and devised its own 'irregular dramaturgy' which developed from ideas and themes rather than texts. It also rejected the administrative hierarchy which was standard in other theatre companies and ran on a one-to-one principle. Its success had been immense, especially with young people, and it received numerous invitations to festivals abroad. Nonetheless — or therefore — the theatre was disliked and feared by the Communist authorities, who were engaged in efforts — hindered by the theatre's high international profile — to weaken Oslzlý's influence and impose their own control.

Müller was hoping that the authorities would assume that involvement in the theatre and other cultural activities was sufficiently absorbing for Oslzlý. As far as we know, they were not aware of his friendship with the Müllers. And Müller considered that these other activities would provide an excellent cover for the seminars. Few people in Brno had such a wide range of cultural contacts, both domestic and foreign, as Petr Oslzlý. Müller also considered the stability of Oslzlý's marriage to be an important factor. Eva possessed the firm principles and stubbornness of her country homeland in the Vysočina highland between Brno and Prague. She had specialised in French language and literature in the late 1960s but never been allowed to teach it as a subject, and now taught Czech to foreign students.

In his published account of the establishment of the Brno seminar Oslzlý remembers how their involvement began: 'Jiří, with whom our bond of friendship and cooperation went back many years, this time introduced his visit by saying that he wanted to discuss a serious matter with Eva and myself. I can't say that we'd ever spent much time discussing matters that weren't serious, but this time he laid especial emphasis on its importance.'[15] The Oslzlýs tried to guess the nature of Müller's news, but were taken by surprise by his proposal. Müller explained that the seminars were to be set up in such a way that, if they ever were to be exposed, the students would still not be at risk. There would, however, be a serious risk for the organisers, and he wanted them to be aware of this. The Oslzlýs' immediate response was positive, but initially Müller did not accept their agreement; he insisted first of all on examining every argument for and against, and then leaving the decision for the two of them to make together.

Petr Oslzlý explains in *Podzemní univerzita* (The Underground University) his personal reason for wanting to be involved: members of his generation, born at the end of the war, had been students at the time of the Prague Spring, and had briefly experienced the freedom it brought. They had been taught by better-qualified teachers, travelled more, and been more open to foreign experiences than those born a little earlier or a little later. Except for those who had deliberately embraced the Communist ethos, they were regarded as a 'lost generation', one which had mistakenly been allowed to enter the universities in the late 1960s on the basis of academic ability and not political affiliation. These students had also missed Marxist-Leninist indoctrination, since when it was reintroduced in 1972 at the end of their studies they had made a mockery of it. They had still had the opportunity of studying under such teachers as Oleg Sus, who were not dismissed until the early 1970s. From the moment they graduated, the Communist authorities knew that they must on no account be allowed to enter the field of education where they might contaminate the minds of the young. It would be a great experience for them at last to contribute towards the educational process. In addition, Oslzlý admitted, he welcomed the opportunity himself again to be involved in the philosophical and political debate which had been part of his university studies.

Before news was sent back to the Jan Hus Foundation, the concept for the seminars had to be worked out between the four of them. Philosophy had been offered, but what kind of philosophy? As they probed the question Oslzlý came to the conclusion that deeper than the crisis in philosophical thought was the crisis in ethical standards. They therefore decided to ask that whatever the subject, the speaker should be asked to orient his or her talk to the ethical point of view, to the 'horizon of being'. And in accordance with their wider activities in Brno, they decided to ask the British whether it was necessary to confine themselves to philosophy and political science, or whether they could ask for subjects from a broader, more 'universal' range — literature, music, theatre, art.... Another important theme for Brno, at the heart of the old Habsburg Empire, was, they believed, the subject of Central Europe. Even if not presented as a subject in itself, they wanted each lecturer to remember it in their presentation.

Practical arrangements were worked out at the start. These proved to be one of the most important contributions made by the Brno group to the whole practice of the underground university, since it was through these that the Brno seminar was able to run for an uninterrupted five years. It was agreed that the seminars would be held at the Oslzlýs' home on a deliberately irregular basis, and would be offered to the students on the basis that 'a friend of Petr's, met through the theatre, happened to be visiting Brno'. No more information than this would be given; therefore if a seminar were raided, no one other than Petr and Eva would have to safeguard what they knew. The Oslzlýs' fourth floor flat was an ideal venue for secret meetings, since the entrance could be reached directly by lift from a little-frequented passage. The lecturers, instead of travelling via Prague, would come through Vienna. That way they would avoid any 'contamination' from meetings in Prague; they would also take advantage of the more relaxed controls of the border crossing at Mikulov, instead of being interrogated by alert officials at Prague airport; and they could present themselves as long-stay holiday-makers in Austria, rather than week-end visitors making the suspiciously long flight to Czechoslovakia. They would be met on arrival in Brno, but spend the first night in a hotel in order to obtain the necessary police registration. It was agreed that to make the best use of the visitors' time, seminars would be held at the weekend (the Prague custom of holding seminars on week nights and disappearing at the weekend had been a problem for JHEF academics, tied to the timetable of their home universities).

The choice of students was important. Before that could be

decided, came the question of the interpreter. All four agreed that the seminars should not be confined to English-speakers, but in order to do the job adequately, the interpreter would have to prepare the texts, and would be aware that these lecturers were not simply 'chance visitors'. The Oslzlýs had a candidate in their friend and fellow-student, Miroslav Pospíšil, the best student of English in his year. Pospíšil, after refusing to join the Communist Party in the late 1970s, had been sacked from his post in the Arts Faculty of the Purkyně University and, like Eva, was frustrated by the routine teaching into which he had been forced at the state language school. After initial reluctance, Müller agreed that Oslzlý could tell him about the project, and Pospíšil became a member of the organising team for the next five years, with a number of the seminars being held at his family home. His wife Yvona decided that, although she approved of the work and was willing to host the seminars, she did not want to know any names or anything about the organisational arrangements: '...because if one day, two men ring our bell and take us away, no matter what they do to me, if I don't know, I won't be able to tell them.'[16] Also important was the Oslzlýs' friend and neighbour, the graphic artist Rostislav Pospíšil (unrelated to Miroslav), who was responsible for many of the practical arrangements. For security the Müllers decided that neither the Oslzlýs nor any of the Pospíšils should know the name of the Jan Hus Foundation nor, for as long as possible, the names of any of the organisers in Britain.

With this arranged, the choice of students could be made; the Müllers left this to the Oslzlýs, since they were the ones who would be taking the risk. Oslzlý realised it was a more sensitive issue than he had anticipated; they were talking about a group which was intended to work together for several years. Eventually he made his choice and was glad to see how, over the coming months, members of that first small group brought with them more and more friends, until the potential attendance for any seminar numbered over 50.

In August 1984, JiříMüller wrote to Roger Scruton (through Vilém Prečan's underground channels) that they were ready to start: 'We are interested in lectures on ethics. We should like the first teacher to come and arrange the whole programme of lectures on ethics. We don't know, what possibilities exist. Our concern is for example a history of ethics, a political ethic, ethics of art, Christian ethics and so on. You see, it is a very broad concern. We suppose one visit during a quarter of year and the stay of teacher from 3 to 5 days. We suppose two or three lectures during the stay... I should like to point out that the organization of lectures will be other and with other aim than the one in Prague. It will be lectured only for people employed in such institutions like university, secondary schools, theatre, research institutions and so on. Dissenters must be excluded. It is necessary to form proper conditions for it. Lectures must not be connected with me and you... As you think politically, I want to add something for your personal information. Our foreigner friends often want to support dissenters, their independent culture and their independent way of life, first of all. But dissenters are living in a ghetto. It is important to support the life of that ghetto, but it is more important to seek and to discover bridges from the ghetto to society. The organization of lectures, as I suggest it, is one such potential bridge.'[17]

In mid-October 1984 Jessica Douglas-Home visited Prague and took the bus to Brno to tell Müller that the first lecturers were ready, although the exact dates had still to be arranged. In late November a postcard arrived which told the Oslzlýs that they could expect David Levy on Friday 14th December. That afternoon Eva Oslzlá telephoned her husband at the theatre to tell him that Levy had arrived; as agreed, he had travelled via Vienna, but by train instead of bus. Consequently, he had been searched by customs officials, and a paper cutter, intended for the Müllers' samizdat press, had been discovered. Levy claimed to have been carrying it as a gift for Petr's theatre, but the books he was carrying also roused suspicion. When around 20 guests gathered for the first seminar on the Saturday evening, the Oslzlýs could not be certain that they had not made a terrible mistake. Petr Osolsobě (who in the 1990s became senior lecturer in aesthetics at the Masaryk University) remembers that the 'visiting friend' was kept hidden in the study until all the guests had arrived; it was only gradually that Oslzlý revealed that he would be talking about the anthropological foundations of politics. It was at this point that Osolsobě realised that the occasion was not 'just a matter of a cup of tea'. He remembers Levy as being 'very subtle, quiet and calm'. For Levy the event was as though he were 'coming back to home ground' — the home ground of Central Europe. 'Most of the participants were young,' he wrote in his report to the trustees. 'They were philosophically curious and very politically oriented; though as might be expected, more away from something they knew than toward any particular unknown other.'[18] Levy reflected later that he had never had such a warm response to his ideas as that which he experienced during this and his two subsequent visits to Brno. His talk on this first occasion was on 'The Political Condition' (on his second visit he spoke 'On Being Right: Tradition, Reality and Utopia', based on his book *Political Order*). In February the second lecturer, John Keane, arrived in Brno to speak on 'Civic Society and the State' and 'Civic Society and the Crisis of the Left'. Osolsobě remembers with amusement that it was the first time most of those in the room had ever heard about the concept of privatisation, one of the most critical public issues in post-revolution Czechoslovakia.

Both the first lecturers had already experienced the Prague seminars and understood the situation in Czechoslovakia; Levy had, on his return, briefed Keane about the specific nature of the Brno seminar. Over the next few years their visits to Brno were held in parallel, with the intention of presenting a balanced view of right and left politics. Some of the regular students, such as Petr Fiala (who in the 1990s became head of the Department of Political Science at the Masaryk University) inclined towards Levy's philosophy; others, such as Pavel Barša (who became his colleague), towards Keane's. Fiala had always wanted to study political science, but knowing the sort of political science taught at the Czechoslovak universities, had chosen instead to read Czech and history. His fellow student in the Arts Faculty was Aleš Filip, Petr Oslzlý's nephew,[19] who had invited him to join the group at its inception; at the age of 20 they were the youngest members. Fiala had already been attending underground seminars run by the Dominicans, but was excited and stimulated by the new group. He found Levy's lecture liberating and surprising, full of new ideas; Levy's manner of expression was also very different from that of his lecturers at the Purkyně University. Pavel Barša was older than Fiala and had graduated at the end of the 1970s, spending a year in the Academy of Sciences, before leaving by his own choice to become a cleaner, nightwatchman and then stoker. He was a musician in the 'unofficial culture', and part of his attraction to John Keane's philosophy was his feeling that they belonged to the same culture and reacted in similar ways. He was also excited by the intellectual ideas — it was the first time he had heard anyone define the term 'civic society' — and by the flamboyance of Keane's delivery. Both Fiala and Barša believed that one of the things which the Brno seminar helped to teach them was the principle of respect and tolerance for differing political opinions. Barša, although francophone and politically close to the French left wing, developed a great admiration for the British ability for academic communication. Fiala, meanwhile, was fascinated to learn about British Conservatism; he had already heard of Mrs. Thatcher, but only through the third visitor to Brno, the Nottingham University professor David Regan, did he hear about the writings of Edmund Burke on the foundations of Conservatism.

David Regan came in March 1985 precisely to speak on 'Edmund Burke and Conservatism', and was followed in May by the philosopher Francis Dunlop on 'The Objectivity of Values'; Dunlop, like Levy and Keane, became a key teacher, returning twice more before the revolution. Both Regan and Dunlop could be described as having a right-wing orientation, but they were followed in the autumn of 1985 by Paul Flather and John Keane, who tended to the left. The 'right-wing/left-wing' opposition did not become an issue until 1990, when John Keane, interviewed by Michael Ignatieff in a BBC2 programme about the Jan Hus Foundation, accused it of propagating right-wing propaganda in the Brno seminars.[20] However, this is not how it was perceived by Oslzlý and Pospíšil, nor by Fiala and Barša, the most politically aware of the students. Fiala found the whole approach of the British lecturers, whatever their orientation, a revelation. Barša thinks with Keane that the seminars were asymmetrical, with the balance to the right; on the other hand, he counters, the balance of the seminars led by the Association Jan Hus in Brno (which he also attended) was to the left. One or two of the British lecturers annoyed him by being too didactic, giving the seminar 'right-wing schooling'; but this, he believes, was inevitable, given the vacuum of the 1980s and the fact that the Czechs and Slovaks lacked any political culture of their own. Pospíšil does not believe that the asymmetry lay in the programme of visits at all; if anything the balance of speakers tended to the left: 'I would argue that the imbalance described by Barša was in the group, not in the lecturers or their presentations. There was more curiosity, more fascination, in right-wing political philosophy, and most of the group were more attracted to the right.'[21] Jiří Müller remembers that the question of right and left was essentially irrelevant; there was one important issue, which was the destruction of Communism. In the early 1980s he wrote to Roger Scruton: 'It is not important from my point of view, when I am criticised by Czechs, emigrants or Englishmen, that a "socialist" associates with "one of the most reactionary philosophers". The important thing is, that your and my political efforts allow it. I think, that the deepest and widest political conflict inside east societies is formed by controversy between the state need to control everything and individuals' need to get away from state totalitarian ambition. This conflict afflicting great part of society is actual and independent from other possible conflicts, and I am interested in it first of all.'[22]

Although the members of the seminar were chosen on the basic criterion of trustworthiness, they were very varied in age and inclination, ranging from catholics to former Marxists. There were among them teachers, students, artists, architects, ecologists, theatre people. A core group formed; Fiala remembers that he was present at almost every seminar, even when on national service. Although it was never openly said that the lectures were planned, it became apparent from about the third lecture that this was a question of a systematically organised series. The reasons for attending also varied. For some of the older members of the group, it was at first as though the visiting lecturers could provide them with a political solution, a way out of the blind alley of totalitarianism. For the younger people, it was more a question of a spiritual dimension to life, in several cases linked with experiences provided by the Theatre on a String. Karel Pala, a third year student of English at the Purkyně University, came because he wanted to learn more about the Anglo-Saxon world; the lectures were for him a window on adventure, on philosophic searching. Marie Blažková believed that the seminar caused a breaking down of barriers, 'a great refreshing inspiration' whereby they were able to regain a taste for learning about new things. Zdeněk Merta similarly felt that what the lectures provided was an awareness of values. For him, and for many of the others, not only the lectures but the circle was important, the fact that these people were meeting in a spiritual but non-denominational atmosphere, and had the freedom to talk about issues that were officially forbidden. Petr Fiala, on the other hand, found that some of the students' contributions tended to be self-indulgent; he wanted to hear above all what the speaker had to say, and was grateful to Oslzlý for his guidance of the discussion. Petr Oslzlý remembers that whereas in the early discussions reactions tended to be polarised — 'I agree'; 'I don't agree' — in the course of time people learnt how to consider a variety of views, and to think through their own responses.

Between 1984 and the velvet revolution, 28 lecturers from the Jan Hus Educational Foundation gave 62 seminars in the course of 40 visits to Brno.[23] All of them were chosen in consul -tation with Müller, the Oslzlýs and Pospíšil; often they would suggest the field or subject, and the appropriate speaker would be found. Oslzlý had hoped from the beginning that one of the key speakers would be Roger Scruton; however, on 7th June 1985 the Brno police broke up a conversation between Scruton and the Müllers and expelled him from Czechoslovakia. Nevertheless, for the next four and a half years he remained in close contact with the Brno seminar, being responsible for briefing almost every one of the 41 lecturers and couriers. Each visitor had to be briefed before leaving Britain, not only in connection with security, but also about the seminar itself. The briefing was continued by Oslzlý and Pospíšil in the 24 hours between their arrival on the bus from Vienna and the start of the seminar. Petr Fiala remembers that all the lecturers arrived with a good understanding of the situation (which he contrasts with the 'arrogance' of many foreign academics who turned up in Czech universities after 1989). Nevertheless, the visits to Brno were as much a revelation for the British as they were for the Czechs. In 1987 the playwright Julian Mitchell wrote: 'I enjoyed the visit enormously. It was my first time behind the Iron Curtain and if we had done nothing more than talk to Mikin and Petr, Eva and Yvonna, for the three days, it would still have been extremely rewarding and instructive. I was very moved by their courage and strength. Their histories are so completely different from ours. I had known, intellectually, from books about the 'Central European experience' before I went. To go there, to see it in the faces, watch it on the streets, discuss it with those who've actually lived it — that was to feel it for the first time.'[24] Petr Oslzlý remembers another visitor who expressed amazement at the cars in the streets, the bright windows of apartments, and the voices of children running in to school: 'So you have this here too!'

Not all the seminars were in the homes of the Oslzlý and Pospíšil families. The aim was to take them to a wider audience where this was possible. In 1986 the 'English Club' — a popular venue before the Second World War — was revived by Pospíšil, Petr Antonín of the State Language School and Don Sparling of the Purkyně University.[25] It was established in trade union premises, the Bedřich Václavek Club, and held monthly sessions given by native English speakers. Between 1986 and 1989, eight of the JHEF speakers, usually those with a non-political orientation, stayed in Brno for an extra Monday night to lecture to an audience of between 100 and 150. Occasional talks were also given at other small clubs which existed as islands of relative freedom in their totalitarian surroundings. It came about that quite specific seminar fields were developed, parallel and interlinked with the programme of political philosophy; between 1985 and 1989 the programmes initiated covered art, music, ecology, literature, architecture and medical ethics (just one visit took place on medical ethics, by Richard Rowson in 1987). Jiří Müller raised the idea of 'parallel subjects' when writing to Roger Scruton (by underground channels) in April 1985: 'we are interested that the visits from England will go on and above all political philosophers will arrive. It would be nevertheless useful if among them also art-historians or artists make a visit. It is partly because of weakening of visits' political character, and partly on account of the fact, that for such a meeting another circuit of people could arise. But "an unpolitical" visit should be also in connection with common questions of man, society, ethics. We would be glad, for purpose of uncomplicated course and good preparation, if would be always possible to arrange with every visitor the firm date of the next visit and how long the following guest could stay.'[26] This was one of the subjects Müller discussed with Scruton during his interrupted stay in June 1985. Scruton, in his first letter to Müller after the incident, wrote (inter alia): 'We are prepared to obey any instructions that you care to give us concerning security. However, we are not certain that the proposal to stay at Marxova Ulice is a good one. Is this not likely to attract more attention rather than less? However, as I say, if these are your considered instructions we shall obey them. JG [Jessica Gwynne, i.e. Douglas-Home] would prefer the following: to come on the express bus from Prague, at 8 a.m. (arriving 11.30?) on Saturday the 21st September [1985]. She will then meet you wherever you want. However, if you wish her to come on the bus from Mikulov, as suggested, she will do that, and it will not be too much trouble. Please send back precise instructions. The title of JG's talk is 20th Century British Painting and its background. Should she talk about her own painting? (She is very shy and would prefer not to, but again will obey instructions.) If JG stays in Prague, she will see no dissident or other suspect person before coming to you.'[27] Douglas-Home visited the Brno seminar on two occasions, the second time in January 1987 to talk about 'German Expressionism'; she was followed by the Oxford artist Helen Ganly. Meanwhile, the composer David Matthews had inaugurated a music programme in January 1986 with talks on Mahler's Tenth Symphony and on 'English Music Today'; later that year Tom Burke had given the first lecture on 'Environmental Protection in Britain' and Dan Jacobson had been the first of a series of writers to visit both Brno and Jaroslav Kořán's group in Prague. The architecture programme, which began in conjunction with the semi-official architectural seminars arranged by Prague architects in the Hlahol auditorium, reached Brno in 1989 with a visit by the British architect Quinlan Terry. Each programme developed its own dynamic, expanding into the world beyond the seminars, and is described elsewhere.

As in Prague, the underground seminar in Brno was closely related to publishing activities. It was as a result of the seminar that Petr Fiala, in cooperation with fellow-students Roman Ráček and Jiří Voráč, began to produce a student journal, *Revue 88* for circulation at the Purkyně University. Oslzlý considers this to have been one of the most important and courageous publishing ventures of the whole 20 years; as a result, Fiala acquired a police file and was unable to find work in Brno after he graduated (he worked in the small Moravian town of Kroměříž until December 1989). František Rychlík, publisher of the Brno version of the Prague samizdat *Střední Evropa* joined the seminar in the late 1980s. Even closer was the link between the seminar and Jiří Müller's samizdat project, Prameny ('Sources').

Once the seminars had been established, Müller felt it was time to set up his samizdat operation again, and this time his priority was to professionalise production. He knew about the rapid advances being made by information technology in the West, and was determined that the 'unofficial culture' should take advantage of this before the moribund, bureaucratic 'official culture' even understood what it was all about. Photocopying machines had reached Prague by the 1980s and there were even some public photocopying services, but the regime exercised strict control not only over the registration of machines but even over the making of copies. The ownership of every machine was registered by law, and it was difficult to make large quantities of illicit copies. (Nevertheless, by June 1985 at least three photocopiers had been acquired by the Czech 'opposition'.) At the beginning of the 1980s the regime was similarly disinclined to make other equipment — such as computers and printers — available to the general public. Where computers were in use, they were often antiquated models acquired before the clampdown of the early 1970s. (In the 1960s Ivan Chvatík's employer had sent him to Sweden for training in the use of such a model; when in the 1980s the police tried to force his dismissal, his employer pointed out that no one else knew how to maintain the computer.) The idea of walking into a shop and buying a personal computer was for most people beyond the bounds of possibility.

Roger Scruton had paid his third visit to Jiří Müller in Brno in April 1984. He reported back to the Trustees about a discussion which covered, among other things, the grants made by the British and American trusts; the cassette tapes needed for recording Milan Uhde's seminars; the possibility of a stipend from the Institut Slave in Paris for Milan Jelínek; and the provision of book catalogues and other materials. About the samizdat press,

Scruton wrote: 'I brought back a specimen of JM's excellent work, which proceeds constantly in his basement (I helped him finish the binding of memoirs from the First Republic).[28] They have done a superb edition of Popovski's book on Soviet science recently, and are clearly not averse to "left" wing ideas, since they have also done an edition of Bahro's new book. (Alena [Hromádková] thought this a sign of how cut off they are!) They would love to have a typewriter with memory, and would certainly make good use of it. Also a binding and a cutting machine (both available in Germany).... They are presently contemplating Konrad Lorenz and Popper. They promise to make an archive of all that we support.'[29]

It was essential that equipment purchased by the Jan Hus Foundation for Jiří Müller's samizdat operation should be 'robust, simple to operate, need little servicing, must not be bulky, must use paper available in Czechoslovakia...'[30] The first item purchased was a memory typewriter, sent through Vilém Prečan's underground channels at the end of 1984: 'Further to our recent telephone call, I now have the information you require: The typewriter that we wish to send to Czechoslovakia has the following dimensions: 613x453x177 mm, and weight 20.6 kilos. It is to go to JiříMüller in Brno.'[31] The first book published in the Prameny series was written on an ordinary typewriter; the second and third on the memory typewriter. (When the typewriter broke down half way through the preparation of the next text, Müller was somewhat disgruntled by the Foundation's inability to trace and send in a repairman from Vienna.) Müller soon found the typewriter's 10 page capacity to be inadequate; at the time of David Levy's first visit he was already asking about the possibility of writing on diskette. In May 1986 he looked into the possibility of purchasing an Atari computer from the foreign currency store, Tuzex; although it seemed likely that these machines were not equipped for work in the Czech language. By the time of Wolfgang Stock's visit in August a change in Czechoslovak customs law had made it feasible to import an Amstrad computer with a high-quality printer. (The change had come about because the Czechoslovak authorities had belatedly realised how far their country was falling behind in information technology; the aim was now to get as many computers into the country as possible, regardless of into whose hands they fell.) Müller confirmed the details during Barbara Day's visit later that month; he could see new potential for samizdat production if the Foundation in Britain acquired a compatible model.

In October 1986 the Foundation agreed to purchase the new technology; Newton-Smith was responsible for choosing the models and Barbara Day for clearing the paper work for export. The computers were bought in December: two Amstrads 1512 with printers. One was for the Foundation's home 'office' (Day's London flat), whilst the other was driven by Stock from Oxford to Munich, and from there by Marie von Spee to Brno, in March 1987. Von Spee was obliged to give Jiří Müller's name as recipient when crossing the border; consequently, she and the Müllers were followed by police during the visit. Nevertheless, the customs officials followed the correct procedure, apart from being unable to determine the machine's kilobytes on which the amount of duty depended. There remained a major hurdle; that of writing in Czech characters. None of the Foundation's advisers knew of any Czech language programme in existence. In Sweden, František Janouch of Charter 77 Foundation was developing a Czech chip as part of a computer's hardware, and most computers donated to the Prague dissidents carried this chip. In Brno they were convinced that a software programme could be developed which could be used by any machine. In January 1987 the Executive Committee of the Foundation agreed to Newton-Smith's proposal that: 'a commercial programme should be adapted for the Czech alphabet, instead of writing a new programme.'[32] In April 1987 the Foundation sent a computer expert from Oxford, Duncan Watt, to Brno as messenger; in conditions of secrecy he was introduced to Jiří Zlatuška, Vice-Director of the Computer Science Department at the Purkyně University. Zlatuška had been successful, in spite of being the son of 'politically unreliable' parents, in obtaining a technical education and was now one of the country's indispensable experts in computer technology. His identity as one of Jiří Müller's network had to be guarded as carefully as that of Petr Oslzlý or the environmentalists. Watt returned to Britain on 5th April, having promised Müller 'to write a WP for them and provide JZ with relevant documentation, source code and compiler';[33] he also observed in his report that 'delays are...

keenly felt in Czechoslovakia'. Wolfgang Stock wrote to Scruton on 21st April: 'They are very frustrated with the fact that the computer is still standing idle due to the missing Czech alphabet/programme that has not yet been produced by DNS [*sic*]. They ask for the quickest possible transportation. It would be possible to send the programme by mail to the computer expert DNS met.'[34] Barbara Day, returning to England on 25th April after a visit which included a meeting with Müller, reported on 'Jiří's great disappointment that [the computer] won't yet write in Czech. He is desperately keen to get on and use it, and hopes that we can send the programme at least with the June messenger.'[35]

However, by June the programme was still not ready, James de Candole (the June messenger), reporting: 'J.M. says that they could almost certainly construct alphabet if provided with relevant manuals from England. His Computer man however is leaving for the U.S.A. in September for 1 Year and therefore prompt action is required. He suggests that I could bring them in in July depending on size. Relevant manual information enclosed. J.M. stressed the absurdity of being in possession of such a valuable piece of equipment and yet being unable to take advantage of it.'[36] In August Müller wrote to Stock that they were expecting to receive the programme from Watt 'in the course of the second week of September.'[37] The problem, according to a message from Day to Stock for his visit that month, appears to have been the necessity for 'the suppliers to come up with the necessary parts'.[38] By then the Foundation had discovered that there was a model of computer with a Czech language programme available in Britain, but it was not compatible with the Amstrad. Should this model be purchased and sent to Müller? But with Stock's return from Brno at the end of the month came the message: 'Please cancel all projects in the UK: Jiří's expert has written a genuine and perfect Czech word processing program (disk enclosed) which produces all special characters both on the screen and on a printer.'[39] Zlatuška called his programme 'Morning Star'; it was used for all the samizdat produced in the Prameny series from the fourth volume on, and for all material written on computers subsequently provided by the Jan Hus Foundation for use in Brno, Prague and Bratislava. Zlatuška and Stock anticipated that the programme could be developed in different language versions and used to facilitate samizdat production throughout Central Europe. By January 1989 it was available in English, Czech, Slovak, Polish and Hungarian versions, adapted for use on different computer models and by different printers. Stock also hoped to find commercial users in the West (contact was made with Radio Free Europe) who would help to provide financial support for the programme. Many of its users believed the Morning Star programme to be superior to T602, which in the 1990s became the standard programme for the Czech and Slovak Republics, but Zlatuška did not have the time to develop it commercially. By the end of the 1990s, however, most Czech users were changing over to the Czech language versions of international computer programmes.

Even during the long wait for a Czech language programme, it had been possible for Müller to use the computer to communicate with the world outside Czechoslovakia. There was no more frustration over poor memories or badly transcribed notes; Müller could write letters on disc to Day and Stock and send them when the opportunity arose. Letters sometimes ran to several sides when printed — often with additional pages to and from Scruton, and sometimes with messages for Zlatuška (then at Delaware University in the USA). They covered such subjects as samizdat production, books to be sent, the Jazz Section, the political situation, a Polish-Czech history project,[40] ecology and music projects and a project 'for the documentation of vanishing Christian and Jewish monuments in Bohemia and Moravia'.[41] In April 1987 Stock proposed: 'For their safety, I would like to ask the next (GB) speaker to pass on to him a professional U.S. programme that does both compress and encrypt any given data in a nearly perfect (i.e. safe) form. This does not only reduce the disc space needed for data (or messenges to and from Brno!) by 50 per cent, but, unless in possession of both the programme and the individual code word, makes the discs unreadable. Once this is operational, it might be interesting for you, too, since it would make communications much more independent of messengers.'[42] In June, Day asked de Candole to find out whether 'JM receive[d] and under[stood] the coded discs from Germany brought by Anthony O'Hear and given to PO? Any messages about them for Wolfgang?'[43] From September on, for over two years (until November 1989) nearly every visitor to Brno carried a disc (outgoing discs were packed in a box with nine blanks for use by the samizdat press).

Much of the correspondence concerned new developments in information technology and the provision of new equipment. On 5th October 1988 Müller wrote to Day: 'I got news... that the JHF had allocated money in order to send us an Amstrad 1640 and two Epson printers. I sent James the addresses (senders and receivers) for the Amstrad 1640 computer and another address for the Epson LQ 859 printer. Please try to send them soon because the announcement about lower customs duties is only valid to 31st December 1988 and we don't know what will happen after that. And now concerning the second Epson LQ 850 printer for us. Would it be possible, instead of this, to buy and send another Amstrad 1640? We don't actually want another dot matrix printer at the moment, since we're not experimenting at present... I would be very grateful if you could bring 2-3 ribbon cartridges, model number: Radix 10, printer manufacturer, Star. Apart from this I need more ribbons for the Epson LQ 850, but only the ribbons and not the cartridges. It's possible to change the ribbon five times in one cartridge. It's much cheaper to change the ribbon in the cartridge than to keep on buying new cartridges, that's why I just want the ribbons and I'd like to know how much the whole cartridge costs and how much just the ribbon. I need to know so that I can work out the expenses per book. I think that the two biggest suppliers for computer needs are Misco (telephone London 01-998 9068) and Inmac (telephone London 01-740 9540). The catalogues promise next-day delivery. I assume I can count on these capitalist firms' advertising gimmicks?' [44]

Müller experimented with three methods of reproduction using the dot-matrix printer: 1) putting carbon copies through the printer, as with a typewriter; 2) making cyclostyled copies from a foil produced on the printer; 3) making photocopies from an original produced on the printer. None of these satisfied him from the point of view of cost or speed. He soon came to the conclusion that only the use of a laser printer combined with an offset machine would ensure 'quantity, quality and speed of production combined with low cost' [45]. The possibilities of sending equipment on an 'official' basis for use by the 'unofficial culture' had radically improved with Jiří Zlatuška's return from America to resume teaching at the University. In July 1989 the Foundation agreed to send a photocopier and laser printer (its use to be shared with the new movement, Open Dialogue) to Brno. Transport was arranged from Germany by Wolfgang Stock; by mid-September the photocopier had arrived, but the laser-printer was still in transit. Müller wrote: 'Wordsmith[46] does two things for you: adjusts text written by word-processor through a typesetting programme, and prints the text thus adjusted on bromides. With the help of computers with a hard disc we can now adjust our texts ourselves with a typesetting programme called Tex and we hope soon that we will also be able to use the Ventura programme. We would also be capable of sending the software for Czech letters for the typesetting machine Linotronic 300, which is used in the West. Can you find out if Wordsmith uses this machine? If so, then we would be able to send discs not with Morning Star, but with text already adjusted by the Ventura programme or Tex. Wordsmith would then in fact only print bromides from discs prepared by us. Obviously a cheaper and easier possibility would be to print camera-ready copy on a laser printer. This possibility depends only on having a laser printer here on which to try it out.'[47]

A laser printer had already been agreed by the Foundation, and in October 1989 Müller successfully printed the Brno-produced sociology journal *Sociologický obzor* on the imported printer. From November onwards the printer was used for production of materials for the velvet revolution. In January 1990 Müller took his discs containing the Prameny series around the state publishing houses. 'Print books from computer discs?' exclaimed the professionals, 'What an impossible idea!'

For samizdat works to be easily read and circulated, it was necessary to bind as well as print. Amongst the brochures travelling backwards and forwards were those describing cutting and binding machines, of German, British and American origin; but whatever choice Müller made, the chief problem was how to import the machine. In the mid-1980s the only method was via Vilém Prečan's secret route, and for bulky items this service was booked up months, even years ahead. In 1986 Wolfgang Stock volunteered to find a way, but in January 1987 Michael Potter brought the message: 'JM has found a retired bookbinder who is prepared to sell them his equipment for about £500. This equipment consists of a guillotine, a pressing machine, a set of spine-lettering tools and another piece of equipment whose purpose is too elaborate for BM's English to describe. Of course, all this equipment is very old-fashioned, but JM thinks it will be quite workable.'[48] The equipment was purchased.

The professionalisation of samizdat applied not only to technology but also to content. Müller's editorial board for Prameny, chosen to represent different skills in editing and translating, consisted of two future university Rectors (Milan Jelínek of the Masaryk University and Martin Černohorský of the Silesian University in Opava), the future Dean of the Faculty of Social Sciences of the Charles University (Miloslav Petrusek), the future Director of the Police Academy in Brno (Vladimír Turek) and the future Chairman of Trustees of the Czech and Slovak Jan Hus Foundation (Vladimír Jochmann). The series name Prameny — sources — declared Müller's aim of introducing key works of western philosophy and political science in translation. The selection of the works to be translated was crucial, and for help in this Müller turned to all his western contacts, including the Jan Hus Fund in Canada: '...it is evident that more than the translator's activity the very choice of literature for this activity is important. And I don't know whether it is possible for the committee to find anybody who would be willing to do this work for us.'[49] Gordon Skilling's reply to Müller has not survived ('...your kind letter, that really pleased me, even if it includes also crushing criticism, because my proposals are too unconcrete'[50]); but Müller's subsequent letter of September 1985 contains his first ideas about Prameny: 'We are trying to form an edition with preliminary name "Thinkers of 20th century" and another one "Science of 20th century". Their sense consists in giving information about works of those authors, who are not published here officially, or about those areas of the science research, on which it is kept silent completely or partly... Translations of professional books are of course not easy, therefore it would be important for us to obtain any support, so that we could at least partly pay for the translations.'[51] At this stage the first series was to include two works by Victor E. Frankl and selections of writings by Karl Popper and Michel Foucault.

Although Skilling had reservations about the value of translations,[52] in January 1986 a grant of $600 was approved by the Canadians: 'subject to explanation as to why the books, which seem highly specialist in nature, should not simply be purchased and sent in. Some directors felt that the titles chosen might be read, by those interested, in original. Others, however, stressed the principle that the directors should not interfere in applicants' choice.'[53] The British Foundation, at its own meeting the following month, was asking: 'What kind of support does J.M. want for the translations of political literature? Next visitor to find out. Recommend translation of *Anarchy, State and Utopia* and Rawls in tandem.'[54] In May 1986 Müller sent a message through Cheryl Misak, asking for a copy of Nozick's *Anarchy, State and Utopia*.

Texts published in the Prameny edition included Levy's *Political Order*, Noel O'Sullivan's *Fascism* and E.J. Mishan's *Economic Growth Debate*. The editions circulated widely in Moravia; four of its original subscribers were actually judges in the Regional Court in Brno, and one is now vice-president of the Constitutional Court. In the euphoria following the Velvet Revolution state publishers were eager to obtain the rights to Müller's translations; there followed a period when, with the market overloaded with new publications and the distribution system breaking down, the publishers retreated. Nevertheless, all of Prameny's Czech translations of key western texts have now been published by 'official' publishers, and some of them (works by Karl Popper, Friedrich von Hayek and Raymond Aron) were in the hands of the public almost immediately after the revolution. The last was J.L. Talmon's *Origins of Totalitarian Democracy*, translated by Jana Kuchtová and published by the SLON publishing house with a grant from the Central and East European Publishing Project.

One of the projects which Müller was keen to include in the second strand of Prameny's publications (on science) was a samizdat volume on information technology. He believed it was tremendously important to make information about new methods of communication available to the general public (which was not happening through the 'official' press) because this could be a major factor in making people independent of the totalitarian regime.[55] In early December 1985 a letter arrived via

Prečan's underground route enclosing a three-page project. However, the project moved slowly and on 11th January 1987 Müller wrote to Scruton: 'I am very sorry, but I have not got good news about the project "Information Technology". The author might write a work informing a broad audience. Instead of this he is trying, according to his own words, to write a top scientific work. Of course he has not got for this purpose sufficient conditions and peace. I told him that he cannot receive any support for the future, because he didn't keep several terms we had agreed upon. I can't say at all for the time being, when he will be able to finish his work.'[56] Later that year the project was abandoned.

A proposal which Müller had presented to the Foundation at the same time as the information technology handbook project met with greater success. Headed 'Technics and Politics (Videorecorder in Czechoslovakia)', it concerned the potential of the video machine which, in 1985, was just starting to be known in Czechoslovakia. The Foundation had sent its first machine to the Müllers in April 1985, ostensibly as a gift from Broňa's mother Anna Koutná, then living in Paris. In December 1985 Müller wrote in his proposal: 'Private ownership of this technique has been legalized. Certainly it is not typical for totalitarian regimes. Before production or import of any consumer goods are permitted, their consequences for society control must be considered by Party.'[57] He continued: 'The existing import of films and TV programmes, which Czechoslovak state monopolizes, is subordinated to political purposes, corresponding to the way relations between politics and culture are understood in a totalitarian state. Due to this fact, a great number of artistic and documentary films of high quality is excluded from import. These are programmes, which, in spite of having no relations to the political realities in Czechoslovakia or associated countries, are considered to be unsuitable from political point of view just because they cannot be used successfully for political purposes (art must serve policy of Party!).... It is necessary to realize how wide range of programmes is excluded from import.... This import control does not concern only the import from the West, it concerns equally import from Jugoslavia, Hungary and Poland.'[58]

Müller foresaw that the availability of the private video

machine would change all this. Although only blank video-cassettes could be purchased in Czechoslovakia (the propaganda apparatus had not even thought to manufacture any of its own), the authorities would be unable to keep a check on privately imported cassettes, which could circulate with ease among owners of video machines. 'The only, but temporary barrier is the high price of video-recorders (average yearly salary) and unsufficient interconnection between west offer and east demand for artistic and documentary programmes.'[59] Müller envisaged a number of families in different parts of Moravia establishing 'home cinemas', with the circulation of video-cassettes imported by the Foundation. After overcoming some reservations, the JHEF provided four videoplayers as well as a portable TV which made it possible to show films and docu-mentaries at a number of venues. One of the 'cinemas' was loca-ted at the home of the Pospíšils; around 30 people gathered every Tuesday evening, and the programme was changed monthly. The audience was much wider than that for the semin-ars. Pospíšil remembers that it was usual in the late 1980s for the few people fortunate enough to own a video-recorder to invite friends and neighbours to watch programmes recorded from Austrian or Polish television. What was important was the Foundation's choice of videos.

Every visiting messenger and lecturer took in two or three or more video-cassettes — the latest feature films, classics and documentaries (for example, on Honda, U.S. space research and the Falklands war) — the selection was eclectic, sometimes based on requests from Brno, sometimes on the Foundation's judgment. Some were of political significance, such as Polish Solidarity's *Workers of 1980* (a request from Petr Oslzlý, which the Foundation eventually obtained in Paris), but most were a-political in content (requests in April 1986 included *Amadeus*, *Easy Rider*, *La Règle du Jeu* and *West Side Story* as well as *1984*). In August 1986 Stock reported: 'They would like to get films of the Czech 'new wave' in the 1960s as well as Hungarian and Polish films of which they know nothing... He [Müller] says that the Jan Hus Foundation is the only source for serious films for the whole black market. It will be dominated by such western films with great speed due to the desperate need for quality films. The translation work they do seems to be quite admirable.'[60] Although in September 1986 Müller asked Stock for more German films, most were in English, and more translators were recruited to translate the dialogue. (One of the most important translators of these video films was Rita Klímová, who became the first post-revolutionary Czechoslovak Ambassador to the United States of America. She used to show the Foundation's videos — which included a biography of Friedrich von Hayek — to her circle in Prague, a circle which included future Prime Minister Václav Klaus.) At first the translations were recorded and played alongside the showing of the film; later, the computer specialists started working on subtitling technology. No one in Brno ever asked the Foundation for a fee for such work, or for interpreting the seminars or translating samizdat; it was all done as their contribution towards a civic society.

An associated project involved the purchase of a video-camera. In June 1987 Müller gave the messenger James de Candole detailed instructions on what model to buy, and how it could be legally imported. The most important project for which the camera was used was the recording of interviews with writers, artists and personalities who, under the totalitarian regime, were forbidden to publish or circulate their work; after 1989 the project was expanded to record the experiences of those whose lives had been damaged or destroyed under forty years of Communism.

Jiří Müller is convinced that the Foundation's institution of a regular messenger service was vital to the success of the Brno seminars and other activities, even though it initially met with opposition from some of the Trustees. When the seminars first started, Müller used to meet and de-brief the lecturers, but he soon realised the drawbacks of this procedure. The Foundation had worked by this method in Prague, and in some cases the academics had adapted themselves with great élan, successfully carrying out highly complicated tasks. In other cases failures had occurred when the lecturer, unnerved by the foreign and potentially hostile environment, had confused his or her instructions. It was, considered Müller, unfair to burden a distinguished specialist with a 'shopping list', and a waste of expertise should he or she be searched and refused a visa for the future. It could also bring danger on Petr Oslzlý, should the secret police be watching.

It is not clear how the first proposal for a messenger service originated; it was not mentioned during Jessica Douglas-Home's meeting with Jiří Müller in September 1985,[61] but in a letter from Müller to Douglas-Home in December he wrote: 'John [Keane] will give you the exact details dealing with your friend's visit, which should be realized in January.'[62] A few days later Keane reported: 'The proposal for a messenger was greeted with great enthusiasm, and I therefore took the liberty of arranging time and date of the first such visit.'[63] According to an Executive Committee meeting held on 21st December: 'Brno have requested an independent messenger service, and asked if the first courier could arive on Jan 10. The meeting agreed that it could not confirm a permanent and regular service, but that it would do its best to fulfil needs.'[64] In January the Management Committee observed: 'A large item of expenditure. Six a year would amount to £2000 for Brno alone. Yet see the emphasis in all recent reports for keeping the two functions separate. Look into the possibility of pooling resources with AJH and of operating from Vienna. Agreed that the JHEF would try to do what it could but without commitment.'[65] By October however it is clear that a commitment had to be made, as Roger Scruton is reported as pressing for the two-monthly service, whilst the meeting sanctioned only a three-monthly service. A Prague service was discussed: it was agreed not to set up a regular service but to empower Scruton and Day to send up to three messengers a year.

The first messenger to Brno was Dennis O'Keeffe, lecturer in the department of education at the Polytechnic of North London. Future messengers were not academics but students and young people who in some cases (but not necessarily) had a knowledge of Czechoslovakia. The most frequent visitor was Roger Scruton's PhD student from London University, James de Candole, who made four visits as a messenger to Brno as well as being the Foundation's first visitor to Slovakia, and initiating contacts with the young opposition in Prague.

Müller understood why some trustees of the Jan Hus Foundation were reluctant to spend large sums of money on the messenger service, which could not strictly be considered an academic or cultural activity, and which raised the potential danger of the Foundation being accused of political or illegal activities. He appreciated their agreement all the more. The results were unprecedented: from 1984 to 1989 the Jan Hus Foundation and the Brno network created a unique cooperation across the frontiers of a totalitarian regime. Unsuspected, they established an independent programme of consistent work, organisationally secured and with different thematic elements, combining long-term projects with continual expansion into new areas — an operation which ran for five unbroken years.

France, Germany and Moravia

Whilst working with the British, Jiří Müller had learnt about the French Association Jan Hus, and recognised an opportunity to initiate a parallel seminar focused on French philosophy. The hosts he chose for this seminar were older than the Oslzlýs and more deeply involved in dissident activities. At the start of the German occupation in 1939 Milan Jelínek had been a young man still looking forward to university; he became an active worker in the underground and was imprisoned from May 1944 to the end of the war. After the war he studied linguistics at the Masaryk University in Brno and in the 1960s spent a year at the Sorbonne in Paris. From the end of the war until 1968 he and his second wife Jana (also a French specialist) were Party members, active reform Communists. During normalisation, like thousands of others, they were expelled from the Party and the university and forced to accept low-status jobs. In 1976, with the release from prison of their former colleague and fellow-Party member Jaroslav Šabata, they met Jiří Müller and become involved in samizdat activities; at first as distributors of the Petlice editions (the samizdat operation run by Ludvík Vaculík from Prague) and later as translators (Jelínek also worked on his own linguistic studies). Šabata was one of the most active dissidents in the country; his daughter Anna (also known as Hanička and as Anča) married Petr Uhl, one of those gaoled with Havel in 1979. Jaroslav Šabata was the organiser of the 'unofficial' Moravian Club (M-klub), which Milan Jelínek joined as a member. From 1978 the M-klub met regularly at different venues to hold discussions on political themes. After 1989, Jelínek and Šabata discovered that there had been three informers among their members, but that they had been thoughtfully selective about the information they passed on to the police. The police would have liked to make an informer of Milan; on three occasions he was called in for gentle persuasion. On the third occasion, in 1982, he was warned that if he persisted in his refusal to cooperate (which he did) they would make it difficult, if not impossible, for his sons to go on to higher education.

The Jelíneks had also been involved in Brno literary evenings with writers such as Jan Skácel or Milan Uhde, or visitors from Prague — Ivan Klíma or Eva Kantůrková. In October 1985, when the British seminars had already been under way for a year, Jiří Müller brought to the Jelíneks two visitors from France, Olivier Mongin and Jean-Claude Eslin. Eslin had studied the work of Jan Patočka in Paris; both of them were editors of the philosophy journal *Esprit*, a review of the noncommunist Left, for which Paul Ricoeur was the most influential writer. They had already made several visits to Prague, beginning in 1982, where they had lectured for seminars held by Hejdánek, Kučera and Rezek. They were impressed by the way the Jelíneks had handled the changes in their life, and by their courage and good humour; Eslin noted that absurd conditions can produce good results. Although they did not lecture on that occasion, Eslin and Mongin were to make two more visits to Brno, in 1987 and 1988. They also arranged for the first seminar to be held at the home of the Jelíneks, by Jean-Michel Besnier in May 1986.

Besnier arrived in Brno the weekend when news of the Chernobyl disaster was beginning to emerge. One of the main features which struck him about the seminar gathering was its isolation from events in the wider world; the participants knew little about Chernobyl and did not seem inclined to ask. His subject was Roland Barthes on language, work which related to Jelínek's language studies: 'Without language there is no liberty.' However, he gained the impression that it was more important for him to listen than to be heard; his presence enabled the group to explain themselves, to find reasons for the conditions under which they lived: 'It was as though if they didn't talk they didn't exist.'[1] Besnier's visit passed without incident, but subsequently the interpreter was interrogated. Nathalie Roussarie, making her first visit to Brno later that month, was taken off the bus at the Austrian border, questioned and forced to leave books and videos with the border guards (some but not all of these were returned on her return journey). She was allowed to continue in the commandeered car of a surprised and curious Austrian couple, arriving in Brno late that night.

The seminar by Besnier was followed in October 1986 by a visit from the young couple André Enégren and Claude Habibe, proposed by Olivier Mongin. Both had prepared papers, but there was only time for half of Enégren's paper — on philosopher Hannah Arendt — since, as at Besnier's seminar, most of the time was taken by debate about the application of philosophy to Czechoslovakia, and the devastation of intellectual thought in the country. Milan Jelínek noted in his diary that there was a lively discussion about the translation of the term 'common sense'. They were followed in January 1987 by Miguel Abensour who, when he told the group that he would be lecturing on Utopias, was told that they were 'fed up with Utopias'. He explained that his theme was Levinas' concept of Utopia, and not the socialist Utopia of the Communists.

For the next three years visitors from the Association Jan Hus arrived regularly at intervals of six to eight weeks (as with the English-speaking seminar, no sessions were held between visits). As in Prague, the visitors covered the range of French philosophy. The Jelíneks remember that conflict arose between the French and the Czechs only during the visit of the French Jesuit and philosopher Pierre-Jean Labarrière, who also gave a second seminar for the Dominican study group. The liberal theology of the westerner was out of tune with the more conservative and traditional approach of Roman Catholics behind the Iron Curtain. The first public lecture for the Association Jan Hus took place in May 1989, with the visit of Alain Finkielkraut, who lectured on 'Heidegger and France' at the Arts Faculty of the Masaryk University. It was an exciting occasion, at which he introduced the names of those who had been unmentionable for the past twenty years — Jan Patočka, Ludvík Vaculík and Milan Kundera.

Communication between Paris and Brno took place by the post-card 'week + 1' method — that is, an innocuous post card would mention a date, but the visitor would always arrive exactly one week earlier than the given date. Most French visitors used the same route as the British, flying to Vienna and taking the bus to Brno. There would be around ten to twenty participants in the seminar, fluctuating round a core of regular attenders, all of them friends of the Jelínek family. The majority were secondary school teachers,[2] but the group included personalities such as the poet Jan Skácel.[3] The French philosopher of Brazilian origin, Maria Petit, with her husband Jean Luc Petit visited both Prague and Brno in September 1989. She remembers that they found the Brno group lively and open-minded in comparison with the group of students to whom she spoke in Prague, who struck her as depressed and complaining.

As in the case of the Oslzlý seminar, the Jelíneks always prepared the same explanation for the presence of the visiting lecturers. In this case, the explanation was that Milan had known the visiting professor whilst he was at the Sorbonne in the 1960s, and that they were using the opportunity of his (or her) visit to pass on news of what was happening in French philosophy. Even should anyone suspect anything different, there was no other information they could pass on to the police. Although the arrangements were similar to those for the seminar run by the Oslzlý family, some students were more evidently from the 'ghetto'. The line was often difficult to draw, and caused some heart-searching; Pavel Barša, for example, used to attend both seminars. One of his fellow students at the French seminar was a Charter signatory; when Barša brought him to the English seminar, the organisers had to make the decision as to whether the presence of a Charter signatory might not draw too much attention to this seminar and endanger the future of those who were still not in any way involved with the dissident world.[4]

It is possible, but not certain, that whereas the British seminar maintained its secrecy, the French seminar was known to the police — probably because the Jelíneks and their circle were already closely watched. Unlike the British, the French travellers were searched far more often than the British, although they were frequently able to smuggle in books and videos by leaving them in plastic bags and picnic baskets under their seat in the bus. (Bernard Fabre, however, successfully delivered a large suitcase of books.) Not only Roussarie, but also the philosopher Yves Geffroy was taken off the bus at the border; he completed the journey in a Polish van, which dropped him on the motorway and left him to hitchhike into Brno. The Jelíneks' telephone was tapped; on one occasion a samizdat translator found herself in difficulties as a result of an incautious reference. The inhabitants of their block of flats were loyal, and did not speak to the police; but in July 1989 the StB gained access to an empty flat below and installed listening equipment. It was removed on 26th November 1989.

If the British, French and Dutch became an established part of the underground philosophy seminars in Prague and Brno in the early 1980s, then it seems strange that the same thing did not happen in the case of the Germans and Austrians,[5] so closely linked geographically and historically. Less than a century earlier German had been the language of government, business and society in Prague and Brno, and as recently as the 1930s Brno had been, to a large extent, a German-speaking city. Even though the Sudeten German population was expelled after the war, German language remained a second language for many of the older generation. Much of the educational system followed (and still follows) the German model. The Czech and Slovak study of philosophy has inherited many German traditions and elements. In July 1981 the American philosopher Richard Rorty suggested to Hejdánek that he might be able to arrange for visitors from Heidelberg; Hejdánek: '...seemed to like the idea. He seemed to regret that they had none but Englishmen and Americans and Frenchmen, and seemed to wonder where all the Germans were.'[6] Rorty, however, 'anticipate[d] some resistance, since it is somehow a worse thing for a German academic to get his name in the papers as having been flung out of a country than it is for us Anglo-Saxons.'[7] (In September 'Hejdánek wondered whether some of the difficulties for the Germans might not be of a psychological order.)[8] It was partly as a result of Rorty's efforts that a visit by Jürgen Habermas and Ernst Tugendhat[9] took place in March 1982; Habermas gave one seminar; Tugendhat gave one for Rezek and one for Hejdánek. He noted that there were two policemen stationed at Hejdánek's flat, but otherwise the visit passed without incident. However, the occasion remained an isolated event.

In October 1984 the British Foundation decided that Ralph Walker of Magdalen in Oxford, organiser of the Kant seminars held by Petr Rezek, should approach Jürgen Mittelstrass about setting up a German trust. Walker diligently corresponded with other leading German philosophers — Dieter Henrich, Willi Vorsenkühl, Rolf Hastman — with the two aims of involving them in the visiting programme and of founding a 'Jan-Hus-Stiftung'. (Their involvement was still being pursued in 1989, when Walker reported to the JHEF Management Committee that Professor Wolfgang Carl was expecting to hear from Wolfgang Stock.) From the British point of view, it did not seem unreasonable to expect German visitors to travel the short distance by land instead of flying in British philosophers for 'tourist weekends'. But as Jürgen Mittelstrass pointed out in his reply to Walker in January 1985, there was no tradition in Germany of such charitable foundations as the Jan Hus.[10]

It was the Oxford connection which led to the organisation of what became de facto the 'German Jan Hus'. In autumn 1984 Wolfgang Stock, a student of history and international law at Würzburg University, escaped from his extra-curricular activities for a period of concentrated study at University College, Oxford. He had since 1977 been involved in sending support to Communist countries — first to East Germany (as a co-founder of the Brüsewitz-Zentrum) and then to Poland. Since the declaration of martial law in Poland in December 1981 Stock had, with friends and support from the International Society of Human Rights, been leading convoys of trucks across East Germany to church centres in Poland. Concealed amongst the shipments of permitted humanitarian aid were equipment and literature smuggled in for Solidarity leaders.

It was not long before Stock's contacts in Solidarity put him in touch with the Polish-oriented Jagiellonian Trust in Britain, which shared with the Jan Hus Foundation several founders (including Roger Scruton and Kathy Wilkes) and a similar mission. This led, in early 1985, to Stock making his first visit to Prague. He visited several personalities active in samizdat and the seminars: Pavel Bratinka, Václav Benda, Ladislav Hejdánek, Radim Palouš, Rudolf Kučera, Petr Rezek and Petr Pithart. In August 1986 Stock made another visit whilst on honeymoon with his co-worker Oriana (née von Lehsten). This visit was to Jiří Müller in Brno (who also took him to meet the Jelíneks), and marked the beginning of active German involvement. In a last moment crisis in September, Oriana Stock took the place of a British messenger to Brno who had unexpectedly informed the Foundation he could not travel; in November her brother acted as a courier to Prague; in March 1987 Marie von Spee drove to Brno with the first computer supplied by the British to Jiří Müller; and in April Stock went to Brno again himself. It is also noted in the October 1986 Minutes of the Foundation that: 'the two parcels of Heidegger[11] had arrived in Munich during the summer, and Wolfgang Stock should be getting them to Prague any time now.'[12] One major project in which Stock became involved was the Brno samizdat technology programme.

The year 1987 also saw the start of regular visits by German lecturers to the underground seminars, organised by Wolfgang Stock. Although the first visit, by Professor Alma von Stockhausen, was to Petr Rezek's seminar in Prague,[13] the programme concentrated on Brno. The themes of the seminars were planned in co-operation with Milan Jelínek, the host for the French visitors, but the lectures were held at the home of Jaroslav Blažke, a secondary school teacher, and his wife Marie. The programme was essentially different from the philosophy programme organised by Petr Oslzlý and the Jan Hus Foundation trustees, Müller and Jelínek giving priority to themes connected with constitutionalism and human rights. The first visitor, in December 1987, was Magdalena Kaufmann of the International Society for Human Rights. The Jelíneks remember that initially there was some surprise that, rather than the academic visitor to which they were accustomed, Kaufmann was an activist. She noted that the most unexpected issue to be raised in the discussion concerned the right to return to one's own country after an absence. Several of the participants in the seminar were, she observed, surprised that such a meeting and discussion with a representative of the ISHR could even take place.

Further visits followed in the spring of 1988; in August, the law student and activist Alexander von Bischoffshausen[14] lectured on West German federalism and noted that Jelínek's group was studying constitutional questions. Jelínek, he reported, seemed optimistic about developments, and drew comparisons with the reform Communism of 1968. In

December Elisabeth von Werthern, managing director of the Club of German Parliamentarians in Bonn, spoke on German parliamentary traditions. The programme continued through 1989, culminating in October with a visit from Bernd Posselt,[15] a visit which Stock had discussed with Müller as early as September 1987. At that time Posselt was the vice-chairman responsible for central and eastern Europe in the international presidency of the Pan European Union, and had made a number of visits to Poland and Hungary which had given him an opportunity to meet European-minded Czechs and Slovaks. Posselt's family was originally Sudeten German, and he still had relations in northern Bohemia whom he had last been able to visit in 1979.

The Paneuropa movement, in which Stock also played a major part (himself speaking to the Brno seminar on European integration), was at this time spreading rapidly in Central and Eastern Europe. The network had connections with the underground church, and with people such as Rudolf Kučera, publisher of the samizdat journal *Střední Evropa*, whom Stock had first visited in 1985 and whom Posselt was to meet on the continuation of his journey from Brno to Prague. In Brno Posselt gave two seminars — one in German at the home of Jaroslav and Marie Blažke, the other in English at the home of Petr and Eva Oslzlý; he also spent half a day with Milan Jelínek, discussing the history of the First Republic. At both the seminars he addressed three main themes — the collapse of Communism, European integration and the European Parliament, and Czech-German relations. He remembers that only a few of the students could bring themselves to believe that they were living in the last days of Communism; Posselt, however, brought them information that had not yet reached Czechoslovakia, still isolated in comparison with Poland and Hungary. He told them, for example, of his visit to Budapest the previous month in company with Otto von Habsburg, president of Paneuropa, when von Habsburg had addressed an audience of Hungarians at a public meeting. The Czechs found this extraordinary, and discussed at length the situation developing in Hungary.

In his organisation of the German-language seminar in Brno, Stock did not entirely follow the wishes of the 'parent' Jan Hus Foundation in Britain in that he never initiated the foundation of a 'Jan-Hus-Stiftung'. He found a more pragmatic alternative by (in April 1987) enlarging the Academia Copernicana e.V., established in February 1985 for work in East Germany and Poland, to include Czechoslovakia. Nor, to Ralph Walker's disappointment, did the German philosophers become involved in the Brno seminars, although Stock had made some attempts to contact them in 1988. These seminars of the late 1980s rode on a new wave of German thought and action; not that of traditional academic contacts, but of a European movement which saw the countries of the former Habsburg lands as being part of the same Central Europe, and which looked forward to a time when European integration would include the countries still trapped behind the Iron Curtain.

Music, Art and Literature

Moravia is a land to itself, and the haunting wildness of its folk music is a world away from the pretty, dancing melodies of Bohemia. The Moravian countryside had its own tradition of music-making, stemming from the times when every village had its own kantor who was both schoolmaster and musician. Brno is a musical city, the home of Leoš Janáček whose pupils' pupils are themselves music teachers at the Janáček Academy of Performing Arts. It was not surprising when in autumn 1985 a message came from the Brno seminar, asking the British to become involved in a music programme.[1]

It was not the first occasion on which the Foundation had concerned itself with musical life in Czechoslovakia. In autumn 1981 Roger Scruton met in London Mirka Zemanová of Early Music, who made several suggestions of areas in Czech music with which the Foundation might concern itself; one of them involved Michal Kocáb[2], the son of the dissident protestant priest and seminar leader Alfréd Kocáb. From October 1981 onwards requests were received for support for the Prague composer Karel Sklenička; and in October 1984 Pius (Karel Palek) sent from Prague a report on the state of contemporary Czech serious music, which the Foundation commissioned Petr Rezek's former student Karel Hubka, now living in London, to translate. The report summarised the roles of the different official organisations involved in serious music and concluded that 'without party membership it is neither possible to reach any significant function in the music institution nor to play any major role on the musical scene. It is a condition sine qua non even for such positions like the musical publisher and the music school teacher. Surveyance over the performing, assessing and payments awarding of the prevailant majority of Czech serious music is carried through by the responsible ideological department of the Communist Party. The only thing which cannot be prevented by the party is that new works of art might arise and be performed abroad.'[3] (The report also noted that 'some exceptions from the above rule can be explained by the fact that the functionaries of the above institutions are to a great extent corrupt.'[4])

The request from Brno was welcomed by the Foundation, and it did not have to look far for a British composer. In 1984 Roger Scruton had published an article in *The Times* about his discoveries in a run-down second-hand music shop in the centre of Prague: 'Behind a dirty window papered with dust-jackets and record sleeves lies a single room, with an adjoining sanctum. The shelves that line this room are piled high with bound editions of the classics: piano sonatas, opera scores, chamber music of every kind, lieder and folk song; even (just occasionally) the full score of a symphonic masterpiece.'[5] The article attracted a response from David Matthews, a classics scholar turned composer, who had worked for three years as assistant to Benjamin Britten, collaborated on the Performing Version of Mahler's Tenth Symphony, and written a considerable body of work himself. Scruton now rang Matthews to ask how he felt about visiting the underground university. It was to be Matthews' third visit to Czechoslovakia — but, he recalls, very different from the first two. He set out on 23rd January 1986 with doubts and anxieties; but remembers his first meeting with Petr Oslzlý as being an overwhelming experience. He describes Oslzlý as being the prototype of the central European intellectual, combining an incredible seriousness of purpose with the warmth of friendship, family life and a close community. He found in Brno an independent musical life, flourishing in spite of censorship.

Matthews' first Brno seminar lasted for six hours; he talked on two subjects, Mahler's Tenth Symphony and contemporary English music, to an audience of around 35 made up of both the regular students and Brno musicians and composers — whom he was surprised to find already knew some of his work. As part of the programme Matthews left behind books, scores, and cassette tapes of 32 pieces, and listened to the works of contemporary Czech composers. He was able to follow in the tracks of two Moravian-born composers who were very important to him: Leoš Janáček and Gustav Mahler. Matthews travelled with Oslzlý and Pospišíl to Mahler's birthplace, the village of Kaliště in the Vysočina where Mahler's father once kept the inn. This inn, rebuilt after a fire in 1937, was still kept by 'a marvellous old peasant woman who with great animation produced sheaves of cuttings and photographs for us to see'.[6] At the Music Information Centre back in Brno, Alena Němcová played for him the first-ever recording of Janáček's Danube symphony, recently reconstructed by the Brno musicologist Miloš Štědroň: 'it must have been more problematic than the Mahler Tenth as the ms. is virtually illegible.'[7]

In the same way as Oslzlý and his colleagues were engaged in pushing back the barriers in Brno, in narrowing the gulf between the 'official' and the 'unofficial', so the Foundation resolved to follow suit. The music programme presented the perfect opportunity. In 1985 Barbara Day had organised a festival of Czech culture through Bristol University, with the primary aim of bringing Petr Oslzlý's Theatre on a String to Britain as part of the cultural agreement between the British and Czechoslovak governments. She now made use of her contacts (without mention of the Foundation) by inviting the Czechoslovak Cultural Attaché Líbor Telecký to meet David Matthews in Jessica Douglas-Home's home in Notting Hill Gate.[8] The meeting took place on 7th July 1986. Telecký was accompanied by an official of the Embassy's visa department who was assumed to be a member of the secret police — a matter of protocol foreseen by Douglas-Home and Day, who had made a point of inviting him to 'bring a colleague'. At the time it was assumed that the Czechoslovak secret police was unaware of the Foundation's existence, or at least of Douglas-Home and Day's involvement; this was only partly true, but no damage seems to have been done. As a result of the meeting Matthews was invited as an official guest to the October 1986 Brno International Music Festival, and Jiří Müller is convinced that the smooth running of the music programme was in part due to this initial vetting by the Embassy. Matthews, indisputable prestige in the international world of music, and his 'clean' record vis-à-vis Czechoslovakia must also have played a major role.[9]

Miroslav Pospíšil took advantage of the 'officially correct' nature of Matthews' visit to invite him to give the inaugural lecture at the newly-created English Club. Matthews spoke on 'The Englishness of English Music' to an audience of over a hundred — the largest yet for any of the Foundation's lectures. The fact that Matthews was now a guest of the Ministry of Culture enabled Oslzlý and Pospíšil to use their contacts in the radio and press, who conducted innocuous but useful interviews. In an interview with J. Kuchtová[10] published in *Svobodné slovo*, Matthews owned that: '...through Mahler something of the Czech countryside got into my music. And the chief among Czech music-makers is Janáček. *Kaťa* was the first opera I ever heard in the theatre. But to see it here in your country is a fantastic experience.'[11] On his return Matthews wrote about the festival for *The Independent*, devoting nearly a third of the article to 'the most exciting new event',[12] Theatre on a String's Ballet Macabre, in which Oslzlý had used Brecht's *Arturo Ui* to highlight certain universal aspects of totalitarian regimes.

On this occasion, some of the Foundation's 'underground' agenda had been undertaken by the composer Nigel Osborne, who joined Matthews for the last five days of his stay. Osborne, more experienced than Matthews in travel behind the Iron Curtain, began his visit in Prague with a meeting with Jaroslav Kořán,[13] and during the second weekend in October gave a seminar for around 20 composers and musicians in Oslzlý's flat: 'I talked about different faces of post-modernism in British music, and tried to encourage debate by provo-Socratic methods (I'm not sure how well this went down!).'[14] Both Osborne and Matthews encoded or memorised the usual load of messages concerning books and other printed materials, videos ('Mikin reported that his dubbed translation of *Doctor Zhivago* had been well received'), potential visiting lecturers, and special projects concerning the Theatre on a String and scholarships for young composers. One important subject was the impending trial of the Jazz Section committee; it was in discussions between Oslzlý, Matthews and Osborne that the first idea of an international petition of musicians was born.

Osborne concluded his report: '...I would like to tell you how impressed I am with the work you are doing. As someone who has been familar with aspects of life in the other half of Europe for some time, I feel it is extremely useful and exactly right. The circle of people you support in Brno is one of value and principle.

'I was most grateful for the care and hospitality of Mikin and Petr. Also I feel you have an excellent ambassador in David, who clearly enjoys considerable trust there, and embraces the situation with real sympathy and intelligence.'[15]

For David Matthews, one of the most useful results of his two-week visit was the opportunity to hear so much music by Brno composers: 'I have a clearer idea of the Janáček tradition which is still very much alive for the middle and younger generations. The outstanding composer is clearly Miloslav Ištvan,[16] who has adopted a number of Janáček's techniques but has created out of them his own highly individual style. Ištvan and his fellow teachers at the Janáček Academy, notably Alois Pinoš, have passed on the tradition to the younger generation. One of Ištvan's outstanding pupils is Pavel Novák. I visited him at his home and talked at length with him; his mother, who speaks English well, acting as interpreter. I was able to reassure him of my conviction that the tradition deriving from Janáček is still valid in Brno, and that the isolation from the West that most composers there feel is not such a bad thing as it might seem. By being restricted in their exposure to new music they've at least avoided some of the dangers of eclecticism, and even more, fashion.'[17]

Matthews returned from Brno with the determination to present some of the work by Brno composers, especially 'unlicensed' composers in Britain: 'I should like to put on a concert of music for oboe, cello and piano, next spring or summer, possibly at the October Gallery in Bloomsbury. I am also writing to the King's Lynn Festival to see if they would be interested in including this concert next year as a companion to Theatre on a String... At the moment I have scores of two very good pieces for oboe, cello and piano by Pavel Novák and 'Peter Graham',[18] three piano pieces by Graham, a piano piece by Michal Košut and a sonata for cello and piano by Ištvan. Alena Němcová is bringing with her more scores and some tapes in November, including a solo cello piece and a trio by František Emmert, who is probably the most 'advanced' composer in Brno, and oboe and piano pieces by Parsch and Košut. There should be more than enough material here for a concert. William Howard[19] of the Schubert Ensemble has agreed in principle to be the pianist, and we are looking for an oboist and a cellist (we have ideas).'[20] From this point onwards Matthews' work with his Brno colleagues proceeded in several parallel lines: the first was a continuation of the Brno music seminars; the second, the promotion of British composers in Brno; and the third, the promotion of concerts in Britain featuring the works of Brno composers. (A fourth line was his work on behalf of the Jazz Section, in which he concealed his name in order not to draw attention to the Brno link.) British composers who visited Brno included, as well as Matthews and Osborne, Gordon Crosse (March 1988); Judith Weir and Anthony Powers (September-October 1988); Michael Berkeley (December 1988); and Simon Bainbridge (February 1989). (For a long time it was hoped that Sir Michael Tippett would visit the Brno seminar, but this was never realised.)

The first success in promoting Brno composers came with the King's Lynn Festival in July 1987, which was based on a Czech theme. Matthews and Howard with Melinda Maxwell (oboe) and Jane Salmon (cello) presented a programme of music from Brno which included new works by Košut, Emmert, Graham, Ištvan and Novák, as well as Janáček's Sonata '1.x.1905'. In March 1988 Matthews and the Schubert Ensemble secured the Purcell Room in London for a concert in which three works by Michal Košut, Peter Graham and Pavel Novák were repeated, and Miloslav Ištvan's 'Canzona for alto flute, cor anglais, cello and piano' given its British premiere. Košut's 'World of Jan Zrzavý' was inspired by the work of the Czech surrealist painter; Novák's 'Garden of Delights' was based on Hieronymous Bosch; whilst Graham wrote of his 'Dumky' that 'the title refers to Dvořák, but the music refers rather to the terms of traditional Japanese aesthetics and to a silent meditation.'[21] *The Independent* critic Bayan Northcott described the 'striking play of the simplest elements — modal lines and declamatory figures isolated in washes of piano resonance'[22] in 'Dumky'. The 'Canzona' was described by Matthews as showing 'Ištvan's lighter, more whimsical side',[23] whilst Northcott wrote that it 'sometimes got trapped in minimalistic patterns — but the provenance of these seemed more like Janáček than Steve Reich.'[24] Northcott concluded: 'Whether or not Mr. Matthews was hinting that *avant gardistes* nearer home would do well to take the lesson to heart, the way all this music found fresh, unpretentious things to do with accessible materials was a distinct plus — together with its common lucidity of texture.'[25] The trio later recorded the programme for the BBC.

Howard, Salmon and Maxwell also performed at the Second Brno Biennial Festival of Contemporary Music, which coincided with the visit to Brno of Weir, Powers and Matthews[26] to Brno in autumn 1988; music by Ištvan, Novák, Graham and Matthews was performed in the Festival. 'Characteristically,' wrote Matthews, 'Petr [Oslzlý] had organized an unofficial fringe festival at the same time as the main festival. This took place in the Academic Club near the university, which was turned into a temporary art gallery, with a big totemic sculpture by Šimek in the centre. The atmosphere was evocative of the 1960s. Peter called his festival 'Dialogues', and arranged a series of evening events, each one dedicated to one of the arts. ...at the music dialogue on 4 October... there were performances of my Aria for violin and piano, Three Studies for solo violin and Duet Variations for flute and piano, interspersed with taped performances of pieces by Radoslav Ištvan, Michal Košut (an electronic piece) and Pavel Novák. Petr, the three Brno composers, Mikin [Pospíšil] and I sat round a central table, drinking cups of tea — a gesture towards England. We all introduced our pieces and there was a certain amount of 'dialogue' between us, prompted by Petr, though sadly none involving the (largely young) audience who were perhaps too polite to say what they thought of my music: did they find it too old-fashioned, I wonder? The evening ended in true ICA style with a Japanese dancer, Min Tanaka, performing a slow, mesmerising dance to improvised piano music by Ivo Medek.'[27]

One of the mutual interests which preoccupied Matthews and Oslzlý was the early life of Gustav Mahler. Matthews' first lecture in Brno had been on the reconstruction of Mahler's 10th Symphony, in which he had been involved; and the scenes of Mahler's early life in the Vysočina highlands were not far from Eva Oslzlá's home village. With the Foundation's provision of a video-camera in August 1987, the idea of making a documentary film became a concrete possibility. In the August of 1989, Matthews, Oslzlý and Pospíšil travelled to Kaliště with the cameraman Aleš Záboj. They were joined by a local teacher, Jiří Rychetský, who (Pospíšil remembers) 'was the best-informed and most active Mahlerite in the country... (he) took us to every cross, house, bridge, linden tree, stream and grove associated with Mahler's life and music'.[28] The loquacious old lady who kept the Mahlers' pub was still there: 'She is a tiny woman of 75 who talks non-stop in a high, complaining voice. She took no notice at all of the camera, and obviously enjoys her fame as the curator of Mahler's birthplace (she talks of him as if he were a son).'[29] The group continued to Jihlava, where they filmed the distillery which Mahler's father later ran, and the apartment which the family occupied and the salon of the Hotel Czap where some of Mahler's earliest compositions were played. The Hotel Czap had turned into a 'run-down pub and community centre' and, wrote Matthews, the 'salon too will soon disappear, as the building is about to be turned into a post office and the salon divided up into offices'. They also filmed the surrounding countryside, Mahler's two schools, 'the site of the synagogue (destroyed by local Nazis in 1939) and the Jewish cemetery (also ransacked by the Nazis and much overgrown; we were unable to find the grave of Mahler's parents)'.[30] The documentary material still exists on video; Matthews approached several television companies who refused to work with it on the grounds that the technical equipment used was inferior to their standards. A number of the buildings filmed by Matthews and the Brno team (including the Mahler family's distillery and apartment) have since been demolished.

The Foundation's music programme had a higher profile than the art, theatre or literature programmes. With good will on both sides, the links between the official and unofficial became increasingly blurred. By the time of the velvet revolution, the music programme had become one of the most successful in finding its own feet.

In the field of the visual arts, independent, 'unofficial' art flourished in Czechoslovakia in the 1980s, but was seen by few beyond the circle of those who knew where to find it. Many of the young artists involved were 'unlicensed' — that meant, in practical terms, that they were not allowed to earn their living as artists, but had to be employed in some other work to avoid being accused of 'parasitism'. The criteria for their acceptance were not based on artistic quality, but on their political views, and on whether they joined the Youth Union or the Communist Party. (The ban did not necessarily prevent them from selling their work, even abroad if this were possible, but such sales were heavily taxed.) Most of them attempted to find some congenial and undemanding work which gave them the greatest possible opportunities to pursue their art on a non-commercial basis. Although it was sometimes possible to work as a 'commercial' graphic artist, other types of work would often be manual and low-status; unlike the situation in the West, the teaching profession was absolutely closed to such artists. Little in the way of published material was available on new trends in art, although the Jazz Section did what it could with slim, black-and-white brochures on contemporary Czech and Slovak artists (the Situace series). Otherwise, artists relied on journals brought back by occasional travellers; Western art journals could not normally be bought in Czechoslovakia, and subscriptions were both prohibitively expensive and (by post) unreliable as to delivery. An art book ordered from a western publisher could cost half a month's salary.

This lack of context seriously affected the development of artistic standards. Personal courage and an impeccable moral character were not guarantors of talented work. Without means of comparison, evaluation and open debate, it was difficult for a small, enthusiastic but uneducated public to distinguish between the outstanding and the run-of-the-mill. Artists had no way to measure their achievements except by purely subjective criteria. Exhibitions of their works could be held only in small informal galleries with limited space — corresponding to the 'small theatres' of the time, which were permitted greater freedom than the big theatres simply because fewer people saw their work. Sometimes it was possible surreptitiously to slide an exhibition into the programme of a conference or other semi-public event. 'Unofficial' theatre, art and music often shared the same space, such as (from 1981) the Junior klub Na Chmelnici on the outskirts of Prague. Private studios, apartments, gardens and courtyards also became venues for exhibitions and mixed-media events. Petr Oslzlý had studied art history at the Purkyně

University, and amongst his friends were the graphic artist Rostislav Pospíšil and Joska Skalník of the Jazz Section. He and they believed that these individual and occasional efforts could become something more. At the back of Oslzlý's mind was a nostalgic memory of the colourful and atmospheric little galleries in the lanes of Paris.

This was how the Galerie Zlevěné zboží, translated sometimes as the 'Reduced Price Drugstore Gallery', sometimes as the 'Bargain Basement Gallery', came into existence. It was founded in collusion with the manager of modest premises selling bandages, brooms, toothpastes and soap powders at prices lower than those in normal stores. The gallery opened in November 1986 with an exhibition by Rostislav Pospíšil as 'a concept of free exhibitions in an unfree world'.[31] Over the next three years the work of 20 artists was exhibited. News of the 'private view' of a new exhibition would be circulated by word of mouth; guests would arrive and a formal opening with entertainment take place. The artist being exhibited took on the role of shop assistant, wearing the standard white jacket. Chance customers were also invited to participate. An important part of the ritual was the 'video-portrait', made possible by the Hus Foundation's donation of video camera, video recorder and portable television. After the closing hour, the celebration would continue in the pub in which the Brno branch of the pre-war avant-garde group Devětsil had been inaugurated. Inevitably, the drugstore venue attracted the attention of the secret police, who were however hampered by the need to behave like members of the 'general public' in an open but intimate space. As nothing apparently seditious was taking place, they were reduced to making long deliberations over whether to buy a sticky plaster or a rain hat.

Such informal exhibitions went part way to breaking the artists' isolation. However, the space was limited. In 1987 Miroslav Pospíšil offered his farmhouse in the Sudetenland as a venue for the exhibition of the work of several artists. He remembers that Oslzlý directed it as though it was a theatrical event, whilst Rosťa Pospíšil undertook the stage management, installing the exhibits in the courtyard and orchard of the farmhouse. It was September, an Indian summer. Sixty to eighty people came, many in family groups, and around 30 stayed overnight, sleeping on bundles of straw in the hay loft. The following year the exhibition was even larger, with visitors from as far as Prague. Activities were devised to involve the visitors, such as 'Catching the Sun', devised by Rosťa Pospíšil, in which a network of white threads was woven between the orchard trees.

Petr Oslzlý was concerned not only to give the artists opportunities to show their own work, but also to open up the possibilities of international cooperation. The first step came at the end of September 1985, when Jessica Douglas-Home gave two talks, one on her personal experience as an artist and the other on contemporary British painting. ('It went quite well except that after ten minutes their projector broke down and Petr was extremely grateful for the one I had lugged heavily from England. I left it there.'[32]) A few months later she received a request from Brno, with an outline of the need: 'The paralysing pressure is directed not only against the artists themselves but also against theoretical work, publishing and the presentation of works in public. Even though crude "socialist realism" of the 1950's type is not openly imposed at the moment, the regime suppresses with vehemence any activity in any of the above mentioned spheres which does not fit — either in form or content — the official image of modern socialist art.'[33] The document detailed what was and was not available — 'the books published... (sometimes even translations of Western publications) deal solely with classical art, the only things about contemporary art being a few monographs about state-approved socialist-realist modernists' — and described the efforts being made to combat this isolation. The request was for lectures and debates on contemporary western art accompanied by slides, with the hope that these could be seen not only at the home seminars but also in clubs for audiences of young people. Suggestions included: 'Francis Bacon, David Hockney, Louis de Brocquy and any other interesting painters or 'movements', Henry Moore of course, Anish Kapoor and other sculptors as well as architects. Collections of the Tate Gallery would be very interesting as well as catalogues and other material from exhibitions there and at other places, visual material, documentaries of performances, actions, happenings etc.' The request concluded with the thought that the main result would be 'further reinforcement of the defence against the uniformity and schematism of thought... any such activity... is a specific act of "civil spiritual disobedience" towards a totalitarian regime. It is the sum of all the various and varied acts of this disobedience that, struggling hard, only just manages to maintan a sense of cultural continuity.'[34]

Jessica Douglas-Home returned to Brno in January 1987 to lecture on German expressionism, and to visit the studios of both 'official' and 'unofficial' artists. She was followed by the Oxford artist Helen Ganly, who travelled to a snow-covered Brno at the end of February. She too did the rounds of the studios, and gave two seminars, with slides. The first, on art and artists in Britain, was held as one of the regular series of meetings, with an audience of the usual group as well as artists visiting the seminar for the first time; the second, on her own work, was attended only by artists. The lectures were informative and practical; rather than talk about great figures of British art, Ganly chose to discuss the life of such artists as herself, the pleasures, pains and frustrations of working and exhibiting. She had also brought materials: 'nearly £100 worth of catalogues donated by different people, and although all were appreciated the *Artists' Newsletter* aroused most interest.'[35]

To western eyes, such seminars would seem to be routine and matter-of-course. In Czechoslovakia in the 1980s they were unprecedented. Few artists, apart from those who were officially approved, were able to establish contacts with western colleagues, and in these cases relationships were often tainted by the need to propagate an ideologically correct viewpoint. Ganly's visit led to a series of new contacts and activities, which she saw as a 'true cultural exchange', an opportunity to share ideas and experiences. One new project was an invitation for her to exhibit in the Reduced Price Drugstore Gallery. In December of the same year Ganly set out for Brno with photographs, etchings, and three small collages at the bottom of her case and, casually pushed under her seat on the bus from Vienna (to avoid attention from the border guards), a pink bag full of video cassettes on art.

Ganly records in her report of this second visit a considerable easing of tension in Czechoslovakia in 1987, at least for artists. She arrived on the eve of St Nicholas to find the Oslzlýs'

children and their friends dressed as 'St Niclaus flanked by two
devils and an angel. The smallest children were suitably awed
but it was really only a dress rehearsal for the priest who was
expected later after he had been to the children's ward. He came
very late. Many smaller children had gone home. It was very
moving to know that after so many years he could revive this old
festival and walk freely in the streets with his two angels and his
two devils. He wore his full robes and carried the silver and gold
crook from the church. As we walked home the streets were full
of small scurrying child figures — dressed as priests and devils
— a surreal vision...'[36] Ganly repeated her February talk to the
English Club — '[a] full capacity audience with people standing
at the back... probably 175 people'. The 'private view' was fitted in between visits to more artists' studios and another seminar at the Oslzlýs' home. Ganly described the private view as:
'a brilliant and hilarious occasion, with me dressed in a white
chemist's coat standing behind the counter serving cutprice
goods, a cellist playing solemnly in the middle of the shop floor,
artists coming in, looking at the work, theatre people coming in,
bemused ordinary customers coming in for toothpaste and
sticking plasters — the uniformed police hovered outside but
could be seen smiling and chatting with Rostya [Rostislav
Pospíšil]... I was... trying to sell a small "discount" brush to a
rather solemn man in a silver grey anorak — in the end I gave
up, and handed him one of the specially printed cards. ..."that's
a member of the secret police" said the others as he finally left
the shop.... We stopped abruptly at 6. — normal closing time for
these "discount" evenings. As a member of the uniformed police came in the cellist was zipping up her instrument. "We're closed now" said the chemist.'[37]
    The freedom that Ganly sensed in the air was being won at a
price. On December 10th, Human Rights Day, the day after her
departure, a demonstration took place in Prague; Müller was
under suspicion of having participated, and was visited by the
police at the fire-extinguisher factory where he was then
employed.
    The Drugstore Gallery received so many visits from the
police that the manager doubted he could continue with the
exhibitions. Ganly later asked why her (non-provocative)
exhibition had caused so much trouble. 'It's because if the

authorities organise an exhibition it takes two years of fuss and bureaucracy,' replied Oslzlý, 'the whole event of this exhibition happening in the way it did makes a nonsense of the official way of doing things.'[38]

Ganly was back in barely three months time, with a double mission to see the work of artists in Prague and to set up an exhibition of the work of her Moravian artists with the Künstlerforum in Bonn; she was accompanied by the Künstlerforum curator, Ludwig von Winterfeld. Together they were drawn into the underworld of Prague artists, with Magor (Ivan Jirous) giving a spectacular performance in the artists' club in Mánes on the Vltava. They embarked on a (frequently frustrating) quest to obtain materials about Czech artists and, at a gathering in the Oslzlý apartment, noted the difficulty Czech artists had in comprehending the kind of independent co-operative effort that had created the Bonn Künstlerforum (an issue which increasingly concerned Ganly during her visits to the Brno artists in the 1990s). Although plans for the Künstlerforum exhibition went ahead (taking place 27th May-15th June 1990)[39] it was 20 months before Ganly returned to Brno — on 25th November 1989, a week after the start of the velvet revolution. Peter Oslzlý was absent in Prague, where he played a major role in the founding of Civic Forum, and only a handful of artists participated in Ganly's seminar. Nevertheless, she left a record of the revolutionary events of those days — in particular the human chain which reached to Bohunice prison where the activist Petr Cibulka was still imprisoned — in her sketches and writings: 'As the dark crowds marched and half ran through the streets, trams passed with passengers cheering... It was an incredible feeling being swept along the icy roads — if my feet slipped warm strangers' hands tightened their grip and I was held up... Once we stopped before a yellow brown house with peeling plaster. One of the windows upstairs was open. Someone had shoved an amplifier through the lace curtains and was relaying the speeches from Prague. We went on.... We were nearly at the top [by Bohunice prison] when we met people coming the other way. "There's no room up there" they said. "It's jam packed and people are singing hymns."'[40]

Parallel with Ganly's work, another aspect of the art programme had been initiated with a joint visit by Anthony

O'Hear, Professor of Philosophy at Bradford University, and Peter Fuller, founder and editor of the journal *Modern Painters*. They too were taken to see the work of local artists, in particular Karel Rechlík and Milivoj Husák. At one meeting of the seminar O'Hear spoke on 'The Role of Art in Human Culture'; the next evening Fuller spoke on 'The Poverty of Modernism'. Both of them commented on the liveliness of the discussion. Fuller wrote afterwards: 'What we had seen, and heard, led me to want to learn a great deal more about Czechoslovakian culture. I felt that I had already had to shed a number of preconceptions which turned out to be false. For example, I had not understood that the real prohibition was not on modernism, but on those areas of cultural experience which aspire or appeal to what can only be called the spiritual dimension of life.'[41] Three years later, after Fuller's death in a car crash in May 1990, O'Hear remembered the occasion: 'Peter's lecture in Brno surprised his audience. The distinguished critic from the West did not talk about the latest artistic developments in London and New York, news of which might not yet have filtered through to the East. Rather, he reminded his audience of the inexhaustible human richness and spiritual power of the European tradition of figurative and landscape painting, something both capitalist West and Communist East seemed at the time bent on having us forget.'[42] Petr Oslzlý, who had been looking forward to Fuller's second visit to Brno in the month that he died, wrote in the same article: 'After the lecture... he argued late into the night with young philosophers, art theoreticians and a group of artists. In the course of one short weekend he visited many artists' studios and even the independent Reduced Price Drugstore Gallery, under close surveillance, as it always was, by the secret police. He was driven by a desire to see as much as he could, to get to know contemporary art in Brno in its breadth and depth.'[43]

Although Douglas-Home, Ganly, O'Hear and Fuller visited a range of artists' studios, there was one studio which all the visitors to Brno had to visit. This was the studio in the home of Jan Šimek, whose story is told by Petr Oslzlý in the book (with photographs by Petr Baran) *Jan Šimek*. Šimek's first elemental works in wood spoke without words of 'highly charged emotions... transformed into existential cries into the surrounding emptiness, the isolation of an individual in an empty society'.[44]

The apartment he had inherited — three airy rooms opening one into the next — had been gradually emptied of furniture to make room for the sculptures, and was the only gallery in which he was entitled to exhibit. British visitors came to learn here something more about life under totalitarianism, discovering at the same time that Brno society was not as empty as Šimek in his early years of work had experienced it. In the shadow of the sculptures, some of them rising almost to three metres, like-minded people had begun to meet each other, school teachers, technicians, architects. Petr Oslzlý sees Šimek's development as an artist almost as an image of the development of Czech society: 'In the course of the 1980s Šimek moved from the isolation of his studio to the open air of everyday life, to a space where his art interacted with the environment around him.'[45] Although often threatened with prosecution as a 'parasite', Šimek survived with memories of policemen sitting in his studio, urging him to 'find work'. 'Look,' he would ask, turning momentarily from his carving, 'which of us here is "working" — you or me?'

As one way of breaking down the division between the 'official' and the 'unofficial', Šimek's audience had long wanted to set up a proper exhibition of his work. Since this could not be done in Czechoslovakia it would have to be abroad, preferably in Great Britain, and the Jan Hus Foundation was asked to bring it about. After many false leads and disappointments, the exhibition opened in April 1989, in the Gallery of Central St. Martin's School of Art in Southampton Row in London. It was organised as a selling exhibition; a cyclostyled catalogue accompanied a printed brochure containing essays by Petr Oslzlý and Peter Fuller. Arrangements were made through the Slovart agency in Slovakia, which Müller and Oslzlý judged to be a safer partner than its Czech equivalent, Art Centrum (in a totalitarian state, there were no other options). In October 1988, Day travelled to Bratislava for negotiations with the agency. The Jan Hus Foundation began to feel confident that with its music and ecology programmes and two planned art exhibitions, it was beginning to establish itself as an organisation which would be able to carry out these and other programmes without interference from the authorities.

Jan Šimek, who had never travelled abroad, reluctantly agreed to go through the process of acquiring a passport. Shortly before he left for London he was called for interrogation by the police. Müller reported the contents of the conversation to Barbara Day in the next exchange of computer discs: 'They told him that you [Day] were not some nice lady interested in the Czechoslovak theatre, but the representative of a dangerous organisation. Concerning Petr [Oslzlý], they said he was a dangerous political provocateur. Nevertheless, in the end the policeman said: "So we're going to let you go [to England]." And off Šimek went.'[46]

When the Brno seminar was under discussion in 1984, it was planned that one of its cultural themes, alongside art and music, should be literature. The first visitor in this programme was the novelist Dan Jacobson, who travelled to Brno with his wife Margaret in May 1986.

It was not Jacobson's first visit to Czechoslovakia. In April 1983 he had visited Prague on an earlier experiment by the Foundation to set up a seminar between English-speaking and Czech writers. Jacobson, who grew up in South Africa, had long had a curiosity about the lands behind the Iron Curtain. What he found was worse than he had expected — a crushed and eerie silence: 'I was depressed, even horrified, to a degree which I could not have imagined beforehand. The emptiness and darkness of the streets after nightfall, the undisguised slovenliness and decay of everything in them, the drabness and meagreness of the shops... and above all, the subdued wretchedness of the demeanour of the people.'[47] Jacobson remembers riding on a tram at night through the dark streets and, aware of the intense reserve of the people around him, thinking: 'This is what it is like. Here, now, in this tram. This is what it is like.'[48]

On that occasion Jacobson talked at length with the novelist Ivan Klíma about the position of writers like himself, about potential western support, and about western journalists and their political interests; as well as about Kafka and the history of Prague: 'the kinds of things,' Klíma said, rather poignantly, 'that I like talking about.'[49] Jacobson was, however, disappointed in his hope of meeting a circle of people interested in literature. In 1986, visiting Brno, his experience was quite different. He gave two seminars: the first, to the regular home seminar, was on

'Fantasy and Ethics', which he related to his own *Story of the Stories* ('I felt that many of the questioners found disappointing my reluctance to concede that what I called our "hunger for transcendence" necessarily showed that we were endowed with a capacity for transcendence.'[50]) As the evening drew on a discussion developed about the situation in South Africa. 'The people there (all but one of whom, incidentally, were younger than I had expected) were extremely sceptical of every aspect of the official line on the crisis in that country (to put it moderately).' The second seminar 'Mirek [Miroslav Pospíšil] had optimistically hoped... could be held in one of the rooms of the university, but since I was not there at their invitation, this suggestion had been turned down flat by the authorities.'[51] Most of this audience were teachers of English, and Jacobson spoke on writing in general, and writing stories in particular. For the Jacobsons, one of the major differences from the Prague visit was their sense of experiencing Brno society in their relationships with the Pospíšil and Oslzlý families. Jacobson was also surprised by Brno's rich aesthetic, having anticipated an industrial city (although Julian Mitchell, a later 'literary' visitor, considered it 'a sad, grimy city'[52]). During his visit Jacobson met Jaroslav Kořán, who was to be responsible for organising a Prague extension to the literary seminar.

Writers who undertook the joint Brno-Prague literary programme included the novelist Piers Paul Read,[53] the poets Carol Rumens and C.H. Sisson, the playwright Julian Mitchell, the novelist and political writer David Pryce-Jones, the literary agent Deborah Rogers and, once more, Dan Jacobson. All except Mitchell[54] and Rogers visited both Prague and Brno, and spoke to the English Club as well as to Petr Oslzlý's seminar group. The serious intention of the Prague stage of the visit was to explore possibilities of translation and publication; in the event, it turned into something of a whirl of sightseeing, parties and meetings with Cultural Attachés and publishers as well as with such celebrated figures as Ivan Klíma, Miroslav Holub, Zdeněk Urbánek[55] and Kořán's friend Michal Žantovský.[56] The working part of the visit took place in Brno, with audiences of around a hundred at the English Club and discussions late into the night at the home seminar. One of Pospíšil's main aims was to penetrate the university; teachers and students from the

English department were invited to the seminar, and sometimes an additional meeting was arranged with his students. Most of the seminars dealt with the writers' own work, relating that to the wider context of English literature. Pryce-Jones spoke on two occasions about Arabs and their society, the first time culturally, the second time more politically: 'I was at once asked intelligent questions... We had a good passage about terrorism, which is imposed by the Party in the Soviet system for the purpose of advantage, but inheres in the Arab system, where it means only that an emergency is at hand justifying the use of a measure only marginally more extreme than the usual violence... We also had a good discussion of the likely outcome of the Iran-Iraq war, and whether Great Power intervention would have results.'[57] Both Read and Rumens noted that very often the audience would be less interested in finding out what was happening in other countries than in relating what they were being told to their own situation under Communism. (Read observed that many themes and issues current in the West were mystifying for his audience and that feminism baffled them; whereas Rumens reported that 'the girls [university students] had plenty to say about the poor position of women in Czech society!'[58]).

Jacobson noted a major change in atmosphere between his first visit to Brno in 1986 and his second in February 1989. On both occasions he was aware of a strong sense of urgency, of life going on 'under the crust' conducted by 'impressive, attractive people who were not crushed at all'.[59] In 1986 he had realised how the Iron Curtain stretched as a physical barrier from Greece to the Baltic Sea, and wondered what kind of government had so little faith in its people that it must lock them inside the country. His seminars and discussions convinced him that a regime which drove such dynamic and interesting people out of its institutions was completely bankrupt, worthless. But whereas in the early and mid-1980s these activities had been 'bolted down under hoods of steel', by 1989 these were fractured. The urgency and impatience was coming to the surface and the question being voiced, 'Why hasn't it ended yet?'. [60]

The Jazz Section

One form of resistance to the oppression and conformity of totalitarian regimes has traditionally been the jazz culture — free and individual improvisation on universal themes, in which music has been the expression of desire for an independent way of life. From the founding of the Republic to the second world war, Czechoslovakia had a jazz tradition of which it was proud. It is best known from the compositions of Jaroslav Ježek for the Liberated Theatre of Voskovec and Werich, in the jazz revues which became increasingly political in the 'Dark Blue World' of the 1930s. In the eyes (or ears) of both Nazis and Stalinists, jazz was decadent and dangerous. From 1948 onwards the Communists promoted folk music as a medium with the potential to gather the flock of nations into one fold. It was not until the late 1950s that young people, listening to the distorted voices of Jimi Hendrix and Janis Joplin on Radio Luxemburg, began again to improvise for themselves, on home-made instruments. Some of them found ways to perform in public, and it was from the cellar of the Reduta jazz club in Národní třída that an important branch of the small-stage movement developed, leading to the founding of the Balustrade and Semafor theatres. In the mid-1960s the first big jazz festivals took place, in Prague, Karlovy Vary and Slaný; long hair became the fashion, and beat groups such as the Matadors and Primitives became the idols of young people indifferent to the principles of Communism which had guided their parents.

These 'beatniks' were amongst the most vehement protestors against the Soviet invasion of 1968, which led to the emigration of many, if not most, of the leading jazzmen of Czechoslovakia. From 1971 onwards the Communist authorities tried to work up public feeling against the 'beatniks'; the general public were taught that such attitudes were degenerate, and that any clean-living family would regard them with disgust. Groups were forbidden to have English names; English texts were banned from performance on radio and television, in concerts and recordings. The 'examinations' which had to be undergone before permission was given to perform in public became ever more stringent. In March 1974 an open-air concert near České Budějovice by the Plastic People of the Universe and DG307 was broken up by police, with hundreds of young people arrested, injured, and later expelled from school and work. The trial of the Plastic People in 1976 was the culmination of this campaign; ironically, it brought together in the corridors of the court house many of the people who were to be founder-signatories of Charter 77. One member of the Plastic People, who was expelled rather than brought to trial, was the Canadian Paul Wilson; he later became a founder member of the Jan Hus Educational and Cultural Foundation in America and the Jan Hus Fund in Canada.

The Jazz Section had come into existence during the aftermath of the Prague Spring, when the old organisations had been disbanded and the regime was trying to ensure that each genre was controlled through one centrally structured organisation. The Jazz 'Section' was therefore an offshoot of the Prague branch of the Musicians' Union; it was launched in 1971, at the 8th International Jazz Festival held in Lucerna on Wenceslas Square. It grew in popularity when two members of its committee, Karel Srp and Joska Skalník, prepared a regular cyclostyled bulletin with the title *Jazz*. Limited by printing capacity to around 5,000 members, the Jazz Section reached thousands more in the most distant parts of the country, through word of mouth and the passage of materials from hand to hand. By nature of the genre, the young people it attracted tended to be non-conformist — those who did not care about joining the Socialist Youth Union or turning up for May Day parades. In 1974 the Section initiated the Prague Jazz Days, which year by year attracted the interest of national and international jazz enthusiasts and, by 1976, of the Communist authorities. By 1978 attempts were being made, through its parent body the Musicians' Union, to abolish the Jazz Section; but it had assumed an independent existence by joining the UNESCO-accredited International Jazz Federation. Meanwhile, the quality of the bulletin had rapidly professionalised both in presentation and content, and Skalník and Srp were preparing further publications: Situace, a series in A4 format about contemporary Czech artists; and Jazzpetit, an imprint which over the years published titles on a range of subjects not covered by the official press — surrealism, dada, minimalist art, the Living Theatre, music in the Terezín ghetto, a rock encyclopedia and Bohumil Hrabal's novel *I Waited on the King of England*, which had previously only appeared in samizdat. As well as music and publishing, the Jazz Section was actively involved in contemporary art events; in 1984 Joska Skalník initiated the Minisalon project, in which he appealed to Czech and Slovak artists, asking them to prepare an exhibit to fit a box measuring 10 x 10 cm. Two hundred and forty-four artists responded and their works appear in the exhibition; others, he comments wryly, suddenly 'remembered' the invitation after November 1989, and were not included. The exhibition — which could not be seen in public until 1990 — toured the USA with great success in 1994.

In 1984 the Ministry of the Interior began to increase pressure by means of Law No. 126, passed as a temporary measure sixteen years previously to deal with the 'crisis phenomena' of 1968. The Musicians' Union was itself suspended and in October 1984 the Jazz Section's registration was cancelled. On the basis of its existence as a member of the International Jazz Federation, it continued to operate. By now it was fighting openly by turning to its members, who were invited in a detailed questionnaire to express their views on contemporary cultural life and the work of the Jazz Section. Through the generosity of an elderly couple it had acquired rent-free premises in a house near Kačerov metro, which thanks to the enthusiasm of its members had been transformed into a busy cultural centre. On weekly open days, members came from all over the country to drink coffee, look through Srp's magnificent collection of American jazz magazines, exchange videos and talk about life beyond politics.

Srp reflected in later years that, as individuals, it would have been easy for them to 'go underground', to live a life of adventure and evasion. Instead, they attended their interrogations when called, consulted lawyers, and did everything possible to make sure their members did not engage in illegal activities. Nevertheless, in July 1985 legal proceedings were initiated against members of the committee for dereliction of duty in disposing of funds and property. The whole process was confused and complicated by the efforts of the authorities to find an appropriate law which could be applied to the case. According to them, the Jazz Section 'did not exist'; but it was a difficult charge to maintain in the face of thousands of young people who stubbornly continued to occupy themselves with activities and publications. In September a large proportion of the Jazz Section's correspondence and documentation was confiscated; as a result, it was impossible for them to continue to mail members, and an appeal was sent by word of mouth for members to stay in touch with them. Nevertheless, their publications continued to come out, since Karel Srp was in contact with three or four printers who had not (apparently) received formal notice of the ban. A year later, in September 1986, the Jazz Section's five committee members together with its treasurer and his nephew were arrested and charged with 'unlicensed trading' under paragraph 118, sections 1 and 2a of the Criminal Code. The Jazz Section's premises were sealed and the remainder of its property (including the American jazz magazines) confiscated.

The Jan Hus Educational Foundation had for a long time been in contact with leading members of the Jazz Section such as Petr Oslzlý in Brno and Petr Rezek in Prague. It had recognised the importance of the Jazz Section's activities in the field of the 'unofficial' culture, where it had encouraged young people to think and act independently, and had kept them abreast of what was new in the outside world in the fields of art, music and theatre. It had been impressed by the Jazz Section's publishing programme. Petr Rezek had been the author of essays on contemporary art published as Jazzpetit volume 17, *Tělo, věc a skutečnost v současném umění* (Body, Thing and Reality in Contemporary Art), whilst volume 21, *Případ Wagner* (The Wagner Case), had been edited anonymously by another of the Foundation's beneficiaries, Pavel Kouba. This publication consisted of the Wagner/Nietzsche confrontation, and was the only publication of any of Nietzsche's writings in Czechoslovakia during that time. Kouba had been listed in the Foundation's stipend book since 1983 under the rubric 'Anonymous (Nietzsche scholar)'. In spring 1988 the query 'Is this Pavel Kouba?' appears in the book; that autumn the Foundation agreed to make a grant for him to lecture on Nietzsche at the International University Centre in Dubrovnik the following summer.

The first member of the Foundation to make contact with the Jazz Section committee was Jessica Douglas-Home, who on 1st October 1985 was taken by Petr Oslzlý for a three-hour meeting with Karel Srp. Srp, who survived on an ebullient enthusiasm welling up from an inner source, anticipated a prison sentence, and appreciated the potential of international publicity and legal assistance that Douglas-Home was able to offer. On her return Douglas-Home worked with Roger Scruton to realise the promise. Contact was made with Charles Alexander, president of the International Jazz Federation, to ensure his commitment to the Jazz Section, since the Czechoslovak Ministry of Culture was putting pressure on the IJF to disown the Jazz Section. On 24th February 1986, in a note smuggled out of the country, Jiří Müller wrote to Douglas-Home: 'When the official Czechoslovak delegate recently returned from the last session of European Jazz Union in Warsaw, our minister of culture Dr. Klusák invited him and said: "I have only one question for you. What is this about the Jazz Section?" The delegate answered, that the Jazz Section membership in the European Jazz Union was acknowledged. Our minister reacted with peak indignation: "How is it possible, when everything has been arranged, so that the membership would be cancelled?" Yes. How is it possible? Yours, J.'[1]

Media publicity was vital, and the Foundation worked to place articles in the western press. The freelance writer Christine Verity visited Czechoslovakia and wrote about the Jazz Section for *The Times*; Müller sent a message to say that her article was so good it was used by the Jazz Section as a source of information for foreigners. In February 1987 the Canadian radio journalist Nancy Durham[2] travelled to Brno and Prague, ostensibly to report on Czech culture, but in reality — after an initial briefing by Oslzlý and Pospíšil — to make a programme on the Jazz Section.[3]

Approaches were made to lawyers and legal organisations

for their support. Politicians were lobbied. In autumn 1985 Norman St. John Stevas attended the Budapest Cultural Forum (part of the follow-up to the Conference on European Security and Co-operation, with the job of discussing the cultural aspects of the so-called 'basket three'of the Helsinki conference covering human contacts and exchanges) as leader of the British delegation. Before leaving Britain he had been briefed in person by Douglas-Home[4] and stunned the Czechoslovak delegation with his references to the Jazz Section. Karel Srp, with the help of the American Embassy, had been present in Budapest to enjoy their discomfiture. Returning through Prague, St John Stevas was present at a meeting with the Jazz Section committee arranged in the magnificent art deco Municipal House by the British Embassy. The following September, shortly after Srp's arrest, David Mellor (as Minister of State) again raised the question of the Jazz Section at the CSCE Vienna follow-up meeting.[5]

The unexpectedness of the arrest of the entire Committee left an administrative hole at the heart of the Jazz Section and, as the authorities probably intended, threatened its communication structure with the West. There had been no contingency plans. Oslzlý and Jaroslav Kořán (co-author with Oslzlý of *Jazzpetit* volume no. 15, on the Living Theatre) consulted the most active Prague members of the Section, and within days a working committee had been formed with Jiří Exner at its head. A parallel committee was created in Brno. Exner was invited to Brno, where he met Müller for the first time. Müller briefed him on all the actions taking place in the West (without mentioning the Jan Hus Foundation by name) and on whom he would be dealing with on behalf of the Jazz Section. From then on, Exner became the main contact person for the Foundation and other western organisations.

Alongside Douglas-Home, Scruton and Durham, the fourth JHEF trustee to adopt the cause of the Jazz Section was the composer David Matthews. His second visit to Brno took place in October 1986, a month after the arrests. He was accompanied by the composer Nigel Osborne and, in long talks with Petr Oslzlý, they decided that their best method of support was a petition on behalf of British musicians. It was agreed between them that the petition should be addressed to President Gustáv Husák and courteously worded, drawing attention only to 'a fundamental misunderstanding of the role played by the Jazz Section of the Musicians' Union, whose activities have brought such liveliness and inspiration to the Czech cultural scene and helped make it an object of admiration throughout the world'.[6] During October, November and December Matthews and Osborne worked feverishly to collect sixty signatures, including those of Sir Colin Davis, Bob Geldof, Elton John, Paul McCartney, Simon Rattle, Sir Michael Tippett, Pete Townshend and Andrew Lloyd Webber. Matthews' own signature did not appear; there was the risk that he was already known to be associated with the Jan Hus Foundation, and that the action could be traced back to Petr Oslzlý. The letter was written on behalf of the Britten-Pears Foundation and at the end of December 1986 was presented to the Czechoslovak Embassy at Notting Hill Gate with a request that it be delivered to the President. A few days later a copy of the petition appeared in *The Times*. Similar letters were sent by writers, including Tom Stoppard, Iris Murdoch, Malcolm Bradbury, Seamus Heaney and Graham Greene.

Meanwhile, Roger Scruton wrote to Jiří Müller: 'We have arranged for a lawyer to come to Prague on the weekend of the 24th [October 1986] to visit Dr Průša.[7] He is not an expert in Czech property law (who is?) — but he is an enthusiastic advocate of human rights, and an influential person. His name is Geoffrey Robertson. He will bring with him money (5 x 150 pounds) for the families of those in prison, as suggested. Where should he meet Dr P? If you do not say anything to the contrary, we will assume that he should simply go to Dr P's house on arrival. Meanwhile, we should like a curriculum vitae for Dr P, and as much information as possible, concerning his recent dismissal from the Czech Society of Lawyers, etc. The Swiss institution for the independence of lawyers is interested in his case.'[8] Geoffrey Robertson Q.C. travelled to Prague on October 24th, where his guide was Jaroslav Kořán. In the course of the weekend he met, as well as Dr. Průša, Václav Havel (who advised on tactics); Rostislava Křivánková[9] (wife of one of the imprisoned); and several Jazz Section members. Robertson analysed the case being brought against the seven men, their defence tactics, and the opportunities that could be used in publicising the case. 'It is also important,' he wrote 'that "official guests" from Britain take the opportunity to raise the issue. A vital opportunity was lost last weekend when jazz bands from the U.S. and Britain (Herbie Hancock and Mike Westbrook) failed to dedicate songs to the defendants. I suspect they were dissuaded by Western diplomats, ignorant of how significant such messages would be for the local audience.'[10] He considered the role of Charles Alexander and the IJF to be crucial to the defence strategy.

The international pressure was beginning to have some effect. On 1st November a report appeared in the Communist Party newspaper *Rudé právo*, 'Under the guise of "jazz lovers"' by Václav Doležal. The writer hits out at 'some instruments of the bourgeois media [who] are trying to shift another meaning onto this illegal activity [of the Jazz Section]. For example, the BBC, the Voice of America, Reuters and some other agencies are showing much consideration towards these wrongdoers. They are asserting that it is all an attempt to terrorise the lovers of popular music, in particular of jazz, in our country.

'This is a meaningless, lying assertion. It is well known that there are many friends of modern music in our country... It is well known that the interest of genuine and disinterested lovers of jazz is not in the least circumscribed. There would be no reason to do this.

'The British newspaper *The Guardian* in its Thursday edition tried to connect the detention of the seven Czechoslovak subjects with the forthcoming Vienna Conference on European security and co-operation. It ponders the "mystery" of why the Czechoslovak authorities decided to take these measures not long before the Vienna Conference "reviewing the fulfilment of the Helsinki undertakings". This British paper asserts that the arrests of these persons should conform to the Closing Act...

'Everyone, whether a lover of jazz or not, whatever his hobby may be, whatever sector his work involves him in, has the duty to keep the laws of our country and therefore to conform to the State's rulings. That applies to these seven citizens as well. The law applies to everyone, and at all times of the year, both before and after any international conference.'[11]

A month later, the philosopher John Rose, lecturing for the Foundation at Hejdánek and Bratinka's seminars, was briefed to meet Rostislava Křivánková. She reported that the prisoners 'were being held on the 3rd floor, where opportunities for mixing are more restricted and conditions generally harsher than in the rest of the prison; wives are denied access; the prosecution can veto any letters sent in; in any case, only 4 pages a fortnight are allowed; it is about a month before replies to letters are received; some have been questioned for as much as 17 hours without interruption; one of them suffers from a heart condition and, although medicines have been sent, they have not been received.'[12]

In February 1987 there was a meeting between Douglas-Home, Scruton, Alexander and Osborne, joined by Zina Freundová[13] and Zuzana Princová.[14] (Princová had been particularly active in the cause of the Jazz Section, and initiated a number of actions independently.) They suspected that the continued delay in setting a date for the trial meant that the Czechoslovak authorities wanted to be sure of their case. They resolved to form the 'Friends of the Jazz Section' and to initiate a programme of activities in support of its defence. One of the decisions was to ask Robertson to make a second visit to Prague, a visit which took place three weeks later; on his return, he wrote:

'The most vital matter is to consider sending observers to the trial, which begins on 10 March and will last at least 3 days. Havel suggests, accurately in my view, that we should try to send one of the signatories to the musicians' protest, which made a big impact. Geldof would be marvellous... We should also consider an eminent lawyer... Could you make sure Amnesty is sending someone?... Charles Alexander is vital. He is going to Czechoslovakia soon in any event, but it would be great if he could attend the trial. Srp's lawyer says he would try to call him to give evidence, but in any event a notorised statement from him would be acceptable. The hand-written note I enclose has been prepared by Exner, who has an identical copy. It sets out 5 alternative train itineraries from German cities — he would like Charles to select one, and he will meet him on the selected train. He fears that Charles will be too closely watched for them to meet in any other circumstances.[15]

'I enclose copies of 3 recent court judgements, together with Exner's summary of events to date and a note about the next case they are going to bring, accusing high party officials of a conspiracy to deprive Srp of his job as publicity officer at a State publishing house.'

Within the next few days the Foundation arranged the travel of Charles Alexander (whom Robertson briefed on the legal aspects of the case), and, to represent the Musicians' Petition, Nigel Osborne and Michael Berkeley. They were met (in the event, at the airport) by Jiří Exner and driven straight to the District Court, where Douglas-Home (or Robertson; this is not clear from surviving records) had arranged through the British Embassy for Alexander to be one of only four westerners to be admitted to the trial. Osborne and Berkeley joined the crowd of around fifty which filled the corridor outside — among them were journalists from *The Times*, *The Observer*, the BBC, the Voice of America and other western media, together with Jazz Section members and supporters, including Olga Havlová. Alexander reported to Douglas-Home:

'As we entered Courtroom 57, there was loud applause and a highly charged, emotional atmosphere. A steady hand-clap was maintained throughout the half-hour or so that we were inside and this was clearly audible — a boost to the morale of those on trial. Karel Srp and Vladimír Kouřil entered handcuffed; the other accused sat on the bench in front of me. It was a small courtroom with only two rows of seats for press and public. The press agency journalists had a translator and I was therefore able to follow the proceedings. The Chairman of the Court entered and read the decision of the Court that they were all guilty of illegal trading since the 25 October 1984 (the date of the J.S. dissolution) and went on to list the sentences. Karel Srp received 16 months and Vladimír Kouřil 10 months. The others all received suspended sentences. Both prosecution and defence confirmed their wish to appeal.

'Throughout the proceedings Karel Srp was radiant and smiling as if his greatest wishes were being fulfilled. He looked fit, healthy and younger than his fifty years. I caught his attention with a wave and he was clearly delighted that I was present... As he was being led by two policemen in the corridor outside the Courtroom, Srp did manage to utter the words "Help Us" into the microphone of the BBC correspondent.'[16]

In the circumstances of the time, the verdict (which was declared invalid in the 1990s) was considered to be a success for the defence. The sentences were relatively light, and the judge's summing-up conciliatory. That evening a clandestine press conference took place in a small apartment, attended by about forty people. Exner, Skalník and Čestmir Huňat spoke first; they thanked the working committee, the IJF and all local and international supporters (the Jan Hus Foundation was not mentioned, for reasons of security). They were followed by Alexander, Berkeley and Osborne with statements of support from the international cultural community. On the same day Minister of State Timothy Renton issued a statement in London, in which he described how impressed he had been by his meeting with members of the Jazz Section, and by their commitment. They had struck him as 'a serious minded-group of individuals dedicated to the promotion of music and other cultural activities as well as to the propagation of information about the CSCE'.[17] He went on to say that although Britain had no intention of interfering in Czechoslovakia's legal processes 'it certainly appears that the State Prosecutor may have used minor technical infringements as a pretext to suppress free expression and perfectly natural cultural and artistic activities which should be regarded as normal in any country whose government is a signatory of the Final Act... I hope that when the case comes to the appeal stage, the sentences will be reconsidered in the light of the commitments Czechoslovakia has undertaken under the Helsinki Final Act.'[18]

At the appeal on 12th May the Muncipal Court rejected the appeals against the District Court's verdicts as baseless. Nevertheless, the international campaign was considered to have succeeded. The publicity had ensured that the accused had to be seen to receive the nearest possible thing to a fair trial, and that the (unjust) sentences were relatively lenient. On June 26th Jiří Müller wrote to Roger Scruton: 'Our ministry would have never negotiated, if such enormous pressure had not been put upon it; the pressure which was so successfully developed by you. Of course, negotiations do not guarantee any result. The JS is prepared first of all for half-legal activities justified by the membership in the IJF (which was also kept thanks to you). The cooperation between the JS and Ch.A. is now good and regular. But I think that in the future the existence of a foreign committee for the support of the JS will be the only "guarantee" for the JS. N.O. sent us a message that the committee could be established already in autumn... The impression of international

interest in the trial with the JS and of the participation of people
you managed to send to Czechoslovakia as well was really
extraordinary. It had an enormous influence not only upon our
institutions (the police had not allowed any intervention against
the people in the court building!) but as well upon the JS
membership. In my opinion everything which has been done is
a good example of our co-operation efficiency.'[19]

Nevertheless, the authorities had succeeded in destroying
something at the heart of the Jazz Section. The necessarily
intense focus on the urgent needs of the imprisoned members of
the committee had turned the focus of the Section inside out.
Relations with the far-flung members of the Section had already
been disrupted when the authorities had made it impossible for
the Section to continue its regular mailings, and broke down
further when it became impossible to go on issuing publications
and organising activities. In the crisis of the moment the natural
inventiveness and creativity of those involved was spent in
thinking-up ever new possibilities of defence and outwitting the
authorities. Relations between Karel Srp and the Working
Committee became strained during the months he spent in
prison, and by late 1988 had completely broken down: 'JM is
deeply depressed by what has happened and says it is
irretrievable.. Exner is the only one trying to do anything for the
4000 members, but he lacks the contacts and the charisma of the
old JS.'[20] Eventually Srp and Skalník founded a new organisation, Art Forum, with an emphasis on publishing and the visual
arts. Exner established Unijazz, which was to pick up the disrupted connections with the old Jazz Section members. The
British, reluctant to take sides in an internal dispute, found
themselves committed to supporting both sides, but to a limited
and cautious extent.

The Jazz Section network was of immense importance in the
revolution of November 1989, when it was used to spread word
of what was happening in Prague to the most distant corners of
the country. Once the revolution had been accomplished some
of the old members began to feel that life had passed them by.
Their earlier refusal to conform to the norms of the totalitarian
society had left them, as Karel Srp put it, with 'no education, no
qualifications, no experience, no opportunities';[21] whereas it did
not take long for their conformist and adaptable contemporaries,

who had completed university studies and served apprentice-ships in socialist institutions, to find well-paid posts with western firms.

Nonetheless, although it is difficult to find businessmen or politicians among former Jazz Section members, after 1989 there were many who transferred the skills they had learnt to the fields of the arts and public service. Skalník, after a short period as cultural adviser to the President, became active not only as an artist, but also in promoting other Czech artists; Srp worked for a while in the Ministry of Culture, and then continued his work with young people in the Jazz Section-Art Forum; Exner, whilst still operating Unijazz, became Deputy Mayor of the City of Prague; Křivánková was made Ambassador to Finland. Of other active members, Jana Chržová became executive director of the Czech Helsinki Committee, whilst Ondřej Hrab (who in 1983 had, through the Jazz Section, organised an 'unofficial' perfor-mance in Prague by the Living Theatre from New York) became the founder and director of the Archa Theatre. Their experience in the Jazz Section had developed in them a particular taste for excitement and creativity in life combined with a sense of responsibility for the community in which they lived.

The Ecology Programme

When the Brno secret police apprehended Roger Scruton and the Müllers on a June afternoon in 1985, they delayed too long; the most important subjects had already been discussed. Amongst them was the environmental issue. Whilst the effects of industrial pollution and acid rain were sweeping across Europe in the 1970s and 1980s, the regimes of the Communist countries were attempting to cover up the results of decades of incompetence, neglect, and corruption. Almost unknown to western environmentalists, there was a band of concerned and knowledgeable people hidden away in the research institutes of Czechoslovakia and working through the 1980s in isolation. Their findings were subordinated to the interests of the Party; for example, a meticulously researched atlas of morbidity in north Bohemia was treated as a purely theoretical treatise. Only 50 copies could be printed, and it had little influence on government policy. The environmentalists were blocked from contact with potential colleagues in western Europe, who at this time did not even know that such data existed.

The green movement in Czechoslovakia, by contrast with that in western Europe, was led by people with a specialist knowledge of the environmental sciences. Initially they lacked the activist and media skills of their western colleagues, but their knowledge of what was happening and the data they collected was detailed and accurate. (During the late 1980s these workers were increasingly joined by their more politically active colleagues, who — the traditionalists felt — naively expected that the environmental problems would be solved with the fall of the Communist regime.) In the early days most of the work was done by small groups, concerned for their own particular locality. These groups came under the central organisations of the Czech and Slovak Associations for Nature Conservation, which had been founded in 1980, to fill the gap which had been left by all the groups which had been banned under the normalisation of the 1970s. In Brno the movement, led by the geographer Miroslav Kundrata, was particularly strong. In 1985 two localities — Brno City and Brno Countryside — combined to publish a newsletter, which they called *Veronika*, which became one of the earliest examples of an independently-minded, semiofficial publication reaching a wide sector of the population. Kundrata remembers that several Party members of the organisation were called to the 'White House'[1] to be censured for the content of the journal, but that it was never actually banned. As well as being involved in a number of environmental projects — both through the Association and as a geographer — Kundrata was also, from an early stage, a member of Petr Oslzlý's seminar, and was one of those who asked for a speaker on an environmental theme. This suggestion gave Jiří Müller the idea for another branch to the Foundation's activities.

One of the most dynamic scientists in the research institutes in Prague was the ecologist and traveller Josef Vavroušek, who had been Müller's fellow student in the 1960s. (They had shared a lathe in the pre-university compulsory year in a factory, and Müller entrusted some of his belongings to Vavroušek during his imprisonment in the 1970s.) After the fall of Communism, Vavroušek became the country's leading environmentalist, rising to the position of federal Minister for the Environment — a role in which he had to deal with the problem of the Gabčikovo dam between Hungary and Slovakia, which he had opposed whilst in opposition. He is remembered still[2] as a powerful political personality and an enormous moral force: 'An extraordinary man, pragmatic and wildly idealistic. He had his strengths and flaws; some of his stuff was wildly impractical, but he inspired a high level of trust, no one doubted him. He had sincerity and vision, a rootedness in the real. He was the heart as well as the brain of the environmental movement.'[3]

In 1985 Vavroušek held a relatively senior position in the Research Institute for Scientific and Technological Development in Prague, but was subject to political control. Although there were those in the State Planning Commission who knew the value of his work, he had refused to join the Party and it was therefore impossible for him to establish international contacts through official channels. Müller asked Scruton, in the conversation interrupted by the secret police, to make known Vavroušek's published work on methodology (methodological questions were the only ones that could be publicly discussed) in Britain. Scruton commented in his report: 'The political point of this does not need spelling out.'

Ecology was a new field for Scruton, but it happened that his friend and neighbour William Waldegrave had recently been made Minister for the Environment. Waldegrave recommended Scruton to contact Tom Burke, director of the Green Alliance. In January 1986, Scruton sent a message through Dennis O'Keeffe, travelling to Brno as messenger, in which he suggested that Burke should visit Czechoslovakia. Müller asked for clarification; was Scruton expecting that Burke would be able to meet 'their ecological friend' at this early stage? (Vavroušek had not yet been mentioned by name.) '[He] works in the Government ecology office,' reported O'Keeffe, 'All connections with him must be prepared carefully and officially. He has a key position. He has written an article on government methods in ecology. It will be published in an official journal. The same journal will carry an English summary. This would supply a pretext for an English ecologist to write officially saying he is interested and would like to visit him and to form an official link. Their friend will get permission for such connections. Then he could come.'[4] Scruton was anxious that Burke should gain experience of the situation in Czechoslovakia as soon as possible; whereas Müller was afraid of jeopardising the main aim, and wanted to find the best way to work from below to infiltrate Burke into the official situation. One of his main preoccupations was to find the most logical links from the unofficial through to the official world. Every link had to be worked out and tested from every angle to ensure it would withstand pressure from the authorities. Environmental pollution was a sensitive subject, and the planning would have to be extremely precise. Nevertheless, Müller agreed that Burke should come to Brno in March to talk on 'Conservation of the Environment in Great Britain'. Oslzlý and Pospíšil discussed the visit with Miroslav Kundrata, and a weekend's programme was drawn up, including both a seminar in Kundrata's home — the first of its kind — and a visit to one of the environmentally threatened areas of Moravia.

In April 1986 the next messenger (Craig Kennedy) reported that: 'JM would like to arrange another opportunity for Burke — or an ecologist of his selection — to meet in Prague with the two Czech ecologists. JM counsels that it would be pointless for Burke to try to correspond from England with the Czech ecologists; only in a face to face meeting will they be able to express their needs and make their queries. JM proposes a trip on Monday through Wednesday 23-25 June, beginning in Brno and moving on to Prague for the meeting.... Both of these ecologists are quite prominent in their field and will be organizing a two-day conference in December of this year. One of them is on open speaking terms with JM; through him JM would like to arrange for British ecologists to attend this conference. Invitations, however, would be a complex matter demanding a good deal of time. Hence, JM would like the proposed meeting to take place as soon as possible.'[5]

Burke crossed the Czechoslovak border from Vienna on the evening of Sunday 22nd June 1986; his briefcase, stowed under his seat on the bus, was bursting with 176 press cuttings on Chernobyl. The Müllers had booked a table in a night club: 'apparently the only place to go on a Sunday night in Brno. Actually, it turned out to be a perfect place to talk — dark, noisy enough to prevent others overhearing conversations but not too noisy to prevent them occurring.'[6] (Müller later admitted it was the first time he had ever visited a night club.) Burke was briefed on exactly how to manage in Prague without drawing attention to himself, and how to make his approach to the ecologists. They moved on to a general discussion of environmental issues. 'On returning to the hotel I passed on the tapes, press cuttings, magazines etc. that I had brought. I was impressed by both of them. They are clearly cautious, committed and clever. Jiří in particular has an almost palpable sense of moral purpose.'

Burke presented himself at the Research Institute for Scientific and Technological Development early the following afternoon and told the porter on duty that he was visiting Prague on holiday, knew of Vavroušek's work, and had called on the off-chance he was available. 'It was clear from my reception that I was expected. There were no difficulties and I was taken up to Vavroušek's office immediately. I was not even asked to sign in.' After an hour's discussion Vavroušek suggested he should give a seminar the next day, and introduced him to his head of division: 'having carefully briefed me on how to present myself. I was to emphasise my professional interest and to concentrate on my concern with methodological approaches. I was particularly and repeatedly warned not to express an interest in substantive data.' The discussion continued through the afternoon and was continued in the evening as they walked around the Old Town and Prague Castle. Burke observed: 'There appears to be a layer of people who are not overtly oppositionist, who have important professional appointments and who are permitted a certain independence of mind and unorthodoxy of behaviour because of the high level of their skills. I was told two or three times that there was no one else capable of carrying out Vavroušek's work and that he was regarded as something of a star of his Institute. He is also a mountaineer of some distinction and has climbed in the Pamirs, including an ascent of Mt. Communism.'[7]

The following morning Burke arrived at the Institute to find his seminar had been cancelled. It had been necessary to obtain permission from the State Planning Commission, and the member responsible for security had refused 'as the correct procedures for permission, which seem to require at least a week's advance notice, had not been taken.' Burke left the Institute, with an arrangement to meet Vavroušek's colleague, Jan Tauber, for lunch. Tauber brought with him 'a Polish economist married to a Czech and living in Prague'. This was Josef Zieleniec,[8] about whom Burke noted: 'he is clearly an economist of some distinction in Czechoslovakia. He is very much a market oriented person himself and describes himself as a conservative. He was in the middle of reading one of Roger Scruton's books which had been translated into Czech.[9] He came to the slightly unsettling conclusion during our conversation that I was a conservative and looked very unconvinced when I explained that I was actually a Social Democrat. I suppose from where he sits the differences appear very unimportant. He is convinced that the Soviet economy will not survive the stresses of the next decade and foresees a rather cataclysmic collapse of the Soviet empire for internal reasons.'[10] Burke observed that Zieleniec was potentially the most valuable of the people he had met: 'He is intellectually formidable and sound in his judgement.' [11]

Burke had more encounters before leaving Prague, concluding with a meeting with Vavroušek to discuss future plans. His aim was to put the relationship on a semi-official basis, and to that end he asked Burke to write to the Director of the Institute. On his return, Burke prepared a follow-up proposal for the Foundation, which he estimated would cost approximately 3000 pounds a year.[12] In August Müller passed on a message from Eva Kruziková, one of the ecologists Burke had met and trusted in Prague. It was a warning for his colleague Dr. R. Brabazon Macrory of Imperial College, who, on Burke's recommendation, had been invited to attend the congress proposed by Müller in April: 'A certain Dr. [****] (top level functionary and superior of hers) will be his watch dog. He, although not a party member, is known as a security police agent. Eva would very much like to meet Dr. Macrory, but could do this only without this Dr. [****]. Would TB please advise his colleague.'[13] Later the same month, Müller told Day that: 'He was extremely pleased by the success of T.B[urke]'s visit, and had had good reports back from Prague. He emphasised that security was vital — it would be a catastrophe if any of the people visited by T were known to be connected with J [Müller]. He would like to see this work expand under T's guidance, and further visitors and organisations to be involved, but emphasised that connections should be consistent; once key persons were established, these would be trusted and substitutions should not be made.'[14] Müller emphasised this again to Oriana Stock in September: 'For Czech scientists, contacts with different foreigners are suspicious and/or dangerous. Therefore it has to be TB again, at least for this next time... TB not necessary forever, but under these circumstances 'the' important institute in Prague... must be done by him. Please don't let chances slip. Other representatives would be most welcome to contact other institutes existing (and waiting) there! Situation is progressing well, some ecology institutions are already envisaging foreign contacts.'[15] Müller eagerly asked: 'How long can he stay??? Programme depends very much on this information. And with which coach is he going to arrive (first/second) in Brno? Please send postcard to JM and his mother respectively, saying "Many greetings from our (number of days stay in ČSSR)-days holiday in Holland. First/second child is well again."'[16]

The next JHEF meeting was not until October; Burke's November visit could not be confirmed before that time. In the meantime, Burke and Scruton visited William Waldegrave, who agreed in principle to making a ministerial visit to Czechoslovakia if the conditions were right. At the October meeting members of the JHEF Management Committee expressed concern about the political implications of the ecology programme in the light of the Foundation's charitable status. Nevertheless, they agreed that for the time being the programme should be continued, and Scruton wrote by underground (under the code name 'Elizabeth') to tell Müller to expect Burke in November, and that Waldegrave was following the situation. (Possibly the agreed postcards were sent as well.) Scruton added: 'Our journals are of course interested in all ecological matters. What is most interesting to them is facts: especially statistics concerning health, death-rates, pollution and forestry. An article simply surveying the whole field, written with a Western audience in mind, and remembering that people here are entirely ignorant of the communist system, would be immensely useful. It would be politically very striking also.' [17]

On the 8th November 1986 Burke flew to Prague, noting the air pollution as the bus travelled from the airport into the city. Müller was waiting for him at the terminal and, briefing him on the situation, told him that from then on Josef Vavroušek, who was to join them shortly afterwards, would be his contact and coordinator. Over that day and the next they discussed potential relationships with Great Britain, including the possible ministerial visit. On the Monday afternoon Burke gave his postponed seminar, talking about the development of environmental policy in western Europe. Vavroušek was particularly excited to see colleagues from other institutes present at the seminar.

Amongst the people Burke met the next day was Bedřich Moldan from the Academy of Sciences, who was to hold the post of Czech Minister of the Environment in the early 1990s. Burke observed: 'He is the key figure in ecology in Czechoslovakia.... He is someone WW[aldegrave] must see if he goes to Prague. He has played a part in the development of all the principal texts on Czech environment policy. He is the only person I met who has already developed a network of Western contacts.'[18] That evening Burke renewed his contact with Zieleniec: 'We discussed health problems in Czechoslovakia and in particular how their kind of society was going to handle AIDS.' The next day, before leaving for London, he talked to two women from the Economic Institute who were studying the economic impacts of environmental problems. 'Although many of the perceptions and policy themes are the same as they are here there are impossible problems in achieving anything. Every attempt to look at penalties or incentives simply runs into the sand. For instance, far from there being an incentive to save energy in a country with relatively limited supples, the way a concern's budget is calculated penalises someone who doesn't use all their allocation of energy.'[19]

Müller gave his evaluation of the situation with the messenger who travelled in the New Year of 1987: '..the fact that [Burke's] acceptability was achieved by unofficial means can form a basis for further development of official contacts without people being afraid that such contacts are too risky. [Müller] thinks that communication has now been opened up in such a way that the Czech government can no longer control it. In his opinion this strategy is fundamental (and not just in the field of ecology). He hopes that this unofficial communciation will enable Western governments to become aware of all shades of opinion in Eastern European societies (rather than just the two poles, government and dissidents, as at present) and to use this awareness in shaping their policies.'[20]

Burke returned to Prague in September 1988. He reported that in the two intervening years Vavroušek had become 'pessimistic with regard to the state of the environment which has continued to deteriorate, but optimistic with regards to developments within the environmental organisations'.[21] Vavroušek introduced Burke to members of these organisations, some of them in the course of visits to northern Bohemia and to Slovakia. He lectured twice on the development of the EEC's environment policy: first in Prague, at the Institute for State and Law, and secondly at the Research Institute for Social Development and Labour in Bratislava. The lectures were attended by senior officials, followed by discussion (which in Prague led to 'another, somewhat more focused lecture'), and reported in the press. All this might seem unremarkable were it not happening in what was still, in 1988, one of the most tightly controlled countries in Europe. These meetings and exchanges of information had not developed from any official inter-governmental programme, but through the underground network and from Jiří Müller's first request to the Jan Hus Foundation. On his return from Prague, Burke requested a meeting with the British Foreign Office, reporting back that: 'They seem very interested in the whole environmental issue in Czechoslovakia but not to know a great deal about it. They were certainly unaware of who the key players were and not very familiar with the notion that there might be something between the Party members and the outright opposition.'[22]

Tom Burke believes the Foundation's environmental programme was less threatening to the Communist regime than the JHEF programme in philosophy, since it did not involve influencing people through ideas. In his view, the environmental programme concerned mainly practical issues to do with breaking down the hegemony of the Party, overcoming bureaucratic obstacles and publicising the shortcomings of official policy. In the late 1980s, however, both Müller and the JHEF trustees believed that these were the very issues which translated most directly into political action. This was borne out by the situation reported in December 1987, when the Brno circle sent a message to London to say that, following official action taken against conservationists who had published a report on the state of pollution round Bratislava, they had had to postpone all further ecology lectures. The increased support for the environmental movement in the late 1980s was counter-balanced by increased vigilance by the authorities, who were prepared to allow environmentalists, professional and amateur, to collect data but not to publicise them. Many of the environmentalists with whom the Jan Hus Foundation was in touch were active in other 'grey zone' activities such as the Jazz Section; initially such links were kept secret from Burke, but in 1988 part of his report was devoted to Jazz Section problems. Organisations such as the Czech and Slovak Associations for Nature Conservation and the younger 'Brontosaurus' provided ground where concern for the environment eroded any distinction between the 'dissident' and the 'ordinary citizen'. Charter 77, however, with its specifically political links with the German Greens, tended to stand outside this general movement.

Burke used his experiences in Czechoslovakia to build up a network of contacts in eastern Europe, in particular Poland, Romania and Hungary. These contacts he introduced to environmental organisations in the European Community such as the European Environmental Bureau, and invitations began to be sent directly to Burke's nominations, rather than through official channels. In 1988 his 'follow up actions' include an exchange programme for the Czech Brontosaurus organisation and a twinning arrangement with the Slovak Union. Exchange of information was vital: 'Push Moldan article with New Scientist,' he notes, 'Send Vavroušek information on: PCBs, problems of system build, EEC policy formulation, growth of NGO movement in West, key environmental texts, e.g. Fourth Action Programme, Single Act etc.'[23] The western Europeans, whose previous contact with eastern Europe had been through official delegations and Party functionaries with little expert knowledge, became increasingly excited at the discovery of this unsuspected layer of articulate, well-informed East European environmentalists. What mattered most, Burke recollects, was 'for someone from outside to be paying attention to what they were doing; for people to authenticate their efforts and to make connections'.[24] Burke is convinced that without this groundwork it would have been impossible for European co-operation on environmental issues, especially between NGOs, to have developed as swiftly and efficiently as it did after 1989.

Bratislava Seminars

The roots of opposition to Communism in Slovakia were quite different from those in the Czech lands. Whereas in the Czech lands the unifying force was, from the late 1970s, the Charter 77 movement, in Slovakia the unifying force was Christianity, specifically Roman Catholicism. The historical reasons for this date back to the time of the Habsburg Empire, and earlier. In Bohemia the Hussite movement had led to a strong protestant tradition among the nobility, violently crushed after the Battle of the White Mountain in 1620. Re-catholicisation brought much beauty and distinction to Bohemian art, architecture, music and literature, but an underlying equation of protestantism with national identity persisted, and produced an ambivalence in Czech culture. Slovakia on the other hand, which as part of Hungary had retained its Catholic traditions, experienced none of this ambivalence. Roman Catholicism was and is part of the Slovak national identity, especially for the agricultural community which makes up the larger part of the population. In the summer of 1987, in conversation with the Keston College representative Dominic Farrell, Ján Čarnogurský identified a basic difference of outlook: 'In Eastern Slovakia, Christians expect to suffer hardship for wanting to bring their children up as Christians and expect regular harassment and intimidation from the police and it does not really occur to them to complain about it.' Čarnogurský maintained that 'the notion of human rights and freedoms is not readily understood, whereas it is in Bohemia and Moravia and that is why people complain so vociferously when these rights are violated.'[1]

A further difference between the two republics was that Slovaks never felt as 'Communist' as the Czechs. Unlike the

Czechs, the Slovaks did not, in the 1946 elections, vote in large numbers for the Communists, and were far more nominal in their acceptance of the Communist regime. Although some Slovaks such as Alexander Dubček achieved high office in Prague, the movement towards reform in the 1960s was consequently less significant in Slovakia, leaving very few 'reform Communists' around to join Charter 77. The purges of universities, cultural institutions and the civil service which took place in Prague and Brno were emulated only on a much smaller scale in Bratislava and Košice. As a result, there was no substantial community of disaffected intellectuals naturally gravitating towards the established underground seminars and the production of samizdat.

Of more than a thousand signatories of Charter 77, only a few were from Slovakia. Amongst them were the writer and 'honoured artist' Dominik Tatarka and the former Communist Party member Miroslav Kusý. Kusý had taught for many years at the Comenius University, and was the author of such works as *Marxist Philosophy*; after signing the Charter he was forced to become a manual worker and wrote for samizdat. In 1980 he compiled the samizdat work *Big Brother and Big Sister: On the Loss of Reality in the Ideology of Real Socialism* in co-operation with the political theorist Milan Šimečka, a Czech who was dismissed from his post at the Comenius University after the August invasion. Like Chartists living in isolation in provincial parts of Czechoslovakia, Kusý and Šimečka (who was not himself a signatory) maintained direct contact with Prague, and were involved in Ludvík Vaculík's samizdat operation. The two of them used to meet with a third, Július Strinka, for a weekly game of chess; although not a 'dissident' meeting, the date was known by others (including the police) who would know where to find them on a Thursday evening.

One of the group which used to meet in this way was the historian Jozef Jablonický, who had worked in the Institute of History of the Academy of Sciences until his expulsion in 1974. His specialisation had been the Second World War and the Slovak National Uprising, a subject where his writings, tenaciously relying on the results of original research, differed from the official Communist version. Even with the archives closed to him he continued to work, using his own notes and materials. These had to be hidden outside his flat, which was subject not only to regular house searches but also to visits from the secret police whilst he was out; his various hiding places included a garage and a friend's flat outside Bratislava. His own typewritten work was hidden in the same way until it could be distributed; one copy would go to Miroslav Kusý, who would arrange for more copies to be made, a second to Milan Šimečka who knew the route whereby it could be smuggled to Vilém Prečan's Documentation Centre in West Germany. (Jablonický, his passport confiscated, did not visit Scheinfeld until after 1989, when he discovered a whole cupboard full of his own work.) Isolated from the other Slovak historians, who preferred to accept the Party line, the only like-minded colleagues he was able to meet were in Prague. As with the other Slovak dissidents, the secret police did their best to intercept his visits to Prague, either by stopping his car on the motorway or detaining him as he stepped off the bus at Florenc bus station.

In the early 1980s this small group essentially made up the political opposition in Slovakia. The weight of the 'independent culture' belonged elsewhere. The organisation of the 'underground church'[2] began in the early 1950s, with the consecration of secret bishops to replace those sentenced in the Communists' show trials. By a law passed in 1949, permission from the state was a condition of every ecclesiastical activity; only services of worship inside a church building were permitted. Therefore, although congregations still met as part of the 'visible' church, an independent structure came into existence to take care of such pastoral responsibilities as were now illegal. A few parish priests were involved in the activities of the underground church, but not many. It had its own structure, with bishops, priests, lay organisers and religious orders, but it always considered itself (and was considered by the Vatican) to be a part of the worldwide church. In the 1970s its activities expanded. Groups consisting of between five and fifteen people met secretly, usually once a week for prayer, readings, meditation and discussion which covered social as well as theological issues. The network was extended by students who had become involved in the underground church in Bratislava and then returned to their home towns where they themselves organised Christian groups. In the mid-1980s the underground church began to manifest itself in pilgrimages, on a scale (numbers of pilgrims ranged from 3,000 to 250,000) which made intimidation by the Communists impossible.

The underground church maintained a strict discipline and forbade those involved in its organisation to take part in political activities. However, one man who spanned the two worlds was Ján Čarnogurský, who had trained as a lawyer and practised until 1981, when his defence of the Charter signatory Hana Ponická led to him being struck off the register. He took a job as a driver, but carried on giving legal advice to political dissidents and to the underground church. Čarnogurský belonged to a prominent Roman Catholic family; his father Pavel was a well-known historian. He had been in contact with the underground church from the late 1970s, and was also involved in other strands of underground activity which did not begin to merge until the late 1980s. He maintained clandestine links abroad, including Radio Free Europe and Keston College, and was a member of Polish-Czechoslovak Solidarity. In July 1987 Alexander Tomsky's successor at Keston College, Dominic Farrell, brought the Foundation news from Bratislava that Čarnogurský would be interested in the possibility of seminars on legal and historical matters. The Trustees of the Foundation, especially Roger Scruton, had long wanted to expand its activities eastwards, although Jiří Müller in Brno had advised that the situation was different in Slovakia and the time was not ripe. However, it was agreed in Britain that a messenger should be sent, and James de Candole, travelling to Brno at the end of the month, was asked to take a bus to Bratislava to visit Čarnogurský and propose a trial run of one visitor in the autumn. Čarnogurský asked for a lecture on either Conservatism or the concept of legality, to take place on 24th October.

Čarnogurský had previously held political discussions with speakers from as far away as Prague (such as Václav Benda) but this venture with the British lecturers was something new. The participants for the seminar were carefully chosen, both from the ranks of political dissidents and those of the underground church. That first audience, of between 15 and 18 people aged from 24 to over 70, included Miroslav Kusý and the elderly forestry expert Miroslav Lehký,[3] who later became an important link in the Bratislava connection. Nearly all the group were

serious Catholics with a political orientation which was, according to Čarnogurský, 'roughly W. German mainstream, ranging
from Social to Christian Democrats, with most of them inclining
towards the rightwards end of the spectrum.'[4] The speaker was
Robert Grant of Glasgow University, who had already visited
Prague for the Foundation in 1984 and 1986. He was asked by
Čarnogurský to talk about 'the political philosophy of conservatism and its relation, if any, to the current practice of the British
Conservative Party. In particular [Čarnogurský] asked about the
apparently paradoxical espousal by Tories of liberal economic
policies. He wanted also to know about Conservative views of
the EEC and NATO.'[5] Grant found the group to be more homo-
genous but politically less sophisticated than the groups he had
met in Prague. 'They were genuinely puzzled by my presenting
British (and indeed historic) conservatism in entirely secular
terms,' reported Grant, admitting that his repetition of Lord
Melbourne's quip that he was not a pillar of the Church, but a
buttress which 'supported it from outside' had not been a success. 'Here someone interrupted, only half-laughingly, with
"Then you will all go to hell!". I was wrong-footed by this
stroke of unconscious Lifemanship, and decided I should not
have been (or rather seemed) so airy about the whole thing.'[6]

Grant returned with requests for equipment, periodicals,
books (including Chautard's *L'Ame de tout Apostolat* and
Rawls's *A Theory of Justice*) and further speakers. He also
brought information about practical aspects of the journey: the
bus ride from Vienna, the hotel situation (catastrophic), how to
find Čarnogurský's flat (in a high rise block near the terminus of
a tram route),[7] registration with the police, and where to eat ('a
more deadly dump than Bratislava is hard to imagine'). He also
reported on the warmth and generosity of Čarnogurský and his
wife Marta.

Over the next two years the Foundation sent eight visitors to
the Bratislava seminar: Professor John Finnis (Natural Law);
David Selbourne (his own political odyssey); Professor David
Regan (Christianity and political ideology); Father Edward
Yarnold[8] (the state of the churches in Britain); John Marks (the
basic structure of school education in Britain); David Pryce-
Jones (see below); Mark Almond (Western perceptions of
Gorbachev's foreign and defence policies); and Dennis

O'Keeffe (Education in the Free Societies, and Political Aspects of Education in the Free Societies).[9] Reflecting the interests of the Bratislava group, the subjects covered primarily religious and political studies (Finnis's theoretical lecture proved something of a struggle for the assembled group, but in discussion they drew him on to a description of Oxford, its university structure and history, and the recent climate of its philosophy).

Over the months the visitors built up a knowledge of the group, its needs and interests; the topics requested were almost all connected with current political and social issues — the Middle East, the East-West military balance, western European integration, church life in western Europe. David Regan, visiting in April 1988, complained that earlier visitors had underestimated the group's intellectual calibre; whilst in January 1989 John Marks commented on the wide range of questions asked, in a session lasting nearly five hours. Friendships were built up in the course of the brief, two-day visits. David Regan spent most of one day with Milan Šimečka and concluded: 'He is a very impressive man — an attractive personality, a powerful intellect, a major writer — but a tragic one. He was dismissed from his academic post in 1969 following the Soviet invasion the year before and has never had another. Nor is he allowed to travel abroad although he receives many invitations... Šimečka has lived partly by manual labour and partly by his writing for 18 years. He was imprisoned for a year in 1980 but released without being tried. His wife has also suffered... She is a brilliant English scholar, a specialist on E.M. Forster... She did not sign the Charter in 1977 but the University asked her to write an attack on the Charter which she refused to do. She was then dismissed.'[10] For Miroslav Kusý, the subject of the seminar was secondary to the quality of the visitors. Most westerners who had found their way to Bratislava had been of student level, or independent lone travellers — interesting as individuals, but not part of the European intellectual and academic network. Now, at last, the Slovaks were coming out of isolation and being linked into that network; they were debating at their proper intellectual level, and news of what they thought was being circulated in the West.

Life was also opening up for Ján Čarnogurský, a man with high ambitions who, as the months went by, was clearly thriving on the sense of urgency driving through Czechoslovakia in the late 1980s and on the expanded network of contacts his western visitors were able to provide. He and Kusý were now broadcasting regularly on Radio Free Europe, taking advantage of improved international telephone connections which meant that calls made from phone boxes could not be traced. Čarnogurský had, with another seminar member, František Mikloško, started the first regular Slovak samizdat, *Nabožensto a súčasnost* 'Religion and the Present'which he edited from 1982 until 1985 when, after a home search by the police, he realised it was unsafe. However, as early as 1984 he had begun to think about the publication of *Bratislavské listy* (Bratislava Newspaper), with the aim: 'to facilitate free discussion of problems in society and the state and of alternative future form of development in Czechoslovakia.'[11] The discipline of the underground church did not allow Mikloško to participate; Čarnogurský found a partner in Ján Langoš,[12] one of an independently-minded group working in the arts and sciences whom he met through the underground church. Langoš — who was close to the writer Dominik Tatarka — had been involved in other, semi-official, literary activities, and was responsible for the practical side of production. *Bratislavské listy*, when it eventually appeared in 1988, was unique in Slovakia for two reasons: it was the first political samizdat, and it carried Čarnogurský's name and address as editor, a revolutionary procedure which had recently been initiated by the Prague samizdat periodical *Lidové noviny*.

Čarnogurský's energy and activity inevitably drew the attention of the secret police. In the first half of the 1980s he was considered to be a religious activitist, and in searches of his home police looked for evidence of the underground church. In the second half of the 1980s he was reclassified as a political activist. Čarnogurský estimates that during this period he went through 20 to 25 interrogations, and was several times held for 48 hours. He always maintained his right not to answer questions, and remembers that the police behaved correctly, knowing that he was a lawyer. (However, other methods of pressure were used; for example, his chronically ill son was refused permission to visit a clinic in Yugoslavia.) The day before John Marks arrived in January 1989, Čarnogurský was called to police headquarters and formally warned that if he continued his present activities he might face criminal charges of working to undermine the Republic, which would carry a prison sentence of 8-12 years; two days later their car was tailed by police, probably to ensure that Čarnogurský did not join the Jan Palach demonstration taking place in Prague. Later that year, in June, police prevented David Pryce-Jones' seminar from taking place by detaining Čarnogurský when on his way to meet Pryce-Jones, and sending Pryce-Jones a false message to the effect that the seminar would not take place.

On 14th August 1989 Čarnogurský and Kusý were arrested after issuing a plea to Slovak citizens to mark the 21st anniversary of the Soviet-led invasion of Czechoslovakia by laying flowers in Bratislava; they were charged with 'incitement' and 'subversion'. Two weeks later Čarnogurský's charge was changed to the more serious one of 'subversion in collusion with foreign agents'. Mark Almond, returning from Bratislava in early October, brought two type-written extracts from Čarnogurský's letters from prison to give to the BBC and a message from Marta Čarnogurska asking for as many visitors to the trial as possible. After postponements, the trial of Kusý and three others (including Hana Ponická) was fixed for 11th-15th November; Čarnogurský's for 22-23rd November. The Foundation arranged for Christine Verity, the journalist who had written about the Jazz Section case, to travel to Bratislava to cover the first of the trials.[13] It was a bleak arrival: 'Bratislava's tower blocks make the city a windswept nightmare.... Dense fog and the undistinguished architecture made orientation difficult.' The Bratislava authorities were suspicious and uncooperative,[14] and Verity talked her way into the court building only by waving a piece of the Foundation's writing paper, with its impressive heading.[15] She noted how important was the presence of herself, Helsinki Watch and other westerners for the defendants' families. Kusý received a suspended sentence and the others were acquitted, but it was not expected that Čarnogurský would escape so lightly.

Čarnogurský spent the first week of the Velvet Revolution in prison. His trial began on 22nd November to demonstrations calling for his immediate release, and in the presence of Alexander Dubček. Acquitted on the 23rd, he was detained pending appeal and finally released on 25th November. When

Barbara Day arrived a week later he was one of the most active participants of the Slovak movement Public Against Violence, whilst simultaneously establishing the Christian Democratic Party (office hours were 10.00 a.m. on the pavement outside the National Theatre in Hviezdoslavovo Square). Within a few weeks Čarnogurský left for Prague, where shortly afterwards he became Deputy Prime Minister of the Federal Republic of Czechoslovakia.

The Cambridge Diploma

In Bohemia as well as in Slovakia, the underground church and its related seminars grew up not in opposition to the established church but parallel with it. Most of those involved were loyal members of their local church, catholic or protestant, and not afraid of the risks this involved — loss of promotion, limited educational opportunities for their children, the impossibility of travelling abroad. But most of them wanted something more — the opportunity to practise and study their faith without looking over their shoulder at the Communist regime's spies and tell-tales. The larger the congregation and the more the participants tried to create a spirit of celebration and fellowship, the more likely it was that amongst them were some who were reporting back to the police the names and activities of those present. It was difficult, in these circumstances, to look for a spiritual dimension in the established churches.

Many of them felt that their church had been, if not irredeemably corrupted, at least tainted by compromise with the régime. In the worst case, this involved the Roman Catholic priests who had joined the *Pacem in Terris* movement, which worked closely with the Communist authorities and had been denounced by the Vatican. *Pacem in Terris* was steadfastly opposed by the veteran Cardinal Tomášek, and the stand of the Roman Catholic church was at least more independent than that of the evangelical (or protestant) church. The surbordination of church to state was often more than its own members could tolerate. The evangelical priest Jakub Trojan, who lost his licence early in 1974 on the grounds that he 'did not fulfil requirements', has described how the long pressure on the church drained its resistance and left it only with the desire to survive. To this end, he recalls, it even adapted its theology and preached forebearance in the face of suffering, but not the need to stand against evil. Parents whose children were not allowed to attend university were advised not to protest, but to 'bear their cross'. Trojan's own seminar met fortnightly through the academic year in the 1970s and 1980s, and was the venue for many of the lectures by western visitors — British, French, German, and especially the Dutch. Hebe Kohlbrugge of Amsterdam visited several times until she lost her visa, and in the 1980s Henri Veldhuis organised a series of visits by theologians parallel with the visits by Dutch philosophers to Ladislav Hejdánek's seminar. Trojan's seminar was based on different themes, often Biblical concepts such as faith, hope and love (some students remember that one of the most consistent themes was that of power). It was an ecumenical seminar, including Catholics such as Alena Hromádková and Tomáš Vlasák.

There were always some priests and churches, both catholic and protestant, involved in the organisation of parallel 'unofficial' activities. Sometimes, as in the 'unofficial arena' in cultural life, the border between what might be tolerated and what might not was difficult to define. In some circumstances, seminars on religious themes could be held and material distributed without interference; in others, such activities were talked of only among participants who trusted each other. At the deepest level of security were those whose identities were known only to the Vatican and its immediate representatives, the underground priests. Amongst them was Tomáš Vlasák, who became one of the most powerful personalities of the Cambridge Diploma seminar.

Not all of those who were concerned with a study of spiritual values turned to the Christian religion. Judaism had a long tradition in the Czech lands, but many old Jewish Czech families had been transported via the closed town of Terezín to the death camps in Poland. Some of the survivors, returning after 1945 to their family homes in the Sudetenland, were swept up in the mass expulsion of the German-speaking population and found themselves refugees in Germany or Austria. Nonetheless, in the first decades of Communism there was still an active Jewish community, many of whom could be met in the dining room of the Jewish Town Hall in Prague. But many of the most active emigrated in the course of the 1970s.[1]

However, there were Czechs of both Jewish and non-Jewish origin who were drawn not only to the study of Judaism, but also of the Hebrew language. Some of them attended the seminars of the protestant clergyman and Hebrew specialist Milan Balabán. Balabán was one of the first, in December 1976, to sign Charter 77; he remembers that as he walked down Národní třída with Jakub Trojan that night they were exhilarated but also apprehensive, knowing they had taken a momentous step. Soon afterwards Balabán lost his licence as a priest, and for the next 12 years went from one job to another for as long as his employers were allowed to keep him, working as a coal heaver, greengrocer, book-keeper, restaurant cleaner, and in the sewers. After losing his licence he began to hold a regular seminar at his own home on Hebrew thought and language, attracting up to 40 students. Held on Tuesday evenings, his seminar was considered to be one of the most important on the underground circuit; among those who attended were Václav Havel, Karol Sidon (the future Chief Rabbi of Prague), and the philosopher Egon Bondy (who also had his own seminar). One of Balabán's students, Jan Schneider, later said that he didn't just teach them Hebrew, he taught them to think in a Hebrew way. He was also often invited to lecture at other home seminars: on Judaism, the Old Testament, and occult and esoteric studies. (On one occasion he was detained by police on his way to deliver a lecture to Ivan Havel's seminar. The paper in his briefcase was on 'Black and White Magic'. The police, somewhat alarmed, released him. If the lecture had been on a philosophical or theological theme, Balabán later reflected, they would probably have made a lot more trouble.)

The first member of the Jan Hus Foundation to make contact with Milan Balabán was Roger Scruton in October 1983. Scruton noted that Balabán had been ill and was unable to take on heavy work, but neither could he practise as a priest or publish his works. In November the Foundation agreed to award him a 6-month stipend of 50 pounds a month. The first initiative for the setting up of the Cambridge Diploma course appears to have grown out of the encounter in April 1986 between Alena Hromádková and the Reverend Dr. Andrew Lenox-Conyngham, clergyman and scholar. It was given impetus by the failure, in

1986, of the Open University and Buckingham University to respond to the needs of the students of the underground university. The simple and dignified way in which the University of Cambridge Local Examinations Syndicate took on the responsibility of guiding a small group of students, existing beyond the framework of the known world, through its examination programme will always be appreciated by the Prague students.

Lenox-Conyngham, when the story opened, was Chaplain and Fellow of St Catharine's College in Cambridge. He had learnt of the persecution of Christians in Communist lands through an address given by the Romanian Lutheran pastor Richard Wurmbrand, and in 1969 a pamphlet published by the Reverend Michael Bourdeaux came into his hands. In 1970 Bourdeaux set up the Centre for the Study of Religion and Communism which, in 1974, was established as Keston College.[2] Keston College became renowned in the West for its meticulous collection and analysis of religious samizdat and other information from behind the Iron Curtain. (Like the Jan Hus Foundation, it was registered by the Czechoslovak secret police as an 'ideodiversní centrum' — a Centre for Ideological Subversion.) Lenox-Conyngham was a member from the beginning, and from 1983 sat on Keston's Managing Committee.

In 1978 Lenox-Conyngham was asked to smuggle Bibles into the Soviet Union for an associated organisation, Aid for Russian Christians. Mildly shocked by the proposal but unable to think of any good reason to refuse, he travelled there on four occasions with not only Bibles but more books, tape recorders, jeans, children's clothes, medicines and — on one occasion — a fur coat. In 1982, whilst at the University of Heidelberg, Lenox-Conyngham was asked by the Czechoslovak specialist at Keston College, Alexander Tomsky,[3] to take books to Prague. With the same nonchalance with which he had travelled to Moscow he accepted boxes of religious and emigré literature, taking them into Czechoslovakia by train and coach and — on one occasion — in the converted petrol tank of a large American car. On his return journey, the concealed space was packed with samizdat; if the hiding place had been discovered on the inward or outward journey, a prison sentence would have been very possible.

On the fourth trip, in early April 1986, Tomsky asked Lenox-Conyngham to give a series of seminars, two in German (interpreted by Milan Balabán) and three in English (interpreted by Alena Hromádková and Pavel Bratinka). Each took place in a different apartment; the subjects included the philosophy of St. Augustine, St. Ambrose and the question of church and state, and Early Church History. Tomsky, hoping that Lenox-Conyngham might obtain some financial support from the Jan Hus Foundation,[4] put him in touch with Roger Scruton. Lenox-Conyngham had, in any case, a message to deliver from Hromádková, to the effect that in Prague they were trying to set up 'a course in Theological studies for mature people, i.e. those over about 30, the course to last about six years and to finish with an examination and the award of degrees. At the moment, however, the project is frozen because of a certain amount of opposition from within their own ranks, but a group of them including of course Alena herself, are determined to try to get the project going sometime. She would like to receive details of curricula of theological courses in English universities because this would help them in working out their own curricula.'

At that time the Chartists were thinking in terms of their own Evening University; Scruton and Lenox-Conyngham, however, saw other possibilities. Initially Lenox-Conyngham considered whether the students might be interested in the Lambeth Diploma, and arranged for them to see the appropriate materials; the general feeling was that the syllabus was too church-based. On 20th June 1987 Lenox-Conyngham wrote to the Foundation: 'I was wondering whether the Cambridge Diploma and Certificate in Religious Studies might be more suitable? I have only just thought of this — and confess I am surprised that I hadn't thought of it before, since I have been one of their examiners for two years and am on the Managing Committee.' Six days later he sent materials and asked whether he could pursue the idea with the Syndicate: 'Obviously the situation in Czecho is quite unlike anything they have encountered before — the Czech Ministry of Education is hardly likely to be very helpful for example!' The Foundation gave its approval and on 18th September Lenox-Conyngham discussed the project with the Assistant to the Secretaries of the Syndicate, Stephen Blunden.

The question of security was a delicate one. Various measures involving the Foreign Office or the British Council were discussed and rejected. It is unlikely that the project would have got off the ground had not Stephen Blunden been willing to go to Prague to see the situation for himself. The visit was arranged by the Foundation and took place in March 1988; on his return Blunden reported to both the Foundation and the Syndicate. Blunden met Milan Balabán and six of the proposed students in an artist's studio, where he talked to them about the requirements of the Cambridge Diploma, and made sure it would suit their needs. Balabán had already written to the Syndicate about the students: 'The theological group consists of ten people whose age ranges from 24 to 52 years. Four of them are university-educated people, five of the group are graduates of secondary or technical schools and just one person of the group passed through basic school only.'[5] He emphasised their commitment to the project, and the fact that they had already been following his courses in Hebrew and Greek studies: 'The lectures are held twice a week for four hours for each combined subject (Hebrew and the Old Testament, Greek and the New Testament). The rest of theological studies will be added step by step.'[6]

It was a remarkable and heterogeneous group. As well as the six who eventually passed through the course, nine others were seriously involved in the project. They included two of Balabán's colleagues from the sewers, one of whom — Pavel Čalek, a Chinese specialist — was murdered in 1988, possibly by the secret police. František Volek, who studied Hebrew, became a manager of a large Prague department store in the 1990s. Pavel Turnovský became an astrologer and JiříHolba an Indian specialist, whilst Jan Placák (brother of Petr Placák of the 'Czech Children') later ran a second-hand bookshop. Ladislav Moučka was an artist whose chief interest was in the cabbala; in the 1990s he became increasingly absorbed in esoteric mysteries and astrological charts. In these days his studio was often used for the seminar; Iva Vodráčková's studio was also well-known as a seminar venue. Rostislava Křivánková and Jana Chržová were both involved in the Jazz Section; Chržová was also a specialist in Celtic cultures, and her exceptional English benefited the whole group.

The six who eventually graduated included two brothers, Jan Schneider and Jiří, eight years younger. Although the family was originally Jewish, their father had been a protestant priest and in the 1950s spent eighteen months in prison — 'in the days when you could be imprisoned for lending someone a book'.[7] In the 1990s Jan Schneider was selected for a high position in the police department of the Ministry of the Interior, whilst Jiří became a Parliamentary Deputy and then Ambassador to Israel. Jan had been introduced to Balabán by Jan Kozlík, with whom he had attended secondary industrial school in Mladá Boleslav; in 1978 they were sharing a flat in Prague. At this time Schneider was working as surveyor on the railways, a position where the secret police had stopped pursuing him 'because I was right down among the dregs'.[8] Kozlík was meanwhile working in a hospital boiler-room, one of the coveted havens with gas-powered boilers which required only the occasional press of a switch and allowed plenty of time for study; he remembers the 1980s as a golden age, when the situation had stabilised to a point where they knew they would be able to survive. (After the revolution, a chauffeur-driven Mercedes waited outside the Cambridge Diploma examination room to speed Kozlík back to his post at the Ministry of the Interior.) The fourth member of the group was the research physicist Petr Krejčí[9] who (with Jiří Schneider) had learnt ancient Greek, and the fifth Marta Chadimová, a specialist in textile conservation. In the early 1990s Chadimová was at the centre of a property restitution scandal, and was released from prison only after being granted a pardon by President Václav Havel; a pardon she refused to accept on the grounds that it assumed her guilt. Subsequently she was the first to validate the Cambridge Diploma at the Charles University, and gained a doctorate in Jewish embroidery. The oldest member of the group was Tomáš Vlasák, a metalworker in heavy industry who in February 1977 was ordained a priest in the underground church. It was Vlasák who at Hejdánek's seminar in 1981 had asked Jacques Derrida the improper but pertinent question: 'What use is that sort of philosophy?'

In the strange world of the underground university, this late seminar was maybe the strangest of them all; a fact acknowledged by Milan Balabán, who finds it astonishing that it was never interfered with by the police. A special atmosphere seemed to surround this gathering of highly-charged and original people; Balabán remembers that the group bonded like a family, in the positive sense. They always met in the flat of one of the group, usually that of Marta Chadimová whose husband, Mikoláš Chadima, was a musician involved in the 'unofficial' world of rock music and underground concerts. Photographs show the group clustered round a table in a room filled with books and *objets d'art*, the table covered with papers and tea mugs, Jan Schneider in a skull cap, Hebrew characters on the blackboard.[10] (The Canadian journalist Nancy Durham, who attended a seminar in 1988, reported that: 'They sat around a huge table and behind them were seven life-size statues including one of a naked man playing a saxophone.'[11]) No one is smoking in the photographs, although visiting lecturers remember that they all smoked except for Tomáš Vlasák, who would declare in his booming voice that they were committing a mortal sin. Stephen Blunden observed after his visit: 'I was impressed by the breadth of interests of the seminar members — Judaism, Buddhism, philosophy, and the Hermetic tradition, as well as Christianity. By no means all those present appeared to be Christians, in the sense of being paid-up members of a particular denomination. Indeed, I sensed that they regarded sectarian differences as a luxury which the circumstances did not permit.'[12]

Blunden categorised the difficulties involved in establishing a Cambridge Diploma Religious Studies centre in Prague as 'resources, language and security'. Resources covered the practical problems both of providing the necessary specialist texts, and of preparing the students for the requirements of the examinations themselves: 'I think that their enthusiasm and breadth of interest is such that some of the students may find it difficult to limit their answers to the field required by each paper.' He advised those whose English was weak not to embark on the examinations until they had sufficient competence in the language, since 'sitting a paper when there is no hope of passing could lead to a delay of five years before one could begin again with a clean sheet'. As to security: 'On the one hand there are the normal requirements regarding the confidentiality of the question papers and the orderly conduct of the examination. On the other hand, there is the extraordinary requirement that the identity of the candidates and their teachers must remain confidential.'[13] For this reason he proposed that the candidates' papers should be submitted through the St Catharine's College Centre where Lenox-Conyngham was Local Secretary, under numbers rather than names.

The Jan Hus Foundation set up a sub-committee to handle the details of the theology programme, and on 18th May 1988 Stephen Blunden, Andrew Lenox-Conyngham and Roger Scruton met at St. Catharine's College. In the course of a long and complex meeting, the subjects they discussed included the choice of papers to be taken (after consultation with Balabán, it was settled that these should be Old and New Testament Theology, Old Testament: General, New Testament: Christian Origins, Judaism and Early Church History); conditions for admission to the course; the timetable; the structure of teaching and submission of essays; the provision of books;[14] visiting lecturers; security; and organisational matters. It was agreed that although all the students must necessarily know English, the Foundation would pay for the intensive sessions with the visiting lecturers to be interpreted. The interpreter chosen by Balabán, Miloš Calda, became an important link in the project.

The plans were made subject to the approval of the Chairman of the Managing Committee, the Regius Professor of Divinity Stephen Sykes,[15] who had already shown his interest in the success of the project, and who later (in December 1989) became one of the visiting lecturers on the course. Further support was given to the project by the M.P. David Mellor, who had been at university with Lenox-Conyngham, and who was now Minister of State at the Foreign and Commonwealth Office.[16] The entire project was eventually submitted to the Vice-Chancellor of the University of Cambridge, Michael McCrum. All this had to be done without revealing Balabán's identity or those of his students, or any detailed information of how the project was to be carried out. In September 1988 Lenox-Conyngham wrote to Professor Sykes: 'I am very anxious that the V-C [Vice-Chancellor] should not get the impression that there is anything illegal or unnecessarily secretive about this matter... The Czech government does not like these [academic] contacts and has sometimes attempted — illegally according to its own constitution and all the more so according to the Helsinki agreement of

1976 — actively to discourage them... What has now happened is that some people, who have every qualification to do so, wish to enter for the Cambridge Diploma in Religious Studies. They have as much right to do this as any one else in any other part of the world... It could potentially be highly embarrassing for this University if it were to be seen as, in effect, discriminating against a particular group of people on what would amount to be no other grounds than that their own government does not wish them to gain this qualification.'[17]

The first visiting lecturer for the Cambridge Diploma course was Lenox-Conyngham himself, in September 1988. He set the timetable for the coming months, which would be spent in preparation for the examinations on Old Testament: General and New Testament: Christian Origins, and observed that 'the main difficulty will be not that of intellectual capacity or of knowledge of the topic but of examination technique'.[18] In December the group was visited by David Sanders, a friar of the Dominican order from Blackfriars in Cambridge. (Travelling on a Čedok package holiday, he was weighed down with duplicate copies of the Jerome Biblical Commentary and Rowland's *Christian Origins*.) In the course of a week's visit he led five long seminars; it was a pattern which made heavy demands on the teacher, but even more on the students, who did not dare to take a holiday from work for fear of attracting attention, and managed to survive the week on two or three hours sleep a night. (Fr. Sanders sensed 'a subdued response' on the last evening.) Sanders' assessment was that 'the group are impressive, and have ability and enthusiasm'. He continued: 'Milan [Balabán] clearly thinks this is an important project for the individuals, the church and the culture at this time. There is a risk that they may not be prepared enough [for the examinations], but provided the practical problems are overcome, it is a risk worth taking.'[19]

Father Sanders returned at the end of May 1989 to find that Balabán had changed his job and was now 'washing up heavy pans in a restaurant'.[20] Sanders was pleased to find that the group had completed the mock exam and that all of them had essays ready to hand in. '[Balabán] explained that the group had been working hard although they had been distracted by the political events.... Everyone was very conscious about the exam and rather nervous too.' Sanders reported that after three hot and sunny weeks they all looked well. However, on marking the essays he noted the recurrent problem: 'Most of them were good efforts reflecting hard work but not always answering the question exactly.... Miloš [Calda] who knows both cultures well explained the differences in attitudes to writing.'[21]

The necessity of writing essays and examination questions on the British model became a major issue with the students, one which they vehemently discussed out of earshot of their visiting tutors. They had been educated in the German tradition, in which 'a piece of writing only 50 pages long is not worth reading, a mere prologue'.[22] Lenox-Conyngham remembers that the students tended to pick key words from the question, and discourse on those. Balabán agrees that this was the case; that the students used the question as a basis to develop their ideas creatively, and that at least two of the teachers appreciated this and said that they learned much from this approach for themselves. Nevertheless, again and again the visiting lecturers had to implore the students to 'answer to the question', the students sometimes beginning to feel terrorised by the pressure. In the German tradition, examinations are held orally; there is no concept of writing against the clock. It was particularly difficult for the 56-year-old underground priest Tomáš Vlasák, whom Balabán describes as 'brilliant, but not always to the point... the Slavonic type, chaotic and unsystematic'.[23] However, successive visiting lecturers record that he was the hardest working and most productive of the students and Lenox-Conyngham recalls his contribution as being 'lively, vibrant and spiritual'. Jan Kozlík's later observation about the essays and exams was that 'the English tradition seems to ask for good craftsmanship, not revolutionary thought'.[24] Nevertheless Jan Schneider considers that the British academics taught them a discipline and precision which proved invaluable in their new posts after the revolution.

The first two rounds of exams were sat in June 1989; the answer papers were photocopied on one of the dissidents' secret photocopiers[25] (in case of confiscation by police) and brought back to be marked by the Cambridge Diploma examiners. It turned out that the efforts of the previous year had been worthwhile; most candidates had achieved reasonable results, Jiří Schneider in particular with impressive success.

No one yet guessed, at the beginning of the new academic

year, that those first exams would be the last to be held in conditions of secrecy. The exams towards which the group was now working were Old and New Testament Theology. The first visitor, the Regius Professor of Divinity Stephen Sykes, arrived on the 8th December — in the middle of the excitement surrounding the Velvet Revolution. No exams were taken in the summer of 1990; in retrospect it is amazing that in that totally changed society the group should still have held together. Virtually all other 'home seminars' came to an end with the Velvet Revolution, but the group sitting the Cambridge Diploma exams was determined to achieve its aim. In June 1991 Krejčí, Kozlík and Vlasák passed two papers each; Chadimová three, and Jiří Schneider four. (Jan Schneider — with a wife and three children in Havlíčkův Brod and a responsible post in the Bureau for the Defence of Democracy[26] in Hradec Králové — postponed the exams for another year.) In 1992, the first five candidates completed the course, and were joined by Jan Schneider in 1993. Two of them — Jiří Schneider and Petr Krejčí — were awarded the full Diploma; the remainder obtained the Cambridge Certificate with Credit. (Jan Schneider, who was awarded Grade I for Old Testament Theology, was offered the rare opportunity to upgrade to Diploma by re-sitting his weakest paper; but by now he was overworked and exhausted.) The British academics who taught the course in the 1990s included Canon John Sweet, of Selwyn College, Cambridge; Father Henry Wansbrough, a Benedictine and Master of St. Benet's Hall, Oxford; and Hyam Maccoby of the Sternberg Centre for Judaism.

The Cambridge Diploma course is unique in the history of the underground university as the only case where students were able to follow regular teaching which enabled them to sit, in secret, the external examinations of a western university. This had for a long time been an aim of the Jan Hus Foundation, and the major regret of the students is that the project did not start three or four years earlier, when they could have devoted much more time and energy to their studies.[27] A major role in the project was played by Milan Balabán, the Hebrew specialist who came from the sewers to take some of Prague's most colourful and talented individuals through to a western academic qualification.

The Philosophers and the Secret Police

The issue of how the Jan Hus Educational Foundation was to deal with the security of its operations had been a concern from the time of Kathy Wilkes' first visit, when the philosophers found themselves between the extremes of Julius Tomin's openness and Jan Kavan's secrecy. Everyone understood the purpose of security, but no one was certain as to how it could be achieved without being reduced to inaction. Differences of opinion had existed amongst the 'dissident' community before the JHEF ever became involved. The earliest home seminars, consisting of small groups of closely-knit friends, were left alone by the police, either because they did not know about them or because they had more important matters to pursue. Some seminars were raided by police as early as the beginning of the 1970s. From the mid-1970s most seminar organisers did everything they could to keep their work secret, arguing that a raided seminar was a wasted seminar, and that it was the duty of the organiser to provide appropriate conditions for study. When Julius Tomin stood against this, his principle of openness (for example, his invitations to President Husák[1]) was condemned by some as publicity-seeking. At the same time, Tomin warned that one fundamental principle of working in a totalitarian state was never to forget the microphone under the table. He remembers that the student Jan Bednář objected: 'But then we can't talk about anything at all!' 'We are free people,' Tomin responded: 'we can say anything we like about our own opinions, about what we think and what we believe. There are only two things we can't talk about: what is to happen, which may be endangered by what we say; and other people, who may be endangered by what we say. But you can talk about your own opinions, with the full awareness that you are taking the responsibility for them yourself.'

Zdena Tomin still remembers one of the Thursday gatherings in the Slavia café when, in Julius's absence, she attempted to defend his activities. On that occasion it was the elderly historian Václav Černý, who usually sat in silence, who pronounced: 'Philosophy that hides is not worth its name.' In the winter of 1978, when the writer Ludvík Vaculík attacked Tomin's methods, he was defended by Václav Havel; even so, the Vaculík sons stopped attending the Tomin seminar. The arrival of the western philosophers exacerbated the debate. The first Oxford visitors had been influenced by Jan Kavan, whose fertile brain was constantly hatching new methods to outwit authority. Tomin maintained that 'playing games with the secret service' was 'pernicious, fundamentally morally wrong, undermining the whole work.'[2] Visitors were often startled when he insisted on talking English with them in the street, openly, and often loudly. Disputes would sometimes erupt during a seminar, such as the occasion at Christmas 1979 when, at a lecture given by Alan Montefiore, Tomin and Alena Hromádková argued over the presence of a Swedish news photographer. Tomin maintained that as it was a free assembly there was no reason why photographs should not be taken. Hromádková believed strongly that such publicity not only destroyed the atmosphere essential to serious study, but that it also attracted students for the wrong reasons. Her feelings were confirmed by her experience in April 1980, after the raid on Anthony Kenny's lecture. Hromádková was one of those detained, sharing a police cell with a young girl from the north Bohemian town of Ústí nad Labem who had attended the seminar in deliberate defiance of her parents, and was delighted by the turn of events.

It is likely that the intention of the authorities was to prevent the spread of the seminar movement rather than to stamp it out altogether. This was why the action taken in the first months of 1980 was directed against seminars which showed signs of dynamics by attracting young people, welcoming participants from outside the 'ghetto', and inviting foreign lecturers. Seminars where the same group had met for years were left in peace. In most cases, the police attempted to use persuasion rather than violence. However, after an incident in between the raids on seminars led by Bill Newton-Smith and Anthony Kenny

(March and April 1980) the student Pavel Šmída adressed the following complaint about his treatment to the Ministry of the Interior and the General Procurator:

After five minutes two plain clothes men came to collect me [from the cell], one slim, of medium height and with dark hair, the other heavier and taller with light brown hair. These two elegantly dressed men had prepared a surprise which previously I had experienced only in films about the animal bestiality of the Gestapo during the second world war. One of the most recent was the film about Maruška Kuděříková shown on TV on Sunday 8.4.1980,[3] an interval of only three days. What is all the more shocking is that this year is the 35th year since we rid ourselves of the horrors of fascism.

This began on an unlit staircase between the first and second floors of the StB[4] building, when the heavier man turned on me with the words: 'Well then, my little Pavel?' and kicked me hard and accurately with his pointed shoe in one of the most sensitive places on a man's body, in the crotch. The pain was terrible, I couldn't stay on my feet, apart from that I desperately wanted to be sick. When I fell to the ground they both started kicking me roughly, during which my right arm was badly bruised, forcing me to stand up and follow them into the interrogation room. But that was an almost impossible demand, and so it required more shoving and pushing, during which I fell heavily on the stairs and the floor. Finally they got me into the office where, I foolishly thought, things would be all right.

Once I had been roughly pushed into a chair two more plain clothes men, who up to then had been content to stand unheeding in the corridor, came in. Without further ado these two men — one of whom smelt strongly of alcohol — started hitting me in the face with the backs of their hands and their open palms, whilst one of them pulled my head back by my hair so I had no way of avoiding their blows. My hands were occupied with protecting another part of my body, because the heavier man of the original two was indicating that he intended to present me with another kick in the same place as last time.

While this beating was going on one of the men asked for the window to be closed, so that no one would hear the noise and outpouring of profanities which accompanied the whole process.

The questions from the two newly-arrived — put to me in such an engaging way — were somewhat surprising in their content. They were about my private trip to the German Democratic Republic, from which I had returned about ten days earlier. What was interesting was that neither the questions nor the relevant answers appeared in the written protocol. The protocol only concerned the philosophy seminars. During the questions, which involved rather more than basic data about my person, I held to my legal right to remain silent. During the interrogation they also asked about the place where I live, which gave my interrogators the opportunity to use expressions about my landlady which would shame even the roughest sailor. (The phrases used were along the lines of swine, whore, bitch, etc.) I also learnt a few interesting facts about the authority of the StB. I was told, amongst other things, that it all depended on how 'sensible' I was during the negotiations concerning my application to move, and that if they didn't want it, it could take ten years. And it seems they don't want it, since it's exactly four months since I handed in the application and I've heard nothing.

During this first interrogation I was also threatened that difficulties would be made for me at work and school, and also for my parents and brother, with whom, as they very well know, I've been completely out of contact for a long time.

Around half past nine a form was filled in for my temporary detention and under 'reason', after a long pretence of thinking it over, they wrote paragraph 2C2, i.e. breaking the peace. That was it for one day and I was locked in a cell under temporary detention. I was awake nearly the whole night, suffering from nervous and physical shock and wanting to be sick.

The next day I wasn't called to interrogation until the afternoon. This interrogation was carried on in a completely different way. The young interrogator carefully attached the handcuffs and led me to what was, by their standards, an elegantly furnished office. The impression however was spoiled by the fact that I was still where I was and that on the way to the office I met the man who had kicked me so crudely the previous evening. He was probably pleased to see me, since he gave me a big smile. In the office I was offered a leather chair. At the head of the table sat a shortish man with the air of being of higher rank. The interrogation was led by the younger StB man. First of all he gave me a lecture on what was good for me, what I should do and how I should behave. Then he used the phone to call the secretary and we got on to the questions in the protocol. Once they had confirmed that I still wasn't going to answer there was another lecture about my loose morals and my relationship to my native socialist land. To my complaint about the way the interrogation had been carried out the previous day came the shocking reply: 'You know, a lot of our people are sometimes nervous, so it can happen that...' and that was it. He also told me that I should lodge a complaint. As usual! On the other hand, he threatened me that if I didn't stop behaving the way I had up to now (for example '...meeting people like Věra Vránová and Anča Šabatová') then I would be banned from living in Prague. That was about it for Thursday.

On Friday the interrogation was much as the day before. I was however threatened with worse sanctions if I carried on attending the philosophy seminars. It was also written into the protocol that I refused to answer and that I did not sign the protocol.

After the interrogation I was returned to the cell and released about an hour later than the 48-hour limit, that is, at 21.25.[5]

The threat of violence often worked in the case of young people who believed, with Hromádková, that the object of the seminar was serious study rather than the need to make a political point. Their hope had been that such an education would help to integrate them into society, not isolate them from it. It also seems probable that the police used more subtle tactics against the students; it is difficult to prove specific cases, but it is clear that if a student were told by police that a fellow-student had offered information, it would be difficult for him or her to know whether it was the truth or a trick of the secret police. In spite of the courage of the young people, police tactics were successful in breaking up Tomin's seminar and, in the early 1980s, almost destroyed Hejdánek's seminar as well.

When Hejdánek adopted the principle of the 'open seminar' he hoped that by being open he could bring the police into the open as well; at every interrogation he asked the police for a written statement as to why they were taking action against the seminar. If an agreement could be reached with the police, he intended to apply for permission to register his seminar as an official event to which foreigners could be invited. Hejdánek never obtained a written statement, and after the arrests of May 1981 (following the discovery of materials in Jan Kavan's van) broke off attempts to come to an agreement with the police. The police raids and consequent fall in attendance at Hejdánek's seminar (the few still attending included Aleš Havlíček, Jan Kozlík and Tomáš Vlasák) were among the reasons deciding the British to focus their efforts on seminars where greater security would ensure continuity of teaching. The lecturers also knew that in the event of rough treatment it was not they who would be manhandled (Derrida was the only one of Tomin or Hejdánek's visitors to be treated as a criminal) but their hosts and students. Those lecturers who were detained (Newton-Smith, Kenny, Wilkes, Procopé, de Boer) were usually treated with restraint, the emphasis of the interrogation being on their error in visiting Trotskyites and criminal elements instead of accepting official invitations.

In the early 1980s, visitors to Tomin and Hejdánek were routinely followed by police, largely as an attempt at dissuasion, and often with comical results. Kathy Wilkes remembers that in August 1980 she accompanied the American philosophers Tom Nagel and Anne Hollander to the American Embassy to discuss what could be done for the student Tomáš Liška. As they strolled around Hradčany and the Malá Strana, Wilkes amused herself by pointing out how the number of secret police following them had grown from two to six. Nagel was dismissive: 'They're just tourists.' On Kampa Island the group briefly separated; when they rejoined, Nagel's eyes were, in Wilkes's words, as round as saucers; he had seen, as he put it in his New York accent, 'that guy talking into his handbag'. In 1981 Ralph Walker, sightseeing on his final day, was followed by one 'young and particularly miserable policeman' whom he attempted to engage in conversation. Such incidents amused rather than disturbed visitors, and it seems as though for several years after the Tomins' emigration the Communist authorities believed the visits from western academics to be ad hoc and uncoordinated.

There were times when those working within the Foundation felt that the precautions they were taking were ridiculous and even paranoid. However, they did not want to take the risk of underestimating the power and influence of the secret police. Research undertaken since 1989[6] shows the extent of police control in Czechoslovakia: for example, the office which issued passports and visas was a police department directly responsible (in the period up to 1989) to Deputy Federal Minister of the Interior Alojz Lorenz[7]; likewise, the directorate responsible for military espionage, was not — as one might expect — a part of the Ministry of Defence, but under Lorenz's control. In army offices as in those of local administration and large firms, impassive, anonymous men were answerable to a hierarchy concealed from other employees, but throwing a permanent shadow over everyday routine. This will for control extended beyond the sphere of employment into the education and leisure pursuits of Czechoslovak citizens. The revelation of 'Operation Isolation'[8] makes it clear that the police fully intended to discredit the students, organisers and foreign visitors of the home seminars.

In the mid-1980s files were opened on some Jan Hus philosophers by the 10th directorate SNB, responsible for political surveillance of the 'internal enemy'. They were kept by the 1st section, which covered 'antisocialist forces and enemy groupings'. In August 1988 the 10th directorate SNB was combined with the 2nd (which had previously been responsible for the 'external enemy'), the combined directorate covering counter-espionage generally. The files that have survived were amongst those archived when the merger took place; it is assumed files which were still active were hurriedly destroyed in December 1989.[9] The files were opened on the grounds that these 'visa foreigners' had been in contact with a dissident who at that time became the subject of a police operation. Most of the reports are of conversations which took place in this subject's apartment. They purport to be from informers who have gained the confidence of the subject of the police operation; the code names of four different agents appear. It can be questioned as to whether these agents really existed. In two cases, the Jan Hus Foundation holds the visitor's own report of the conversation in question, and in neither case is there mention of another person being present. An alternative possibility would be the use of listening devices, which is possibly borne out by the nature of the reports. They are long, and full of sometimes garbled detail which seems to relate to what is heard rather than seen. An item at the end of the report generally warns other police departments against attempting to make contact with the informer 'because of the risk of deconspiration'. If material gained by microphone were attributed to an informer, presumably the reason would be that the policeman concerned was trying to show evidence of his success in recruiting agents. However, it is also argued that bureaucracy within the secret police would make this kind of deception impossible (a separate directorate, no. 6, was responsible for technical monitoring) and that it would in theory be possible to trace the identity of the informers through the code names.

In April 1984 the police opened a file on Roger Scruton,[10] as a contact of the object of the police operation. By June it was known that he was involved in organising foreign visits, that a samizdat edition of *The Meaning of Conservatism* was in preparation, and that he was planning to visit Czechoslovakia that August. The London agent of the StB was despatched to check Scruton's employment at Birkbeck College and his address in Notting Hill Gate, and the 4th directorate SNB[11] was asked to find out whether Scruton had made a reservation at one of the hotels 'covered' by the secret police. Scruton, however, alerted by the hostile attitude of the Embassy officials, cancelled the visit. By the following spring the StB was able to connect him with the visits of David Levy, Alan Montefiore and Steven Lukes, and with Jan Kavan and others in London. They also knew that he had visited Czechoslovakia frequently in the past,[12] and that he wrote notes in Turkish.[13] The inquiries inclined the police to the view that the British visits were in some way supporting the underground church, but what concerned them most was the forthcoming seminar to be given by Scruton in Prague to mark the samizdat publication of *The Meaning of Conservatism*. On 6th June 1985, the day on which Scruton entered Czechoslovakia at Mikulov on the Austrian border, the secret policeman responsible for Scruton sent an order to the Mikulov customs post that on his departure Scruton must be thoroughly searched for written material connected with the activities of the 'so-called' Czechoslovak opposition and for personal notes written in a foreign language (especially Turkish). It was thought that such material might have a 'conspiratorial' import; if anything was found, Scruton was to be held for further questioning.

The morning after Scruton's arrival in Brno the secret police had an agent (or agents) waiting outside the Müllers' small terraced home; he (or 'they'; it is less likely to have been 'she') must have seen the family leave for work and school before trailing Scruton into town where, to the agents' probable disappointment, he failed to meet any 'interesting' person (Broňa remembers that he bought strawberries for the children). In the afternoon the Müllers took the children to their grandparents and drove Scruton to a nearby park (Jiří, as on every journey, checking the mirror of the Trabant to see whether he recognised any following cars). As they settled down to serious discussion, Scruton looked up to see 'two sinister young men looking down at me from what seemed — in the momentary dismay — a supernatural height'.[14] Scruton sat looking blankly at Müller, who stared back; both avoided the eyes of the policemen, till one ('taller, ruder and more dangerous-seeming than his companion') said: 'We know very well that you speak Czech, Mr. Scruton. We should like you to come with us for questioning.'[15] The next few moments were confused; Scruton remembers chiefly the courage and calm of the Müllers. Scruton's passport was in the Müllers' home. The police agreed to let him return, but not in the Trabant with the Müllers; he would follow in the police car. Three hundred metres on Müller was stopped by a traffic policeman and ordered out of the car; conscious of the compromising documents he was carrying and aware that this could lead to a house search, Müller gestured towards his escort and put his foot on the accelerator. In Chudobova Street: 'We lept from the car without even closing the doors, tore into the house and slammed the front door behind us. We destroyed everything we needed to,[16] and waited to see what would happen next...'[17] What happened next, according to Scruton, was that: 'Three minutes of banging finally brought [Müller] to the door-step, but he refused absolutely to allow the police to enter, or to fetch my belongings. It was for me, he said, to collect what was mine, and finally this was acceded to, on condition that one of the policemen follow me everywhere. Fortunately it was the milder and more easily embarrassed of the two who was chosen; hence I was able to contrive a moment alone, so as to destroy the incriminating pages of my notebook.'[18] Other pages he passed to Broňa, whilst Jiří distracted the policeman.

Scruton was taken to the police station, where it was clear that the Brno police were acting under orders; after a brief inter-rogation he was charged with having failed to register the address where he was staying, and ordered to leave the country (by the Mikulov crossing) within three hours. The Müllers were allowed to drive him to the border, followed 'by squads of cars, all containing the kind of gum-chewing heroes who in England would be doing their bit for Liverpool Football Club'. In Mikulov they spent the last hour in the old Jewish cemetery, 'falling silent every time a young hero strode out of the bushes across our path'.[19]

At the border the guards carried out the instructions from Prague, and stripped and searched Scruton. All they found was the address in Paris of Broňa's mother, and the outline of John Keane's book on 'civil society and socialism'[20] which, he assured the guard, 'defend[ed] socialism against the charge that it must inevitably replace the functions of society with those of the state'.[21] Scruton noted that the guard was interested and wanted to know more; the guard was sufficiently interested to report the conversation to Prague: 'During the search he asked if we thought he was a British spy, adding that he was only a philosopher and that he had his own opinion about socialism which he would always assert. He went on to say that socialism was a concept which had had some meaning at the end of the second world war but that at the present time there was no future in it.[22] When asked why he was visiting Czechoslovakia, which was a socialist country, he said that he'd been coming for a long time and had many friends in Brno and Prague, even some at the Charles University. He'd intended to get in touch with them, and with others in Brno, if he hadn't been thrown out on technical grounds.'[23] Scruton then 'walked through the border and along the quiet road with a deep sense of the peace to which I had come, and of the war which I had left and by which the Müllers were still surrounded'.[24] Broňa Müllerová watched him disappearing: 'There was this broad empty space between the two border posts, absolutely empty, not a single human being in sight except for one soldier, and across that broad empty space trudged an English professor, Roger Scruton, with his little bag into Austria... and after that the Communist authorities never allowed him back.'[25]

On 17th June Scruton was placed on the Index of Undesirable Persons, one of the grounds given being that he was involved in sending 'emissaries' to 'internal enemies' in Czechoslovakia. At the time, the Foundation and the Müllers were concerned that the authorities suspected the existence of the Brno operation. It is apparent from the police file that this was not the case; their main concern was to prevent him reaching Prague. By chance, a week after his expulsion the Ministry of the Interior wrote to the police with a request from the Polish 'friends' for information about Jessica Douglas-Home, née Gwynne, wife of the editor-in-chief of *The Times*, and Roger Scruton, doctor of philosophy, who were allegedly carrying out an 'anti-Polish' activity. The police were able to reply, with some satisfaction, that Scruton had been expelled and placed on the Index for giving illegal lectures on the premises of internal enemies, sending emissaries of 'Centres for Ideological Subversion' and, above all, being responsible for the samizdat edition of *The Meaning of Conservatism*, intended as a platform for the 'illegal church' and other anti-socialist groups. About DOUGLAS-HOME Jessica, they added as an afterthought, they had no information.[26]

In November 1985 an event occurred which shook the Foundation, and which had serious consequences for Petr Oslzlý, but which does not seem to have alerted the police to the existence of the home seminar in Brno. On 14th November, the journalist and post-graduate student from Balliol, Paul Flather (who was later to become one of the Foundation Trustees), travelled to Brno, where he gave two seminars, on Gandhi's philosophy of non-cooperation and its implications for East and Central Europe, and on the links between democracy and technology. Oslzlý observed that 'the general opinion was that our national or regional mentality tended towards passive resistance rather in the intellectual sphere than in the physical. So one could not say that the flickering spark evoked that afternoon was blown into a flame. It could be described rather as one of the drops of understanding which eventually flowed into a river of enlightenment'.[27] It was a busy few days in Brno — including, as well as the seminars a meeting with Jiří Müller, a visit to the Theatre on a String, and to Jan Šimek's studio — and for some reason the precaution of registering accommodation with the police was omitted. Flather continued to Prague, where he met and exchanged messages with Fraňková, Hromádková and Bratinka, leaving 24 hours later on the night train to Vienna. The border was crossed in the early hours; Flather was taken off the train and kept under guard for two hours before being questioned. The first interrogation focused on Brno, and where he had stayed. At 8.30 a.m. he was escorted to another building where a 'a tall younger man dressed in full uniform' (who 'refused requests for a phone call, tea or food') opened the interrogation with the words 'You don't like our country, do you, Mr. Flather?'.[28] This interrogator had been through Flather's luggage, and unsettled him by laconically commenting on what he found there. Amongst the materials discovered were messages from Brno and Prague to Kathy Wilkes and Jan Kavan, a list of theological books requested by Milan Balabán, a catalogue of Jan Šimek's sculptures, and a diary containing addresses. Questions were asked about Flather's contact with Czech emigré circles. Later in the morning they were joined by two other men 'wearing those revolting leather jackets and high heels'[29] whose questions, directed through the first, English-speaking interrogator, were more brutal and, based on a reference in Flather's notebook to Pardubice,[30] made the assumption that he was a military spy. At 1.30 p.m. Flather was told he could leave, and continued his journey to Vienna.

The same day the 'worker for special purposes' (i.e. the StB agent) of the Brno State Theatre notified Petr Oslzlý that he had to attend an interrogation the following afternoon at 'Leninka' — the Brno headquarters of the secret police.[31] For 15 minutes they kept him waiting whilst they 'kept coming and going, shuffling their papers, looking into files, joking between themselves, making tea and, when I complained that they were wasting time, saying it was all up to me.' Eventually they began to suggest to Oslzlý that maybe he had something to confess to them; something that was 'weighing on his mind'. Finally they asked him about Paul Flather, and asked why he had not reported his meeting with Flather: 'I held my ground and repeated that they would have to get used to the fact that the Theatre on a String was internationally known and visited by lots of foreigners and I was never going to write any reports since they had now made it clear that these reports really were for the secret police.' The interrogation lasted an hour and was not repeated, but from then on Oslzlý was banned from travelling abroad with the theatre: 'The ban was very frustrating, and although I adjusted to it, there were occasions when I got very angry. When I say I adjusted to it, what I said to myself was: "If I can't go out into the world then I will do everything possible to bring the world here to me." From this basic idea valuable consequences can flow, all kinds of things can become possible that aren't confined to life under totalitarianism, that reach out into a broader sphere. It's possible that the philosophical concept of the seminar was enriched by this, and I am very certain that I was personally enriched.'[32]

Six weeks after Flather's expulsion, Alan Montefiore and Catherine Audard travelled by train from Vienna directly to Prague. A police file on Montefiore, under the code name LOGIK, was opened on the day of their arrival (Sunday 29th December 1985) although the police, in their usual chauvinist way, dismissed Audard as 'an English-speaking woman whom the source believes to be Montefiore's wife'.[33] The source (whether informer or listening device[34]) reported that the first part of the conversation turned on security issues arising from the apprehension of Flather, at that time still one of Montefiore's students. Surprisingly little about these security issues is mentioned in the police report, which is more concerned to record information about future visitors from France, Germany and Britain and about the samizdat press. The usefulness of the Vienna route was mentioned, but apparently not in connection with the Brno seminars. The reporter found it worth recording Montefiore's statement that he and Roger Scruton 'did not agree on matters of social policy and politics, but otherwise had a good personal understanding'. The police concluded that: 'MONTEFIORE (was) the representative of a charitable society which provides help for the internal enemy — financial and technical. The information confirms information already gained about mutual connections between visa foreigners visiting (name blacked out), whose activity is coordinated from one centre (IDC) operating on the territory of Great Britain. The information confirms the hostile activitiy of Montefiore on the territory of the ČSSR and the task of (name blacked out) as one of the coordinators of hostile activity in the ČSSR in the field of creating dangerous material and the organisation of the so-called anti-universities.'[35]

It is evident from both Roger Scruton and Alan Montefiore's files that at the end of 1985 the police had not yet identified the Jan Hus Educational Foundation as the Centre of Ideological Subversion for which they were looking. They appear to have done so by July 1986, when the 31st section of the 1st Directorate SNB (espionage), investigating the Foundation as a hostile IDC in Great Britain, applied to the 1st section of the 10th Directorate SN. for material from Scruton's file. Information was supplied concerning Scruton's contacts with internal enemies in the illegal church and those oriented towards philosophy, sociology and historiography, and that he had carried out illegal lectures. His name had already occurred in 1981 in connection with the Palach Press. He was responsible for sending lecturers from British universities under tourist visas to help Charter 77, which visits had been arranged with the financial support of the Jan Hus Foundation. In 1985, the report claimed, he was increasing his activity with the publication of *The Meaning of Conservatism*, for which reason he was placed on the Index of Undesirable Persons.

Scruton had not however ceased in his hostile activities, the report continued, which he carried out through, on the one hand, the Jan Hus Foundation and, on the other, employees of British universities such as Barbara Day, secretary of the Jan Hus Foundation.[36] For this reason, the department would be grateful for any information on Scruton unearthed during the compilation of the intelligence report on the Jan Hus Foundation. This would be particularly useful in connection with Alena Hromádková, who shared in the organisation of the 'anti-universities', and who received British lecturers.

The police file on the Jan Hus Educational Foundation is either still held in a closed archive or has not survived. Hundreds of secret police files which should have been handed over to the Ministry of the Interior after the Velvet Revolution are assumed to have been destroyed in the chaos of November and December 1989. In some cases a record of their existence remains. That is the case with Barbara Day's file — or files, as it appears that by an administrative error two were opened by different police departments under different registration numbers and code names in June and September 1982 (before she was in contact with the JHEF). The files were presumably set up in connection with Day's research visit from October 1982 to February 1983.[37] The first file was opened by the 3rd section (education, foreign students and sport) of the 10th Directorate SNB (surveillance of the internal enemy), the second by the 3rd section (Great Britain and France) of the 2nd Directorate SNB (surveillance of the external enemy). Presumably they cannot have been very active files, as the duplication was not discovered until June 1986, when it was noted in the register as a 'basic error', and the first file destroyed (probably by incorporation into the second). However, according to the report of 17th July 1986 on Roger Scruton, Barbara Day was by then under the surveillance of the 31st section of the 1st Directorate SNB, responsible for spying on the JHEF.

Without access to this file we can only guess as to how in spring 1986 the StB discovered the existence of the Foundation. It may be relevant that in January 1986 the JHEF received its first grant from the National Endowment for Democracy in Washington. Because the Foundation was a British organisation[38] the grant was channelled through the SVU, a Czech and Slovak emigré organisation, with branches throughout the world. Although the grant came via the American branch of the SVU[39] and the JHEF had little to do with the British branch, the committee of the latter occasionally received reports from its American colleagues. Sitting on the committee was the StB's leading agent in Great Britain, a man who had been planted in London after 1968 and became an active member of the emigré community. From references dated 1987 and 1988 in files of the 10th Directorate SNB relating to other matters it would seem that the only material he obtained was scanty and confused; but nevertheless, what little he knew found its way to the StB in Prague. This discovery, made in 1998-99, confirms the wisdom of the early decision by Trustees of the Jan Hus Foundation to make it a purely British operation, without the involvement of emigré Czechs and Slovaks. It was a decision which some members of the emigré community found unjust, but which was understood and appreciated by others.

In spite of the enormous resources of the secret police, and the disturbing evidence that there were conversations which they managed to overhear, it would appear that they gained very little information about the operations of the Jan Hus Foundation. They seem to have had no knowledge of the English-speaking seminar in Brno which Oslzlý and Pospíšil ran securely for five years and which was undoubtedly the most effective, both in the short and the long term, of all the Foundation's actions. They do not seem to have realised that the Foundation was working in Slovakia, although in many ways that was one of the most dangerous operations, since Čarnogurský, Kusý and Šimečka were all closely watched by the police.

In October 1987 Robert Grant, from Glasgow University, made his third visit to Czechoslovakia and his first to Bratislava. A file had been opened on him in Prague in May 1986, when he had been known to visit Alena Hromádková and had been searched on leaving the country. He was pleasantly surprised to be allowed to cross freely into Slovakia from Austria, and his main problems were the difficulty of finding accommodation and the impossibility of registering with the foreigners' police: 'Č[arno-gurský] drove us to Police HQ at Februárového víťazstva 45; it was shut for the whole weekend. A pair of policemen were lounging in a small sort of caretaker's office round to the left of the building, and we asked them what to do. They said just to say, if asked, that we had done our best to register.'[40] Grant's return crossing was as smooth as his arrival.

And yet, unknown to Grant, the Prague authorities had been notified of his arrival on Friday 23rd October and had issued an order to all border crossings and airports that GRANT Alexander Dickson Robert should be thoroughly searched on departure. At the same time the Bratislava police were asked to find Grant and report on the contacts he made. However, it seems not to have been a working weekend for the 10th Directorate SNB, since the orders were not issued until Monday 26th October, by which time Grant was safely back in Vienna. On the 24th November, the Bratislava police laconically replied that there was no trace of Grant having been in Slovakia, and that he had made no official or unofficial contact with anyone at the Comenius University, the School of Economics, the Technical University, the Academy of Performing Arts or the Academy of Fine Arts. If they do ever hear of him, they add helpfully, they will let Prague know.[41]

The secret police service in Communist Czechoslovakia frequently blundered and evidently suffered from lack of commitment, indifference and self-interest among its work force. It was a low-status profession which looked more impressive than it really was. In the late 1980s its premier directorate, the 1st directorate SNB, (Intelligence) was rehoused in an imposing new building on the heights of Kobylisy, with panoramic views of Prague. It was hardly necessary for employees to leave the premises, where they could enjoy a restaurant, bar, swimming pool and fitness centre. Presumably it was hoped that by improving working conditions a better quality of candidate would be attracted and the standard of the intelligence service raised. However, nothing can be certain about the way the secret police operated. Their business was disinformation, and their aim to sow mistrust amongst members of the community. Lists of informers released by Petr Cibulka, the former Brno dissident who set up *Necenzurované noviny* (Uncensored News), have been condemned as manipulated by the secret police; but then again, was the rumour itself initiated by the secret police? Many Czechs prefer not to dwell on such issues, and not to consult their files even where these are still in existence, apprehensive of doubt that may be cast on people with whom they still live and work.

It is hard to shake off habits acquired whilst living in a police state. Amongst these is a reluctance to pass on information. The first aspect of this concerns knowledge relating to one's own situation, whether personal data or views and opinions; to release these is to increase one's vulnerability. The second concerns knowledge of the outside world, knowledge which confers power and becomes an instrument that can be manipulated to one's own advantage. When the western philosophers visited the home seminars, the students were amazed by how prodigal they were with their thoughts and opinions, views and experiences; they responded by opening up their own lives, their deepest doubts, longings and hopes for the future. Both sides were enriched by the mutual exchange of gifts. From this point of view the home seminars — and not only those visited by the foreigners — were the first steps on the slow reconstruction of trust and interdependence which is taking place in the Czech and Slovak Republics today.

The Fracturing of the Bolts

In the spring of 1987, one night after audience and actors had left the Brno art gallery which was home to the Theatre on a String, Milan Uhde and Petr Oslzlý sat talking in the chaotic basement room which served as office and dressing room. The evening's performance, *The Bartered and the Bought*, had been advertised as by 'a collective of authors', but was really by Uhde. It told the story of Smetana's librettist Karel Sabina, whose misfortune was to turn informer when the Austrian authorities no longer cared. The subject naturally led them to the current situation, Uhde commenting that there had never been such a long period of cultural darkness in Bohemia as the present age. But, he added, there were signs that the system was beginning to break; there were tensions in high places between people who wanted to change things and those who were afraid, but the conflict was still hidden. In the last two and a half years of the Communist regime in Czechoslovakia the Foundation was made aware of the revival taking place in Czech and Slovak culture and society by means of an intensifying stream of communications and requests, expressed with increasing confidence, and making increasingly larger and more varied demands on the Foundation's resources.

The ten years of secret work by the Jan Hus Educational Foundation could never have happened without the raising of large sums of money, all found by the Trustees through patient letter-writing and making of contacts. They were not easy years in which to appeal for money for projects in Eastern Europe; the attitude of some funders was to ask why they should provide support for work in Communist countries. On the other hand, the Trustees were unable to appeal for funds by presenting themselves as fighters for the overthrow of such regimes. They were barred from that both by their Deed of Trust under the Charities Law of Great Britain, and by their own principles. The Foundation had been set up: 'to facilitate the free flow of information in Czechoslovakia...; to provide books, lectures, articles, educational materials, meetings and discussions...; to support the free press in Czechoslovakia... and to facilitate publication of material written by Czechs and Slovaks...; to provide stipends for independent scholars, and to help in the running of classes and discussion-groups...; to assist all Czechs persecuted for their religious or political beliefs.'[1] If a totalitarian regime felt threatened by this (which of course it would) then the fault was was with the regime. But if the Foundation had given any indication that the discomfiture of a foreign state might be one of the intended outcomes of its work, then it would have incurred the wrath of the Foreign Office and the possible loss of its charitable status. The consequences of this policy were that, for those unable to understand conditions in the Communist bloc, most of the Foundation's activities appeared to be low-key and small in scale. In financial terms this was true, since the Foundation's greatest resources were the talents and energies of its trustees and visitors, which were never included in the modest balance sheets. A small but regular income had been ensured in the early days when a number of individuals committed themselves to paying, under Covenants, a sum of between 5 and 100 pounds a year for a period of seven years, thus providing some continuity in the work. In May 1982 the Treasurer reported approximately 3,500 pounds in the bank, but added that 'response to the latest appeal had been disappointing'; in September 1983 the Trustees agreed that they would aim to raise and spend between five and six thousand pounds in the academic year 1983/84.

In the early days of Julius Tomin's seminar the philosophers had not been inhibited about publicising the philosophy seminars and the needs of their students. The main emphasis had been on the legality of the seminars. As the work expanded it was clear that, for the protection of those inside Czechoslovakia, confidentiality had to be maintained about names, identities and activities. The annual reports of the Jan Hus Foundation therefore described hypothetical case studies, put together from different elements and scrutinised to ensure no recognisable

personality emerged from the account. Even so, there was concern about the circulation of the reports, and Trustees found
themselves in the frustrating position of having to classify the
Foundation's publicity material as 'Highly Confidential'.

Nevertheless, by diligent networking they continued to raise
funds. A large part of the business of every meeting was a discussion of possible sources, and how they should be approached. One of the most active fund raisers was Jessica Douglas-
Home, who became involved in the Foundation when, in May
1983, Scruton arranged the publication of an article by Petr
Pithart in *The Times*, at that time edited by her husband Charles
Douglas-Home. In these years it began to be possible to raise
what were, for the Foundation, substantial amounts of one, two,
even three thousand pounds from British sources. The work was
expanding; more and more requests were arriving, whilst at the
same time it was increasingly difficult for the philosophers to
carry out the administrative work themselves. The future would
have been in doubt had it not been for two major sources of
sponsorship, both of them from America: the financier George
Soros and the National Endowment for Democracy.

Soros's name first apears in the Foundation Minutes in
October 1982, when Roger Scruton reports that: 'he and WHNS
[Bill Newton-Smith] had tried in vain to see Soros, but WHNS
might arrange to see him eventually; he would be supplied with
an account of the JHEF's achievements and future prospects.
RVS and WHNS would prepare such an account, making special
reference to samizdat and tamizdat[2].' In December it is noted
that 'ACRGM [Alan Montefiore] will sign and send the letter to
Soros soon'. The letter consisted of two detailed requests, one
on behalf of Petr Pithart's history project and the other for 'a
pair of sociologists who have been working for a long time on a
highly sensitive project, cataloguing and analysing the language
of totalitarianism, and its use of propaganda'[3]. This seems to
have been followed by a revised application which has not survived; on 12th April George Soros replied to Roger Scruton's
'letter of February 23', approving two projects — Karel Palek's
'Anamnesis' and the translation of Scruton's own work, but
rejecting a third proposal, on the grounds that it was dangerous
to confuse the merit of an individual with the merit of his work.
By the following May it appears that $4,000 had arrived from

Soros, Scruton reporting that: 'Soros had agreed to provide £1000 to support Pius's samizdat Anamnesis, and another £1000 for Pithart's translation of *The Meaning of Conservatism*'.

A meeting took place between George Soros and Roger Scruton in early December 1983 when they discussed among other matters the project for printing and re-importing samizdat which eventually became the Athenaeum Press.[4] From this time until the end of 1989 Soros's Open Society Fund provided regular support for the British Foundation's projects, as well as making grants to the French association and the Canadian fund. The support, however, was never automatic, and always relied on certain criteria being fulfilled. One of them was that the Foundation would never become reliant on Soros's funding; there always had to be income from other sources, and the Trustees never relaxed their fund-raising efforts. The projects Soros supported had to be concrete and, whilst never asking for detailed accounts of how the money had been spent, he liked to know and see the results of the activities. In April 1989, when it was clear that the political and social situation in Czechoslovakia was undergoing major change, Soros attended the Foundation's Annual General Meeting held in the Old Common Room of Balliol College, and joined in the discussion of 'Future Policy and Activities'. The Trustees had reviewed their activities of the previous year, noting in particular the success of the music and ecology programmes, and the creation of Open Dialogue. They were now considering the possibilities of operating in the 'grey area', through contacts within the universities and other official institutes. 'George Soros recommended that as a long-term aim the JHEF should try to find an official counterpart and ways of operating in Czechoslovakia officially. He emphasised the need to make new contacts, particularly with young people; it was agreed that the following items would go on the agenda for the ExC [Executive Committee] and ManC [Management Committee]

- The Czech Children
- Public lectures
- Operating openly
- Creating official visits.'[4]

At an informal gathering after the meeting, Soros referred to Petr Oslzlý's activities for the general population of Brno as the sort of work he would be interested in supporting.

Soros's policy, particularly by the end of the 1980s, seems to have been to work within the system by finding pockets of independent thought within institutions, and exploiting these to subvert the whole structure. The other major player in the field of support for independent culture under totalitarian regimes was the National Endowment for Democracy, a non-governmental organisation based in Washington DC. Working with relatively limited funds, the NED sought out institutions and individuals which operated on the basis of democratic values. The aim was the promotion of freedom of thought, pluralism, independent action, free exchange of information and the mobilising of international support. It was apparent to the NED that in countries with totalitarian regimes, the carriers and disseminators of democratic values and ideas were those operating outside the official structures, and in the circumstances of the 1980s they did not consider working with governments in any form. Support was given on the basis of personal assessment — meeting those involved, sensing their excitement and being convinced that they could achieve what they proposed. They were looking, not for administrative competence, but for quality and substance in the work itself. They also looked for variety and pluralism, and preferred to support several small groups rather than a few large ones. Amongst their beneficiaries were Keston College, the Hungarian Cultural Foundation, Vilém Prečan's Documentation Centre, Jan Kavan's Jan Palach Information and Research Trust, František Janouch's Charter 77 Foundation, and the Škvoreckýs' Sixty-eight Publishers.

The first application to the NED on behalf of the Jan Hus Foundation was made in October 1984, after a meeting between Scruton, Douglas-Home and Nadia Diuk of the NED. The Foundation applied for $50,000 over two years, budgeted under three headings: secretarial support; the republication in the West of samizdat intended for teaching purposes and its reimport;[5] ongoing support for existing activities in the field of seminars and samizdat. Over the next 15 months the proposal was redrafted, but on 14th January 1986 Douglas-Home wrote to thank the NED for a grant of $25,000 for one year, to cover the costs of secretarial assistance and publications, and of equipment to include photocopiers, cutting and binding machines, video recorders and video equipment. In October the NED programme officer Yale Richmond helped the Foundation prepare its application for the following year: '[Richmond] advised that the proposal be as specific as possible, and should concentrate on what the JHEF does best, which cannot be emulated by emigré groups — i.e., the seminar programme.'[6] In January Richmond wrote to advise on the confidentiality of the Foundation's reports: 'The evaluation plan also tells us more than we would want to have on the record. We are subject to the Freedom of Information Act which means that anyone (US or foreign) may request access to information in our files on a particular subject, and we are obliged to make such information available or to show why it should be withheld... For this reason, I hope you will be able to give us an edited version of the plan, telling us only in general terms how you will evaluate the success of the activities conducted with our grant funds.... And neither your evaluation plan nor your quarterly reports should contain any information which you would consider confidential.'[7] The NED continued to support the Foundation's work on the basis of annual applications, including its critical programmes in ecology, samizdat, video and music, and its support for the Jazz Section.

The late 1980s were marked by an expansion in the Foundation's resources which was paralleled by the expansion in its activities. Specialists in an ever wider range of subjects were recruited as visiting lecturers and advisers. Many of them knew little about the Communist bloc and less about its independent activities, so for the purpose of orientation Roger Scruton put together a book, *Czechoslovakia. The Unofficial Culture*, with contributions from Barbara Day, Jiří Gruša, Jessica Douglas Home and David Matthews. It was one of the first publications of the Claridge Press, precariously produced in conditions only marginally better than those of the samizdat press. An increasing number of requests arrived for support for samizdat and seminar projects. Visiting Prague in July 1988, Jessica Douglas-Home discussed another new venture, a seminar in architecture, with Alena Hromádková, Petr Pithart and a British architect of Czech origin, John Robins. The first visitor was Léon Krier, known in Britain as the architect who had advised the Prince of Wales on the Poundbury project near Dorchester. Krier gave two seminars; at the first, the discussion turned on architectural developments in Prague, in particular the construction of housing estates on the periphery of the city. Hromádková, who had made the initial connections, was aware of a sense of hushed unease; the audience consisted mainly of architects in official positions and, maybe out of fears of microphones or informers, the host had not provided an introduction for the visiting speaker. Krier had mixed feelings about the audience: 'only two or three people spoke, the others were silent, some approving and others showing blank faces.... There were a few young people who nodded very very approvingly but obviously didn't dare say a word. While Alena seems to me to be an interesting and honest person, neither B. [the host] nor B.'s wife nor C. [another architect] (of others I cannot speak for no-body else spoke to me) are interested in ideas of traditional Architecture and City.'[8]

The architects were better prepared in May 1989 for a visit from Graham King, County Planning Officer from West Glamorgan. His seminar was held in the hall belonging to the Society of Prague Artists — a wonderful secession building on the banks of the Vltava — and advertised by a handbill. This small flier was a landmark for the Foundation, since until this time the only public venue for its lectures had been the English Club in Brno (although Burke's talks at the Research Institute for Scientific and Technological Development could be described as 'semi-public'). King spoke to an audience of 25 on British urban planning and architecture: 'inevitably, the discussion afterwards warmed up as time went on and... broadened into considerations of British Government policies today under Mrs. Thatcher and their possible relevance to the situation in Czechoslovakia. It was apparent from those present that Mrs. Thatcher had obtained a kind of hero status for the Czechs in their current situation of oppression.'[9]

Five months later Quinlan Terry, known in Britain for his traditional style of design, gave three lectures on the contemporary development of architecture. His lecture in the hall of the Society of Prague Artists attracted an audience of 40, whilst in Brno 200 came to hear him at the English Club, and 50 architects attended his lecture at the Design Centre. Amongst the questions he fielded was one from a West German student of architecture who objected to Terry's concept of traditional architecture and called for a society which was 'free of all these [class] differences so that we are free to live together happily and equally'. The reply came from 'three strong minded Bohemians'[10]: 'An egalitarian society is a theory: a theory which is popular in some circles in Western Europe. If you want to see how the theory works out in practice we invite you to live a little longer in Czechoslovakia.'[11]

In May 1988 Alena Hromádková wrote to Roger Scruton about 'a course in Czech studies which I consider to be the second part of the project already known as "Language and Faith"'.[12] The project description was by Miroslav Červenka, a leading scholar in Bohemian studies who had been thrown out of the Czechoslovak Academy of Sciences in 1970 and since then had worked as a librarian, and secretly on samizdat and seminar activities. Červenka wrote that 'like the Czech Hebrew specialists — whose activity is already under way — we will found an evening university for the teaching of Czech studies.'[13] He wrote of 'the one-sided manipulation of the Humanities at official places of learning' which had destroyed the academic standing of Czech and Slovak universities, and the use of non-objective criteria which excluded talented young people from higher education. Červenka announced a three-year course on 'The Czech Tradition'. Fourteen subjects were to be studied, taught by specialist teachers. The intention was that the students should be examined at the end of every term and, in the long term, validation obtained through a western university. Červenka wrote that 20 students had presented themselves, the maximum that could be accommodated in the private apartments which served as lecture rooms.[14] The students included Saša Vondra[15], Jáchym Topol[16], and Petr Placák of the 'Czech Children'; many of them were grouped around the young, iconoclastic, samizdat publications *Respekt*, *Vokno* and *Revolver revue*. (Hromádková reported that she was 'amused at the contrast between the polite young men and their journals'.) The Hus Foundation was asked to contribute towards the cost of purchasing and copying texts, and towards fees for the teachers. A sum of £2,000, to include a small photocopier, was recommended at the July meeting of the Foundation's Executive Committee.

The course was conceived ambitiously, and at the end of the first year, in an evaluation for the Foundation, it was admitted that the material had proved too demanding for the students; they had read only a small number of the works of 19th century literature, and some had not sat the exam. The reason given was their participation in other activities, including samizdat: 'Concentration is not only a question of time but also of an individual's intentions, of the inner hierarchy of tasks which these courageous people create out of their activities, people who are active in the fate of their country and who are living a difficult life to the full.'[17] On the other hand, lectures had been well-attended and had attracted other students: 'The course has a good reputation among young people who are dissatisfied with the regimented official institutes of learning.'[18]

These students who were now — under what proved to be the dying days of a totalitarian regime — 'living life to the full', were the new generation which George Soros was eager to support. Samizdat was proliferating and was openly passed around and discussed in public places. An increasing number of requests was reaching the Foundation from new initiatives such as the Eastern Europe Information Agency, represented by Jan Urban[19], which asked for a fax machine, and the Club of Czech Intelligentsia, which included Josef Vavroušek. At the same time, the reactions of the authorities were becoming unpredictable and potentially more dangerous; in spring 1989 Václav Havel and Ivan Jirous were amongst those arrested in Prague; in the autumn, Ján Čarnogurský, Miroslav Kusý and others in Bratislava.

In September 1989, the Foundation's regular courier to Brno, James de Candole, spent a student month in Olomouc. One of his tasks was to make contact with the young people initiating new projects. He brought back stories of meetings with Petr Placák and the Czech Children, and their 'wonderfully impossible manifesto... which calls for the return of the Bohemian Crown (the motto of the Czech Children is... God, King and Country) and the replacement of power stations with windmills, draws attention to the desperate need in Czechoslovakia of responsible political leadership, a 'king' who will fulfil the duties traditionally invested in a monarch at his coronation by serving rather than enslaving his people, leaders who will love and protect their inheritance which they hold in trust for future generations.'[20] He joined in the activities of the Society for a Jollier Today, including the daily 'jog' down Politických vězňů (Political Prisoners' Street), and heard about the mock attack by 'policemen' with water melon helmets and cucumber truncheons. This mock attack was dangerously close to reality; de Candole also witnessed police with loudspeakers and dogs dispersing a peaceful gathering of families in Stromovka Park.

Water cannon and riot police had featured in action taken against demonstrators in Wenceslas Square and the Old Town Square on 28th October 1988, when the celebration of the founding of Czechoslovakia in 1918 was reintroduced into the calendar. As a precaution, the authorities had detained 122 dissidents for the weekend; a first stage in Deputy Minister Lorenz's contingency plan, Operation 'Norbert'.[21] The arrests resulted in some absentees (including Václav Havel himself) in the audience for Theatre on a String's performance at the Junior Klub Na Chmelnici of *Rozrazil o demokracie*, a living newspaper devised by Petr Oslzlý and other Brno theatre workers which referred on stage to the death of Jan Patočka, and included a short (unattributed) play by Václav Havel[22].

Amongst the new movements of 1988-89 there was the 'Open Dialogue' declared by Petr Oslzlý, Joska Skalník, Petr Rezek, Jan Šimek, Jaroslav Kořán and other artists and philosophers. Open Dialogue was deliberately conceived as a 'non-organisation': a free association of all those who subscribed to its manifesto, similar to the Devětsil movement of the 1920s. Those involved had learnt from the problems of the Jazz Section that official registration was no protection, since it could be claimed that the organisation had broken the conditions of its registration. If there were no registration there could be no conditions to break. Oslzlý discussed the concept with David Matthews and Nigel Osborne during their visit in October 1986; the aim of Open Dialogue was not to challenge or revolt against the existing system, but to provide living, indigenous entertainment for audiences. To do this, it would turn to the memories and experience of those who had worked in the arts before the war or during the 1960s — regardless of whether or not they were officially 'approved'. Open Dialogue was initiated during David Matthews' visit in October 1988, when — parallel with the Brno International Music Festival — Oslzlý organised the alternative 'Dialogues' festival[23]. That autumn more than 300 writers and artists signed Open Dialogue's manifesto: '...We want to revive continuity of culture, to make contact with artists abroad, and to invite them to take part in our dialogue. We shall make our activities widely known through publications and audio and video recordings. Our association is not a formal organisation and will not be restricted to artists and writers of a single generation. Adherence to our OPEN DIALOGUE does not exclude membership of other groups, associations or unions. The activity of the free creative association OPEN DIALOGUE will begin with a dialogue about its aims and their realisation. It is through this dialogue that the programme and vitality of our association will be continually redefined and renewed...'.[24] The Foundation, in consultation with Jiří Müller, agreed that the computer and equipment donated to the Jazz Section should be shared with the Open Dialogue team.

The Foundation also maintained its original mission of support for the teaching of philosophy and related subjects. It became a partner in a new venture, George Soros's scheme to bring young Czech and Slovak scholars to Oxford University, providing grants for the purchase of books. New opportunities opened in cooperation with the Inter-University Centre in Dubrovnik, with which Bill Newton-Smith and Kathy Wilkes were involved. In the mid-1980s, when the Foundation was looking for invitations for scholars not affiliated to the Communist Party to attend conferences abroad, the Inter-University Centre was one of the possible venues. In 1984, the Foundation was asked to consider a grant for Ladislav Tondl, who had been expelled from the Charles University in 1958 and from the Academy of Sciences in 1970. Trustees arranged an invitation to a philosophy of science conference in Dubrovnik for him, but he was refused an exit visa; the visit was realised in 1986.[25] In spring 1988 visits were arranged for Pavel Kouba, the 'anonymous Nietzsche scholar', and Ivan Chvatík, the translator of Heidegger.[26] In April Wilkes wrote that: 'Neither in fact attended the courses we had originally thought they were attending, but were both enthusiastically attending the "Nietzsche course".

They walked around with their faces split by huge grins, and were immensely glad of, and grateful for the opportunity. I had a chance to talk to one of the Directors of that course, who had much valued their participation. This seems to have been a thoroughly successful innovatory move by the JHEF, and one which I hope we shall repeat. (As a member of the Dubrovnik Executive, though, I would remind the JHEF that the IUC paid for board-and-lodging for one of them, and cooperated willingly with the somewhat unorthodox manner of their invitations).'[27] In May Kouba wrote to the Foundation: '...I had the opportunity to meet some distinguished interpreters of Nietzsche's work, to discuss with them my own paper and to establish connections that surely will become the basis of a long-term cooperation. My participation in the course has become not only a very valuable experience to me personally, but also a stimulation to spread the unofficial contacts with foreign philosophers which are of great importance for us.'[28] In 1989 visits were arranged for Chvatík and Josef Moural; Wilkes noted in the summer that the latter was 'the sole person who moved with equal ease between official and unofficial circles'.[29] Visits by other young scholars were supported. The necessarily 'unorthodox' manner of the invitations extended to the financing of the visits, to make it possible for the scholars to leave Czechoslovakia at all; since permission to leave the country was dependent on money arriving through the right channels at the right time. Even with permission, the journey was not always trouble free; Hungarian border guards confiscated diskettes and materials from Pavel Kouba on his way from Prague to Dubrovnik.

It was the Inter-University Centre which led to Bill Newton-Smith and Kathy Wilkes's return to Czechoslovakia. The Centre accepted not only the Hus Foundation's 'unofficial' scholars, but also others who still held influential positions in academic life. Such a contact enable Wilkes to return to Czechoslovakia in June 1989 for the first time after 7 years: 'My brief was to go both "officially" and "unofficially" (I had an invitation from the Vysoká Škola Ekonomická and the Institute of Philosophy and Sociology of the Academy....) The "official" invitation got me a visa over the counter with no trouble.[30] Equally, entrance and exit at the airport were simple and swift. It will be interesting to see whether I can now get a normal tourist visa.'[31] She lectured to Hejdánek's seminar on 'Death and the Future': 'Discussion vigorous... the Continental tradition in philosophy very present: 'reason', 'faith', 'the self/subject', all interpreted very differently.... Great fights about the reality of Hamlet, time, quarks, numbers, beauty. It was excellent to see Ladia [Ladislav Hejdánek] again.... He introduced me to his group with a 10-minute speech, describing in detail the ancient history of British visitors to Prague unofficial courses and my role as the first such visitor. I am canonised as the 'mother' of the courses; WHNS may be surprised to hear he is canonised as the 'father'. If the apartment is bugged, alert STB officials would have learnt a great deal.'

Wilkes was, appropriately, the first of the Foundation's academic (as opposed to cultural) visiting lecturers to penetrate the official structures. She observed that 'the "grey" area is dissolving into the "white" area. Younger scholars who... are not actively in the "unofficial" groups are not outside them because they are afraid; but because they have their own battles to fight in their own institutes. Signing the Charter, and going to unofficial lectures, does not seem relevant to them. They are militant, articulate, and going their own way. Not all of them, of course; but a goodly proportion.... From a group of 8 or so in several hours in Prague bars I heard as many radical opinions expressed, and ideas for action proposed, as I heard from the unofficial groups.'[32]

All the Foundation's visitors to Czechoslovakia noted the changing atmosphere of the last two years of Communism — the increasing sense of expanding horizons, of future possibilities. The threat of reprisals did not diminish, and some people remained afraid; nevertheless, the barriers between the 'ghetto' and the 'grey zone' were crumbling, and ever more proposals and requests were put before the Foundation's Trustees at their meetings — samizdat projects, history projects, film projects, computer technology projects, book requests, proposals to visit the Inter-University Centre in Dubrovnik... In the summer of 1989 inhabitants of Prague saw with their own eyes East Germans taking refuge in the West German Embassy. Nevertheless, it was hard to see how this forty-year regime would come to an end. Most Czechs were still trapped in their private lives; there was no apparent opposition to take a lead. In mid-October Ladislav Hejdánek sent a message to the Foundation: 'The last days of this regime will be difficult.' In Britain, the Foundation Trustees held their breath as they wondered what occasion would precipitate the inevitable overthrow of Communism in Czechoslovakia, what form it would take, and how their colleagues would cope. The Berlin Wall fell on Thursday 9th November. The following Monday, Nancy Durham flew to Prague on a journalist's visa secured with some difficulty at the Czechoslovak Embassy in London. Durham had previously (February 1987, March and July 1988) reported for the CBC and BBC, using her JHEF contacts to prepare broadcasts on the Jazz Section and the unofficial culture. Her reports had earned her the enmity of the Communist authorities, leading to interrogations at the airport and shadowing by the secret police. At the beginning of that bitterly cold week in November she found Prague more depressing than ever, with no apparent signs of the Czechs having been inspired by the example of the Germans. On Wednesday, still wondering whether to cut short the visit, she became involved in an environmental demonstration on the Charles Bridge and was chilled by the screams of demonstrators attacked by riot police in a neighbouring street. The next day word was travelling round Prague of the student procession planned for the Friday. Marching alongside the students, Durham saw men putting down their beer mugs to join the demonstration, women leaving their shopping, actors waving from the windows of the National Theatre. 'This is not a demonstration,' the student alongside told her, 'this is an uprising.' Here, trapped between cordons of riot police, she found Marta Chadimová from the Cambridge Diploma seminar[33] with her husband Mikoláš, and witnessed the violent beating of students by the People's Militia.

Trapped in the same crowd was a theatre student from Brno. As soon as he escaped he made his way to the Junior Klub Na Chmelnici where Petr Oslzlý and Theatre on a String were preparing a performance of *Rozrazil o demokracii*, the first since it had been banned a year earlier. The student, shocked by what he had seen in Národní třída, contributed his eye-witness account to the 'living theatre'. The next day, Saturday, at a meeting in the Realist Theatre, students and theatre people decided for a strike. On Sunday evening at 8.00 p.m. Oslzlý was one of those on the stage of the Činoherní Klub when Václav Havel announced the foundation of Civic Forum as an open opposition made up of representatives from a variety of civic initiatives[34] prepared to begin negotiations with the Communist authorities. Oslzlý said later that as they sat there he estimated they had a 50% chance of being arrested and a 10% chance of being shot.

Oslzlý — one of the team responsible for organising the manifestations in Wenceslas Square and on Letna — was not the only one of the Foundation's colleagues directly involved in the first activities of Civic Forum. Records show that founder members of the Co-ordination Centre included Pavel Bratinka, Ivan Dejmal, Jaroslav Kořán, Daniel Kroupa, Martin Palouš, Petr Pithart, Joska Skalník, Josef Vavroušek and many others known to the Foundation.

Meanwhile in Brno, Jiří Müller and Milan Jelínek helped to set up their counterpart to the Prague Civic Forum, whilst at the Purkyně University[35] Miroslav Pospíšil was one of what was, initially, a handful of teaching staff who joined the students in the occupation of the university buildings. In a 24-hour frenzy of activity they published and circulated posters, fliers and news-sheets, keeping contact with Prague through telephone and relays of cars on the high road to Prague. In Bratislava, thousands demonstrated against the continued imprisonment of Ján Čarnogurský. On 26th November, immediately after his release, Čarnogurský appeared at the manifestation organised by Public Against Violence. On 3rd December, in response to Roger Scruton's message that he should return to legal practice, he laughed: 'I have much bigger ideas than that!'. A few days later he was in Prague, and in the New Year was made Deputy Prime Minister of Czechoslovakia.

The turn of the year was a strange and wonderful time. The Foundation's colleagues, its seminar students and writers of samizdat, came out of their secret existence and faced the public, addressing them in theatres and factories and from stages constructed in the squares of cities and towns across the country. In late November and early December the weather was icy; their words shimmered in the frosty orange air, and the listening crowds glowed from excitement and solidarity. Many of the dissidents were directly involved in negotiations with the Communists; the battle was not yet won, and everyone feared a counter-attack. All the equipment laboriously imported by the Foundation — computers, printers, photocopiers — was being used at white heat to produce literature which would explain to the public (especially in the country and small towns) the issues being discussed at the manifestations taking place in the major centres.

Almost a decade earlier Dan Jacobson had arrived in Communist Czechoslovakia to find it 'bolted down under hoods of steel'. It was a country where too close an interpretation of Hamlet's remark 'Denmark's a prison could cost a theatre director his career, a land surrounded by barbed wire fences, search lights, watch towers and armed guards, positioned not to keep the enemy out, but its own people in. Its most intelligent and independent citizens were isolated not only from contact with foreigners but from contact with the general public, by means of blocks to their employment in the fields of education, politics or the media. In extreme cases, they were isolated by twenty-four hour police guards on their homes, eventually by prison sentences or banishment. In most societies, children whose parents provide them with opportunities for creative study and research can expect an advantage over those whose education is left to indifferent teachers; under Communism, the opposite was the case - talented and inquiring children had little hope of a higher education in anything other than purely technical and scientific subjects.

Over and over again, past students have testified that the underground seminars were 'windows open to the world outside', that the visits by foreign lecturers brought 'a breath of fresh air' to the foetid prison of Communism. Life under Communism meant daily subscription or resistance to principles in which, in the 1980s, no one any longer believed, but which were proclaimed in school, at work, in the press, on television and from the house tops. No one who has spent their life in a free society can entirely appreciate what it meant to the students to sit in a freely gathered group, to debate new ideas, and to carry these ideas into their daily life. They found in philosophy the key to their prison, in study of the thinkers of the past an understanding of their present situation. From this came the urge to share their experience with their friends and colleagues, a process fraught with the risk of betrayal and punishment. And yet this is what happened; the ideas were spread through samizdat and 'semi-official' seminars, through celebrations and festivals, through art and drama. The bolts which held the 'hoods of steel' were fractured; the prisoners were freed.

Epilogue

'The past is a foreign country:
they do things differently there.'

(L.P. Hartley, *The Go-Between*)

One of Václav Havel's most controversial decisions in the early
days of his presidency was to amnesty prisoners countrywide, to
free those whom he felt had been imprisoned by an unjust and
arbitrary legal system, and amongst whom he had himself spent
much time. There was some alarm among the population at the
unanticipated consequences of his action, and the idea of
bemused and disoriented amnestied prisoners roaming the
towns and countryside.

And yet a large part of the population shared the same dis-
orientation. Freed after forty years from the prison of
Communism, free to make their own judgments and decisions,
they could no longer be sure which way was 'Forward!'. Some
clung as long as they could to familiar patterns of work and
behaviour, whilst others assumed that the lifting of restraints
gave them licence to do as they pleased. The corruption, envy
and fear endemic in the Communist system undermined genuine
efforts towards free and fair enterprise. After years of living by
the principle 'he who does not steal from the state steals from
his own family', many found it difficult to understand that there
could be such a thing as a voluntarily accepted moral code.
Under Communism, an older generation which had adapted its
traditional values to accommodate 'survival techniques' lost
sight of the boundary between what was and was not ethical.
Meanwhile, a younger generation — the product of a
Communist education — grew up unaware that any such bound-

ary existed, regarding the free market as a place to better oneself at the expense of others; the expression 'business ethics' was for them a contradiction in terms.

The issue was largely one of national and personal identity; the generation of the '*chata* culture' which had loyally voted Communist at every election of its voting life now expressed horror at the crimes committed by 'those Communists'. Sometimes it seemed as though the violence of the repudiation was in equal measure to what the person had to hide. It was a topsy-turvy world, in which a doctorate in Marxist-Leninist studies was still academic currency, graduates of the police academy used their 'law' degrees to set up lucrative practices in international law, and former secret policemen appealed against dismissal on grounds of 'violation of their human rights'.

Nevertheless, those who during the 'dark years' had continued to think independently and to act according to values which were older than the last fifty years of totalitarianism, did manage to influence public and political life. A nation with memories of the democratic government which existed from 1918-1938 could understand that there were standards which identified a mature society. Paths had to be opened through the débris of the old regime, through the negative modes of thought and behaviour. One clear route was through the influence of education and the not-for-profit sector. That was why Czech and Slovak philosophers and teachers appealed once more to their colleagues abroad.

The first appeal had arrived in December 1989, during a Christmas party in Roger Scruton's flat in Notting Hill Gate whilst Jan Hus Trustees were toasting the restored democracy and looking forward to the disbandment of the Foundation. First, there were the immediate practical needs of Civic Forum; at the same time long-term needs in the fields of education and publishing were discussed. In 1990 the British Foundation, under the Chairmanship of Anthony Smith,[1] decided it would gradually transfer responsibility to the Czechs and Slovaks, whilst still offering support and advice. On 22 October 1998, at a ceremony held in Magdalen College, Oxford, President Václav Havel awarded three Commemorative Medals of the President of the Republic to Kathy Wilkes, Barbara Day and the Jan Hus Foundation as a whole. Roger Scruton received a State

Honour, the Medal for Merit [First Class] of the Czech Republic. Gordon Skilling had previously received the Order of the White Lion.

Meanwhile, in May 1990 Miroslav Pospíšil registered the new Czechoslovak organisation in Brno, and became the first Director of the Vzdělávací nadace Jana Husa, whose Board of Trustees was largely composed of colleagues who had been active in the underground university in the 1980s. Initially working with the British and French organisations, Pospíšil worked to raise funding from Western and eventually from domestic sources. Scores of projects to improve and restore educational standards were carried out in the 1990s, mainly in the universities and institutes of higher education, but also in the arts, in the voluntary sector, and in further education. Even when, after the division of Czechoslovakia in 1993, it was necessary to register the Slovak foundation separately from the Czech — as the Vzdělavácia nadácia Jana Husa — the two foundations still remained inextricably interwound. During the 'Mečiar years' the Foundation became central to the alliance of non-governmental organisations in Slovakia; whilst in 1998 Jiří Müller was made adviser to the Minister of the Czech Republic responsible for the development of the non-profit sector.

In 1979, during her first visit to the underground university in Czechoslovakia, Dr. Kathy Wilkes had led a seminar on the theme of the identity of human personality. Whereas the cells of the body are renewed throughout life, she had taught, memory endures and accumulates. Human personality is like a rope made up of fibres of experience — principles, desires and hopes. The longer the fibres, the stronger the personality. The individual can deliberately cultivate certain elements whilst resisting other influences. 'Personality' is not something which is permanent and limited: it is the expression of its own development. Twenty years later, the meaning of her seminar is just beginning to be understood.

'...My first surprise was that an Oxford professor could be so young and feminine, and at the same time so confident and wise...'. [2]

APPENDIX I

Jan Hus Educational Foundation
1980-1990

Trustees
Catherine Audard
Frank Bealey
Jessica Douglas-Home
Nancy Durham
Paul Flather
Helen Ganly
Stuart Hampshire (Chairman 1981-1984)
Andrew Lenox-Conyngham
David Matthews
Alan Montefiore
Claus Moser (Chairman 1984-1989)
Iris Murdoch
W.H. Newton-Smith
Jonathan Ruffer
Roger Scruton
Anthony Smith (Chairman 1989- present)
Tom Stoppard
Charles Taylor (Chairman 1980-1981)
Christopher Taylor
Ralph Walker
Kathy Wilkes

Patrons

Professor Sir Alfred Ayer
Sir Robert Birley, KCMG
Sir Adrian Cadbury
The Rt. Revd. and Rt. Hon. GE Ellison, PC
Norman Franklin
Lady Antonia Fraser
Dame Helen Gardner
Professor Ernest Gellner
Sir Stuart Hampshire
Yehudi Menuhin, KBE
The Rt. Revd. Hugh Montefiore
Sir Claus Moser KCB, CBE, FCA
Professor Sir Roger Mynors
The Duke of Norfolk
Harold Pinter, CBE
The Hon. Victoria Rothschild
Dr. the Hon. Honor Smith, OBE, FRCP
C.H. Sporborg
Professor Charles Taylor
Rosalyn Tureck

APPENDIX II

Lists of Visitors: Jan Hus Educational Foundation

(For the first year these visitors were travelling under the auspices of the Oxford Sub-Faculty of Philosophy or independently; the Foundation did not come into existence until the summer of 1980. There were almost certainly more visits during this period than are listed, but no records were kept. There are probably names missing in the later period as well, where no report was made and no correspondence has survived. All the visitors in the first year talked to Julius Tomin's seminar, and often some other seminars as well. In other cases they usually travelled to speak at one seminar, but often spoke at others. The following short forms are used: LH = Ladislav Hejdánek; RK = Rudolf Kučera; PB = Pavel Bratinka; DK = Daniel Kroupa; PR = Petr Rezek. All the visitors to Brno spoke at Petr Oslzlý's seminar [some also at the English Club and other venues] and all those to Bratislava spoke at Ján Čarnogurský's seminar.)

1979

April	Kathy Wilkes
June	Charles Taylor
July	Richard Hare
September	Thomas Mautner?
	Roger Scruton
	Anthony Savile
Sept/Oct	Ian Pearson
	Jessica Strauss Pittman
November	Thomas Mautner
December	Alan Montefiore, Catherine Audard, Steven Lukes

1980

January	Kathy Wilkes
February	Roger Scruton
March	W.H. Newton-Smith
April	Anthony Kenny
	Pat Kerans?

	David Cooper
May	Kathy Wilkes
	Roger Scruton
July	David Armstrong
	Christopher Kirwan
	Roger Scruton
	Tom Nagel & Anne Hollander
August	Kathy Wilkes
	Alan Montefiore, Catherine Audard
October	Roger Scruton (LH)
	Kathy Wilkes (LH)

1981

January	Christopher Kirwan (LH; Neubauer; Sousedík)
	Roger Scruton (LH; Němec)
February	John Procopé (LH)
	J.R. Lucas (LH)
March	Jack Skorupski (LH)
	Dan Dennett (LH)
April	Roger Scruton (LH, Vašíček)
	Gwill Owen (LH)
	Heather Allen (proposed setting up of ELT seminar)
June	Roger Scruton (LH)
July	Richard Rorty (LH)
September	Alan Montefiore & Catherine Audard (LH)
	Ralph Walker (PR)
October	Jonathan Ruffer (seminar for Trojan did not take place)
	Roger Scruton (seminar for LH did not take place)
	Dorothy Edgington (PR: Analytical Philosophy)
November	Roger Scruton (LH)

1982

January	David Levy (LH)
February	Jon Elster (PR: Analytical Philosophy)
March	Jürgen Habermas & Ernst Tugendhat (LH; PR)
April	unsigned report (LH)
	Kathy Wilkes (PR: Analytical Philosophy)
	Anthony O'Hear (seminars for LH & PR did not take place)
June	Michael Flynn (PR: Analytical Philosophy)

	Christopher Taylor (PR: Analytical Philosophy)
	Christopher Kirwan (PR)
July	John Dunn?
September	Brenda Cohen (PR: Analytical Philosophy)
	Kathy Wilkes (PR: Analytical Philosophy/Aristotle;
October	LH)
	Steven Lukes?
November	Matthew Hutton (Harvest Trust)
	T.L.S. Sprigge (PR: Analytical Philosophy)
December	Matthew Hutton
	David Charles (PR: Analytical Philosophy/Aristotle)
	Richard Sorabji (PR: Analytical Philosophy/Aristotle)

1983

January	Roger Scruton (PB; PR: Analytical Philosophy; DK)
	Michael Baxendall (PR: Art)
March	David Levy (RK)
	Sally Shreir (seminar for RK did not take place)
April	Dan Jacobson (Klíma)
	Ralph Walker (PR: Kant)
	Ronald Beiner (RK)
May	Alan Wynn (LH: visiting human rights activist, no seminar)
	Christopher Taylor (PR: Aristotle)
July	Matthew Hutton (Harvest Trust)
	Jacques & Hélène Brunschwicg (PR: Aristotle)
	A.C.Montefiore & Catherine Audard?
	David Stark
October	Roger Scruton (PB; RK)

1984

January	Timothy Garton Ash (RK)
	Ralph Walker (PR: Aristotle)
	Lars Bergström (PR: Aristotle; LH)
February	Bob Grant (PB; RK)
March	Klaus Nellen
April	Christopher Kirwan (PR: Aristotle; LH)
	Roger Scruton (as Trustee; PR: Kant; Brno)
	Christopher Taylor
June	Jessica Strauss Pittman

July	Matthew Hutton (Harvest Trust)
	Frank Bealey (RK)
	Paul Flather (Prague: courier)
October	Jessica Douglas-Home (Prague, Brno: courier)
	Dorothy Edgington (PR: Kant)
December	David Papineau (LH)
	David Levy (Brno)

1985

January	Michael Rosen (PR: Kant)
February	John Keane (Brno)
March	Wolfgang Stock (Prague: courier)
	David Regan (Brno)
May	Ralph Walker (as Trustee; PR: Kant)
	Richard Rorty?
	Francis Dunlop (Brno)
June	Roger Scruton (Brno as Trustee; seminar for RK did not take place)
	Donald & Margaret Davidson (LH)
	Dan Raff (Prague: courier)
September	John Hale (seminar for LH did not take place)
	Jessica Douglas-Home (Prague, Brno as Trustee)
November	Paul Flather (Brno, Prague as Trustee)
December	Joanna Hodge (PR: Kant)
	John Keane (Brno)
	Alan Montefiore & Catherine Audard (Prague as Trustees)

1986

January	Dennis O'Keeffe (Brno; courier)
	David Matthews (Brno; music)
February	Grant Gillett (PR: Kant)
March	Tom Burke (Brno; ecology)
	Bob Grant, John Rose (RK)
April	Barbara Day (Prague, Brno as secretary; courier)
	Craig Kennedy (Brno; courier)
	Louis Greig (Prague)
	Andrew Lenox-Conyngham (Prague)
	David Levy (Brno)
	Christopher Kirwan (Prague as Trustee)

	Fiona Hughes (PR: Kant)
	Dan & Margaret Jacobson (Brno; literature)
May	Cheryl Misak (Brno; courier)
	Howard Robinson (PR: Kant)
June	Herman Parret (LH)
	Tom Burke (Brno, Prague; ecology)
	Gunnar Skirbekk (LH; RK)
	John Keane (seminar for RK did not take place)
July	Wolfgang & Oriana Stock (Brno; couriers)
August	Barbara Day (Brno, Prague as secretary; courier)
	Steven Lukes (RK)
September	Oriana Stock (Brno; courier)
	David Matthews, Nigel Osborne (Brno; music)
October	Geoffrey Robertson (Prague; Jazz Section)
	Francis Dunlop (Brno)
	Ralph Walker (as Trustee; PR: Kant)
November	Tom Burke (Prague; ecology)
	John Rose (RK; LH)
	Norman Podhoretz (RK)
December	Tony Judt (LH; seminar for RK did not take place)

1987

January	Michael Potter (Brno; courier)
	Jessica Douglas-Home (Prague, Brno as Trustee)
February	David Selbourne (RK)
	Michael Rosen (PR: Kant; seminar for LH did not take place)
	Helen Ganly (Brno; art)
	Geoffrey Robertson (Jazz Section)
	Nancy Durham (Jazz Section, journalist)
March	Charles Alexander, Nigel Osborne, Michael Berkeley (Jazz Section)
	Francesca Murphy (LH)
	Piers Paul Read (Brno, Prague; literature)
April	Duncan Watt (Brno; courier)
	Barbara Day (Prague, Brno as secretary; courier)
	Michael Banner (Brno; courier)
	Wolfgang Stock (Prague, Brno; courier)
May	Anthony O'Hear, Peter Fuller (Brno)
	John Marks (Prague; courier)

June	Barry Stroud (PR: Kant)
	Angelo Petroni (LH)
	James de Candole (Brno; courier)
August	David Matthews, Maggie Hemingway (Brno as Trustee; music, literature)
	James de Candole (Brno; courier)
September	Wolfgang Stock (Prague, Brno; courier)
October	Nora Beloff (RK)
	Carol Rumens (Brno, Prague; literature)
	Robert Grant, Graham Capper (Bratislava)
	Sholto Douglas-Home (Prague; courier)
November	Julian Mitchell, Richard Rowson (Brno; literature, medicine)
December	Helen Ganly (Brno as Trustee; art)

1988

January	James de Candole (Brno; courier)
	Christopher Kirwan (as Trustee; PR: Plato)
	John Finnis (Bratislava)
	David Pryce-Jones (Brno, Prague; literature)
	Onora O'Neill (LH)
February	Stephen Beller (RK)
	David Selbourne (RK; Bratislava)
March	Nancy Durham (as Trustee; Jazz Section, journalist)
	Charles Alexander (Jazz Section)
	Gordon Crosse (Brno, Prague; music)
	Lesley Brown (PR: Plato)
	Gerald Cohen (LH)
	Helen Ganly (Brno, Prague as Trustee; art)
	Stephen Blunden (Cambridge Diploma)
April	Barbara Day (Brno, Prague as secretary; courier)
	David Levy (Brno)
	David Regan (Bratislava)
	John Keane (Brno)
May	Lindsay Judson (PR: Plato)
June	C.H. Sisson (Brno, Prague; literature)
July	Jessica Douglas-Home (Prague as Trustee)
	Nancy Durham (as Trustee; Jazz Section, journalist)
August	James de Candole (Brno; courier)
September	Tom Burke (Prague, Bratislava; ecology)

	Andrew Lenox-Conyngham (as Trustee; Cambridge Diploma)
	Philip Steen, Charles Foster (Cambridge Diploma couriers)
	Edward Yarnold (Bratislava)
	David Matthews (as Trustee), Judith Weir, Anthony Powers (Brno; music)
	Robin Holloway (Prague; music)
October	Christopher Taylor (PR: Plato)
	David Cazalet (Prague; courier)
	Léon Krier, John Robbins (Prague; architecture)
	J.E. Tiles (PR: Plato; LH)
	Barbara Day (Prague, Brno, Bratislava as secretary; courier)
November	Michael Woods (Prague, PR)
	Paul Helm (LH)
	Michael Berkeley, Deborah Rogers (Prague, Brno; music, literature)
	Steven Lukes with Ira Katznelson, Jonathan Fenton & Jeffrey Goldfarb (LH; DK)
December	David Levy (RK; DK)
	David Sanders (Cambridge Diploma)

1989

January	Ralph Walker (as Trustee; PR: Plato)
	Marek Matraszek (Brno; courier)
	John Marks (Bratislava)
February	Dan Jacobson (Prague, Brno; literature)
	Eric James (Prague; courier)
March	Simon Bainbridge (Prague, Brno; music)
	Norman Barry (Brno)
	Mark Almond (RK)
April	Angus Cargill (Prague; courier)
	Susan Marsh (Brno; courier)
May	Graham King (Prague; architecture)
	Francis Dunlop (Brno)
	David Sanders (Cambridge Diploma)
June	Frank Bealey (as Trustee; Brno)
	Kathy Wilkes (as Trustee; LH)
	Barbara Day (Prague, Brno as secretary; courier)

	David Pryce-Jones (Bratislava; seminar did not take place)
August	Angus Cargill (Bratislava, Prague: courier)
	Gavin Harris (Prague: courier)
	David Matthews (Brno as Trustee; music)
September	Wolfgang Stock (Brno; courier)
	James de Candole (Brno, Prague: courier)
	Quinlan Terry (Prague, Brno; architecture)
October	Mark Almond (Bratislava)
	John Marks (Prague: courier; seminar for RK did not take place)
November	Christine Stone (Bratislava; journalist)
	Nancy Durham (Prague as Trustee; journalist)
	Helen Ganly (Brno as Trustee; art)
December	Barbara Day (Bratislava, Brno, Prague as secretary; courier)
	Stephen Sykes (Cambridge Diploma)
	Dennis O'Keeffe (Bratislava; seminar in Olomouc did not take place)

Association Jan Hus

(The first part of this list is very incomplete, as no records were kept, and many philosophers travelled independently. There is a note in the early part of the files that orginally visits took place every two months, and subsequently monthly. Unmarked visits were to Prague, usually to Ladislav Hejdánek's seminar; there were also visits to Rudolf Kučera's seminar and to other seminars. All the visits marked 'Brno' are recorded in Milan Jelínek's diaries.)

1979
December   Catherine Audard

1980
June   Paul Ricoeur
August   Catherine Audard

1981
May   Jean-Pierre Vernant

September   Catherine Audard
November   Roland Brunet
December   Jaques Derrida

1982
?   Michele Bernhard?
May   Jean-Claude Eslin & Olivier Mongin
May?   Antonia Soulez & Charles Malamoud
June?   J.J. Lecercle?
September   Anne Baron & Didier Fouillard
October   Jeanette Colombel
November?   Louis Marin?
December?   Jean-Francois Lyotard

1983
January?   Edouard Fernandez Bollo?
April   Michel Deguy
May   Pierre Lantz & Pierre Livet
June   Nathalie Roussarie, Jacques & Hélène Brunschwicg
(June/Oct?)   Marie-Claire Boons?
September   Pierre Lantz and Livet
October?   Claude Imbert?
Oct?/Dec?   Jean-Claude Schmatt
November   Jacqueline Rousseau Dujardin
            Jean-Claude Eslin & Olivier Mongin?
            Pierre Kaufmann
            Mikel Dufrenne?

1984
January   Jean-Claude Schmidt
February   Etienne Balibar
            Jean-Pierre Vernant?
            Georges Labica?
March   Maurice Agulhon
April/May?   Jean-Francois Lyotard
            Jacque Merleau-Ponty?
            Jean-Claude Eslin & Olivier Mongin?
            Hervé Martin?
May   Louis Dumont?
            Jean-Jacques Lecercle?

	André Miguel?
June	André Jacob?
	Louis Dumont
	Jeanette Colombel
June?	André Jacob?
October	Pierre Kaufmann
Nov/Dec?	E. Leroy-Ladurie?

1985

February	Louis Marin & J. Luc Nancy
	Ph. Lacoue-Labarthe?
June	André Glucksmann
	Paul Thibaud?
September	Jean-Francois & Mme. Lyotard
October	Jean-Claude Eslin & Olivier Mongin (RK; Brno)
November?	Lautmann?
December	Catherine Audard (Prague)

1986

February	Psychoanalysts (Rousseau Dujardin, Trilling, Frécourt, Cachard, Rebuffat)
March	Paul Ricoeur
April	Marcel Gauchet
	C. Leforte
May	Jean-Michel Besnier (Brno)
	Emmanuel Terray
	Nathalie Roussarie (Brno)
	Jeanette Colombel
June	LeRoy Ladurie?
September?	E. Terray
September	Leroy Ladurie
October	André Enégren & Claude Habib (Brno)
November	Stanislas Breton & Irene Jami

1987

January	Miguel Abensour & Françoise Coblence (Prague; Brno)
	Emmanuel Terray
February	J.L. Thébaut (Brno)
April	Pierre Kaufmann (Brno; Prague)
May	Jean-Pierre Vernant

June	Yves Geffroy, N. Cavallero
September	Pierre Cartier
October	Yves Geffroy (Brno)
	André Comte Sponville
November	Catherine Challiere & Chantal Demonque (Brno)

1988

January	Bernard Fabre (Brno)
February	Nathalie Roussarie (Prague; Brno, as Secretary)
	M. Ferro
March	Pierre-Jean Labarriere (Prague; Brno)
May	Vincent Descombes
	Marc-Vincent Howlett (Brno)
June	Pierre Jacob
September	Jean-Claude Eslin (Prague; Brno)
October	Bernard Fabre (Brno; Prague)
December	Etienne Balibar?

1989

January	Sabine Bollock (Brno; courier)
February	André Comte Sponville
May	Alain Finkielkraut (Brno; Prague)
June	Pierre Jean Labarriere & Gwendolyne Jaczyk (Prague; Brno)
September	Jacques Message (Brno)
	Jean-Luc & Maria Petit (Brno; Prague)
October	Paul Ricoeur
November	Charles Malamoud (Prague; Brno)

Academia Copernicana
(This List is believed to be complete)

1985

March	Wolfgang Stock (Prague: courier)

1986

August	Wolfgang & Oriana Stock (Brno; couriers)
September	Oriana Stock (Brno; courier)
November	Hugo von Lehsten (Prague; courier)

1987

February	Alma von Stockhausen (Prague; PR)
March	Marie von Spee (Brno; courier)
April	Wolfgang Stock (Brno, Prague; courier)
September	Wolfgang Stock (Brno, Prague; courier)
December	Magdalena Kaufmann (Brno)

1988

April	Alexander von Bischoffshausen (Brno, Prague)
June	Reinhard Brandt (Brno, Prague; Kant)
December	Elisabeth von Werthern (Brno)

1989

May	Mark von Campenhausen (Prague; courier)
September	Wolfgang Stock (Brno)
Sept/Oct	Bernd Posselt (Brno)

APPENDIX III

Interviews (and Correspondence)
for the Jan Hus Educational Foundation:

(Interviewed in connection with the activities of the British Jan Hus Educational Foundation)

Heather Allen, David Armstrong, Catherine Audard, Tom Burke, David Cooper, Nadia Diuk, Jessica Douglas-Home, Nancy Durham, Paul Flather, Helen Ganly, Carl Gershman, Robert Grant, Dan Jacobson, Jan Kavan, John Keane, Anthony Kenny, Christopher Kirwan, Andrew Lenox-Conyngham, David Levy, Steven Lukes, David Matthews, Alan Montefiore, Bill Newton-Smith, Roger Potocki, Vilém Prečan, Anthony Savile, Roger Scruton, Ralph Walker, Kathy Wilkes.

For the Association Jan Hus:
Catherine Audard, Miguel Abensour, Jean-Michel Besnier, Jacques Derrida, André Enegren, Roger Errera, Jean-Claude Eslin, Bernard Fabre, Claude Habibe, Maria Petit, Nathalie Roussarie, Jean-Pierre Vernant.

For the Jan Hus Educational and Cultural Fund:
Vratislav Pechota, H. Gordon Skilling, Peter Steinfels, Jessica Strauss, Charles Taylor, Paul Wilson.

For the Jan Hus Fund/Le Fond Jan Hus
H. Gordon Skilling, Charles Taylor, Paul Wilson.

For the Academia Copernicana:
Martin Leitner, Bernd Posselt, Oriana Stock, Wolfgang Stock.

Holland:
Theodore de Boer, Henri Veldhuis.

Austria:
Klaus Nellen (for the Insitut für die Wissenschaften vom Menschen)

Czech Republic:
Milan Balabán, Pavel Barša, Jan Bednář, Ludvík Bednář, Jaroslav Blažke, Marie Blažková, Jaroslav Borecký, Pavel Bratinka, Ivan Dejmal, Jiří Fiala, Petr Fiala, Markéta Fialková-Němcová, Jana Fraňková, Zina Freundová, Jiří Gruntorad, Ivan Havel, Aleš Havlíček, Ladislav Hejdánek, Alena Hromádková Milan Jelínek, Jana Jelínková, Ivan Chvatík, Pavel Kouba, Jan Kozlík, Daniel Kroupa, Rudolf Kučera, Daniel Kummerman, Miroslav Kundrata, Jiří Müller, Broňa Müllerová, Eva Oslzlá, Petr Oslzlý, Karel Palek, Martin Palouš, Radim Palouš, Petr Pithart, Miroslav Pospíšil, Vladimír Prajzler, Miloš Rejchrt, Petr Rezek, Jan Schneider, Karel Srp, Jiřina Šiklová, Jan Šimek, Julius Tomin, Zdena Tominová, Jakub Trojan, Zdeněk Vašíček.

Slovak Republic:
Ján Čarnogurský, Jozef Jablonický, Ján Langoš, Miroslav Kusý Miroslav Lehký (Snr), Miroslav Lehký (Jnr.).

Appendix IV

Funding bodies, emigré organisations and other support groups working in the West:

(This is not a complete list; it includes only those with which the Jan Hus Educational Foundation cooperated between 1980 and 1989)

Academia Copernicana e.V. (West Germany)
Amnesty International (UK)
Association internationelle de défense d'artistes (France)
Association Jan Hus (France)
Central and East European Publishing Project (UK)
Charter 77 Foundation (Sweden)
Charter 77 Foundation (USA)
Československé dokumentární středisko nezávislé literatury (West Germany)
Fondation pour une entraide internationelle (France)
Index on Censorship (UK)
Jagiellonian Trust (UK)
Jan Hus Educational and Cultural Foundation (USA)
Jan Hus Educational Foundation (UK)
Jan Hus Fund — Le Fond Jan Hus (Canada)
Jan Palach Information and Research Trust (UK)
Helsinki Watch (USA)
Keston College (UK)
National Endowment for Democracy (USA)
Open Society Fund (USA)
Palach Press (UK)
Rozmluvy (UK)
Solidarity Fund (UK)
Svědectví (France)
SVU (USA/UK)

BIBLIOGRAPHY

This bibliography includes the following types of books and articles: Material in English (including translations from Czech and Slovak) which relates directly to the context in which the seminars took place and samizdat was produced; works in English, French, German and Dutch which were written or partly written as a direct or indirect result of experiences at or around the seminars; works originally in Czech or Slovak which were published in English, French and Dutch as a result of contacts made through the seminars; Material in Czech and Slovak which relates directly to the context in which the seminars took place and samizdat was produced; listings in Czech and Slovak of seminars and samizdat.

'A Correspondent' (Jessica Douglas-Home): 'Art in Czechoslovakia', *The Salisbury Review* (London), July 1987
Allen, Kimberly Ann: *Compromise, Collaboration and Betrayal: The Legacy of the Czech Secret Police Cadre*, unpublished dissertation, Princeton University, New Jersey 1997
Anonymous (Petr Pithart): 'In Search of Central Europe: To Those Who March for Peace', *The Salisbury Review* (London), October 1983
Armstrong, David: 'Letter from Prague', *Quadrant* (Australia), January 1981
Beller, Stephen: 'Zrodil se moderní svět zde?' (Was the modern world born here?), *StředníEvropa* 1990/16 (Praha)
Birkett, Julian: 'If Books Could Kill...', *The Listener* (London), 31 May 1990
Brabenec, Vratislav and Jirous, Ivan: 'Banned in Bohemia', *Index on Censorship* (London), 1/83
Bratinka, Pavel: 'The candles that freed Prague', *The Times* (London), 15 December 1989
de Candole, James: 'Václav Havel as a Conservative Thinker', *The Salisbury Review* (London), December 1988
Čarnogurský, Ján: 'In Search of Central Europe', *The Salisbury Review* (London), June 1989
Čarnogurský, Ján: 'Czecho-Slovakia's Road from Serfdom' in *The Salisbury Review* (London), September 1990
Císařová, B., Drápala, M., Prečan, V., Vančura, J. (ed): *Charta 77 očima současníký — po dvaceti letech* (Charter 77 in the Eyes of its Contemporaries — Twenty Years Later), Ústav pro soudobé dějiny AVČR, Praha 1997
Day, Barbara: 'Theatre on a String' in *Index on Censorship* (London), 2/1985
Day, Barbara: 'In Prague' in *Plays International* (London), April 1989
Day, Barbara: 'Small war in Absurdistan', *The Spectator* (London), 26th August 1989
Day, Barbara: 'Velvet Philosophers' in *The Times* (London), 20 August 1998
Douglas-Home, Jessica: *Once Upon Another Time* (forthcoming, 2000)
Drápala, Milan (ed): *Minulost a dějiny v Českém a slovenském samizdatu 1970-1989* (The Past and History in Czech and Slovak Samizdat), Doplněk, Brno 1993.
Dunlop, Francis: 'Objektivita hodnot' (The Objectivity of Values) in *Proglas* (Brno) 5-6/91, and *Podzemní univerzita* (ed. Oslzlý)
Durham, Nancy: 'Czechoslovak artists pessimistic about change' in *The Globe and Mail* (Toronto), 1985

Eslin, Jean-Claude: 'Katolická cirkev před volbou jménem osvětím', *Střední Evropa*, 1990/14 (Praha)

Fiala, Jiří (compiled): 'Pondělky 85' (Mondays 85) in *SCIPHI* (Praha), February, May, October 1991, June 1992, November 1994

Fiala, Jiří (compiled): *Katětovův seminář* 1970-1995 (Katětov's Seminar 1970-1995), privately published, Praha 1995 (1997)

Fidelius, Petr (Karel Palek): 'In Search of Central Europe: Totalitarian Language' in *The Salisbury Review* (London), January 1984

Fidelius, Petr (Karel Palek): 'In Search of Central Europe: On Handling Words' in *The Salisbury Review* (London), April 1984

Fidelius, Petr (Karel Palek): 'In Search of Central Europe: Right versus Left, The Limits of Intransigency' in *The Salisbury Review* (London), October 1984

Fidelius, Petr (Karel Palek, tr. Erika Abrams with a foreword by André Glucksmann): *L'esprit post-totalitaire*, Bernard Grasset, Paris 1986 (trans lation of *Jazyk a moc* (Language and Power), Arkýř, Munich 1983)

Flather, Paul: 'Philosophers' open warfare for freedom of thought' in *The Times Higher Educational Supplement* (London), 29 February 1980

Flather, Paul: 'Politics and philosophy: the unlikely course Oxford took to Paris' in *The Times Higher Educational Supplement* (London), 6 June 1980

Flather, Paul: 'Philosophy behind a flight to freedom' in *The Times Higher Educational Supplement* (London), 12 September 1980

Flather, Paul: 'The post-Tomin tribulations of Czechoslovakia' in *The Times Higher Educational Supplement* (London), 15 May 1981

Flather, Paul: 'Britský imperialismus v Indii' (British Imperialism in India) in *Proglas* (Brno) 8/91

Frankel, William: 'An Eye on Gorbachov - 1, Why Czechs Do Not Move Their Feet' in *The Statesman* (Calcutta & Delhi), 17 September 1986.

Frolík, Jan: 'Nástin organizačního vývoje státobezpečnostních složek sboru národníbezpečnosti v letech 1948-1989' in *Sborník archivních prácí*, Vol XLI, no 2 (Praha) 1991

Ganly, Helen: *The Wolfman and the Clown*, André Deutsch, London 1990

Goetz-Stankiewicz, Marketa (ed): *Good-bye, Samizdat*, Northwestern University Press, Evanston, Illinois 1992

Gruntorád, Jiří (compiled): *Informace o Chartě 77: článková bibliografie* (Information about the Charter: Bibliography of Articles), Doplněk, Brno 1998

Guppy, Shusha: 'The Clandestine University' in *The Daily Telegraph* (London), 6th October 1990

Hanáková, Jitka: *Edice českého samizdatu 1972-1991* (Editions of Czech Samizdat), Národní knihovna České republiky, Praha 1997

Havel, Ivan: 'ANote on the book *The Matter with Truth*' in: Robert McRae *The Matter with Truth*, Oikoymenh, Praha 1990

Havel, Václav: 'In Search of Central Europe: Politics and Conscience' in *The Salisbury Review* (London), January 1985

Havel, Václav: 'In Search of Central Europe: Slaughter-house' in *The Salisbury Review* (London), October 1986

Havel, Václav (tr. Paul Wilson): *Letters to Olga*, Faber and Faber, London 1988

Heidegger, Martin (tr. Ivan Tomáš [Ivan Chvatik] et al): *Konec filosofie a úkol myšlení* (The End of Philosophy and the Task of Thinking), Athenaeum - Rozmluvy, Oxford - London 1985

Hejdánek, Ladislav: 'Offering a variety of views' in *Index on Censorship* (London), 3/86

Hejdánek, Ladislav: *De filosofie en haar verhouding tot de waarheid* (Philosophy and its Relationship with Truth), Eburon, Delft 1988
Hemingway, Maggie: *The Postmen's House*, Sinclair-Stevenson, London 1990
Heneka A., Janouch J., Prečan V., Vladislav J. (ed): *A Besieged Culture —* *Czechoslovakia Ten Years after Helsinki*, Charta 77 Foundation/ International Helsinki Federation for Human Rights, Stockholm-Vienna 1985
Hird, Sam (Barbara Day): 'Silencing the Jazz Section' in *The Spectator* (London), 27 September 1986
Hitchens, Christopher: 'Oxford's Unlikely Liaisons' in *New Statesman* (London), 21 March 1980
Hitchens, Christopher: 'Lock up your philosophers' in *New Statesman* (London), 28 March 1980
Hlušičková, Růžena and Otáhal, Milan: *Čas Demokratické iniciativy 1987-1990* (The Time of Democratic Initiatives 1987-1990), Nadace Demokratické iniciativy pro kulturu a politiku, České Budějovice 1993
van der Horst, Klaas: *Een Scheur in het Gordijn. Kerkelijke Nederlands-Tsjechische contacten 1959-1989* (A Tear in the Curtain. Contacts between Dutch and Czech Churches 1959-1989), Eman, Heršpice 1997
Jacobson, Dan: 'Revoluční Street' in *New Society* (London), 14 July 1987
Jones, Derek (ed.): *Censorship: An International Encyclopedia*, Fitzroy Dearborn, London 1999
de Jong, B. (ed.): *Wie zijn je vrienden in Oost-Europa?* (Who are your Friends in Eastern Europe?), Amsterdam 1985
Kavan, Rosemary: *Freedom at a Price: An Englishwoman's Life in Czechoslovakia*, Verso, London 1985
Keane, John: 'Občanská společnost a stát' (Civil Society and the State) in *Proglas* (Brno) 3-4/91, and in *Podzemní univerzita* (ed. Oslzlý)
Keane, John: 'Protistranická politics' (Anti-party Politics) in *Proglas* (Brno) 3/92
Keane, John: *Democracy and Civil Society*, Verso 1993
Kershaw, Alex: 'The Trial of Jan Kavan' in *The Independent on Sunday* (London), 20 September 1992
Kenny, Anthony: *An Oxford Life*, John Murray, London 1997
Kohák, Erazim (ed): *Patočka*, University of Chicago Press, 1989
Kořán, Miloš (Pavel Bratinka): 'In Search of Central Europe: Survival as a Way of Human Life' in *The Salisbury Review* (London), April 1987
Korda, Jan: 'In Search of Central Europe: Prostitution in Czechoslovakia' in *The Salisbury Review* (London), September 1989
Korder, T.R. (Radim Palouš): *Voegelin & Patočka*, Athenaeum - Rozmluvy, Oxford - London 1988
Kroupa, Daniel: *Svoboda a řád (sváteční rozhovory)* (Freedom and Order [Occasional Conversations]), Éós, Praha 1996
Levy, Alan: 'Family Man From The Catacomb Culture' in *The Prague Post*, 11-17 January 1995
Levy, David J.: 'The Rediscovery of Central Europe' in *The World and I*, September 1986
Levy, David J.: 'Politické bytí' (Political Being) in *Proglas* (Brno) 1/91, and in *Podzemní univerzita* (ed. Oslzlý)
Lukes, Steven: 'After Tomin, the ambiguity remains' in *The Times* (London), 5 December 1980
Machala, Lubomír (ed): *Česká a slovenská literatura v exilu a samizdatu* (Czech and Slovak Literature in Exile and Samizdat), Hanácké noviny,

Olomouc 1991
Málek, Jiří and Zikmundovský, Zdeněk: *Přehled o činnosti a struktuře StB v letech 1988-1990*, unpublished paper, Prague 1991
Matthews, David: 'The flourishing tradition of Janáček and bear steaks' in *The Independent* (London), 21 October 1986
Matthews, David: 'Mahlerova 10. symfonie' (Mahler's 10th Symphony) in *Proglas* (Brno) 4/92
Matthews, David: 'In Search of Mahler's Childhood' in Philip Reed (ed): *On Mahler and Britten: Essays in Honour of Donald Mitchell on His 70th Birthday*, The Boydell Press/The Britten Pears Library, London 1995.
Müller, Jiří: 'Prý mám hroší kůži' (Apparently I have the skin of a rhinocerous) in *Lidové noviny* (Praha), 24 May 1990
Müller, Jiří: 'Epilog československého samizdatu' (An Epilogue to Czechoslovak Samizdat) in *Duha* (Brno), year 4 (summer 1990) no 2
Navarrete, Nilda: 'Search for a perfect tutor; Czechoslovakia' in *The Times Higher Educational Supplement* (London), 13 October 1995
Němec, Jiří and Souček, David (compiled): *Jan Patočka, Bibliografie 1928-1996*, Oikoymenh, Praha 1997
Neubauer, Zdeněk and Palouš, Martin (ed): *Academia: Commemorationes et Consultationes. Sborník k sedmdesátinám Radima Palouše* (Festschrift for the Seventieth Birthday of Radim Palouš), CTS-Dušický L.P., Praha 1994
Newton-Smith, W.H.: 'Isolation in Prague' in *New Statesman* (London), 14 March 1980
Nietzsche, Friedrich (tr. Pavel Kouba, Jan Krejčí): *Nečasové úvahy* (Untimely Reflections), Athenaeum, Oxford - London 1988
O'Hear, Anthony and Oslzlý, Petr: 'Peter Fuller: a light in the night' in *The Sunday Telegraph* (London) 10 June 1990
Oslzlý, Petr (ed.): 'Podzemní univerzita' (The Underground University) in *Proglas* (Brno), 2/91, 3-4/91, 5-6/91, 7/91, 8/91, 1/92, 2/92, 3/92, 4/92, 8/92
Oslzlý, Petr: *Drogerie Zlevněné zboží*, illustrated brochure to accompany exhibition held by the Ville de Rennes, 1992
Oslzlý, Petr et al: *Podzemní univerzita* (The Underground University), Centrum pro studium demokracie a kultury, Brno 1993
Oslzlý, Petr: *Jan Šimek: Případy soch* (Jan Šimek: Stories of Sculptures), Atlantis, Brno 1999
Pithart, Petr et al.: *Acta contemporanea; K pětašedesátinám Viléma Prečana* (For Vilém Prečan's 65th Birthday), Ústav pro soudobé dějiny AV ČR, Praha 1998
Podhoretz, Norman: 'Journey to the evil empire' in *New York Post*, 9 December 1986
Pokorná, Terezie: *Revolver Revue* No. 33, January 1997
Posselt, Bernd and Stock, Wolfgang: 'Paneuropäische Wendejahre' in *Paneuropa-Deutschland*, 3/1992
Procopé, John: 'An evening in Prague' in *Outlook* (Oxford), 1981
Pryce-Jones, David: 'Czech Rule of Lawlessness' in *The Spectator* (London), 7 October 1989.
Racek, Václav: 'In Search of Central Europe: Totalitarianism in 1983' in *The Salisbury Review* (London), April 1983
Read, Piers Paul: *A Season in the West*, Secker and Warburg, London 1988
Regan, David: 'Edmund Burke a konzervatismus' (Edmund Burke and Conservatism) in *Proglas* (Brno) 3-4/91, and in *Podzemní univerzita* (ed. Oslzlý)
Ricoeur, Paul: 'Etika a politika' (Ethics and Politics), *Střední Evropa* 1993/29

(Praha)
Robertson, Geoffrey: *The Justice Game*, Chatto and Windus, London 1998
Scruton, Roger: *Untimely Tracts*, The Macmillan Press, London 1987
Scruton, Roger et al: *Czechoslovakia - The Unofficial Culture*, The Claridge Press in association with the Jan Hus Educational Foundation, London 1987
Scruton, Roger: 'Intellectual stokers gave power to the people' in *The Sunday Telegraph* (London), 21 January 1990
Scruton, Roger: 'A Catacomb Culture' in *The Times Literary Supplement* (London), 16-22 February 1990
Scruton, Roger (trans. Petr Pithart): *Smysl konservatismu*, Torst, Praha 1993
Scruton, Roger: 'Co je konservatismus?' (What is Conservatism?), *Střední Evropa* 1993/34 (Praha)
Selbourne, David: 'Czechs hunt elusive spring' in *The Sunday Times* (London), 8 March 1987
Selbourne, Davis: 'The Pope's divisions line up in Prague' in The *Sunday Telegraph* (London), 27 March 1988
Skácel, Jan (ed. Sabine Bollock, Bernard Fabre): OPÉRATEURS 4, Paris 1989.
Skilling, H. Gordon: *Charter 77 and Human Rights in Czechoslovakia*, George Allen and Unwin Ltd., London 1981
Skilling, H. Gordon: *Samizdat and an Independent Society in Central and Eastern Europe*, Macmillan Press in association with St Anthony's College, Oxford, 1989
Slavická, M., Pánková, M. (ed): *Vytvarné umění - The Magazine for Contemporary Art 3-4 95: Zakázání umění I* (Forbidden Art I); *1-2 96: Zakázáné umění II* (Forbidden Art II)
Smith, Simon: *Movements of resistance and transformation in Czechoslovakia during the 1970s and 1980s* (unpublished dissertation, July 1996)
Srp, Karel: *Výjimeční stavy: povolání jazzové sekce* (States of Emergency: the Calling of the Jazz Section), Pragma, Praha 1994
Strauss Pittman, Jessica: *Apolitical Politics: The Role of Alternative Culture in Czechoslovakia* (unpublished dissertation, Fall 1983)
Suk, Jiří: *Občanské fórum* (2 volumes), Ústav pro soudobé dějiny AV ČR-Doplněk, Praha-Brno 1997
Ševčík, Václav et al: *Na Babě 12*, privately printed, Praha 1995
Šimečka, Milan: 'In Search of Central Europe: My Years with Gorbachev' in *The Salisbury Review* (London), October 1984
Šimečka, Milan: 'In Search of Central Europe' in *The Salisbury Review* (London), September 1989
Šimečka, Milan (tr. A.G. Brain): *The Restoration of Order*, Verso, London 1984
Šimulčík, Ján (ed.): *Svetlo zpodzemia: zkroniky katolíckeho samizdatu 1969-1989* (Light from the Underground: from the chronicles of Catholic samizdat 1969-1989), Vydavatelstvo Michala Vaška, Prešov 1997
Škvorecký, Josef: 'Jazz hot, punk-rock et socialisme réel' in *L'Autre Europe* (Paris), No. 9, March 1986
Špirit, Michael (ed): *Tvář* (visage), Torst, Praha 1995
Taylor, Charles: 'There is a hidden psychic cost involved in having constantly to play one's part in a systematic lie' in *New Statesman* (London), 6 July 1980
Tomin, Julius: 'Inside the Czech security state' in *New Statesman* (London), 7 March 1980.
Tomin, Julius (int. Gordon Clough): 'The World this Weekend' in *The Listener*

(London), 18 September 1980

Tomin, Zdena: 'The typewriters hold the fort' in *Index on Censorship* (London), 2/1983

Tomin, Zdena: *Stalin's Shoe*, Everyman Paperbacks, London 1986

Tomin, Zdena: *The Coast of Bohemia*, Everyman Paperbacks, London 1987

Trojan, Jakub: *And Nightingales Sing: theological reflections and dialogues*, Oikoymenh, Praha 1992

Vaculík, Ludvík: *Český snář*, Sixty-Eight Publishers, Toronto 1983.

Vaculík, Ludvík: *A Cup of Coffee with my Interrogator,* Readers International, London 1987

Verity, Christine: 'Jazz which rocks the Eastern bloc' in *The Times* (London), 18 October 1985

Verity, Christine: 'Trial of Czech wreath-layers shows 40 years of frustration' in *The Sunday Telegraph* (London), 19 November 1989

Vladislav, Jan (ed.): *Václav Havel or Living in Truth,* Faber and Faber, London 1987

Vladislav, Jan (ed.): *ACTA: Quarterly of the Documentation Centre for the Promotion of Independent Czechoslovak Literature,* 1/1987, 2/1987, 3-4/1987, 1-4/1988, 1-4/1989 (Scheinfeld)

Vladislav, Jan (ed.): *ACTA: Čtvrtletník Československého dokumentačního střediska nezávislé literatury,* 1/1987, 2/1987, 3-4/1987, 1-4/1988, 1-4/1989 (Scheinfeld)

Wilkes, Kathy: 'Talks with the philosophical nightwatchman of Prague' in *The Guardian* (London), 10th May 1979

Wilkes, Kathy: in *New Statesman* (London), 19th October 1979

Wilkes, Kathy: 'An Empty victory for the Secret Police' in *New Statesman* (London), 30 May 1980

Wilkes, Kathy: 'Report on Academic Freedom in Czechoslovakia' in *Proceedings and Addresses of The American Philosophical Association* (Delaware), August 1980

Williams, Kieran: 'The StB in Czechoslovakia: the evolution of a political police under communist rule' in Denis Deletant, Paul Latawski, Kieran Williams: *Security Forces in New Democracies: Poland, Romania and the Czech and Slovak Republics*, Macmillan London (forthcoming)

von Winterfeld, Ludwig (ed.): *Offener Dialog: Eine Ausstellung Tschechischer und Slowakischer Künstler aus der Region Mähren/Brünn* (Open Dialogue: An Exhibition of Czechoslovak Artists from Brno/Moravia), Künstlerforum, Bonn 1990.

Wyclif, John (ed. Ivan Mueller, tr. Anthony Kenny): *De Universalibus*, Clarendon Press, Oxford 1984.

Žáček, Pavel (ed): *Securitas Imperii 1; Sborník k problematice bezpečnostních služeb*, Úřad dokumentace a vyšetřování Činnosti Statní bezpečnosti při Úřadu vyšetřování Police ČR ve spolupráci s Odborem Public Relations a prevence MVČR ve Vydavatelstvía nakladatelství MVČR, Praha 1994.

Žáček, Pavel (ed): *Securitas Imperii 2; Sborník k problematice bezpečnostních služeb,* Úřad dokumentace a vyšetřovánízločinů kom munismu, Themis (nakladatelství MVČR), Praha 1995.

Žáček, Pavel (ed): *Securitas Imperii 3; Sborník k problematice bezpečnostních služeb,* Úřad dokumentace a vyšetřování zločinů kommunismu, Themis (nakladatelství MVČR), Praha 1996.

Žáček, Pavel; Benda, Patrik (ed): *Securitas Imperii 4; Sborník k problematice bezpečnostních služeb* (3 volumes), Úřad dokumentace a vyšetřování zločinů kommunismu, Themis (nakladatelství MVČR), Praha 1998.

NOTES AND REFERENCES

INTRODUCTION

1 John Hale, Visitor's Report, September 1985 (JHEF/RVS)

2 1952; Rudolf Slánský had been Secretary General of the Communist Party. Ten of the eleven were Jewish – in other words, suspected of being part of a worldwide conspiracy.

3 The office responsible for collecting information, the Bureau for the Investigation and Documentation of the Crimes of Communism, works against a current of former Communists with an interest in concealing the past.

4 In summer 1968 I was teaching English to a group of Czech teachers. When I asked them what the political changes really meant to them, this was their answer.

5 *Ideodiversní centrum.*

6 *Index nežádaných osob.* The only exception to this was Roger Scruton in June 1985, who was however deported in connection with the samizdat publication of *The Meaning of Conservatism* (see the chapter: 'The Philosophers and the Secret Police).

'BOLTED DOWN UNDER HOODS OF STEEL'

1 Author (under the pseudonym Petr Fidelius) of *Jazyk a moc* (Language and Power), (Arkyř, Munich 1983 translated into French by Erika Abrams as *L'esprit post-totalitaire* (Bernard Grasset, Paris 1986). Editor of *Kritický sborník*, 1981-89 (samizdat), 1990-present.

2 Edmund Husserl (1859-1938) studied in Germany and became professor at Freiburg University. His philosophy of the investigation of 'essences' or meanings, termed phenomenology, became a method widely used among philosophers on the mainland of Europe.

3 Martin Heidegger (1889-1976)

studied under Husserl and in 1928 became his successor at Freiburg University, of which he was briefly Rector. His early support for the Nazi regime led to his being forbidden to teach in Germany in the immediate post-war period.

4 For example, in October 1985 Václav Havel's brother Ivan gave a series of three lectures on Goldschlager's model of higher brain functions.

5 Conversation with Markéta Fialková (née Němcová) 12th February, 1997.

6 Skilling: *Charter 77 and Human Rights in Czechoslovakia*, 1981

7 Ibid.

8 Work in the uranium mines in northern Bohemia was a form of punishment not only for political prisoners but also for 'politically unreliable' young men who were not thought worthy of doing their National Service in the army; they were known as the 'black brigades'. The work was not only arduous but injurious to their health.

9 At this time Roger Scruton, graduate of Cambridge University, was Professor of Aesthetics at Birkbeck College of the University of London. He had founded *The Salisbury Review*, and written many articles (often controversial) on philosophy, aesthetics and politics.

10 *Sunday Telegraph*, 21.1.1990.

11 Ernest Gellner, review of *The Power of the Powerless* edited by John Keane, *Times Literary Supplement*, 3.10.86. The book centres around Václav Havel's essay of the same name.

12 Many of those who had experienced the Communist takeover of 1948 remembered Hájek as the person who engineered the fusion of the Social Democrat Party with the Communist Party.

13 Mlynář and Klímová were husband and wife, parents of Vladimír Mlynář, who in the 1990s became editor of *Respekt* and later a parliamentary deputy. Zdeněk Mlynář left for Austria soon after the appearance of the Charter. Klímová became the first post-revolution Ambassador to the USA

14 Such as František Janouch, a nuclear physicist living in Sweden. Janouch established the Charter 77 Foundation, which raised money in the West to provide humanitarian aid for Czech and Slovak dissidents.

15 Havel and Patočka were replaced in September 1977 by Ladislav Hejdánek and by Marta Kubišová, a popular singer in the 1960s who, because of her opposition to the Soviet invasion, was banned from performance for 20 years.

16 I use the Czech form 'Tominová' when referring to Zdena's activities in Czechoslovakia in the 1980s, the western form 'Tomin' when referring to her life in Britain.

17 The police term for the home seminars was the 'anti-university'.

18 One of the seminar students who became a journalist after 1989 and in 1999 was appointed Ambassador to Israel to succeed Jiří Schneider (see the chapter: 'The Cambridge Diploma').

19 Then and now a philosopher at St. Hilda's College, Oxford; the first Oxford lecturer to visit Julius Tomin's seminar.

20 Kathy Wilkes: 'Unofficial Philosophy Courses in Prague', duplicated brochure, undated, probably June 1980.

21 Radim Palouš was to become the first Rector of the Charles University after the Velvet Revolution.

22 Information compiled by Jiří Fiala.

23 Jiří Stráský became the last Prime

Minister of the Federal Republic of Czechoslovakia in 1992.

[24] Jan Patočka's son-in-law. In 1990 he became a Parliamentary Deputy; later he returned to the Charles University, and in 1998 was Minister of Education.

[25] Information compiled by Jiří Fiala.

[26] Minister of Education after the Velvet Revolution.

[27] Information compiled by Jiří Fiala.

[28] Vilém Prečan's *ACTA* (1987-1989), Skilling's *Samizdat and an Independent Society in Central and Eastern Europe* (1989), Goetz-Stankiewicz's *Good-bye, Samizdat* (1992).

[29] Wilson in Goetz-Stankiewicz (ed., 1992).

[30] Nevertheless, Nadia Diuk of the National Endowment of Democracy has noted that the Czechs were computerising their samizdat whilst the Poles were still working with off-set machines. (Conversation with Nadia Diuk, 20th March 1998.)

[31] Zdena Tomin, *Index on Censorship*, 2/1983.

[32] *New Statesman* 19.10.79.

[33] Ibid.

[34] Letter from Julius Tomin to the University of Oxford, Great Britain and Harvard University, USA, 20th May 1978. Tomin's original is in English. The letter was summarised in Czech in *Informace o Chartě 77* 18-29th May 1978.

[35] Ibid.

[36] Ibid.

[37] The dissidents were well aware themselves of this conflict, and it was a subject of debate during their gatherings in the Slavia café.

[38] Many British people were so shocked by the August invasion and moved by the plight of the young Czechs and Slovaks that a scholarship fund was set up to enable them to attend British universities; it was a unique opportunity.

[39] It is from this date that the controversy as to whether or not Kavan was recruited as an informer by the StB agent František Zajíček at the Czechoslovak Embassy begins.

[40] Press release issued by The Solidarity Fund, 4th April 1981.

[41] Named after Jan Palach, the Czech student who burnt himself to death in protest against the nation's increasing apathy towards the Soviet invasion.

[42] Press release issued by the Palach Press Ltd., 20th December 1980.

[43] Uhl, who described himself as Trotskyite, was on the left wing of the dissidents. In 1998 he became Commissioner for Human Rights for the Czech Republic.

[44] Introduction to *Informace o Chartě 77, Doplněk* 1998.

[45] *Výbor na obranu nespravedlivých stíhaných* (Committee for the Defence of the Unjustly Prosecuted/ Persecuted).

[46] Anna Šabatová was the daughter of the Brno dissident Jaroslav Šabata. In 1998 she received one of the rare awards made by the United Nations

for her work in human rights.
[47] Letter from Jan (Kavan) to Kathy

(Wilkes), 7th July 1980.

OXFORD COMES TO PRAGUE

[1] Cf Christopher Hitchens in the *New Statesman*, 21.5.80. (Hitchens was an ex-Balliol student.)

[2] Minutes of the Meeting of the Sub-Faculty of Philosophy, Oxford University, 29th January 1979.

[3] Minutes of the Meeting of the Sub-Faculty of Philosophy, Oxford University, 5th March 1979.

[4] She stayed at her post at the Inter-University Centre in Dubrovnik through most of the siege of 1991, and was subsequently awarded the Freedom of the City.

[5] Kathy Wilkes, diary for 1978-79. (KVW)

[6] Kathy Wilkes: 'Visit to Philosophers in Prague, Spring 1979'; this report has the note: 'The subfaculty of philosophy at its meeting of 7th May asked me to write out my verbal report and circulate it to members of the philosophy subfaculty and Lit. Hum. Board.'. (KVW)

[7] Kathy Wilkes, diary for 1978-79. (KVW)

[8] Kathy Wilkes: 'Visit to Philosophers in Prague, Spring 1979', op.cit.

[9] This old cottage (a *chalupa* rather than a *chata*), dependent on its own well for water, surrounded by mountains and reached by a rough track across a field, was typical of many

acquired by Prague intellectuals in the early 1970s. When its elderly owners died their three children, preferring the town, were eager to sell the property; when *chata* dwelling became fashionable in the 1980s, they would have been only too glad to buy the family house back again.

[10] Split brain surgery, performed on people with extreme epilepsy.

[11] The *emigré* journal published by Jiří Pelikán in Rome.

[12] Ludvík Vaculík, *Český snář* p. 193. (tr. Day)

[13] In the 1950s and 1960s Pavel Kohout was a convinced and enthusiastic Communist. After 1968 he opposed the regime and lived in exile in Austria.

[14] Wilkes, *New Statesman*, 19.10.79.

[15] Kathy Wilkes: 'Visit to Philosophers in Prague, Spring 1979', op.cit.

[16] Ibid.

[17] 'A Special Correspondent', in *New Statesman*, 4th May 1979

[18] Kathy Wilkes: 'Talks with the philosophical nightwatchman of Prague' in *The Guardian*, 10th May 1979.

[19] Sandra Emstaff in *Isis*, 31st May 1979.

[20] Kathy Wilkes, diary for 1978-79. (KVW)

21 Jiří Gruša is a writer who in 1978 was arrested for the samizdat publication of his novel *Dotazník* (The Questionnaire). He was subsequently stripped of his citizenship and lived in exile in West Germany. From 1993-97 he was Ambassador, subsequently Minister of Education, and is at present (1999) Ambassador to Austria.

22 *Infoch* year 2, no. 9 (29.5/ 11.6.1979).

23 Ibid.

24 According to Tomin this information came from Ludvík Vaculík, and he (Tomin) passed the information on to Taylor; Taylor remembers hearing it from Lukáš Tomin.

25 Photographs were always a contentious issue, and even on this occasion some of those present refused to be photographed.

26 The American philosopher and logician, Willard Van Orman Quine.

27 Letter from Charles Taylor to Barbara Day, 21st January 1997.

28 On 6th July Taylor's article on conditions in Czechoslovakia appeared in the *New Statesman*; it put an end to the possibility of him giving any more seminars for the Prague students.

29 Meeting of the Sub-Faculty of Philosophy, Oxford University, 11th June 1979.

30 When Prajzler and Bednář visited the Technical University in 1990 the copies of their letters of expulsion were no longer in the archives; where they should have been, there was a break in the numbering system of the files. 'Goodness,' said the official then in charge, 'there must have been something serious going on here.' 'But,' Prajzler noted in 1997, 'the people who did it are still teaching there.'.

31 It was not the first time they had discussed the central European situation; the subject had arisen at a Christmas dinner in New York in 1978 with the philosopher Tom Nagel (himself of Czech origin) and his wife Anne Hollander. Nagel and Hollander were to meet the Tomins in Prague in summer 1980.

32 Quoted in letter from Kathy (Wilkes) to Tony (Kenny), 4th December 1979. (AK)

33 Ibid.

34 Author of (among others) *Mé přítelkyně v domě smutku* (My Friends in the House of Sorrow) and winner of a number of literary prizes.

35 Tomin, *New Statesman*, 7.3.1980.

36 Ibid.

37 Zdena Tominová remembers that there was a period when hair cropping was quite regular, the excuse given that the person did not resemble the photograph on their identity card.

38 Such a late start seems to have been unusual but not exceptional.

39 In the mid-1990s, after several years as Czech Ambassador to Poland, Němcová-Fialková entered the Law Faculty of the Charles University as a first year undergraduate.

40 In the 1960s a successful theatre and film director and playwright.

41 Letter from Kathy Wilkes to Tony (Anthony Kenny), 8.10.79. (AK)

42 Alan Montefiore's postgraduate student at Balliol College; he later became a Trustee of the JHEF.

43 *The Times Higher Educational Supplement*, 2.2.80.

44 *The Times*, 11.3.80.

45 Ibid.

46 Although many people condemned the use of the telephone as foolhardy, Tomin approved its use (when in working order) as being consistent with the principle of openness. There are several references in Wilkes's diary to telephone conversations between Oxford and the Tomins in Prague.

47 *New Statesman*, 7.3.80.

48 Ibid.

49 Ibid.

50 *New Statesman*, 14.3.80.

51 Now abandoned and derelict.

52 *New Statesman*, 14.3.80.

53 *Cherwell*, 14.3.80.

54 Kathy Wilkes: 'Unofficial Philosophy Courses in Prague', duplicated brochure, undated, probably June 1980.

55 *Infoch*, year 3, no. 6 (30.3./27.4.1980) (tr. Day)

56 Letter from Dr. Anthony Kenny to Dr. F. Telicka, 19th March 1980. (AK)

57 Ibid.

58 *Infoch* year 3, no. 6 (30.3./ 27.4.80) (tr. Day)

59 See the chapter : 'The Philosophers and the Secret Police'.

60 Kenny, *An Oxford Life*, 1997

61 *The Daily Telegraph*, 14.4.80.

62 *Infoch* year 3, no. 6 (30.3./27.4.80) (tr. Day)

63 *The Daily Telegraph*, 14.4.80.

64 *The Times*, 19.4.80.

65 Letter from Christopher Mallaby, Eastern European and Soviet Department, Foreign and Commonwealth Office, to Dr. Kenny, 16th May 1980. (AK)

66 Peter Blaker, Minister of State

67 *The Times*, 22.4.80 and memorandum of telephone conversation between Anthony Kenny and Christopher Mallaby. (KVW)

68 Letter from Christopher Mallaby, op.cit.

69 *Infoch* year 3, no. 6 (30.3./27.4.80) (tr. Day)

70 Dr. Kenny's M.P., John Patten, also protested on behalf of both his constitutents, Dr. Kenny and Bill Newton-Smith; as a Canadian citizen, the latter did not come under the jurisdiction of the British Foreign Office.

71 Meeting of the Sub-Faculty of Philosophy, Oxford University, 5th May 1980.

72 Kathy Wilkes: 'Unofficial Philosophy Courses in Prague', (op.cit.)

73 Julius Tomin: *Musilo to být?* (Did it have to be so?) in *Infoch* year 3, no. 7 (27.4./10.5.80) (tr. Day)

74 *New Statesman*, 30.5.80.

75 Letter from Roger (Scruton) to Kathy (Wilkes), 5th June ('or thereabouts') 1980. (KVW)

[76] Quoted in letter from Jan (Kavan) to Kathy (Wilkes), 7th July 1980. (KVW)

[77] Meeting of the Sub-Faculty of Philosophy, Oxford University, 9th June 1980.

[78] However, the name must have been discussed much earlier than this. On 28th February 1980, Paul Wilson wrote to Jessica Strauss Pittman about the incorporation of the American branch, referring to the 'Jan Huss [sic] Educational Trust or whatever it's to be called' (see the chapter on the North Americans).

[79] Letter from Roger (Scruton) to Kathy (Wilkes), 5th June 1980. (KVW)

[80] Kirwan, a philosopher from Exeter College in Oxford, later became a Trustee of the JHEF.

[81] Zdena Tomin: 'The typewriters hold the fort' in *Index on Censorship*, 2/83.

[82] *The Listener*, 18.9.80.

[83] *The Doll* (1992), *Ashtrays* (1993) and other works published by Twisted Spoon Press, Prague.

PRINCIPLES AND POLICIES

[1] The Charter was not read aloud or made available to those present; a number of them later argued that what they had signed was an attendance list, not their agreement to any document.

[2] Quoted in Skilling, *Charter 77* p. 133.

[3] *Times Higher Educational Supplement*, 29.2.80.

[4] Letter from Kathy (Wilkes) to Alan (Montefiore), undated, probably September 1982. (KVW)

[5] *Outlook* (Oxford), 1981

[6] *Index on Censorship*, 3/1986.

[7] See Bibliography.

[8] *Outlook* (Oxford), 1981

[9] Letter from Dan (Dennett) to Kathy (Wilkes), 31st March 1981. (JHEF/RVS)

[10] Roger Scruton, Visitor's Report April 1981 (JHEF/RVS) and conversation with Ladislav Hejdánek, 10th July 1997.

[11] Letter from Bill (Newton-Smith) to Jessica (Strauss Pittman), dated Sunday (probably November/ December 1980). (JHECF/JS)

[12] Although Maxwell was born on the pre-war territory of Czechoslovakia, he came from Ruthenia beyond the eastern end of Slovakia, a region subsequently absorbed into Ukraine and in the 1980s part of the Soviet Union.

[13] Letter from Bill (Newton-Smith) to Jessica (Strauss Pittman), op.cit. (JHECF/JS)

[14] Bruce Chatwin's novel of Prague, *Utz* (1988), is dedicated to Diana Phipps.

[15] Alan Montefiore, Visitor's Report September 1981. (JHEF/RVS)

[16] Briefing for 'Sally' (Shreir) unsigned (certainly by Roger Scruton), undated (around

March/April 1983). (JHEF/RVS)

[17] An example was Daniel Kroupa, who was awarded a stipend intermittently between 1985 and 1989, for his organisation of one of the most consistent of the teaching seminars.

[18] Litomiský became Mayor of Pelhřimov in the 1990s.

[19] RS. (Roger Scruton): 'A note on validation', undated, probably 1984. (JHEF/RVS)

[20] In 1993 he supported the campaign led by Jessica Douglas-Home for the academic independence of Trnava University in Slovakia. (*The Times* 27.1.93)

[21] Roger Scruton, Visitor's Report January 1981. (JHEF/RVS)

[22] Jarmila Křivanová, Director, Acquisitions & Processing Department, to Jane Long, 25th May 1981. (JHEF/RVS)

[23] Wilkes: 'BOOK BUYING: SUGGESTIONS ABOUT POLICY', 26.4.1984.

[24] Letter from Jan Kavan to Roger Scruton, 28.4.1981. (JHEF/RVS)

[25] 'REPORT' issued in America as part of press pack by Debra Black (Jessica Strauss Pittman) on behalf of Jan Kavan and the Palach Press, 21st July 1981. (JHECF/JS)

[26] Tigrid, one of the circle of Prague intellectuals in the 1930s, was now producing the *emigré* journal Svédectví in Paris. In the 1990s he became Minister of Culture in the Klaus government.

[27] Alan Montefiore, Visitor's Report September 1981. (JHEF/RVS)

[28] 'REPORT' op.cit.

[29] In the 1990s Ruml became Minister of the Interior in the Klaus government, and was subsequently co-founder of the Freedom Union party.

THE FRENCH PHILOSOPHERS

[1] Almost immediately after the trial, Ariane Mnouchkine in France and Patrice Chéreau in Germany prepared a stage presentation; the English version (*The Prague Trial 1979*) was not staged until a year later (22nd October 1980), when Julius Tomin participated in the BBC recordin g.

[2] For example, the Comité des mathématiciens (Michel Broué), the Ligue des Droits de l'homme and La libre Pensée.

[3] Pierre Fougeyrollas, quoted by Paul Flather in *The Times Higher Educational Supplement* 6.6.80.

[4] Jacques Derrida, quoted by Paul Flather in *The Times Higher Educational Supplement* 6.6.80.

[5] Document in the Archive of the Association Jan Hus; undated, but item 4) concerns the meeting to take place on 21st December 1980.

[6] The JHEF had more success than the AJH in raising funds, partly because of its easier access to American donors (although both organisations were given substantial

support from George Soros [see final chapter]). Unlike the JHEF, the AJH did not have a paid secretary; all the work carried out by Nathalie Roussarie was on a voluntary basis.

[7] The apprehension in Prague of Jan Kavan's transport, driven from Paris by Françoise Anis of the Ligue des Droits de l'homme and Gilles Thonon of La libre Pensée.

[8] Letter from Catherine Audard to members of the Association, 15th May 1981. (AJH/CA)

[9] In the period up to 1990 the Jan Hus Foundation received no financial assistance at all from the British government.

[10] Le Comité directeur de l'Association Jan Hus: 'ASSOCIATION JAN HUS POUR LE SOUTIEN AUX UNIVERSITAIRES, ÉTUDIANTS ET ENSEIGNANTS TCHÉCO-SLOVAQUES'. (AJH/CA)

[11] Ph.Dr. Karel Vykypěl (his doctorate was in psychology) was one of the more professional and sophisticated officers of the secret police. At this time, as head of the first section of the Xth directorate SNB, he was responsible for most of the visiting lecturers who acquired files (see the chapter: 'The Philosophers and the Secret Police'); he later rose to a high position in the IInd directorate SNB, and his last promotion was in Jan

1990. Later that year he was charged with crimes committed against Czechoslovak citizens in the course of police actions in 1988 and 1989, and subsequently received a prison sentence.

[12] Quoted in Jiří Gruntorad: 'StB proti Chartě – akce "Izolace" in *Listy* 27 (1997) No. 1. (tr. Day)

[13] Errera belonged to the Assocation Amis sans frontières and had made several trips to Prague, usually at Christmas time, with bags of books, newspapers and other presents.

[14] Letter from Catherine Audard to members of the Association, 23rd May 1983. (AJH/CA).

[15] Ivan Jirous known as Magor, artist and poet, was first imprisoned in 1973 and then as 'manager' of the Plastic People of the Universe in 1976. He was rearrested and sentenced in 1977 and again in 1981. In 1976 he was described at his trial as 'the chief organiser of all unofficial cultural activities in the country'. (*Index on Censorship*, 1/83)

[16] Paul Ricoeur was the most influential writer at *Esprit*.

[17] Described by Alena Hromádková as: 'a generous and good person who undertakes everything' – Roger Scruton, Visitor's Report January 1983.

[18] Conversation with Jean-Claude Eslin 23rd February 1997.

SEMINARS AND SAMIZDAT

[1] Conversation with Kathy Wilkes, 30th November 1996.

2 Eva Stehlíková, of the Cabinet for Greek, Roman and Latin Studies of the Academy of Sciences, confirms that the organisers were unable to give any information as to how they had received Wilkes's name.

3 Alan Montefiore and Catherine Audard, Viitors' Report September 1981.

4 Pavel Bratinka, however, always considered that the behaviour of both the French and German governments during the Cold War 'gave hope and encouragement to the USSR'. The British were better, but 'stuck to out-dated concepts and didn't understand the nature of power'; the Americans (without any real understanding either) knew the importance of values and acted correctly on instinct. (Conversation with Pavel Bratinka, 26th May 1998.)

5 This would appear to have been a verbal warning. There are however references to it in Visitors' Reports, such as that from Jon Elster, March 1982. (JHEF/RVS)

6 Minutes of Meeting of Trustees of the Jan Hus Educational Foundation, 14th October 1982. (JHEF/RVS)

7 Roger Scruton, Visitor's Report October 1983. (JHEF/RVS)

8 Christopher Kirwan, Visitor's Report April 1984. (JHEF/RVS)

9 David Papineau, Visitor's Report December 1984. (JHEF/RVS)

10 The theory is supported by the fact that in the years of work in Brno and Bratislava there was never a single misunderstanding about the date of somebody's arrival. There is also concrete evidence (Gruntorad in *Listy 27*, 1/1997) that the StB had the deliberate intention of discrediting Hejdánek during this period.

11 Dorothy Edgington, Visitor's Report November 1981. (JHEF/RVS)

12 Letter from F (Falstaff, i.e. Petr Rezek) to Lulu (Roger Scruton), undated. (JHEF/RVS)

13 RS (Roger Scruton): 'Archive Report on the Analytical Course', undated. (JHEF/RVS)

14 Karel Hubka: 'Contacts betweeen the Prague Philosophical Circle (PPC) and the English Philosophers', London, 10th November 1984. (JHEF/RVS)

15 Letter from F (Falstaff, i.e. Petr Rezek) to Lulu (Roger Scruton), undated. (JHEF/RVS)

16 Letter from Anita Brookner to Roger Scruton, 28th October 1981. (JHEF/RVS)

17 Michael Flynn, Visitor's Report April 1982. (JHEF/RVS)

18 Kathy Wilkes, Visitor's Report April 1982. (JHEF/RVS)

19 Letter from F (Falstaff, i.e. Petr Rezek) to Lulu (Roger Scruton), undated. (JHEF/RVS)

20 Letter from F (Falstaff, i.e. Petr Rezek) to R (Ralph Walker), translated from German by Walker, dated by Walker June 1986. (JHEF/RVS)

21 C.A. Kirwan: 'Notes for visitors to the Prague Plato course', 14th January 1988. (JHEF/RVS)

22 Christopher Kirwan, Visitor's Report January 1988. (JHEF/RVS)

23 J.E. Tiles, Visitor's Report October 1988. (JHEF/RVS)

24 Rezek himself was highly dissatisfied with the post-1989 state of philosophy at the Charles University, and after spending a few years there in the early 1990s, resigned in order to found his own publishing house (REZEK) to bring out superbly produced volumes of Plato, Aristotle and other philosophers.

25 Ralph Walker, Visitor's Report January 1989. (JHEF/RVS)

26 Letter from F (Falstaff, i.e. Petr Rezek) to Ralph (Walker), translated from German by Walker and enclosed in Ralph Walker's letter to Barbara Day, 13th July 1989 (JHEF/RVS)

27 John Marks, Visitor's Report October 1989. (JHEF/RVS)

28 Bratinka worked as a cleaner and a stoker in the 1980s. In 1992 he became a parliamentary deputy and in 1996 Minister Without Portfolio in Václav Klaus's cabinet.

29 Roger Scruton, Visitor's Report January 1983. (JHEF/RVS)

30 Conversation with Pavel Bratinka 26th May 1998.

31 Ibid.

32 Ralph Walker, Visitor's Report January 1989. (JHEF/RVS)

33 Roger Scruton, Visitor's Report January 1983. (JHEF/RVS)

34 David Levy, Visitor's Report March 1983. (JHEF/RVS)

35 Sally Shreir, Visitor's Report April 1983. (JHEF/RVS)

36 Ronald Beiner, Visitor's Report April 1983. (JHEF/RVS)

37 Minutes of the Meeting of Trustees, 2nd May 1983. (JHEF/RVS)

38 Roger Scruton, Visitor's Report October 1983. In April 1981, Scruton had reported that Kučera was nervous of inviting foreign lecturers to his seminar. (JHEF/RVS)

39 Kučera has throughout the 1990s been head of the Department of Political Science of the Social Sciences Faculty of the Charles University. He was also founder of the journal *Střední Evropa* (Central Europe, see below) and edits it to the present day.

40 *Sunday Telegraph*, 21.1.1990.

41 See Bibliography.

42 Benda had been sentenced alongside Havel at the VONS trial of 1979, and only recently released. In Dec 1989 he founded the Christian Democrat Party; in 1990 he became a parliamentary deputy; in 1995 head of the Bureau for the Documentation and Investigation of the Crimes of Communism; in 1998 a Senator. He died in June 1999.

43 Robert Grant, Visitor's Report February 1984.

44 Professor of Political Science at Aberdeen University, a friend of Alan Montefiore who later became a Trustee of the Jan Hus Foundation.

45 *Smysl konservatismu* was subsequently published as a 'microbook' – the size of a small diary, with a magnifying glass in the spine – by the amazing independent publisher Josef

Jelínek in West Germany.

[46] According to the police files, Hromádková was asked by another of the seminar organisers to leave Prague for the duration of Scruton's visit, to avoid attracting attention to him.

[47] Roger Scruton, Visitor's Report October 1983. (JHEF/RVS)

[48] RS (Roger Scruton), 'Report on Samizdat Journal: Střední Evropa'. (JHEF/RVS)

[49] Ibid.

[50] Minutes of the Meeting of Trustees, 29th September 1983. (JHEF/RVS)

[51] Alan Montefiore and Catherine Audard, Visitors' Report January 1986. (JHEF/RVS)

[52] Letter from R.K. (Rudolf Kučera) to the Jan Hus Foundation, June 1989. (JHEF/RVS)

[53] Roger Scruton, Visitor's Report January 1983. (JHEF/RVS)

[54] Ibid.

[55] Since 1990 Palek has been issuing *Kritický sborník* as a regular journal.

[56] See the chapter on Brno.

[57] Roger Scruton, Visitor's Report October 1983. (JHEF/RVS)

[58] Pius (Karel Palek), 'The Account of my Activities' Autumn 1983 - Spring 1984'. (JHEF/RVS)

[59] Alan Montefiore and Catherine Audard, Visitors' Report January 1986. (JHEF/RVS)

[60] Paul Flather, Visitor's Report July 1984. (JHEF/RVS)

[61] Ralph Walker, Visitor's Report May 1985. (JHEF/RVS)

[62] Ibid.

[63] Roger Scruton: *Dictionary of Political Thought*

[64] Roger Scruton, Visitor's Report January 1983. (JHEF/RVS)

[65] David Levy, Visitor's Report March 1983. (JHEF/RVS)

[66] Barbara Day, Visitor's Report April 1986. (JHEF/RVS)

[67] Jessica Douglas-Home, Visitor's Report February 1987. (JHEF/RVS)

[68] In 1990 Prečan was appointed director of the Institute of Contemporary History of the Academy of Sciences.

[69] Ralph Walker, Visitor's Report May 1985. (JHEF/RVS)

[70] In the 1990s Deputy Foreign Minister and subsequently Ambassador to the U.S.A.

THE NORTH AMERICANS

[1] Josef Škvorecký, who had made a name for himself in Czechoslovakia in the 1960s with the novel *The Cowards*, emigrated after 1968 with his wife Zdena to Canada, where he continued to write, and where they founded '68 Publishers.

[2] Letter to Jessica (Strauss Pittman) from Paul Wilson, 28th February 1980. Archive of the Jan Hus Educational and Cultural Fund, Baltimore U.S.A.. (Hereafter JHECF / JS)

[3] Ibid.

⁴ Letter to Philip Roth from Jessica Strauss Pittman, 9th March 1981. (JHECF/JS)
⁵ The Skillings succeeded in celebrating their Golden Wedding in the Old Town Hall in 1987, in the presence of Václav Havel and other dissidents.
⁶ Professor of Sociology at Duke University, Durham, N.C. (JHECF/JS)
⁷ Executive editor of *Commonweal* and religious correspondent for *The Times*.
⁸ Letter to Directors from Jessica Strauss Pittman, 28th October 1981. (JHECF/JS)
⁹ Minutes, Annual Meeting, 1981, Jan Hus Educational and Cultural Fund, Inc.. (JHECF/JS) According to Strauss Pittman's letter to Directors, it was expected that Jan Kavan would attend the first part of the meeting, but his presence is not recorded in the Minutes.
¹⁰ Jan Hus Educational and Cultural Fund, undated draft document. (JHECF/JS)
¹¹ Ibid.
¹² Ibid.
¹³ Letter to Chuck/Professor C.M. Taylor, copy unsigned, 18th September 1982, with note to Jessica (Strauss Pittman) from Kathy (Wilkes). (JHECF/JS)
¹⁴ Ibid.
¹⁵ Letter from 'Debra Black' (Jessica Strauss Pittman) to Directors, 31st January 1982. (JHECF/JS)
¹⁶ Letter from Debra Black (Jessica Strauss Pittman) to Directors, 19th November 1982. (JHECF/JS)
¹⁷ 'Report on the American Jan Hus', unsigned (certainly by W.H. Newton-Smith), 24th January 1983. (JHEF/RVS)
¹⁸ Minutes, Annual Meeting, Jan Hus Educational and Cultural Fund, Inc. 3rd December 1982. (JHECF/JS)
¹⁹ 'Report on the American Jan Hus', unsigned (certainly by W.H. Newton-Smith), 24th January 1983. (JHEF/RVS)
²⁰ Copy of letter to Dr. (Kathy) Wilkes, copy unsigned (probably from Jessica Strauss Pittman), undated but with minutes of meeting on 3rd December 1982 attached. (JHECF/JS)
²¹ Ivan Kyncl was the son of the journalist and Charter signatory Karel Kyncl, who later followed his son to Great Britain. In the 1990s Karel became Radio Prague's correspondent in London, where he died in 1997; whilst Ivan Kyncl is now a successful theatre photographer, winner of several British awards.
²² Agenda, 1983 Annual Meeting, 11.00 a.m., Saturday 14th January 1984, Jan Hus Educational and Cultural Fund, Inc.. (JHECF/JS) There are no minutes of this meeting in the archive.
²³ Application (in English) enclosed with a letter to the Directors from Paul Wilson, 7th January 1984. (JHECF/JS)
²⁴ Roger Scruton, Visitor's Report April 1984 (JHEF/RVS).
²⁵ David Stark, Visitor's Report July

1983 (JHEF/RS).

[26] H.Gordon Skilling, 11th July 1984, op.cit.

[27] Letter from Gordon(H.Gordon Skilling) to David (Stark), 15th January 1985. (JHECF/JS)

[28] Discussions were reopened in 1998 as to how this sum – between $700-$800 – should be used.

[29] Letter to David (David Stark) from Gordon Skilling(H.Gordon Skilling), 23rd February 1987. (JHECF/JS)

[30] Letter from Jessica(Jessica Strauss Pittman) to Zdena and Josef Škvorecký, 30th November 1981. (JHECF/JS)

[31] A C.B.C. producer with particular interest in plays from Czechoslovakia.

[32] Brought up in Czechoslovakia as the son of Russian exiles, he became professor at the University of Toronto.

[33] 'Jan Hus Fund (Le Fond Jan Hus), Toronto March 15, 1983'. Archive of H. Gordon Skilling, University of Toronto, Canada. (Hereafter JHF/HGS, Toronto University.)

[34] Signed Václav Havel, Praha, 19.6.1984. (JHF/HGS, Toronto University.)

[35] Letter to 'pane profesore' (H. Gordon Skilling) from Václav Havel, 12th July 1984. (JHF/HGS, Toronto University.)

[36] Letter to Václav Havel, unsigned (from H. Gordon Skilling), 4th August 1984. (JHF/HGS, Toronto University.)

[37] Ibid.

[38] Financial decisions following meeting of the Jan Hus Fund, 24th May 1985. (JHF/HGS, Toronto University.)

[39] Vratislav Brabenec, saxophonist with the Plastic People, who went into exile at the beginning of the 1980s.

[40] Letter to 'Milý přítele' (Dear Friend), with handwritten note to 'Milý Gordone' (H. Gordon Skilling) from Václav Havel, 29th June 1985. (JHF/HGS, Toronto University. Tr. Day.)

[41] Minutes of the Meeting of the Jan Hus Fund (Canada), 13th January 1986. (JHF/HGS, Toronto University.)

[42] Letter to Bill (Newton-Smith) from Gordon (H. Gordon Skilling), undated, probably February 1986. (JHEF/RVS)

[43] Minutes of the Meeting of the Jan Hus Fund, 13th January 1986. (JHF/HGS, Toronto University.)

[44] Agenda for the Meeting of the Jan Hus Fund, 7th March 1987 with typed notes added later, original sent from 'P' (Paul Wilson) probably to Charles Taylor, who was absent from the meeting; this copy marked 'GS (copy)'. (JHF/HGS, Toronto University.)

[45] Letter 'To the JAN HUS Foundation, Toronto' from Jaroslav Šedivý, 20th March 1988, with Curriculum vitae attached. (JHEF/RVS)

PHILOSOPHY FROM THE NETHERLANDS

1 Wilkes: 'APPEAL FOR ASSISTANCE TO CZECHOSLOVAKIA PHILOSOPHERS', undated, but issued whilst Wilkes was Secretary of the Sub-Faculty of Philosophy. (Th.deB)

2 Letter from Kathy Wilkes to Th. de Boer, 30th January 1980. (Th.deB)

3 Ibid.

4 Ibid.

5 Van der Horst: *Een Scheur in het gordijn* (A Tear in the Curtain), Heršpice 1997

6 For example, the internationally known dogmatician Prof. Dr. Herman Berkhof.

7 The Catholic foundation Koinonountes sent theology lecturers to the circles around Ota Mádr and the Kaplans; whilst the Dutch Socialist Party (Partij van de arbeid) sent some visitors to Marin Palouš's seminar.

8 Levinas (tr Rejchrt); *Výbor krátśich textů*, Prague 1983.

9 Havel, Václav (translated by Paul Wilson): *Letters to Olga*, Faber and Faber, London 1988.

10 Ibid.

11 Ibid.

12 Hejdánek is convinced that the police were confused, and had not wanted to raid his seminar whilst a foreigner was present.

13 Jiří Němec, father of Markéta Němcová, was now working in the Patočka archive at the Institut für Wischenschaft vom Menschen.

14 Barbara Day: 'Report on telephone conversation with Herman Parret, 26 June 1986'. (JHEF/RVS)

15 Ibid.

16 B.D. (Barbara Day): 'Report on telephone conversation with Herman Parret, 3 July 1986'. (JHEF/RVS)

17 Letter from Barbara Day to Herman Parret, 11th July 1986. (JHEF/RVS)

18 Letter from Barbara Day to Henri Veldhuis, 2nd January 1987. (JHEF/RVS)

THE BRNO OPERATION

1 Milan Uhde, a native of Brno, became the the second post-revolutionary Minister of Culture (1990) and subsequently Speaker of the House of Deputies (1992).

2 On 17th November 1989 Oslzlý was in Prague with the theatre's controversial *Rozrazil – On Democracy*. He became one of the founders of Civic Forum, and remained in Prague for the next two and a half years as one of the President's advisers.

3 The name came from a text by the pre-war Brno writer Jiří Mahen; the Communist authorities forced the theatre to shorten its name to Theatre on a String because 'Husa' was too

close to (President) Husák.

⁴ In the 1990s Kovalčuk became a parliamentary deputy, then Dean of the newly-founded Theatre Faculty of the Janáček Academy, then director of the drama company at the National Theatre in Prague.

⁵ 'M' for Moravia.

⁶ Ivan Klíma the novelist and his wife Helena, psychologist.

⁷ Eva Kantůrková the writer, and Jiří, later head of Czech Television.

⁸ Parents of Jiří Zlatuška, who in 1987 created one of the first-ever Czech-language software programmes for the use of the samizdat press, and in 1998 became Rector of the Masaryk University in Brno.

⁹ Before the war, Brno, like Prague, was an important European centre for structuralism, but its study was not compatible with Marxist-Leninist ideology and was forced underground.

¹⁰ The seminars were recorded by Müller and (with Komárková's texts) published in samizdat in 1980, and after the revolution by the publishing house Eman.

¹¹Šabata was imprisoned in 1971, Charter spokesman in 1978 and imprisoned again the same year, and spokesman again in 1981.

¹² Vašíček thinks there were around 20 present; Scruton remembers 'a small group'.

¹³ Roger Scruton, Visitor's Report April 1981 (JHEF/RVS)

¹⁴ *Sunday Telegraph*, 21.1.1990.

¹⁵ Oslzlý: *Podzemní univerzita*, Brno

1993 (tr. Day).

¹⁶ *Prague Post*, 11-17.1.95.

¹⁷ Letter from 'J' (Jiří Müller) to Roger (Scruton), 12th August 1984 (grammar original, spelling corrected). (JHEF/RVS)

¹⁸ David Levy, Visitor's Report December 1984. (JHEF/RVS)

¹⁹ Another nephew attending the seminar, Martin Filip, secretly joined the Dominican order.

²⁰ 'Late Night Extra', BBC2, Wednesday 30th May 1990.

²¹ Conversation with Miroslav Pospíšil, 8th September 1998.

²² Letter from 'J' (Jiří Müller) to Roger (Scruton), 24th November, probably 1984.

²³ Oslzlý: *Podzemní univerzita*, Brno 1993.

²⁴ Julian Mitchell, Visitor's Report November 1987.

²⁵ Sparling, a friend of fellow-Canadian Paul Wilson, had also settled in Czechoslovakia in the 1970s.

²⁶ Letter from 'J' (Jiří Müller) to Roger (Scruton) 14th April 1985. (JHEF/RVS)

²⁷ Letter from 'R' (Roger Scruton) to 'J' (Jiří Müller), undated, probably August 1985. (JHEF/RVS)

²⁸ These were the memoirs of Václav Havel's father.

²⁹ Roger Scruton, Visitor's Report April 1984. (JHEF/RVS)

³⁰ David Regan, Visitor's Report March 1985. (JHEF/RVS)

³¹ Letter from Roger Scruton to Dr. Prečan, 2nd June 1984.

³² Minutes of the Jan Hus

Educational Foundation Executive Committee meeting, Saturday 17th January 1987. (JHEF/RVS)

33 Duncan Watt, Visitor's Report April 1987. (JHEF/RVS)

34 Letter from Wolfgang Stock to Roger Scruton, 21st April 1987. (JHEF/RVS)

35 Barbara Day, Visitor's Report April 1987. (JHEF/RVS)

36 James de Candole, Visitor's Report June 1987. (JHEF/RVS)

37 Letter from 'JB' (Jiří and Broňa Müller) to 'W' (Wolfgang Stock), 16th August (1987). (JHEF/RVS)

38 Briefing for Wolfgang Stock, September 1987. (JHEF/RVS)

39 Wolfgang Stock, Visitor's Report September 1987. (JHEF/RVS)

40 Set up with funding from the National Endowment for Democracy (see last chapter).

41 Letter from Jiří (Müller) to Roger (Scruton), 14th February (1988). (JHEF/RVS)

42 Letter from Wolfgang Stock to Roger (Scruton), 21st April 1987. (JHEF/RVS)

43 Briefing for James de Candole, June 1987. (JHEF/RVS)

44 Letter from 'J' (Jiří Müller) to Barbara (Day), (tr. Day) (JHEF/RVS)

45 Jiří Müller, 'Epilog československého samizdatu', *Duha* 2/90.

46 A British typesetting firm which the Foundation was using.

47 Letter on computer disc from 'J' (Jiří Müller) to Barbara (Day), 19th September (1989) (tr.Day). (JHEF/RVS)

48 Michael Potter, Visitor's Report January 1987. (JHEF/RVS)

49 Letter from Jiří Müller to Professor Skilling, November 1st (1984?). (JHF/HGS, Toronto University.)

50 Unsigned letter (certainly from Jiří Müller) to 'Mr. Professor' (Gordon Skilling), 20th September 1985. (JHF/HGS, Toronto University.)

51 Ibid.

52 Letter from 'G.S.' (Gordon Skilling) to 'Jack' (Jiří Müller), 16th January 1986. (JHF/HGS, Toronto University.)

53 Minutes of meeting of the Jan Hus Fund (Canada), 13th January 1986. (JHF/HGS, Toronto University.)

54 Minutes of meeting of Executive Committee of the Jan Hus Educational Foundation, 24th February 1986. (JHEF/RVS)

55 Conversation with Jiří Müller 17th June 1997.

56 Letter from 'J' (Jiří Müller) to Roger (Scruton), 11th January 1987 (JHEF/RVS)

57 'Technics and Politics (Video-recorder in Czechoslovakia)', undated, probably November 1985. (JHEF/RVS)

58 Ibid.

59 Ibid.

60 Wolfgang Stock, Visitor's Report August 1986.(JHEF/RVS)

61 Jessica Douglas-Home, Visitor's Report September 1985.

(JHEF/RVS)

[62] Letter from 'J' (Jiří Müller) to Jessica (Douglas-Home), 12th December (1985)

[63] John Keane, Visitor's Report December 1985. (JHEF/RVS)

[64] Minutes of the Jan Hus Educational Foundation Executive Committee meeting, 21st December 1985. (JHEF/RVS)

[65] Minutes of the Jan Hus Educational Foundation Management Committee meeting, Saturday 18th January 1986. (JHEF/RVS)

FRANCE, GERMANY AND MORAVIA

[1] Conversation with Jean Michel Besnier 26th February 1998.

[2] Under the normalisation of the 1970s the secondary schools were not as heavily purged as the universities.

[3] Skácel became a close friend of the French philosopher and poet Bernard Fabre, who had his work translated and published in France as *Observateurs 4*, 1989.

[4] Miroslav Pospíšil remembers that it was JiříMüller who arbitrated in difficult decisions of this kind.

[5] Apart from the Institut für Wissenschaft vom Menschen, where Klaus Nellen, with the help of Ivan Chvatík, created a duplicate Patočka archive. There was however no involvement in the home seminars.

[6] Richard Rorty, Visitor's Report July 1981. (JHEF/RVS)

[7] Ibid.

[8] Alan Montefiore, Visitor's Report September 1981. (JHEF/RVS)

[9] Tugendhat had been born in Brno and left as a child in the 1940s. His family home was the famous Tugendhat Villa, otherwise known as the Mies van der Rohe house. He returned to Brno as a teacher for a short period in the 1990s.

[10] Wolfgang Stock has pointed out that the German operations relied on American money channelled through the British foundation. (Correspondence with Wolfgang Stock, September 1998.)

[11] A samizdat translation printed by the JHEF in Britain and reimported for distribution to seminars in Czechoslovakia.

[12] Minutes of the Meeting of the Management Committee of the Jan Hus Educational Foundation, Sunday 5th October . (JHEF/RVS)

[13] Letter to Roger (Scruton) from Barbara (Day), 18th March 1987. (JHEF/RVS) The visit was a disappointment for Professor von Stockhausen; the JHEF had arranged for her to speak to Petr Rezek's seminar on Heidegger on Sunday 22nd February, but was unaware that Herman Parret (due to speak at Hejdánek's seminar the following evening) was visiting Rezek's seminar on the Sunday.

[14] Von Bischoffshausen later became

President of the International Society for Human Rights.

[15] Posselt is now a Member of the European Parliament.

MUSIC, ART AND LITERATURE

[1] It is not clear how the first request arrived, but according to John Keane's report the visit was already agreed by the time of his visit in December 1985.

[2] In November 1989 Michal Kocáb became one of the leading activitsts of the Velvet Revolution.

[3] A NOTE ON THE STATE OF THE CONTEMPORARY CZECH SERIOUS MUSIC 1983-4, 'Prague, October 1984 Transl. C.P.H.' No author is given. It is possibly the work of the Professor Vojtěch mentioned in Scruton's report of his meeting with Zemanová; a grant was made to him to write a monograph on Czech atonal music. (JHEF/RVS)

[4] Ibid.

[5] Roger Scruton: 'A Feast of Fibich' in *The Times*, 10th January 1984; reprinted in *Untimely Tracts*.

[6] David Matthews, Visitor's Report January 1986. (JHEF/RVS)

[7] Ibid.

[8] On this occasion Jessica Douglas-Home used her maiden name, Gwynne, by which she is known as a professional artist, rather than her married name.

[9] Another factor was the role of the musicologist Graham Melville-Mason, who had many years experience with the country, and who, for example, took over responsibility for inviting Ištvan and Novák to the King's Lynn Festival

[10] The interviewer was Jana Kuchtová, whose exceptional skills in English led her to be recruited as a translator for samizdat publications and an interpreter on occasions when Miroslav Pospíšil could not be available. In 1990 she became the first secretary of the newly-founded Czechoslovak Jan Hus Educaional Foundation.

[11] *Svobodné slovo*, 11th November 1986 (tr. Day).

[12] Matthews, 'The flourishing tradition of Janacek and bear steaks', in *The Independent* 21.10.86.

[13] Jaroslav Kořan, who had a first career as a script writer and a second as translator of contemporary American literature, lived dangerously on the edge of the Prague 'underground'. He was a member of the Jazz Section, and Helen Ganly's guide to the artistic world in her March 1988 visit. He became the first post-revolutionary Mayor of Prague in 1990 and subsequently editor of *Playboy*.

[14] Nigel Osborne, Visitor's Report October 1986. (JHEF/RVS)

[15] Ibid.

[16] A pupil of Janáček's pupil Jaroslav Kvapil.

[17] David Matthews, Visitor's Report

October 1986. (JHEF/RVS)

[18] Peter Graham's real name was Jaroslav Pokorný until he married and became Jaroslav Šťastný, sensibly adopting his wife's name ('pokorný' means 'humble', whereas 'šťastný' means 'fortunate'). 'Graham' was taken from 'graham' – or wholemeal – bread.

[19] The pianist William Howard has done remarkable work in promoting the Brno composers; Matthews believes that his commitment has been one of the most important factors in their subsequent success.

[20] David Matthews, Visitor's Report October 1986. (JHEF/RVS)

[21] David Matthews, programme note.

[22] Bayan Northcott in *The Independent*, 17th March 1988.

[23] David Matthews, programme note.

[24] Bayan Northcott in *The Independent*, 17th March 1988.

[25] Ibid.

[26] Matthews travelled with his partner the novelist Maggie Hemingway, who later wrote a novel *The Postmen's House* based on her experiences.

[27] David Matthews, Visitor's Report October 1988. (JHEF/RVS)

[28] Conversation with Miroslav Pospíšil, 7th September 1998.

[29] David Matthews, Visitor's Report August 1989. (JHEF/RVS)

[30] Ibid.

[31] *Jan Šimek* by Petr Oslzlý, Atlantis, Brno 1999; Day: English summary.

[32] Jessica Douglas-Home, Visitor's Report October 1985. (JHEF/RVS)

[33] Document in archive of Jan Hus Foundation, untitled, unsigned, no translator named. Handwritten note: 'This arrived on 10/1/86 – JD-H (Jessica Douglas-Home)'. (JHEF/RVS)

[34] Ibid.

[35] Helen Ganly, Visitor's Report February 1987.

[36] Helen Ganly, Visitor's Report December 1987.

[37] Ibid.

[38] Helen Ganly, Visitor's Report March 1988.

[39] It was followed by an exhibition by the Künstlerforum artists in Brno.

[40] Helen Ganly, Visitor's Report November 1989. The 'hymns' would not have been religious hymns but the national anthem (národníhymna), 'Kde domov můj'.

[41] Peter Fuller, Visitor's Report May 1987.

[42] Anthony O'Hear: 'Peter Fuller: a light in the night', *Sunday Telegraph* 10th June 1990.

[43] Peter Oslzlý: 'Peter Fuller: a light in the night', *Sunday Telegraph* 10th June 1990.

[44] Oslzlý, Jan Šimek, Brno 1998, Day: English summary.

[45] Ibid.

[46] Letter from J (Jiří Müller) to Barbara (Day), on computer disc, 17.4.(1989). (tr. Day)

[47] Dan Jacobson, Visitor's Report April 1983. (JHEF/RVS)

[48] Conversation with Dan Jacobson, 8th April 1998.

[49] Dan Jacobson, Visitor's Report

April 1983. (JHEF/RVS)

[50] Dan Jacobson, Visitor's Report May 1986. (JHEF/RVS)

[51] Ibid.

[52] Julian Mitchell, Visitor's Report November 1987. (JHEF/RVS)

[53] Piers Paul Read's novel *A Season in the West* was partially based on his experiences.

[54] Mitchell was travelling with Richard Rowson, who gave a seminar on medical ethics.

[55] The septuagenarian writer who in

1990 became Václav Havel's Ambassador Extraordinary.

[56] Žantovský became Czech Ambassador to the U.S.A. following the death of Rita Klímová.

[57] David Pryce-Jones, Visitor's Report January 1988. (JHEF/RVS)

[58] Carol Rumens, Visitor's Report October 1987. (JHEF/RVS)

[59] Conversation with Dan Jacobson, 8th April 1998.

[60] Ibid.

THE JAZZ SECTION

[1] Letter from J (Jiří Müller) to Jessica (Douglas-Home), 24th February (1986), orginal English, spelling corrected.

[2] Durham subsequently became a Trustee of the Foundation, and married Bill Newton-Smith.

[3] 'Czech Jazz' was broadcast on CBC 'Sunday Morning' two days before the Jazz Section trial.

[4] Jan Kavan helped Jessica Douglas-Home with additional information for the briefing.

[5] David Mellor also gave helpful advice in connection with the Cambridge Diploma project.

[6] Letter from Professor Donald Mitchell of The Britten-Pears Foundation to His Excellency the President of the Czechoslovak Socialist Republic Dr. Gustáv Husák, 23rd December 1986.

[7] JUDr. Josef Průša could act only as adviser to the Section's lawyers; he

had been a zealous defender in cases brought against dissidents, and consequently spent five years in prison for 'perverting justice'.

[8] Letter from 'Elizabeth' (Roger Scruton) to 'David' (Jiří Müller), undated, probably October 1986.

[9] Křívánková was also an early member of the Cambridge Diploma seminar; in the 1990s she was made Ambassador to Finland and subsequently became a member of the Czech Helsinki Committee.

[10] Geoffrey Robertson, Visitor's Report October 1986.

[11] *Rudé právo*, 1st November 1986. (tr. Day)

[12] Letter to Roger (Scruton) from John Rose, 3rd December (1986).

[13] Freundová was one of the earliest and most active Charter signatories; she emigrated to England after a life-threatening attack by three members of the StB in her own apartment.

14 Princová was at this time a journalist with the journal *The Economist.*

15 Letter to Barbara (Day) from Geoffrey Robertson, 27th February 1987.

16 Letter to Jessica Douglas-Home from Charles Alexander, 15th March 1987.

17 Jazz Section Trial: Convictions. Statement by the Minister of State, Mr. Timothy Renton: 11th March (1987)

18 Ibid.

19 Letter to 'R' (Roger Scruton) from 'David and B' (Jiří and Broňa Müller), 26th June 1987.

20 Barbara Day, Visitor's Report October 1988.

21 Conversation with Karel Srp, 29.6.1998.

THE ECOLOGY PROGRAMME

1 The Communist Party headquarters in Brno.

2 Vavroušek and his daughter were killed in an avalanche in the Tatra mountains in Slovakia early in 1995: 'An enormous loss to the whole of Europe.' (Tom Burke, 17.7.98).

3 Conversation with Tom Burke 17th July 1998.

4 Dennis O'Keeffe, Visitor's Report January 1986.

5 Craig Kennedy, Visitor's Report April 1986.

6 Tom Burke, Visitor's Report June 1986.

7 Ibid.

8 In the 1990s Josef Zieleniec became Foreign Minister of the Czech Republic in Václav Klaus's government, and is considered nationally and internationally to be one of its leading experts in economic foreign affairs. He is the founder of the Centre for Economic Research and Graduate Education of the Charles University.

9 The samizdat edition of *The Meaning of Conservatism*, which had been responsible for RS's expulsion the previous June.

10 Tom Burke, Visitor's Report June 1986.

11 Ibid.

12 It was hoped that either the Foreign Office or the Department of the Environment would provide financial support, but this was refused in a letter from the Eastern European Department of the FCO to Roger Scruton, 22nd December 1986. (JHEF/RVS)

13 Wolfgang Stock, Visitor's Report August 1986.

14 Barbara Day, Visitor's Report August 1986.

15 Oriana Stock, Visitor's Report September 1986.

16 Ibid.

17 'Elizabeth' (Roger Scruton) to 'David' (JiříMüller), undated, probably October 1986.

18 Tom Burke, Visitor's Report

November 1986.

19 Ibid.

20 Michael Potter, Visitor's Report January 1987.

21 Tom Burke, Visitor's Report September 1988.

22 Ibid.

23 Tom Burke, Visitor's Report September 1988.

24 Conversation with Tom Burke 17th July 1998.

BRATISLAVA SEMINARS

1 Dominic Farrell, Visitor's Report July 1987. (JHEF-RVS)

2 The underground church also existed in the Czech lands, but its significance was greater in Slovakia because of its wider popular appeal.

3 Miroslav Lehký's son, also Miroslav Lehký, was Charter spokesman in 1990 and later worked for the Bureau for the Documentation and Investigation of the Crimes of Communism.

4 Robert Grant, Visitor's Report October 1987. (JHEF-RVS)

5 Ibid.

6 Ibid.

7 Čarnogurský and his family have remained in the same flat to the present day, refusing pressure to move to somewhere more 'appropriate' for a major political figure.

8 Yarnold's visit had been requested by Lehký, who had met him 20 years earlier at Campion Hall in Oxford.

9 As O'Keeffe's visit took place in December 1989 he was able to give his lectures at a public venue.

10 David Regan, Visitor's Report April 1988. (JHEF-RVS)

11 Translation taken from Keston College Newsdesk, 7.11.1989. (JHEF-RVS)

12 Ján Langoš was Minister of the Interior for Czechoslovakia from 1990-92.

13 Christine Verity, *Daily Telegraph* 19th November 1989.

14 Christine Stone (Verity), Visitor's Report November 1989. (JHEF-RVS)

15 Designed by Jessica Douglas-Home.

THE CAMBRIDGE DIPLOMA

1 In 1982 I was taken there to be shown 'the table of the invisible people' – 'all my friends, all of them gone,' lamented my companion, 'all emigrated, scattered over the world.'

2 In the 1990s Bourdeaux moved Keston College to Oxford and renamed it Keston Institute.

3 Tomsky was also the founder of an *emigré* publishing house and journal, both called *Rozmluvy*.

4 'Agreed to allow £50, on condition our support of him should be noted in our publicity, and that he carry out an

item of our business on future trips.' (Minutes of the Jan Hus Educational Foundation Executive Committee meeting, Monday 28th April 1986.) (JHEF/RVS)

[5] Letter from Milan Balabán to the Secretary of the Syndicate, 10th November 1987. (JHEF/RVS)

[6] Ibid.

[7] Conversation with Jan Schneider 25th June 1998.

[8] Ibid.

[9] Subsequently legal adviser to Prime Minister Václav Klaus.

[10] A reconstruction of the seminar, filmed in Marta Chadimová's flat, was shown as part of a programme on the Jan Hus Foundation in 'Late Night Extra', Wednesday 30th May 1990 on BBC2.

[11] Nancy Durham, Visitor's Report March 1988. (JHEF/RVS)

[12] Stephen Blunden, Visitor's Report March 1988. (JHEF/RVS)

[13] Ibid.

[14] The majority of the books provided by the Jan Hus Foundation for the Cambridge Diploma course – around 170 volumes altogether – are now kept in Professor Milan Balabán's office in the Faculty of Theology of the Charles University, and are available to students of that Faculty.

[15] Now Bishop of Ely.

[16] David Mellor also gave valuable support to the Jazz Section.

[17] Letter to the Reverend Professor Stephen Sykes from Andrew Lenox-Conyngham, 10.9.1988. (JHEF/RVS)

[18] Andrew Lenox-Conyngham, Visitor's Report September 1988. (JHEF/RVS)

[19] David Sanders, Visitor's Report December 1988. (JHEF/RVS)

[20] David Sanders, Visitor's Report June 1989. (JHEF/RVS) (The restaurant was the Slovanský dům in Na příkopě.)

[21] Ibid.

[22] Conversation with Jan Kozlík 22nd January 1998.

[23] Conversation with Milan Balabán 7th November 1997. (Vlasák is now a parish priest with particular responsibility for prisons and for St. Elizabeth's Hospital.)

[24] Conversation with Jan Kozlík 22nd January 1998.

[25] The Foundation had in fact purchased a small photocopier for the sole use of the Cambridge Diploma group, and this had been brought into the country in a suitcase by David Levy in December 1988. Unfortunately, the machine was commandeered by another member of the dissident community, who at the time was convinced the gift was for him. It was returned some months later with apologies and an empty toner cartridge.

[26] i.e., the newly purged secret police.

[27] In the Foundation's view, the bureaucratic attitude shown by the Open University in 1986 led to a tragically missed opportunity.

THE PHILOSOPHERS AND THE SECRET POLICE

1 *Infoch* 1980 no. 6.

2 Conversation with Julius Tomin 19th March 1997.

3 If it was the Sunday before this incident, then it must have been 6.4.1980

4 Státní bezpečnost, i.e. secret police.

5 *Infoch* 1980 no 6. (tr. Day)

6 Kieran Williams: 'The StB in Czechoslovakia: the evolution of a political police under communist rule' in Deletant, Latawski, Williams: *Security Intelligence Forces in New Democracies*; Zdeněk Zikmundovský and Jiří Málek in *Přehled o Cinnosti a struktuře StB v letech 1988-90*; the Securitas Imperii series published by the Bureau for the Documentation and Investigation of the Crimes of Communism.

7 Lorenz was sentenced in 1991 for crimes relating to his operational measures in 1988-89.

8 See the Derrida story in the chapter: 'The French Philosophers'.

9 All that is actually known is that they have not been handed over to the Ministry of the Interior; they may be sitting in the wardrobe of a member of the former StB.

10 Most of the following information is taken from Roger Scruton's police file and used with his permission.

11 Responsible for agents who physically followed Czechoslovak citizens and foreigners; this section (no. 5) covered hotels and restaurants.

12 But not *how* frequently; the file

mentions 3 visits in 1981, whereas Scruton was in Prague 5 times that year.

13 This was an error. Scruton had once visited Prague with a Turkish friend, but it was Kathy Wilkes who wrote notes in Turkish and transcribed them into Ancient Greek script.

14 Roger Scruton, Visitor's Report June 1985. (JHEF/RVS)

15 Ibid.

16 On 28th June Müller wrote to Scruton: 'I ask you, please, if you could send me over Mr. V. Prečan as soon as possible the folders again that we had to annihilate – it is the matter of cutter, drilling machine for paper, stapler and microfilm.'. (JHEF/RVS)

17 Oslzlý: *Proglas* 1/92. (tr. Day)

18 Scruton, June 1985.

19 Ibid.

20 *Democracy and Civil Society*, Verso 1993

21 Scruton, June 1985.

22 This opinion was later advanced as one of the reasons for putting Scruton on the Index of Undesirable Persons.

23 StB file on Roger Scruton. (tr. Day) (RVS)

24 Scruton, June 1985.

25 Oslzlý: *Proglas* 1/92. (tr. Day)

26 No file nor any record of a file on Jessica Douglas-Home has been found in the police archives. This would appear to be carelessness on the part of the StB, since they had a clear warning from the Poles that she

would be likely to continue Roger Scruton's work.

27 Oslzlý: *Proglas*

28 Paul Flather, Visitor's Report November 1985. (JHEF/RVS)

29 Ibid.

30 The home town of Semtex.

31 Oslzlý: *Proglas*

32 Ibid.

33 This material is from Alan Montefiore's file, and used with his permission. (ACM, tr. Day) At the end of the report there is a list of people mentioned in the conversation who should be investigated in addition to Montefiore; Audard is not mentioned anywhere.

34 There is no record in Montefiore's Visitor's Report (JHEF/RVS) that any 5th person (ie, other than the Montefiores and the two Czechs

named in both Montefiore's and the police report) was present at this meeting. Other than this, there are no great discrepancies between the two reports.

35 Montefiore, December 1985

36 Day was never an employee of any British university.

37 On research for a PhD thesis on the Divadlo Na Zábradlí (Theatre on the Balustrades) in the 1960s.

38 By 1986 the American JHECF was dormant.

39 The Czechoslovak Society of Arts and Sciences.

40 Robert Grant, Visitor's Report October 1987. (JHEF/RVS)

41 This material is from Robert Grant's police file, and used with his permission. (RADG, tr. Day)

THE FRACTURING OF THE BOLTS

1 Policy statement of the Jan Hus Educational Foundation, undated. (JHEF/RVS)

2 Samizdat work printed in the West and transported back to Czechoslovakia.

2 Letter from Alan Montefiore to George Soros, 25th January 1983. (JHEF/RVS)

3 RS (Roger Scruton) 'Report of a meeting with George Soros', 9th December 1983; Minutes of the Meeting of Trustees, 11th January 1984. (JHEF/RVS)

4 Minutes of the Annual General Meeting of Trustees, Sunday 30th

April 1989. (JHEF/RVS)

5 This eventually became the Athenaeum Press.

6 Barbara Day: 'Report of meeting with Yale Richmond (Programme Officer, N.E.D.)', Thursday 23rd October 1986. (JHEF/RVS)

7 Letter from Yale Richmond to Barbara Day, 19th January 1987. (JHEF/RVS)

8 Leon Krier, Visitor's Report November 1988. (JHEF/RVS)

9 Graham King, Visitor's Report May 1989. (JHEF/RVS)

10 Almost certainly Moravians.

11 Quinlan Terry, Visitor's Report

October 1989. (JHEF/RVS)

[12] Letter from Ester (Alena Hromádková) to Roger (Scruton), 24th May 1988, tr. Day (JHEF/RVS)

[13] Letter from Dr. Miroslav Červenka, Dr.Sc., addressed to 'Váženíkolegové' (Dear Colleagues), undated, tr. Day. (JHEF/RVS)

[14] The main hosts were Petr and Harriet Macek, relations of the Oxford student Jessica Strauss who had founded the American Jan Hus Educational and Cultural Fund.

[15] Vondra became Deputy Foreign Minister in the 1990s, and subsequently Ambassador to the United States.

[16] Son of the (silenced) playwright Josef Topol, and one of the most original writers of the 1990s.

[17] 'Večerní univerzitní studium bohemistiky, HODNOCENÍ PRVNÍHO ROKU', unsigned, tr. Day, received June 1989. (JHEF/RVS)

[18] Ibid.

[19] In 1990 Urban became the third leader of Civic Forum, after Havel and Pithart; he later returned to journalism

[20] James de Candole, Visitor's Report September 1989.

[21] Williams, 'The StB in Czechoslovakia', op.cit.

[22] *Zítra to spustíme*, translated as *Tomorrow!* in *Czech Plays*, edited by Barbara Day, 1994.

[23] See the chapter on music for Matthews' participation. Had it not been for illness, Maggie Hemingway

would have participated in the dialogue on literature.

[24] 'Inaugural declaration by the free association of creative artists: OPEN DIALOGUE' (tr. Day) in *Plays International* April 1989.

[25] In 1989 Tondl was made director of the Institute of the Theory and History of Science at the Czechoslovak Academy of Sciences.

[26] The applications were mediated through Petr Rezek.

[27] Letter from Kathy Wilkes to Barbara (Day), 21st April 1988.

[28] Letter from Pavel Kouba addressed to 'Dear Sirs', 5th May 1988.

[29] Kathy Wilkes, Visitor's Report June 1989.

[30] It is unlikely that either Kathy Wilkes or Bill Newton-Smith were directly linked by the secret police with Operation 'Ali', and it is almost certain that their police files had by now been archived.

[31] Kathy Wilkes, Visitor's Report June 1989.

[32] Ibid.

[33] In accord with the security practised at that time, Chadimová knew Durham only as a radio reporter, and had no idea she was connected with the organisation behind the Cambridge Diploma semina.

[34] Amongst the others on stage were Václav Malý, Dana Němcová, Radim Palouš and Joska Skalník.

[35] Soon to return to its original name of the Masaryk University.

[36] A policy which has resulted in today's drastic dearth of high-quality

teaching staff in Faculties and Institutes of Arts, Humanities, Social Sciences and Law.

EPILOGUE

[1] Anthony Smith CBE, President of Magdalen College, Oxford, was elected Chairman of the JHEF in 1989. Although he was an associate of Petr Pithart from the 1960s, he had not previously been connected with the JHEF: however, he proved to be the most involved and energetic chairman in the history of the Foundation.

[2] Ludvík Vaculík, *Český snář* p. 193.

INDEX